"*Bush Tragedies* is a meticulous, well researched work of brutal and sordid crimes, and accidents of awful, immeasurable and diverse events that tore many outback towns in western New South Wales to pieces.

"In a quiet way, it is an incredible tribute to country law enforcement officers and judiciary 'back in the day'.

"Bill Poulos uses a genre of creative non-fiction to recreate all the happenings in his book. The reader becomes the witness to these scenes. I found the re-enactments noteworthy – 'a cavalcade of vehicles carrying the police magistrate, police officers and the accused and his solicitor made its way into town'.

"The recounting of 'the headless body', left an unusual query hanging as to who exactly was the dead man. The Murulla train disaster of 1926 is quoted from the Newcastle Sun newspaper: The town awoke to pulsing life and the streets were filled with the screech of cars and the shouts of men. Breathlessly they dashed into the bush to succour the victims of disaster.

"Bill, you have mastered – and to quote one of the characters in your book, Inspector Goodwin – one hell of an investigation."

—Judith Flitcroft, author of *Walk Back in Time*

"*Bush Tragedies* is a collection of short stories that brings to life the early settlement of western NSW and south-western Queensland. Bill Poulos does a magnificent job of researching primary source material and bringing it together in a clear and succinct way.

"*Bush Tragedies* will amaze you, shock you and on occasions bring a tear to your eye."

—Ken Price, author of *Broken Lives* and *Kokoda Mist*

BUSH TRAGEDIES

TRUE STORIES OF CRIME, MURDER, MISERY AND HEARTACHE FROM WESTERN NEW SOUTH WALES

BILL POULOS

A Sid Harta publication

This edition published in 2023 by Sid Harta Publishers,

23 Stirling Cres, Glen Waverley VIC 3150, Australia

ISBN: 978-1-922958-40-2

p528

ABOUT THE AUTHOR

Bill Poulos is a former freelance features and sports journalist based at Moree in north-western NSW.

His passion is the thoroughbred racing industry, and he wrote extensively on this subject for numerous magazines, newspapers and websites across the eastern states of Australia for more than thirty-five years.

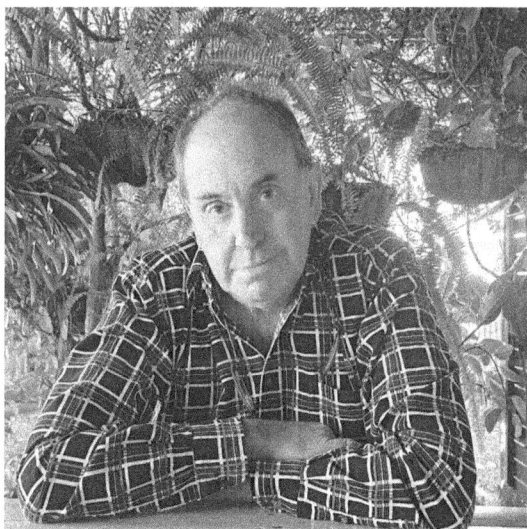

Bill's research for a book on the history of horse-racing in north-western NSW was the reason *Bush Tragedies* serendipitously evolved — historical stories of crime, murder, misery and heartache kept dragging him away from the project at hand.

Bill won the John Newfong Award for Outstanding Indigenous Affairs reporting at the 2016 NRMA Kennedy

Awards for Excellence in NSW Journalism and was also nominated for three Racing NSW Awards for Excellence in Media (2003, 2005 and 2010), winning in 2010.

Bill lives in Moree with his wife Cindy and stepson Yang. Bill and Cindy own and manage a small business in Moree, and Bill writes every chance he gets.

For Zhi Ye

ACKNOWLEDGEMENTS

The stories within these pages have been written in good faith, using information and facts available to anyone. They were compiled over three years using newspaper articles sourced from the National Library of Australia, court and law-related documents from New South Wales and Queensland state archives and military and service records from the Australian War Memorial and National Archives of Australia.

Several ancestry and family heritage websites were referred to as well as private documents and information kindly supplied by family members.

There are many people who helped along the way, none more so than the researchers at Western Sydney Records Centre. My requests for information were never a problem, and responses were prompt, efficient and always on the money.

Historical society members at Moree, Warialda, Inverell, Narrabri and Dubbo were always helpful and a special thank you goes to historian Michael McNamara, an old school friend from way back when. Michael always had the answers I was seeking when roadblocks popped up.

Many people came forward with information about their ancestors and I thank them all. Their input and guidance were invaluable.

Warren Thatcher, a cousin, helped enormously when delving into our family history — the wild and woolly Timmins mob — and a copy of *The Tail Goes with the Hide*, written by another cousin, the late Gene Makim, was never far away.

A special thank you goes to Anne-Marie Carrigan.

Anne-Marie's mother, Amy Fingleton, was shot dead in the family car in downtown Moree in 1948. The man who pulled the trigger was Amy's brother, Paul — Anne-Marie's uncle.

Anne-Marie was a baby in a bassinet next to her mother when Paul pointed a pistol through the sedan's passenger side window and murdered his sister. The tragic death would have been averted had PTSD been recognised in 1940s postwar Australia as a very real mental illness.

I sat on the story for two years before working up the courage to talk to Anne-Marie about her mother's death. Anne-Marie bravely gave me her blessing to publish the story, and for that I am forever grateful.

Finally, thank you to my beautiful wife, Zhi Ye Ou Yang, fondly known as Cindy. You watched and waited patiently for nearly three years as I got lost in a maze of historical murder, intrigue and tragedy. When I emerged from my self-imposed time tunnel, you were there to welcome me home — thank you.

There were 'this is what happened' offerings along the way but unconfirmed anecdotes could not be verified as fact. Therefore, hearsay has not been used. I wanted to make the stories as interesting as possible, but not embellish them with family folklore and half-truths for the sake of a good yarn.

Rather than compile boring, historical essays, I have relied on a style known as creative non-fiction.

To me, they are good, old-fashioned tales from the Australian bush. I hope the reader enjoys them as much as I enjoyed putting them together.

BIBLIOGRAPHY

Chapter 11:

Pratt, Eric. (2015) *Witnesses to History*, published by Strictly Literary (https://www.strictlyliterary.com/), page 154

CONTENTS

Englishman William Ball was the last man hanged at Armidale Gaol after murdering his wife, Louisa, near Bingara in 1912 (Image credit: Museums of History NSW — State Archives Collection)

CHAPTER 1

I JUST WANTED TO PUT HER OUT OF HER MISERY

William Ball was within a few days of skipping Australia and sailing the high seas to England.

He joined the crew of the United Tyser Lines steamer *Star of Scotland* on Thursday 18 January 1912 with a plan to work his way back home.

Ball, twenty-three, was wanted by police on suspicion of murder. He fled the Gwydir district in north-western New South Wales two days earlier.

The young Englishman's last known whereabouts were on 16 January, when he booked into the Commercial Hotel at Bingara and stayed the night. The following morning he travelled by bus to Warialda railway station at Kelly's Gully and caught a train to Sydney.

Ball travelled lightly. He carried only a small Gladstone bag, with a copy of the *Daily Commercial News and Shipping List* tucked under his arm.

The publication listed the latest shipping itineraries of all vessels in and out of Sydney Harbour for the next few weeks. Ball read it from cover to cover.

He marked the tramp steamer *Star of Scotland*, due to leave on Thursday 25 January, as his likely ticket out of Australia.

Back at a property near Bingara, under a pile of smouldering embers doused by a recent shower of rain, laid the charred remains of his pretty young wife, Louisa.

Ball killed Louisa the same day he booked a room at the Commercial Hotel.

They were married five months earlier in England and less than eight weeks before their arrival in Australia.

Also travelling on the bus from Bingara to Warialda was a woman named Annie Rose Martin.

The short bus trip was uneventful but Annie couldn't help noticing the handsome young Englishman's obsession with the newspaper.

Annie watched him read the shipping news repeatedly. Every so often Ball folded the paper and rested it on his lap. But within minutes, if not seconds, he flicked it open and re-read the arrivals and departures columns.

Annie wasn't one to stickybeak, but it all seemed quite odd. The clean-shaven, good-looking young man with brooding eyes was utterly obsessed with the shipping details.

Ball arrived in Sydney on Wednesday 17 January and the following day filled a position on the *Star of Scotland*.

He boarded the steamer and quickly connected with fellow crew members. Ball knew, sooner or later, Louisa's remains would be found and the police notified. But he was confident a ship anchored on Sydney Harbour was the last place police would look when the inevitable manhunt began.

He smiled smugly.

Newspapers would later headline the murder "a carefully planned crime".

There was, however, one slight glitch to Ball's perfect escape plan — the woman by the name of Annie Rose Martin.

Ball was no stranger to Australia. His first trip out was in 1909. He stayed for a couple of years and returned to England to marry Louisa, also known as Lois.

The couple had known one another for about three years but were separated by sea for most of that time. They married in August 1911 at Swanley, a small town in the county of Kent, about sixteen miles from central London.

Ball figured the time was right to settle permanently in Australia. He and Louisa arrived in Brisbane on 10 October 1911 on the *Demosthenes*. Ball worked his return passage as a coal-trimmer; Louisa travelled as a passenger.

His work experience on the *Demosthenes* held him in good stead when enquiring about work on the *Star of Scotland*.

The newlyweds headed to Toowoomba, where Ball signed up with a labour agency. He was offered a job in north-western NSW as a general farm hand and boundary rider. Louisa was offered employment as a cook and general domestic.

The couple made their way to Bingara to start a new life together on the grazing property, The Hill, part of the much bigger Pallal station, owned by Bill and Ellen Mack.

Ball started work at The Hill, about thirteen miles from Bingara, on 9 December.

What should have been a fairytale beginning for the newlyweds took a turn for the worse when Louisa was struck down with severe rheumatism.

She was treated daily by a nurse and finally admitted to Bingara Hospital in a serious condition. She spent eight days in hospital before Dr Emilio Demarco allowed her to go home.

Ball wasn't all he seemed, either. Gone was the dashing young adventurer Louisa thought she fell in love with. Instead, there was an angry man with a shocking temper and violent ways. Ball treated her badly on the voyage to Australia. Even then she wondered whether she was making the right life choices.

Maybe Ball's violent ways and rude manner were there all

along and Louisa simply didn't see the signs — or didn't want to. After all, she had not seen Ball for nearly three years. How well Louisa really knew her husband is a matter of conjecture. The fact remains, she was deeply in love with Ball and willing to travel halfway around the world to be with him for the rest of her life.

Back at The Hill, Ball was furious his gravely ill wife could not perform home duties or help around the place. He also became sullen when Bill Mack refused him a horse and buggy to take to Bingara to collect Louisa from hospital.

Instead, Mack collected Louisa and took her back to the farm. Dr Demarco said Louisa needed at least one week's rest.

On 16 January, the day after Bill Mack's thirty-eighth birthday, Ball was left in charge at The Hill while Bill and Ellen Mack returned to their adjoining property, Pallal.

Louisa was home recovering, and barely able to work. She was exhausted and in pain.

Later that day, Ball loaded a shotgun belonging to Bill Mack and murdered Louisa as she limped across the house yard. The bullet pierced her left side, just below the heart.

Ball callously lifted Louisa's bleeding, lifeless body into a wheelbarrow and wheeled her to a spot about 200 yards from the homestead. He started a small brush fire and burned Louisa's body beyond recognition.

Ball returned to the back of the house and lit another fire. Here he disposed of Louisa's clothes, apparel and personal belongings. He kept Louisa's wedding ring as well as a half-hoop ring and some photographs.

As he watched the body of his wife burn, Ball calmly planned his escape.

He placed the shotgun back in the kitchen pantry where he

had found it. He packed some belongings in a Gladstone bag and wrote a letter of resignation to Bill Mack.

He took a bath and shaved, removing his moustache. Refreshed and clean-shaven, Ball donned a light-grey tweed sack suit with dark stripes and a light-grey, soft felt hat.

He laced up his boots, had a quick look around the empty homestead and walked to Bingara.

The faint smell of a fire hung in the air as he left the property.

*   *   *

Two days later, when Ball was tucked away on the *Star of Scotland* on Sydney Harbour making new friends and thinking of England, Mack returned to The Hill to check on his new employee.

He was convinced William Ball was not the right man for the job.

'He is not overburdened with an enthusiastic love of hard labour,' Mack told his wife, Ellen.

When Mack arrived at The Hill late in the afternoon the homestead was deserted.

Everything seemed exactly the same as when he left two days earlier. There were, however, two huge boxes sitting on the office floor.

Mack found a note on the desk, written by a family friend, Bingara Presbyterian minister Alexander Campbell Greaves.

'Sorry to have missed you. I camped here Thursday night; no-one was about the place.'

There was also a letter from William Ball: 'I've been thinking that if I stop here, I will only be hurting the missus, as she is not in a fit state to work, so we have decided to go. Will you please send the boxes to the parcels' office in Brisbane.'

About 5 pm, Mack returned to Pallal and related the afternoon's odd course of events to Ellen. He was relieved to be rid of Ball, but was concerned about Louisa.

At 7.30 pm Mack telephoned Bingara police sergeant John Byrne.

'Do you know if a young couple, William and Louisa Ball, have been through town the last day or two, or might still be in town? They were working for me. Mrs Ball is just out of hospital and in no condition to travel,' Mack said.

Byrne made enquiries and learned a person fitting Ball's description arrived on foot at the Commercial Hotel on Tuesday night.

Ball apparently told hotel owner Annie Wilkinson he walked in from Pallal station.

He cashed a cheque for £4 and booked a room for the night. The cheque drawer was William Rodney Mack.

He asked Mrs Wilkinson to wake him early, but he never slept a wink that night.

The next morning, Ball jumped on a Smith's Busline coach to Warialda railway station at Kelly's Gully, twenty miles down the road.

Commercial Hotel porter Henry Green told Sgt Byrne that Ball seemed pre-occupied with his luggage when sitting on the bus.

Green said he knew Ball.

'He stayed at the hotel a couple of weeks earlier when the races were on. I tapped him on the back and said, "Going away so soon?"

'He did not reply, but kept his head down between his

6

knees. He fumbled with a bag between his feet. I tried to have a conversation with him, but he kept his head down and pretended to be busy with his luggage,' Green said.

Sgt Byrne and Sen-Constable John Adams accompanied Bill Mack to The Hill to further investigate the couple's disappearance.

They found evidence of a small scrub fire about 230 yards from the house block and a second, smaller fire at the back of the homestead.

There were traces of burnt dress material in the remains of the smaller fire as well as photo frames and other mementos.

'That looks like the same pattern as the dress Mrs Ball was wearing the other day,' Bill Mack said.

Sgt Byrne organised a thorough search of the remains of the larger fire. Several charred bones were found, including a human pelvis, leg and wrist bones, and part of a skull and backbone. They also found several items of women's apparel, including the wire frame of a hat and corset, hooks, buttons, corset busks and hairpins.

Byrne observed the ground surrounding the ashes was swept towards the fire, as if to stop the spread of flames.

The investigation hit a stumbling block when police interviewed the ticket clerk at Warialda railway station.

A young man fitting Ball's description did indeed purchase a ticket, but the clerk could not recall the purchaser's destination.

Police Sub-Inspector James Miller, from Inverell, examined a list of ticket sales made at Warialda railway station on Wednesday 17 January.

There was one ticket issued to Gravesend; one to Delungra; four to Inverell; one to Boggabri; two to Moree; and two to Sydney.

Miller knew Ball would have been at one of those stops.

However, determining the correct stop would take time and patience.

Miller had plenty of patience, but not much time. The longer it took to work out Ball's intended destination, the further away the suspected murderer would be.

Other passengers at the railway station were interviewed, including Annie Rose Martin, the inquisitive woman on the bus the same day Ball travelled from Bingara to Warialda railway station.

Annie remembered the young man only too well. He sat alone and fervently read the shipping details in the *Daily Commercial News and Shipping List*. He had a Gladstone bag tucked between his feet.

'He never took his eyes off the newspaper, and read it over and over again,' Annie said.

Sub-Inspector Miller smiled. He had his man.

Miller informed his superior at Inverell police station, Insp John Evans, and an official police search for William Frederick Ball was launched.

Ball was described as about twenty-three years of age, 5ft 9in tall, slender build, fair complexion and hair, clean-shaven, with blue eyes and prominent teeth.

Sydney detectives were notified. The suspect was most likely on a ship in Sydney Harbour preparing to flee the country.

Sen-Sgt John Wallace, of the Sydney water police, began making enquiries. He was told several men recently joined the *Star of Scotland*, docked at Long Nose Wharf at Snail's Bay.

The ship had arrived from New York, via Melbourne, on 15 January fully laden with general merchandise. It was scheduled to leave Sydney Harbour for England, via New Zealand, on 25 January.

*   *   *

Meanwhile, on 22 January, Bill Mack returned to The Hill with his brother, Alex.

They found several pieces of paper, deliberately torn up, in bushland about a quarter of a mile from the homestead. Bill and Alex connected the jagged scraps of paper, as if assembling a jigsaw puzzle.

They discovered one was a letter of reference for Louisa Brooks (Louisa Ball) from a person in England named Mrs Jones and the other was an agreement between William Ball and the labour agency in Toowoomba that facilitated Ball's employment at The Hill.

The next day, Pallal farmhand Charlie Norris found a gun 'wad', part of a shotgun shell used to separate the shot from the powder.

'I found this between the side gate and the house,' he told Bill Mack.

Mack searched the area and found several traces of blood as well as shot marks on a veranda post near the kitchen.

'The person firing would've been near the pantry and meat safe,' he told Norris.

There were also shot marks in the gate and at the foot of the gatepost.

Mack observed the blood stains were in a direct line with the shot marks.

There were also bloodstains on the axle and inside the rim of a wheelbarrow used to take slaughtered sheep to the meat safe.

Bill Mack passed on the findings to Inverell police.

*   *   *

The same afternoon in Sydney Sen-Sgt Wallace and detectives John Walker and Thomas Malone arrived at Customs House in Circular Quay to enquire about new staff appointments on the *Star of Scotland*.

They were given the names of three men. William Frederick Ball, the man they urgently wanted to speak to, was one of them.

The detectives boarded the steamer around 7.30 pm and spoke at length with Captain Edgar Drewett Beck.

'We believe you may have a new crew member who is wanted for questioning about an apparent murder near Bingara, up in the north-west area of the state,' Sen-Sgt Wallace said.

Captain Beck summoned three newly signed crew members to his cabin. Only two responded to the call.

Wallace went below deck and found Ball playing cards and socialising with fellow crewmates. Wallace called him aside.

'Did you join the ship the other day?' Wallace asked.

Ball nodded. 'Yes, I did.'

'You better come with me.'

Wallace escorted Ball back to Captain Beck's cabin, where detectives Walker and Malone were waiting. The other two men were dismissed.

'Where were you before you came to Sydney?' Malone asked Ball.

'I was in Bingara, working on a station owned by a fellow named Bill Mack,' Ball replied.

Malone asked Ball where his wife, Louisa, might be.

'She's still there, at Mack's place.'

Detective Walker then told Ball about the discovery of human bones in the remains of a fire not far from the Mack homestead.

'We suspect they are the remains of your wife and we are

going to arrest you on a charge of murdering her at the property The Hill, on or about 16 January. It is my duty to warn you that anything you say may be used in evidence against you.'

Ball hung his head for a few minutes, as if deep in thought. What came next was totally unexpected.

'Okay, I will tell you the truth. I could not bear to see her in pain, so I shot her and burnt her. She was in terrible pain all the time we were up there and could not walk about. That is the reason I shot her. I shot her the day Bill Mack and his wife went to Pallal, the head property. It was a Tuesday.'

Detective Walker couldn't believe what he was hearing. He wasn't quite sure which line of questioning to take. He took a second or two to regain his composure.

'What weapon did you use?'

'Mr Mack's shotgun. She was walking in the yard when I shot her. She died straight away. I put the gun back in the pantry then I put her in a wheelbarrow and wheeled her to a fire and burnt her,' Ball replied.

Walker left the cabin and returned a few minutes later with a small Gladstone bag and a sailor's kitbag.

'Are these yours?' Walker asked Ball.

'Yes.'

A search of the Gladstone bag revealed two rings. One was a wedding ring.

'They are my wife's rings. I took the wedding ring off her finger after I shot her so I could show her people in England she was dead,' Ball said.

The kitbag also contained a wedding photo, a woman's handbag and another smaller photo.

'Those are my wife's things,' he told the detectives.

Ball fell silent for a minute or two, then blurted out: 'How did you find out I was on this steamer? How did you find out I burnt her?'

'That's what the police are paid for,' replied Detective Walker.

Ball spent the night at Darlinghurst Gaol and the following day appeared before Sydney Water Police Court and was formally charged with murder.

When having his fingerprints taken, Ball repeated his story to Detective Malone.

'I want you to believe I am telling the truth when I say I only did it to put her out of her misery. I did not do it to get rid of her.'

Ball was remanded to Bingara Gaol ahead of a coronial inquiry into the death of his wife.

Early on Tuesday 23 January District Coroner John Charles Lawson Veness, Sgt Byrne and Government Medical Officer, Dr Emilio Demarco visited the scene of the tragedy.

Dr Demarco made a careful and detailed examination of the bones and pronounced them to be those of a human being.

An inquest into the death of Louisa Ball opened at Bingara courthouse on 9 February 1912 before Coroner Veness, the founder of the *Bingara Telegraph* newspaper in 1884.

Narrabri Sub-Insp Simon Butler appeared on behalf of the police.

William Frederick Ball, charged with the wilful murder of his wife, Louisa, was present, handcuffed and manacled.

Ball surprised everyone in the courtroom when he alleged Louisa deliberately drank poison moments before he shot her. He even suggested she may have been dead before he pulled the trigger.

Poison, or a possible suicide attempt, had never been mentioned before the inquest. Not once, not even on the *Star of Scotland* when detectives nabbed Ball.

Everyone present in the tiny courtroom sat in hushed silence and listened intently to Ball's story.

Ball claimed Louisa attempted suicide and he merely wanted to 'put her out of her misery'.

'Why did you not tell the police (earlier) your wife had poisoned herself,' Sub -Insp Butler queried.

'I was so upset I did not know what I was saying. I did not tell them the next day in court (after being arrested in Sydney) either,' Ball said.

There was in fact no mention of poison until Wednesday, 7 February — two days before the inquest — when Ball was taken to the scene of the crime to assist police officers with enquiries.

'That was the first time I mentioned anything about the poison — when I was with police at The Hill two days ago,' Ball said.

'The only reason I had for shooting my wife was because she was in great pain. I thought she had taken poison. She was very bad with rheumatism. That upset me in the first place. I was kept awake at nights because my wife could not sleep with the pain.'

Ball claimed Louisa drank a strange, strong-smelling liquid from a cup a few minutes before her death.

'She drank this stuff before I shot her. I don't know what was in the cup, but it smelled strongly of carbolic,' Ball said, referring to carbolic acid, or phenol, a poisonous chemical normally used as a disinfectant or antiseptic. The chemical is also known as lysol.

'I shot her because I thought she had poisoned herself and appeared to be in great pain. I didn't think to give her an emetic.'

Ball was referring to a vomit-inducing agent, usually a concoction of various plants including mustard and lobelia.

'There was plenty of mustard in the house but I don't think I knew what I was doing at the time,' Ball said. 'I threw the cup under the house.'

Ball shrugged his shoulders when asked why he hid the cup.

He also couldn't explain where his wife obtained carbolic acid, or lysol.

Butler asked Ball where Louisa was standing when she allegedly drank from the cup.

'She was on the veranda between the tank and the end of the veranda, towards the gate,' Ball said. 'I had just returned from opening the gate for Mr Mack when I saw her drinking the stuff. I asked her what she was doing. She made no reply.'

'I saw there was something the matter and rushed to her. She could not speak, or did not want to speak. I took the cup away from her and rushed to the kitchen to get her a drink of water. When I came back, she was staggering. I returned to the kitchen with the cup and got a gun from the pantry. She was lying down when I went to the kitchen.

'I put two cartridges in the gun and went back to the veranda. She was then standing up, but staggering. I fired at my wife, but the cartridge misfired. I then fired the second barrel and took the empty shell out of the gun and threw it away.'

'What position was your wife in when you fired at her?' Butler asked.

'She was staggering on the footpath a little further towards the gate. I put the gun away and then went down to where she was. She was dead and foaming at the mouth. I was standing just outside the pantry door when I fired the shot,' Ball said.

'My wife was staggering and in a falling position when I fired. I then examined the body to see where I had hit her. I found most of the shot had hit her under the heart — there were a few grains scattered. She was not bleeding much.'

Ball told the inquest how he disposed of his wife's body.

'I put her in a wheelbarrow straight away and wheeled her down to Pallal paddock and burnt her,' he said.

'I did not use much wood. There were two limbs together and I placed her between them. I only stayed about a quarter of an hour after lighting the fire. I burnt everything except the things in the house. I took the ring off her finger immediately after shooting her. She only had her wedding ring on. I found the other ring in the bedroom. I burnt her body because I did not want anyone to know anything about it.'

Ball told the inquest he married Louisa five months earlier in England. It was a happy marriage, he claimed.

'I had never quarrelled with her, and did not quarrel with her that day, either before or after the Macks left to go to the other place (Pallal),' he said.

Police Sgt John Byrne told the inquest Ball was taken back to the scene of the alleged murder on Wednesday 7 February.

Also present were Narrabri Sub-Insp Simon Butler and Sydney detectives John Walker and Thomas Malone, the arresting officers who collared Ball on the *Star of Scotland*.

It was at this moment Ball told the officers about a cup from which Louisa allegedly drank poison.

'Did you find the cup?' Ball asked Butler.

'What cup? The cup I threw under the house?'

Butler crawled under the house where Ball indicated and found fragments of a cup.

Detective Malone reached under and found more fragments.

'I believe the fragments smelled of carbolic acid,' Malone told the inquest.

Ball's employer, Bill Mack, told the court he escorted Sgt

John Byrne and Sen-Constable John Adams to The Hill the day after the alleged murder.

'The sergeant and I found a fire outside the side gate. We examined the fire and found portions of a dress material, partially burnt portions of a raincoat and portions of what appeared to have been a photograph frame,' Mack deposed.

'I recognised the material to be similar to that worn by Mrs Ball. We then went into a paddock of Pallal station, west of the house, and there found the remains of a fire that had burnt right out.

'I concluded it was recent, from the presence of white ashes, and the fact it had gone out after a shower of rain. We found remains of burnt bones. I don't know if they were human bones, but we also saw some wire framework, apparently from a woman's hat, the framework of a purse, the stay busks of a lady's corset, a silk buckle apparently from a lady's belt, and also some hairpins.'

Mack told the inquest about the letters he and his brother, Alex, found a few days after the alleged murder.

There were also bloodstains on the ground and wheelbarrow and shotgun pellets in the gate and gatepost, he said.

'Mrs Ball had been in the Bingara Hospital for about eight days during her employment with me,' Mack said. 'Ball's general attitude towards his wife made it appear that he was irritable on account of her inability to work.'

Mack said there was strychnine and arsenic kept in a hut near the house, but no carbolic acid at the house.

'On the day I left Ball at the house, he asked several times for a cheque to send to Sydney. I gave him a cheque for £4, which more than covered the wages due.'

Mack told the inquest there was always a double-barrelled,

breech-loading gun kept in the pantry.

'Ball had access to the pantry and permission to use the gun, and often used it,' Mack said.

Alex Mack corroborated his brother's evidence.

Several other witnesses were called, including Commercial Hotel owner Annie Wilkinson.

'Ball was shown his room. He was alone; there was no woman with him. He was dusty looking and tired. He told me he had just walked in from Pallal, sixteen miles away. His eyes appeared to be very wild,' Mrs Wilkinson told the inquest.

Also called to give evidence was Annie Rose Martin, who travelled on the same bus as Ball from Bingara to Warialda Rail.

Bus driver James Duff Adams, Commercial Hotel porter Henry Green and hotel patron Phillip Edward O'Brien, a local butcher, also gave evidence.

They all testified Ball was alone at the hotel and alone when travelling on the bus.

The coronial inquest into the death of Louisa Ball concluded at Bingara Courthouse on Monday 12 February.

Coroner John Charles Lawson Veness found Louisa Ball died from the effects of gunshot wounds wilfully inflicted by her husband, William Alexander Ball, at The Hill on Tuesday 16 January.

The coroner committed Ball to stand trial at the Armidale circuit court on 23 April on a charge of wilful murder.

*   *   *

The trial before Justice Richard Sly lasted one day.

Crown Prosecutor Sydney Mack told the jury the crime was 'a most revolting one'.

'The accused is a new arrival from England, having come to Australia with his wife in October of last year. The two obtained employment at The Hill, near Bingara, during which time the accused behaved towards his young wife in a most rude and brutal manner,' Prosecutor Mack told the court.

'Ball made a statement before the Coroner's Court, practically admitting his guilt. He said he shot his wife to put her out of her misery, because she suffered from rheumatism. He also claimed she had taken carbolic acid.

'He put the body in a wheelbarrow, wheeled it away, and burned it.'

Ball was defended by barrister Montague Charles Chubb, as instructed by Crown-assigned solicitor David Claverie, from Armidale.

The accused, in a clear, strong voice, told the jury he was not guilty of the crime.

Evidence was taken from Bertha Hendry, a passenger on the *Demosthenes*, the ship William and Louisa Ball were on board when it arrived in Brisbane on 10 October 1911.

Mrs Hendry travelled from Melbourne to give evidence. She said she came from Scotland on the *Demosthenes* and befriended Louisa Ball on the voyage to Australia.

'During the voyage the accused was very unkind to his wife — he was nasty and cruel in his manner towards her. Mrs Ball was often seasick and he never at any time showed her any attention,' Mrs Hendry said.

'He wouldn't even go to have meals with her and she complained to me about it. There were 1,300 passengers on the ship, including a number of married couples, and I noticed the way all the married men behaved towards their wives.'

Defence counsel Chubb responded: 'You must have been

kept very busy.'

Dr Emilio Demarco told the court he examined burnt human remains and bones at The Hill on 23 January.

'I can positively say they were those of a human being — probably those of a female. They were those of a young person,' Dr Demarco said. 'There were portions of bones from the pelvis, shoulder blades, thighs, arms, face, skull and legs. The fingers were practically intact.'

Bingara police Sgt John Byrne deposed he was present when Dr Demarco examined the remains.

Defence counsel Chubb seemed amused.

'Are you an authority on anatomy?' he asked the sergeant.

'I have had considerable experience with bones. On one or two dozen occasions I have helped doctors dissect bones,' replied Byrne.

'Then you have been practically a medical student,' Chubb guffawed.

When the courtroom laughter subsided, Byrne replied: 'I have never examined burnt bones before.'

Sub-Insp Simon Butler said he sent the cup fragments, a section of concrete footpath bearing bloodstains, and other pieces of evidence to assistant government analyst Dr Thomas Cooksey.

'The cup in question had an odour of carbolic acid about it, but there was not enough of the poison to make a test,' Dr Cooksey deposed.

Butler presented Ball's testimony from the coronial inquest. Ball's statement regarding items he burnt along with his wife's body was read to the court.

'I used that fire to burn up a lot of odds and ends. I can't say if I burnt my wife's wedding dress there. I burnt a white dress.

She had two white dresses. I also burnt a raincoat. I hardly know exactly what I did burn. I can't say for certain if I burnt any pictures,' Ball told Butler.

'I burnt an old skirt and a pair of trousers. I burnt them when I was leaving the house. It was the trousers I was wearing when I placed the body on the barrow and afterwards on the fire.'

Ball refuted Bertha Hendry's evidence, labelling it 'incorrect'.

'She has come to this courtroom to swear my life away. She had a set against me from the very start when I tripped her up on something. She didn't like it. My wife and I were always on friendly terms,' he told the court.

Ball reiterated his statement from the coronial inquest. His full confession was read to the court and submitted as evidence.

There was also the argument Louisa Ball may very well have been dead from carbolic poisoning in the moments before Ball raised the firearm and pumped her with shotgun pellets.

Throughout the trial Ball responded to questions clearly and precisely.

'Is there anything else you'd like to say?' defence counsel Chubb asked his client.

'Yes. I am entirely innocent of murder. I must have been mad at the time or otherwise I would not have burnt the body.'

Chubb said his client should be given the benefit of the doubt.

'He was evidently in a crazy state at the time and unable to say whether his wife took poison or not. I honestly think the jury can only find a verdict of manslaughter,' Chubb said.

Chubb said the jury had only three choices: not guilty on the grounds of insanity; not guilty altogether; or guilty of manslaughter.

Crown prosecutor Mack scoffed at Chubb's summation.

'There is no way there could be a verdict of manslaughter. It can only be murder, or nothing,' he said.

'As to insanity, there is not a particle of evidence pointing that way. The accused has made a statement admitting his guilt. His question to detectives, "How did you find it out?", is practically another admission.'

Justice Richard Sly addressed the jury. He completely dismissed any chance of defence counsel adopting a plea of insanity.

'There was absolutely no evidence given as to the alleged insanity of the accused, and it is really remarkable this "innocent man" should do his utmost to obliterate every trace of his crime and finally seek to leave the country at the earliest possible opportunity,' Justice Sly said.

'Although the accused claims he was insane at the time, there has to be most definite evidence to this effect, and this has not been forthcoming. The law never assumes insanity; it has to be proved.'

Justice Sly doubted Ball's claim his wife possibly died from carbolic poisoning seconds before shooting her.

'If the woman was dead before he shot her, he is not guilty of anything,' the judge told the jury.

'But if she was not dead, as the statement at the Coroner's Court would have it, and which is most damning, it is another question altogether.

'Although the accused now holds she was dead before the shot was fired, he never made such a statement earlier. It is really remarkable, if it was true, that he did not say so before.

'Even if the ill-fated woman had taken poison, it was no excuse for shooting her. It was murder all the same.'

The jury retired at 5.30 pm and returned to the courtroom

two hours later. Justice Sly asked the jury foreman if the panel had agreed on a verdict. 'Yes, Your Honour, we have. We find the accused, William Frederick Ball, guilty of wilful murder.'

There were no recommendations attached to the verdict.

Justice Sly turned to the accused.

'Is there anything you wish to say before I pass sentence?'

'Yes, Your Honour. I went home for the purpose of marrying the girl. Do you think any person in his right senses would have done what I'm supposed to have done? I have nothing more to say,' Ball replied.

Justice Sly addressed Ball: 'The sentence of this court is that you be taken from the place whence you came and that on a day to be hereafter named you are taken to the place of execution and hanged by the neck until you are dead. May the Lord have mercy on your soul.'

* * *

Early on Monday 17 June 1912, Archdeacon Julius Lewis of the Armidale Church of England Cathedral sat in a dank prison cell at Armidale Gaol with the convicted murderer.

The chaplain was there at 6.30 am, praying silently for Ball. He attended the condemned man daily.

Ball's striking good looks and confident air were gone. He now wore a full beard and sat quietly, awaiting his fate.

Once slim and taut, Ball gained nearly two stone in weight during imprisonment.

'From the time the decision of the Executive Council was announced that the condemned man was to pay the full penalty of his crime, to within a few days of his execution, Ball had shown a spirit of utter indifference and callousness,' newspaper reports stated.

'All through, his demeanour was one of stubborn disregard to his awful fate. To the ministrations of Archdeacon Lewis, however, who was in daily attendance, he was most attentive and responsive.' Guided by Archdeacon Lewis's spiritual influence, Ball exhibited genuine interest in his Bible and read it over and over during his final days.

Ball slept little the night before his execution and preferred to chat amiably with the prison warder guarding his cell.

'He talked about anything; about the weather mainly and things like that. He drank a cup of tea and ate a little bread for breakfast. He appeared to have no misgivings and was quite resigned to his fate,' the warder told curious pressmen.

A scaffold was erected in the prison quadrangle, well away from the cells. The scaffold, in storage for nearly twenty years, had not been used since 29 November 1892, when Jimmy Tong was hanged for the murder of Harry Hing at Walcha.

Carpenters were called in from Sydney to carry out the gruesome reconstruction.

The brick-lined pit beneath the scaffold, filled in years earlier, was excavated. Dirt and rubble removed from the pit was piled at the back, not quite out of sight but out of the way.

Just before 9 am, Ball was escorted from the cell block to the gallows.

He was dressed in dark grey prison clothes with his arms bound at the back. A white hood was gathered above his dark mop of hair. The hood resembled a strange-looking cap, but carried a dark, grisly purpose.

Ball was escorted on either side by the hangman and his assistant, both dressed in black and protected by anonymity.

Archdeacon Lewis, gaol governor John James Clifford,

Deputy Sheriff George Atkin and Government Medical Officer Dr Walter Eli Harris were next, followed by a small army of prison warders and police officers.

The sound of crunching feet across loose gravel mesmerised onlookers.

Likewise, newspaper reports mesmerised readers.

'The prisoner walked with a firm, even step. There was not the semblance of a falter, and not the slightest move in the muscles of his face, which was somewhat pallid. He firmly strode to the fatal spot where he was to take the last sad look of this world amidst such sombre surroundings. The rarefied mountain air was laden with sunshine. Thin, white mists curled upward against the dark blue of the distant hills and the parched, frost-touched grass of the rolling pastures shone like yellow silk. But none of the bright spirit of the day entered into the prison on the hill.'

Ball, flanked by the hangman and his assistant, slowly mounted the steps to the drop.

On reaching the top, Ball took a long breath, straightened his shoulders, and turned to face the small gathering.

The hangman placed the noose around Ball's neck and pulled it tight under his right ear. Ball's feet were pinioned at the ankles. The hangman gently tapped the white, pleated hood and watched it unfurl over the condemned man's face.

Ball didn't blink; he stood rigid and determined.

At precisely 9 am the hangman drew the bolt and the drop swung open.

William Frederick Ball fell to his death. The rope snapped tight and his body jerked three times.

Death was immediate.

'Without a pause the bolt was drawn and the unfortunate

man was launched into eternity. It was all over in a flash, without the slightest hitch. A few convulsive shudders passed through the body, and that was all. If such a term can be used, the ghastly affair was admirably carried out,' newspapers reported.

Hardened pressmen from *The Sun* and *Armidale Chronicle* looked away.

A warden, visibly shaken by what he saw, raised a hand to the wall to steady himself, for fear of fainting. Archdeacon Lewis wept. He ministered Ball daily and was certain the condemned man found his peace with God.

'He is indeed penitent — that is beyond doubt — and sorry for his dreadful deed,' Archdeacon Lewis whispered.

Twenty minutes later, after the small crowd of silent, dazed witnesses had dispersed, Ball's body was cut down. The deputy-sheriff, police magistrate George Atkin, conducted an inquest on the grounds of Armidale Gaol before a six man jury. Dr Walter Harris pronounced 'death was by hanging in accordance with the law'.

William Frederick Ball, the last man hanged at Armidale Gaol, is buried at Armidale General Cemetery. His wife, and victim, Louisa 'Lois' Ball, is buried at Bingara Cemetery.

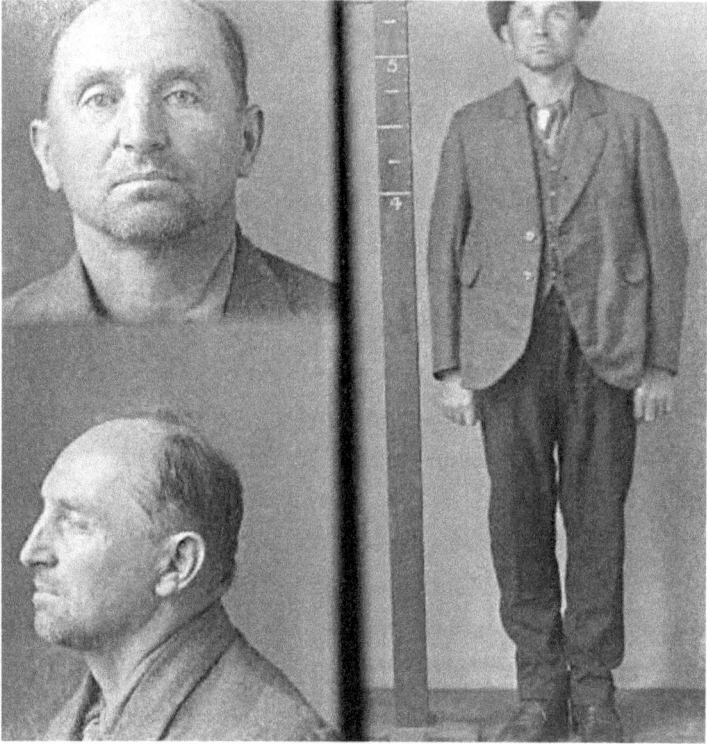

Gaol mugshots of drifter Paul Minel, who killed his mate James Smith in 1929 and dumped his beheaded body in the Narrabri Creek (Image credit: Museums of History NSW — State Archives Collection)

CHAPTER 2

WE HAVE THE HEAD HERE, TOO. WOULD YOU LIKE TO SEE IT?

Rabbit trapper Bill Boyd and his sixteen-year-old son William traipsed along the edge of the soggy creek bed, three miles east of Narrabri in north-western NSW.

It was Sunday 10 November 1929 — a warm, overcast morning — and the trip down from Texas in southern Queensland was proving worthwhile.

Bill wanted to get the traps laid out before rain set in.

'It definitely looks like there's rain coming, son. We'll get as much done as we can,' he said.

A mild spring meant pickings along Narrabri Creek were good and rabbit meat and pelts were in demand.

William ran ahead, setting the traps. As he charged through a clump of she-oaks, he noticed a decaying sack, similar to a chaff bag, partly submerged in an outcrop of river sand about thirty yards from the creek's edge.

As he got closer, the smell felled him. Despite his curiosity, William stopped short of trying to open the sack. The foul smell held him back.

Rather than open the bag, he raced back and told his father about the discovery.

When they returned to the mysterious sack Bill noticed clothing protruding from one corner. The stench was overwhelming.

'Surely not,' he muttered.

Using a hunting knife reserved for skinning rabbits, Bill carefully cut open the bag. He told his son to look away.

Bill Boyd tumbled back in shock as he ripped open the sack, exposing the decomposed remains of a human body.

The head and lower legs were missing and both hands were severed at the wrists. The arms were tied to the torso and the hands were loose in the bag. One hand was bandaged. Both legs were hacked off just above the knees; the ragged remnants of a pair of gabardine trousers clung loosely to the thighs. The torso was clad in a rotting, grey flannel shirt and cardigan-type jacket.

About a dozen house bricks were used to weigh it all down.

Bill and his son ran back to their campsite on a strip of land between the Namoi River and Narrabri Creek, known by locals as The Island.

There were dozens of rabbit carcases neatly laid out alongside their smouldering campfire. They had planned to skin and clean the rabbits that morning and take them to a receiving depot at Boggabri.

But the work ahead was now the furthest thing from their minds.

'We can come back and sort all this out later; we have to get to the police and report this,' Bill told his son.

They jumped in Bill's old lorry and sped back to Narrabri, passing an old shack known as Granny Smith's Hut, one of several derelict cottages and outbuildings near an area called Wall's Paddock.

The hut, with a tiny front veranda and pitched roof, was barely liveable.

Bricks lying around the derelict building, long regarded by superstitious locals as haunted, closely resembled the bricks used to weigh down the bag Bill and his son found in the sandy river-spit off Narrabri Creek.

'Look at those bricks; this will have a few people talking. They reckon that place has ghosts,' Bill half-joked.

He knew this was no time for humour and that local gossip about haunted houses was utter rubbish, but slightly lightening the mood wasn't hurting anyone. William smiled back, but only briefly.

They stared grimly at the road ahead as the old truck rattled and shook its way to town.

Wilf Goodwin, promoted to Narrabri police inspector ten months earlier, was manning the Narrabri station when Bill Boyd and his son ran in and blurted out their incredible story.

'Slow down, boys, slow down,' Goodwin said.

Boyd collected himself. He told Goodwin in detail about the headless, dismembered body on the banks of Narrabri Creek.

Goodwin, along with constables Frank Chalker and Pat McGovern, escorted Boyd and his son back to where the human remains were found.

The body was taken to Narrabri Hospital to undergo a full post-mortem examination by Dr Alex Park.

Insp Goodwin organised more police officers, including Sgt Percy Warburton, Constable John McCann and Aboriginal tracker Ted Dillon, to scour the river banks and drag the creek in case the missing head and legs were still out there.

Grazier Tom Bolton, who leased land close to where the body was found, was certain the bricks weighing down the bag were made locally.

He and Insp Goodwin peered up and down the banks as they watched officers drag Narrabri Creek. Goodwin knew he had one hell of an investigation ahead.

'I'll bet that bag was thrown into the creek about a mile or so from here,' Bolton said. 'Those pinkish bricks are old Narrabri bricks. They were burnt at a kiln near here about forty years ago. I'd pick them anywhere.'

When he got back to Narrabri Hospital, Insp Goodwin had one good clue to work on. The bandage on the dead man's hand was surgical grade and applied professionally.

'We'll need to check all the doctors and hospitals in the district. This hand was bandaged by a medical professional; it's not a home-made affair,' Goodwin said.

It was also unclear whether the body was dumped in Narrabri Creek or further upstream. Recent flooding meant the body could have travelled a considerable distance.

'This poor bugger could've been killed miles from here. What Tom Bolton said about those bricks might be right, though,' Goodwin said.

Constable Wally Mackie was a young, salt-of-the-earth copper with an eye for detail. One of his jobs as a young constable was to make himself known to any strangers that lobbed in town.

Mackie cast his bushman's eye over the remains laid out on the morgue table.

'I met a man a couple of months back and I know this is the trunk of the same man,' he said.

'I have a good idea where he was killed and from where those bricks in the bag were gathered.'

Det-Sgt Frank Matthews, from the Criminal Investigation Bureau in Sydney, was notified. He arrived the following day and began collecting evidence.

The bush telegraph went into overdrive. Within a couple of days, hundreds of people watched from a distance as police dragged the creek, a stop-start operation hampered by wet weather.

Cars lined the road nearly all the way back to Narrabri and children played in the scrub as their parents gawked at the drama unfolding out on the water.

The search took on a carnival atmosphere as police and volunteers combed the area, looking for clues and missing body parts.

The police didn't muck around. By the end of the week, the body was identified and a murder suspect rounded up — and the incredible story of how a pair of drifters fell out had an entire nation mesmerised.

*   *   *

A few months' earlier, German expat Paul Minel and a bloke who went by the name of James Smith arrived in the Narrabri district looking for work.

There were a few watering holes to call in on first, however. They had plenty of money and the folding stuff needed spending.

It was later speculated, but never confirmed, that Smith's actual name was Arthur Sorensen. One story arising frequently was that he used the name James Smith to enlist in World War I, fearing he would be rejected for service if he used his 'foreign' name.

Smith, believed to be of Danish descent, allegedly kept the moniker when he returned to Australia.

Smith and Minel met in 1927 at Quambone, a small outpost about thirty-five miles due west of Coonamble in central-western NSW, but went their separate ways not long afterwards.

For the next two years Minel tramped around the back

blocks of western NSW, picking up work where he could or earning a living as a builder and carpenter.

Smith was doing pretty much the same thing. To get by, he trapped rabbits and sold the skins and meat, and picked up odd jobs here and there.

Smith and Minel knew about lean times. They lived rough, drank hard and barely survived. When they had money, it usually found its way to the cash drawer of the nearest pub.

In June 1929, while breasting the bar at the Terminus Hotel in Coonamble, fifty-year-old Minel bumped into Smith. He recognised him as the bloke he briefly met a couple of years earlier at Quambone.

They got drinking and talking and a friendship of sorts developed. After a two-day booze-up, they teamed up and went rabbiting.

Smith owned an old, grey utility truck, a Willys-Overland Whippet. The truck was registered in the name of Arthur Sorensen, adding weight to the belief that was indeed his real name.

His driver's licence, issued on 13 January that year, also bore the name Arthur Sorensen.

Minel, broad-shouldered, stocky and partly bald with a broad accent, stood a tick over five and a half feet tall and weighed in at twelve and a half-stone . He was born in Leipzig, Germany on 18 June 1879 to Louis and Mena Minel. As a child, he left for South Africa with an uncle and returned to Germany in the mid-1890s. For the next ten years Minel was in and out of gaol for various offences.

In 1896 he spent six days in gaol for 'begging for alms', as well as lending his identification papers to other persons and false pretences. The following year he was given three days' gaol, again for begging.

For two years from 1898, he served in the German army but on 21 March 1900 was charged with desertion and fined 300 deutschmarks.

Twelve months later Minel was again charged with desertion. He was also found guilty of giving away military property, embezzlement, two cases of 'simple' theft, two cases of 'grave' theft and other 'misdemeanours'.

He was removed from the army and gaoled for four years. Six months into the sentence, Minel was found guilty of historic wilful forgery of documents as well as theft and given another three years. Both sentences were served concurrently.

By 1907, he was again before the German courts and given fifteen months' gaol for two counts of embezzlement and one count of false pretences. After his release, Minel opted for a life at sea. For the next couple of years he found employment with various steamship companies and worked chiefly as a fireman.

Minel landed in Queensland in 1912. He went back to sea after three months and returned to Australia on the SS *Port Phillip* in 1914.

He was issued a permit to seek employment in rural areas and for the next twelve years worked his way around NSW, chiefly as a builder and labourer.

Minel was penniless when he met up with Smith at Coonamble.

They jumped in Smith's truck and went looking for rabbits in the Pilliga scrub, a rugged stretch of virgin country midway between Narrabri and Coonamble.

After eight weeks of camping out and trapping rabbits, they sold enough skins to divvy up £50 — about $4000 in new millennium dollars.

Smith and Minel were cashed up and thirsty.

In early August, they headed to Narrabri and camped on the banks of the Narrabri Creek.

Each day they went to town drinking and socialising and to draw money from the Government Savings Bank.

They were told about an empty, rundown cottage near their campsite.

They found the cottage, known as Granny Smith's Hut, and moved in. It stood on ground leased by Tom Bolton who gave them permission to stay.

'You're welcome to camp here as long as you do not do any damage to the place,' Bolton told them.

Minel spoke to Bolton about some work. Bolton wanted a shed built but Minel was in no hurry to strap on the nail bag. Not while there was coin about, anyway.

Oddly, Smith didn't want Minel to take on the building job.

On the way home after a session at the Caledonian Hotel, Smith allegedly told Minel: 'If you take on that job, I'll put a knife in you.'

Minel didn't take the threat too seriously, but decided to return to the pub rather than stay the night with Smith at the hut.

'I'll stay here tonight to be on the safe side; Jim is not in a good mood,' Minel allegedly told hotel licensee, George Brereton, who knew Minel as Jack Booth.

Smith, tall and thin with gaunt features and sunken eyes, had damaged a finger while rabbiting and was treated by a local doctor, who bandaged his hand.

On Thursday 22 August, Smith met up with a woman and took her back to the abandoned hut. Minel stayed in town that night, drinking heavily and regaling locals.

Smith returned the next day and joined Minel at the pub and settled in for another session. The monumental bender continued.

No more was said about Bolton's shed — not until the trip home that night.

Shortly after dusk they loaded up the truck with grog — beer, wine and rum — and headed back to Granny Smith's Hut. The day-long drinking session was far from over — even during the short trip home. Smith and Minel stopped and drank rum and plonk at every gate and nursed beer bottles at every turn.

Again, Smith told Minel not to build the shed for Bolton.

About halfway home, as both men threw back rotgut, the old truck hit a thick tree root, bending the axle and damaging the mudguard and shock absorber.

Both men were shaken but uninjured. Smith, however, was absolutely ropeable.

'You bloody idiot! This truck is the only thing we have. No truck, no money,' he blasted.

The grog-fuelled argument worsened. By the time they got back to the old hut about 11 pm, Smith and Minel were ready to circle.

'Don't you start that job for Bolton, either; I told you what would happen if you did,' Smith warned.

He grabbed a half-brick — they were lying around everywhere — and rushed at Minel. The German raised his hands in self-defence and managed to deflect the missile.

The drunken pair fell to the ground and wrestled violently. Smith roared obscenities, biting Minel on the arm and leg as the free-for-all intensified.

Minel reached out and found the half-brick discarded when

the fight broke out. He raised his arm and struck Smith across the head several times — hard.

Smith fell back, stunned by the blows. The wound began to seep blood.

Smith leaned back on his haunches, dazed by the hit to the head. He nursed the wound and swore under his heaving breath. His rage was intense.

Minel, now suddenly sober, or close to it, sat a safe distance away and brushed himself down.

Both men were out of breath. They slowly calmed down and regained their senses.

Minel watched Smith nervously. He'd only known him a few months and Smith's violent streak caught him completely unawares.

'Please, don't ever do that again; don't ever rush me like that,' he pleaded.

Smith nodded as Minel cautiously approached his injured mate. He helped Smith to his feet and walked him steadily to the hut's front veranda.

Minel unpacked his medicine chest. He bathed Smith's wounds with iodine and bandaged his head. There were deep gashes on either side of the head. Blood oozed through the bandages.

'I've hurt my hand again,' Smith whispered. He could hardly talk.

'The way you hit me, is it any wonder,' replied Minel.

'I'm sorry this has happened Jim, and I'm sorry about the truck, but don't rush at me like that. You frightened the hell out of me. Please, don't ever do that again.'

Minel took a swig from a bottle of rum and passed it to Smith. They sat together silently on the veranda. After a while, Minel helped Smith to the front room and laid him down on an old mattress.

Minel thought it wise to keep well away. He moved to the veranda and sat in an old foldaway field chair, nursing a bottle of wine.

He looked up at the stars, his mind still very much alert despite the drink. Winter was not quite over and a chilly breeze crept across the open plain. A mid-August half-moon shone brightly overhead.

Minel huddled against the cold night air and half-dozed. The grog was starting to kick in, but he was very much aware of his surroundings, and especially mindful of his volatile mate dozing a few yards away. Minel was terrified of Smith's apparent short fuse.

Inside, the badly injured Smith wasn't dozing. He was wide awake. He lay on his back and stared at the tongue-and-groove lining boards above. His aching head rested on an old sugar bag filled with feathers. The moonlight cast a shadow across the papered walls of the ramshackle room.

Smith was very angry. He could hear Minel breathing heavily outside and guessed the German was snoozing.

A loaded hunting rifle rested against the front door jamb, not far from where Minel was sitting.

Smith stared at the rifle and stared at the door. His blood was boiling. His head thumped. He was losing a lot of blood.

Outside, Minel dozed — with one eye open. He saw movement through the doorway and realised Smith was getting up.

Smith appeared in the doorway, explosive with rage. He grabbed the rifle and charged at Minel — but Minel was alert and ready and far too quick.

He sprang from the chair and pushed Smith back across the threshold, snatching the rifle as they wrestled in the darkened room.

Minel blindly pulled the trigger. A single gunshot echoed across Narrabri Creek. Minel ran from the hut, riddled with fear and now completely sober.

He was unsure whether Smith had been hit, but figured it would be a lot smarter to be outside and armed with a gun, rather than inside with an aggressive psychopath.

Minel had no intention of returning to the hut to find out. Not straight away, that was for sure.

Frightened beyond belief and convinced Smith was stark-raving mad, he bided his time behind a clump of bushes. He never let his eyes stray from the hut for too long. The rifle rested half-cocked in the crook of his arm.

After a couple of hours, Minel cautiously made his way back inside. Smith was dead. The old mattress was soaked with blood.

Minel was now in a state of absolute shock. He needed a drink badly. He fell asleep on the veranda of Granny Smith's Hut, nursing a bottle of rum.

The next day, Saturday 24 August, Minel woke early. There was nothing more he could do but head back to town and get on the drink. He needed to get his head together and come up with a plan. He knew there were plenty of deep waterholes in Narrabri Creek.

Minel breasted the bar at several hotels. After one hell of a pub crawl, he returned to the hut shortly after dusk and began cleaning up the mess and disposing of any evidence.

He dragged Smith's body to the rear of the hut as he tried to work out what to do next. He knew no-one would believe his story. He had to get rid of the body and get the hell out of Narrabri.

Minel, with tears streaming down his cheeks, spotted the broad-bladed axe he used for chopping firewood. He picked up the axe and began hacking blindly at Smith's body. He knew he had to get rid of the remains, but Smith was simply too heavy to carry.

The axe wasn't very sharp, but it did the job. The lower limbs and arms were roughly hewn from the torso and with two almighty swings of the axe, Smith's head rolled away and rested against the back wall of the old cottage.

Minel was covered in blood. He drank copious amounts of rum as he carved up the body.

He placed some of the body parts, including the torso, in an old bag and weighed it down with bricks he found lying around the hut.

Minel then dragged the bag down to Narrabri Creek and cast it into the murky, still water.

If Smith's remains were ever found, Minel figured, identification would be much harder if the head was missing. He planned to dispose of the head and lower legs a little later, in a different spot.

Minel collapsed on the banks of Narrabri Creek and wept.

He barely slept a wink that night. Instead, he sat in the old field chair on the front veranda and stared blankly into the night sky. He occasionally read copies of the *Labor Daily* newspaper and *Daily Telegraph Pictorial*.

By dawn, Minel had read both publications from cover to cover — several times.

Later that morning Tom Bolton and his wife, Elizabeth, arrived at the hut to talk to Minel about the shed they had discussed a few days earlier.

They found Minel sitting on the front veranda.

'Where's your mate?' Bolton asked offhandedly.

'He cleared out a day or two ago. I've no idea where he's gone,' Minel replied and quickly changed the subject.

'I can start that building work this week if you like. By the way, I'm going to sell my truck, if you're interested, or know of anybody who might be looking. I'm only asking £70 for the old girl and can probably come down a bit on that — maybe as low as £40. I've got another vehicle, a Ford, back at Orange, down south. I'll head that way soon to collect it,' Minel said.

'Besides, I just can't get used to the gears on this truck and I think the battery is flat as well.'

Tom nodded. 'I can get our son, James, to come over and take a look at it, if you like. He'd have it fixed in no time. Meanwhile, can you come over and have a look at the work we want done; tell us what materials we'll need and give us an idea of how much it will all cost.'

Minel thanked Bolton and smiled. 'I'll be there first thing tomorrow.'

It was at this point, Minel realised the decomposing head and lower limbs of Smith were still in the hut, wrapped up in a sugar bag on the mattress, the bag Smith had filled with downy feathers to use as a pillow.

Saying goodbye to Tom and Elizabeth Bolton couldn't come quickly enough. Once the Boltons were out of sight, Minel went inside and gathered up the ghoulish sack, now clotted with congealed blood.

Hair fragments and feathers were everywhere.

Minel weighed the bag down with more bricks and carried it at arm's length down to the creek. He hiked several hundred feet along the bank before throwing it into the water.

He watched the bag sink and bubble its way out of sight, quite a distance from where he dumped the rest of the body the day before. He offloaded the sugar bag's contents — hundreds of feathers — down a rabbit warren.

Minel began loading Smith's belongings and personal effects on to the broken down truck, including a tent, Smith's mattress and the rifle. He cleaned up the cottage the best he could and frantically began thinking about what to do next.

He spent the next week building the shed for Tom Bolton and camped at Bolton's woolshed.

Bolton's son, Jim, helped Minel tow Smith's truck back to the main gate of the Bolton place. There was no reason not to assume the truck belonged to Minel, and Bolton even took the battery to Narrabri to be checked over and recharged.

The following Tuesday 3 September, Minel drove to Narrabri and met Bolton at the bank, where he was paid £5 for the week's work just completed.

Minel jumped in the truck and left town. He repeatedly looked over his shoulder as he headed south-east to Werris Creek. He bought a bottle of rum at Boggabri to keep him company.

Along the way he sold Smith's rifle, as well as his own shotgun, for £1 to a stranger camped in a wagonette on the side of the road.

He stayed the night at Werris Creek and the following morning drove the short distance north-east to Tamworth.

He camped on the edge of a creek not far from town and meticulously went through Smith's belongings.

Minel found the truck's registration papers in the name of Sorensen, war medals and personal documents including military discharge papers in the name of Smith, and various sales and banking receipts in both names.

He assumed both identities and drove to Tamworth in the truck, which was still registered to 'Arthur Sorensen'.

Minel tried to sell the truck, originally purchased by Smith from Olympic Motors in Coonamble the previous year.

A motoring firm in Tamworth, interested in buying the vehicle, contacted Olympic Motors to confirm ownership of the Overland Whippet and to make sure the vehicle had been paid for in full.

Minel wasn't exactly covering up his tracks as he roamed from town to town.

A Tamworth builder by the name of Jim Ryan gave Minel a job plastering and he later purchased the truck for £40.

On about 16 September, Minel travelled to Orange, about 240 miles south-west of Tamworth.

Minel owned a Ford he'd left there in June but when he arrived he was told by an old acquaintance the police were looking for him.

He scarpered back to Tamworth, where he applied to have the address on Smith's driver's licence changed from Coonamble to Tamworth.

In the meantime, Jim Ryan, who purchased the Overland Whippet believing it belonged to 'Arthur Sorensen', had the name on the registration papers changed to his own.

At some point, Minel told Ryan he changed his name from Sorensen to Smith when he enlisted — a plausible story.

Meanwhile, Minel was again on the move. He said farewell to Tamworth and headed to the New England region. He stopped briefly at Armidale and Tenterfield before settling on Glen Innes, a thriving sheep and cattle town about 200 miles north-east of Tamworth.

Minel's identity alternated between 'James Smith' and 'Arthur Sorensen' as circumstances suited.

He also went by other aliases, including 'Jack Willcox' and 'John Booth'.

Minel gave the axe used to chop up Smith's body to a complete stranger at Glen Innes and found accommodation next to the Royal Hotel, where he shared a room with pub employee, Chris Ince.

He found employment in the area, mainly doing odd jobs and carpentry work, but spent a lot of time drinking.

Minel laid low and kept to himself mostly, but read as many newspapers as he could. He swallowed hard when he saw the breaking story in *The Guardian* about a headless body found by rabbit-trappers in a creek bed near Narrabri. He read how a search was under way for the missing head.

It was now November — more than two months since Smith was killed. Minel realised more than ever that he was nowhere near out of the woods, not by a long shot.

Surely, they won't find Smith's head, Minel reasoned. *That'd be like finding a needle in a haystack.*

The holes in Narrabri Creek were deep and recent flooding meant the head could be miles downstream.

What Minel didn't know was that police were already hot on his trail.

On Tuesday 12 November, two days after the unidentified human remains were found, CIB Det-Sgt Frank Matthews was collecting information about two men who camped in a hut near Narrabri Creek, but were now missing.

There were plenty of Narrabri locals prepared to come forward with stories about Paul Minel and Jim Smith, also known as Jack Willcox and Arthur Sorensen.

Constable Wally Mackie told Matthews he'd called by the old hut about two months earlier to 'feel out' the two strangers.

'One of the men had his hand bandaged,' Mackie said.

'He told me he was a carpenter working in the area.'

Grazier Tom Bolton told Matthews about his dealings with the men.

'They were camped at the hut and one of them started building a shed for me before he left. He told me his name was Jack Willcox and mentioned he was going to Orange to pick up a vehicle after he finished working for me. That was back towards the end of August. I paid him in early September. As far as I know, he left town the same day,' Bolton said.

'The other fellow had his hand bandaged. Willcox told me his mate had left the district. He said he had no idea where he went.

'They were driving an Overland Whippet, grey in colour, and had all sorts of trouble with it. My son helped Willcox get it going again,' he said.

Bricks used to weigh down the corpse were very similar to bricks made at Narrabri Brick Kilns in the late 1800s, and identical to bricks strewn about the hut where the men squatted.

Bloodstains were also found on the floor and walls of the hut and old newspapers, books, empty liquor bottles and cloth bandaging were lying about.

The bandages were similar to the bandage used to wrap the dead man's hand.

Narrabri shopkeepers, the local chemist and hoteliers told Matthews about dealings with the men, now confirmed as James Smith and Paul Minel. The names 'Arthur Sorensen', 'Jack Willcox' and 'Jack Booth' were also mentioned.

Matthews traced the truck to Jim Ryan at Tamworth, who

bought the truck from Minel, thinking he was dealing with 'Arthur Sorensen'.

The torso's bandaged hand also gave police a vital clue; one of the missing men was treated for a broken finger by a doctor in August and Matthews was certain it was the same man Constable Mackie spoke to at Granny Smith's Hut.

The trail led to Glen Innes, where local police were keeping a close eye on Paul Minel. They brought him in for questioning and detained him on suspicion of murder.

Det-Sgt Matthews jumped on the overnight Brisbane Express at Tamworth and arrived in Glen Innes at 6 am on 14 November — four days after Bill and William Boyd found the decomposing, headless body on the banks of Narrabri Creek.

Detective Leonard Allmond, also from Sydney CIB, arrived from Sydney to assist with inquiries.

Glen Innes Sgt Ludwig Schrader and Constable Reg Phillips showed the CIB detectives a bundle of documents including military discharge papers in the name of James Smith, a certificate of qualification to apply for land in the name of James Smith, motor driver's licence No. 286G41 in the name of Arthur Sorenson and a receipt for a Commonwealth Savings Bank passbook in the name of James Smith.

The bank book, issued at the Inverell branch in 1928, was used and stamped at Narrabri on August 10 — two days before the headless body was discovered.

There was a receipt in the name of Arthur Sorensen from the Monarch Garage and Engineering Works at Coonamble and other receipts in the name of James Smith.

There was also a summons in the name of 'Arthur Sorensen alias James Smith' as well as Australian Workers' Union tickets in the name of James Smith.

The documents had been in the possession of Paul Minel, the man now in custody on suspicion of murder.

The same day, nearly 160 miles away at Narrabri, police officers Warburton, McCann and McGovern in company with Aboriginal tracker Ted Dillon were dragging the waters of Narrabri Creek for the fourth day in a row. They'd been at it since dawn. It was now mid-afternoon and they were tired but by no means defeated.

Warm and muggy weather, with intermittent rain, slowed the search. Also the boat, supplied by the local council, leaked badly.

McGovern, shirtless and soaking wet, was at the boat's stern, dragging a grappling iron when he felt it take hold of an object deep down in the swirling water.

'I think I've got it,' he said jubilantly, hauling a rotting bag on to the boat.

The bag broke open and the decomposed remains of a human head rolled across the floor of the boat and rested at McGovern's feet.

The head was in an advanced stage of decay; the face was blackened and cracked and the eyes were cloudy and grey.

McGovern began dry retching. Warburton, McCann and Dillon looked away, horrified.

Constable McCann slowly rowed the boat back to shore.

The *North-Western Courier* reported:

When level with the gunwale, the bag burst, dislodging its contents. The head rolled to the bottom of the boat, frightfully decomposed. The discovery was a sickening one and it was not to be wondered that the searchers were visibly affected. The boat was pulled to the shore with its grisly contents still lying on the floor of the boat, and the spot marked where it was brought to the surface. The crew did not hesitate to step ashore, but did not examine the contents at that moment. From appearances, it looked as if the bag would not be big enough to hold all the missing parts. It could be seen that the head was cleanly cut from the body, and the head was covered in black hair.

Back at Glen Innes police station, detectives Matthews and Allmond, along with Sgt Phillips and Constable Schrader, were interviewing Paul Minel, unaware the head had been found.

They spoke at length with the suspect and obtained a detailed statement. Minel was dishevelled and distressed, but willing to talk.

Most importantly, Minel confessed to the crime. He supplied a full admission and gave the police detailed information.

'I will tell you anything you want to know. I did not mean to kill Jim; he attacked me first,' he whispered.

Matthews stared gravely at Minel. Allmond, Phillips and Schrader looked on.

'Do you mean to say that you were the cause of his death,' Matthews asked.

'Yes,' replied Minel.

'I will caution you now that you need not say anything further unless you wish to do so, as anything you say will be written down and given in evidence.'

Minel slumped back in his chair. The nightmare was over. It was almost a relief. He swallowed hard and fought back tears.

'I want to tell you everything; I want to get it off my mind,' he sighed.

Minel proceeded to tell the officers in stark detail exactly what happened at Granny Smith's Hut the weekend James Smith died. He had a lot to get off his chest.

'We drank three or four bottles of beer on the way home and stopped half an hour at every gate we came to, drinking rum and wine. We got to the hut about 11 o'clock. We had an argument over some little thing. I was frightened of him and he rushed me with a stone or brick. I copped the stone with my hands and we came down on the ground together. He would not let go and I hit him on the head with the stone. He bit me on the arm and on the leg while we were struggling. I let him get up. I remembered his head was bleeding. I washed his head on the veranda with iodine and stuff. I asked him to forgive me and not to rush me again. After I finished the bandaging, he lay down in the front room. I sat outside on the veranda in a little folding chair.'

Detective Matthews listened intently as every word Minel uttered was transcribed.

Allmond, Schrader and Phillips struggled to believe the incredible story.

Minel claimed he shot Smith in self-defence. 'I sat on the veranda. I was half-asleep. He got up. I could see his legs moving. He reached for the gun, which was loaded. He had it in his hand. I reached and grabbed it, too. I pulled it away from him, and pulled the trigger, and he fell back dead on the bed,' he said.

Minel told the officers how he disposed of Smith's body.

'I cut him up with an axe which I had for chopping wood. I cut off his head and legs. I put the pieces in bags and put bricks in them. I then dragged the bags to a tree in front of the hut and threw them in the river,' he said.

When Minel finished, the detectives and police officers needed a few minutes to take it all in.

Detective Matthews breathed deeply. 'I will read your statement over to you, and if you want to correct it, just say so and I will do it.'

Minel nodded.

Matthews read out the lengthy statement verbatim. Minel listened carefully.

'Is it all right, or do you wish to alter it in any way?' the detective asked.

'No, I do not wish to change it,' Minel replied hoarsely.

'Is the statement true?'

'Yes.'

'Has any promise or threat or inducement been held out to you to make this statement?'

'No.'

Minel signed each page of the statement. When finished, he looked directly at Matthews and took a deep breath.

'I am much better now. I have been very worried. I will give you no trouble. I want to get it all over with.'

Detective Allmond produced an axe, handed into police earlier, and other items including a tent and blood-stained clothing.

'Is this the axe that you referred to in your statement — the axe you used to cut up the body of James Smith?' Allmond asked.

'Yes,' replied Minel.

Minel held Allmond's stare.

'I'm sorry,' he whispered.

The following day — Friday 15 November — Minel was formally charged at Glen Innes police court before police magistrate John McCulloch with 'that he did at Narrabri, on or about 22 August, feloniously and maliciously murder James Smith'.

At Narrabri the same day, a post-mortem examination of the body parts was resumed by Dr Alex Park in the presence of Deputy Coroner Herbert Leigh Walker. He had examined the torso earlier in the week.

Dr Park's findings contradicted Minel's version of events. Most importantly, there was no sign of a bullet wound or any indication of gunfire.

Dr Park found a star-shaped fracture on the right side of the skull, above the ear, and an extensive fracture on the left side, running across the crown and down the back of the skull. The right hand was injured and bandaged. Skin on the back of the body was in a dried, mummified condition.

'If the head wounds were caused by a brick, great force must have been used in at least two blows. The wounds on the left side of the head would cause immediate death. It would have been possible for the fractures to have been caused after death,' Dr Park said.

'The legs appear to have been severed with a saw and the head with an axe.'

Dr Park said wounds to the badly decomposed head and torso were possibly caused by a heavy blow from the flat side of an axe head.

A bullet, or wound consistent with being caused by a bullet, was not found.

Back at Glen Innes, Minel was handcuffed and taken to Tamworth by rail. He was escorted by detectives Allmond and Matthews, and Constable Phillips.

The following morning Minel identified Jim Ryan as the man

who bought Smith's Overland Whippet.

Minel told Matthews a police line-up was not necessary.

'I don't want to give any trouble,' he told the detective.

Instead, Minel peered through the lock-up doorway and identified Ryan.

Ryan looked up. 'Yes, this is the man I bought the truck from in the name of Smith or Sorensen.'

Matthews took both men to the police motor garage, where a grey Overland Whippet was parked.

'Yes, that is Jim Smith's truck, the one I sold to Mr Ryan,' Minel said.

Minel was also shown a driver's licence in the name of Arthur Sorensen.

'The address on this licence has been changed from Coonamble to Tamworth,' Matthews said.

Minel nodded. 'Yes, I had it changed.'

That afternoon, Tamworth Constable James Passfield drove Minel and the arresting officers to Narrabri.

'Are you going to take me down to the hut?' Minel asked.

'Would you like to go down there and show us where it all happened?' Matthews asked.

'Yes, I will show you everything. I don't want to give you any trouble.'

Narrabri Police Inspector Wilf Goodwin and Sgt Percy Warburton went with them to Granny Smith's Hut.

Minel sat on an old tree stump and told the officers in graphic detail about the argument that led to the death of Jim Smith.

The November sun beat down. CIB detective Matthews listened to every word.

Minel changed his story several times. The days leading up to the weekend Smith died was one big bender and Minel's mind was foggy. He was unclear about exactly when he found Smith dead in the hut or which night he dumped the body parts in the creek.

After a while, Minel got up and guided the group around the site. Dozens of sightseers and newspaper reporters watched from a distance as Minel identified various objects and locations.

The *North Western Courier* reported: 'It was evident he was imparting something to the detectives and Insp Goodwin and Sgt Warburton. As they walked from one spot to another, an outstretched finger indicated various points about the yard.'

Minel told Matthews about shooting at Smith after Smith allegedly rushed him with the rifle.

He confessed to taking an axe to Smith's body and dumping the head, legs and torso in Narrabri Creek.

'I dragged him outside and chopped him up with the axe. He was too heavy to carry. I put the body and some bricks in one bag, and the head and legs and some bricks in another bag.'

Minel walked the officers to the edge of the creek. 'I threw one of the bags in at that tree.'

'Why did you throw it there?' asked Matthews.

'That is one of the deepest parts of the creek,' Minel replied.

Inside the hut, Minel pointed to a hole on the floorboards of the front room.

'Jim's head would've been about where that hole is; he used to sleep there.'

Minel was taken back to Narrabri police station, where he identified clothing belonging to Smith as well a strip of blood-stained calico cloth.

'That is the piece of calico that I tore off the tent. I used it to bathe Jim's head.'

Matthews looked squarely at Minel. 'We have the head here, too. Would you like to see it?'

Minel shrunk back.

'Oh, no, don't show me the head. I could not look at it. I know it is Jim's. I am not going to give you any trouble,' he said.

Caledonia Hotel licensee George Brereton was called in to identify Minel. Brereton knew Minel as Jack Booth. Brereton also identified the decapitated head of Jim Smith.

'I have no doubt that is the head of the man I knew as Jim, and the mate of the man I have just spoken to (Minel),' he said.

Narrabri local George Huggins came forward.

He told Matthews he'd been out rabbit shooting in early November — about two weeks before William and Bill Boyd found the remains — and saw a bulky bag on the banks of the creek.

'I thought there was a dead dog in it. I took a couple of shots at it and kept moving along the bank looking for rabbits,' he said.

It is unlikely the bag contained the remains of James Smith, given there were no bullets or bullet wounds found at the post-mortem.

District police working on the case were praised by Det-Sgt Matthews.

Within a week of the headless body being found, an arrest was made and the victim identified.

'They worked like a machine,' Matthews said.

'Take the case of the motor lorry. Fifteen minutes after Tamworth police station had been in communication with Coonamble, the lorry was being driven into the police yard at Tamworth. Then, again, at Glen Innes a description of Minel was given over the telephone to stations on Tuesday night, and early on Wednesday morning he was taken to the Glen Innes police station.'

Deep-sea diver Arthur Albert, a celebrity figure well-known in Sydney social circles, arrived in Narrabri to search the deep waterholes of Narrabri Creek. Smith's lower legs were still missing and diver Albert was just the man to find them.

The *Newcastle Sun* reported: 'The presence of diver Albert in the district has caused tremendous interest, and many residents took their children to the scene of operations on Saturday and Sunday'.

'On Saturday, a great crowd gathered around the water holes and gaped as diver Albert came to the surface with his first find — a sugar bag which had no connection with the crime.'

After countless dives to the bottom of Narrabri Creek in various locations, the limbs were never found and the search was abandoned.

An attempt to lower a battery-powered light to the bottom of the creek to improve visibility was also abandoned.

On Monday 2 December Minel appeared in Narrabri police court before Augustus Kieran Loftus on a charge of murder.

Minel was remanded until 9 December, with the inquest into the death of James Smith slated for Thursday 5 December at Narrabri courthouse.

Narrabri auctioneer and former local alderman Herbert Leigh Walker, appointed district deputy coroner in 1913, officiated.

More than twenty witnesses from as far away as Sydney, Coonamble, Glen Innes and Tamworth, were called to give evidence. Dozens of curious spectators angled for front-row seats in the tiny courtroom.

The inquest drew headlines around the country.

The *Sun* reported: 'Stocky, broad-shouldered and outwardly calm, Paul Minel sat in one of the old-time docks that have survived the march of progress in country towns. He was almost hidden by a tall fence of heavy iron bars an inch thick. His build and carriage gave the impression of great strength. His arms are longer than those of most men his size, and his step is alert and springy. Minel is partly bald and the hair is swept across a bald patch above his forehead.'

The *Truth* didn't let readers down:

> Seldom has there been heard in an Australian court a story so gruesome, so fantastic in its very horror, as that which unfolded in the Narrabri police court on Thursday. Present in custody, the cynosure of all eyes, was Paul Minel, who is charged with murder. Short and powerfully built, he sat still and unmoving throughout the hearing. He did not heed the glances that so often wandered, fascinated, in his direction.

Minel, dressed in a serge suit and coloured shirt, was haggard and withdrawn. His thinning hair was neatly combed across his bald head.

Police inspector Wilf Goodwin described the events of Saturday 10 November:

'Bill Boyd and his son William — they were rabbiting in the area — came to the police station at about 12.30 pm and told me a body had been discovered in the creek,' Goodwin said.

'I went with the Boyds, along with constables Chalker and McGovern, and inspected the body, which was later taken to the morgue. A close investigation was made of the locality. We also visited a place called Granny Smith's Hut, where a magazine and piece of calico cloth were found. Both items had apparent bloodstains on them and floorboards inside the hut were splashed with blood. The wallpaper was also stained and little pieces of dried blood fell from the boards when we lifted them. Other articles, including bricks, were found in the hut,' he said.

Insp Goodwin said he was at the hut later in the week when detectives Matthews and Allmond arrived with Minel.

Minel's statement, made to detectives Matthews and Allmond at Glen Innes police station, was read out. Those in attendance hung on every word.

Minel declined to give evidence or make any further statement.

He did, however, apologise repeatedly for killing Smith; he insisted the act was in self-defence.

'I am so sorry,' he told the inquest.

Deputy Coroner Walker found 'James Smith, also known as Arthur Sorensen, died from the effects of blows to the skull and that Paul Minel had feloniously and maliciously slain James Smith.'

The accused lowered his head and wept. His neatly combed hair fell down across his eyes.

Minel was committed to stand trial on one charge of murder at Narrabri circuit court on 15 April 1930 before Justice Augustus James.

Minel was defended by rising young barrister, twenty-seven-year-old Noel McIntosh, the only son of well-known solicitor Herb McIntosh.

Members of the public rushed for seating when the courtroom doors swung open. More than two hundred people assembled outside.

An axe and handsaw, as well as blood-stained planks of timber and a rifle, were among exhibits stacked against panelling in front of the jury box.

Minel's full confession was tendered as evidence and read out by Minel. He pleaded not guilty to the charge of murder and added, 'We drank a good deal while we were camped on the creek and had many rows. I am sorry for what has happened. I did not mean to kill Jim.'

Crown Prosecutor Alf Rainbow told the court the defence 'might be twofold'.

'Either the defendant was attacked and took Smith's life in self-defence or Smith was killed during a fight, probably a drunken brawl. If one of the parties to a fair fight were killed, it might be open for the jury to find the other guilty of manslaughter. If the prisoner killed Smith, the burden of proving that the act was justified rests with me,' he said.

'Minel's story is that, on the night Smith allegedly attacked him with a brick, he took the brick from Smith and hit him with it. The accused also said that later in the night he saw Smith's hand, holding a rifle, come round the door and that he grabbed the rifle, which exploded, and Smith crumpled in a heap. His confession was that, finding Smith dead, he dismembered the body and threw it in the creek,' Rainbow told the twelve-man jury.

'Another statement by the accused was that, after hitting Smith with the brick, the latter pushed him and the explosion of the rifle occurred the following night. There is medical evidence to say that if the injuries to the skull were caused on the first night, Smith could have hardly regained consciousness,' he said.

Dr Park described the post-mortem examination conducted at Narrabri Hospital.

'The figure of a dancing female was tattooed on one arm. I examined the head a few days later and found a star-shaped fracture on the right side and an extensive fracture on the left side, running over the crown and down the back of the skull. I believe the wounds on the left side of the head would cause immediate death,' he said.

'The legs appeared to have been severed with a saw and the head with an axe, and there was a fracture to the right hand, which was bandaged. There were no bullet wounds.'

Detectives Allmond and Matthews gave comprehensive evidence.

Matthews fully detailed his visit to Glen Innes police station and gave a clear statement of his interview with the accused.

'I said (to the accused) I am Detective-Sgt Matthews and with me is Detective Allmond. We have come to see you and question you regarding your movements during the last six months. The accused said: "I will tell you anything you want to know",' Matthews said.

'When we returned to Narrabri the accused showed me where a man (Smith) had been chopped up and the spot where bags were thrown in the river. Both men drank a good deal and often became very quarrelsome.'

Detective Allmond said Minel told him: 'I did not mean to kill Jim.'

Defence counsel Noel McIntosh addressed the jury.

'Did the accused kill Smith in self-defence? It is undisputed that Smith and the accused were wanderers without ties, and both were drinking heavily before the night of Smith's death.'

Counsel suggested it was natural for Minel to dispose of the body and clear out after killing Smith in self-defence.

'It is doubly natural in the case of a foreigner whose mind was confused by drink. While the accused's statements have differed, they have not differed in essential facts and both statements lead to the same conclusion, and to the declaration that he acted in self-defence, without the intention of injuring anyone. The accused still has a mark on his head to show that he was struck during the fight with Smith,' McIntosh said.

Justice James addressed the jury.

'Were it not for the question of provocation, the facts would be very simple,' he said.

'The strong chain of circumstantial evidence which exists was pieced together by the police, who have been doing some very clever work. Where there is a reasonable hypothesis of innocence, the accused is entitled to the benefit, but in this case, the accused had admitted to the killing.

'You, the jury, have very strong evidence of the accused's mistakes. Whether it was intent or reckless indifference, the accused picked up the gun and fired when he could have run away. It is a strange fact the body was found without the head or legs. People don't disfigure bodies without intent and the accused's own statement is contradictive.'

The jury retired at 4 pm and returned three-and-a-half hours later.

There were three possible outcomes — guilty of murder; guilty of manslaughter; or an acquittal.

The foreman informed Justice James the jury could not agree on a verdict.

'Nor is there any likelihood of the jury agreeing,' he said.

Justice James was shocked and visibly irate.

'The evidence is clearly there before you,' he berated. 'This is very unfortunate and means a retrial will be needed.'

'I am sorry, Your Honour, but it is not possible for the jury to agree.'

Justice James ordered the jury be locked up overnight. However, the outcome was the same when the court resumed at 11 am the next day.

The jury was dismissed and Minel placed on remand.

* * *

A new trial was set down for Tuesday 29 April at Armidale courthouse before Justice Percival Halse Rogers, who was elevated to a Supreme Court judge in June 1928.

The case was closely monitored by newspapers across Australia.

The *Armidale Express and New England General Advertiser* reported:

> Minel is a short, thick-set man, typically Teutonic in appearance. He sat almost motionless in the dock, staring straight ahead or studying the faces of the jurymen. He was neatly dressed in a double-breasted grey coat, with soft collar and tie.

Senior Crown Prosecutor Les McKean, as instructed by Bill Sheahan of the Crown Law Department, opened his address by stating the crime was premeditated.

'It was brutal and callous, and deliberately planned and carried out,' McKean told the court.

'In this case, it is admitted, that a man was killed, but the defence is that he was killed in self-defence. The jury must disregard everything that transpired at the previous trial as well as anything they might have heard concerning the previous jury or the previous jury's mentality. The new jury must do nothing in the nature of a compromise. If the facts point to murder, then they must find the accused guilty of murder.'

McKean told the jury about the months leading up to Smith's death.

'James Smith was at Inverell trapping rabbits in 1928. He was next seen at Coonamble in January 1929, with the accused. The victim and the accused were next seen near Narrabri, at a place called Granny Smith's Hut. It appears they were often very drunk and were in Narrabri together fairly often. The next appearance of the accused was at Narrabri when he appeared to be alone.'

McKean argued there was never a clearer case of deliberate murder.

Defence counsel Noel McIntosh, as instructed by Armidale solicitor Bill Murray, delivered an impassioned address to the jury.

'My client admits to killing James Smith, but it was purely a case of self-defence,' he said.

Minel tearfully denied all intent to murder Smith.

'We had a quarrel,' he told the court.

'I saw him moving slowly towards the rifle. I saw him grab it and when I grabbed it, too, I must have pulled the trigger and it went off. I saw my mate fall backwards. I went away and when I returned I saw he was dead. I don't know what I did after that. I can't say more. I didn't intend to kill him.'

Minel sank wearily back in the dock, sobbing uncontrollably.

Narrabri publican George Brereton said Minel and Smith were frequent visitors to the Caledonian Hotel.

Minel stayed at the hotel on the night of Thursday 22 August.

'He was alone and said Smith had gone off with a woman,' Brereton deposed.

'Later that day, Minel and Smith were together and very drunk. I advised them to put their lorry in the pub yard and stay the night. However, they purchased more liquor and drove away. They did a lot of hard drinking and on this night they were both incapable of properly driving the motor lorry,' he said.

Minel returned to the hotel alone the following day and told Brereton that Smith had left for Sydney.

'Minel appeared to be a bit cut up and uncommunicative. Previously, he had been of a cheery and friendly disposition,' Brereton said.

'I remember on one occasion, Minel told me he was afraid to go home to the camp. He told me Smith had threatened to stick him with a knife.'

Depositions taken at the inquest from Bill and William Boyd, the father and son rabbit-trappers who discovered Smith's decaying body on the banks of Narrabri Creek, were presented as evidence.

Justice Halse Rogers said a chief feature of the case was the virtual admission by the defence that all evidence presented by the Crown was true.

'It is solely a question of whether the accused killed the deceased in self-defence or with murder in his heart,' the judge said.

'It is true that standards alter as times alter, but neither now, nor at any other time, was there a more serious crime than that of murder. An assertion of self-defence has to be as closely considered as the actual charge of murder.'

David Cody, the official reader of district river levels, was called to give evidence.

Local rivers flooded in October, about a month after Smith's body parts were dumped in the Narrabri Creek. It was suggested rising waters washed Smith's torso to shore, where it was later found by young rabbit trapper William Boyd.

'Narrabri Creek widened to fifty yards in some places and flooding was quite severe,' Cody said.

After hearing lengthy evidence over three days from more than twenty witnesses, including police officers from Narrabri, Sydney, Glen Innes, Tamworth and Coonamble, the twelve-man jury retired to consider the evidence.

They returned five-and-a-half hours later with a verdict of manslaughter.

Justice Halse Rogers, clearly surprised by the decision, didn't soften his opinion of Minel.

'You are one of the most callous, cold-blooded and calculating individuals that has ever been before the court, but that has nothing to do with me in my duty of passing sentence,' he said.

'The crime is that you took your mate's life. You have taken his life and you have taken everything he had. I cannot conceive a worse case of manslaughter, and I sentence you to imprisonment for fifteen years.'

The judge said it was not for him to inquire what influenced the minds of jury members to reduce the charge from murder to manslaughter.

'I pointed out as clearly as I could that there was no jurisdiction for the jury reducing the charge. You are a lucky man not to have been convicted of murder,' he told Minel.

Defence counsel's appeal for mercy fell on deaf ears.

McIntosh told the judge the verdict indicated there were elements that negated the Crown's case.

'What elements?' Justice Halse Rogers retorted.

'For one thing, they have come to the conclusion, it seems, that the trouble was caused when the men were drunk. I would take it from the verdict that they believe this occurred during a drunken brawl. I do not put it forward as a reason for finding him guilty on a charge of manslaughter, but it certainly has negatived the question of murder,' replied McIntosh.

The judge said an appeal for mercy was rendered ineffective by the events that took place immediately after Smith died — law-abiding citizens simply didn't dismember or behead bodies without intent.

He looked sternly at Minel.

'You have been found guilty of manslaughter. I might say that you are a lucky man that you have not been convicted of murder. It is hard to conceive that manslaughter of a more heinous nature could be committed,' he said.

An appeal against the sentence was heard on Friday 23 May.

Justice Halse Rogers' closing statement from the second trial was read out to the full Court of Criminal Appeal.

The appeal was dismissed and the fifteen-year sentence stood. However, the sentence was backdated to 15 April, the date of the mistrial.

* * *

Confusion over James Smith's real identity deepened a couple of weeks after Minel was sent to gaol.

War medals found in Minel's possession — believed to be originally among Smith's personal effects — were owned by returned Digger Bill Foley, from Inverell.

On Wednesday 18 June 1930, the *NSW Police Gazette and Weekly Record of Crime* noted 'William Edward Foley, or O'Grady, whose military medals were found in the possession of Paul Minel, has been located. The medals were stolen from

Foley, at Inverell, several years ago, and it is inexplicable to him how Minel became possessed of them.'

Smith was rabbit trapping in the Inverell district in 1928, about the time the medals disappeared. He opened an account at the Commonwealth Savings Bank in the name of James Smith.

The timeline overlap casts doubt over Smith's claim he was a returned Digger and that his real name was Arthur Sorensen.

However, Smith's belongings, found in Minel's possession, included army discharge papers in the name of James Smith.

Were the discharge papers stolen as well? Or was James Smith his real name?

It is quite plausible he served under his real name and borrowed Arthur Sorensen's identity, not the other way around.

An Arthur Sorensen did indeed serve in the Great War. He enlisted on 18 January 1916 at the age of twenty-seven and was assigned Service No.4823.

His brother, William, also served.

The Sorensen brothers, from Gympie in Queensland, joined the 26th Infantry Battalion, made up of around 1000 men mainly from Queensland with a smaller number from Tasmania.

Arthur embarked from Brisbane on RMS *Mooltan* on 12 April 1916 and William embarked from Brisbane on HMAT *Commonwealth* two weeks earlier.

William was killed in action in France five months later.

There were also two James Smith enlisted in the 26th Infantry Battalion — Service No.4200 and Service No.6643.

James Smith (6643), from Gympie, enlisted in Cairns and embarked from Sydney on HMAT *Hororata* on 14 June 1917.

James Smith (4200), from Rockhampton, enlisted

in Townsville and embarked from Brisbane on HMAT *Commonwealth* on 28 March 1916.

William Sorensen was also a passenger on HMAT *Commonwealth*.

Arthur Sorensen's age corresponds with that of manslaughter victim James Smith. Sorensen was born in 1889 and Smith was recorded as being forty years of age when killed in 1929, which makes his birth year the same.

However, Private Sorensen died in Queensland in 1939 — ten years after Smith's mutilated body parts were dragged from Narrabri Creek.

There are many unanswered questions surrounding the case.

Chiefly, was the body in Narrabri Creek that of James Smith or Arthur Sorensen — or neither?

It is possible the victim adopted different personas and aliases as he tramped around the backblocks of NSW, using identification papers he 'found' or 'borrowed' along the way.

The identity of the human remains found in Narrabri Creek was never satisfactorily established and 'James Smith or Arthur Sorensen' was buried at Narrabri General Cemetery on 27 November 1929 — and the answers to all the questions went with him.

Paul Minel earned an early release from prison and by the 1940s was in Mudgee, earning a respectable living from building and carpentry work, possibly under the name Jack Willcox.

He died intestate on 13 October 1944 from myocarditis and is buried at the Mudgee Methodist Cemetery.

He left cash, property and jewellery valued at £62, or about $4500 in new millennium dollars.

Postscript:

The Narrabri murder in 1929 established a mystery about the true identity of the victim. Herbert Leigh Walker, the deputy coroner involved in the trial, also left a few questions unanswered.

Walker, a well-known Narrabri resident and highly regarded public figure, was a local stock agent and auctioneer.

He arrived in Narrabri in 1895 and in 1897 was appointed council clerk and inspector of nuisances, a type of health inspector responsible for keeping the town 'clean, sanitary, and safe'.

He later became a Narrabri council alderman.

During the next thirty years Walker held numerous positions in public office, including treasurer of the Local Government Association, deputy-coroner, deputy-sheriff and guardian of minors.

But on 7 November 1932, he was found dead in his Maitland Street office by an employee, Gladys Moore.

An empty glass was near the body.

Walker was due to appear in court that morning to face a charge of fraudulent misappropriation.

The same day, he purchased half a pound of cyanide from chemist Archie Pratt.

Walker told Pratt he needed the cyanide for a client trying to get rid of an ant infestation. He gave Pratt a letter verifying the request.

'I wrapped up the cyanide and gave him the parcel,' Pratt told District Coroner Arthur Hardwick at the subsequent inquest.

Police Sgt James Lambert said Walker was to appear at Narrabri police court the day he was found dead.

'His name was called but he did not appear,' Lambert said.

Dr Les Cook told the coroner he was called to Walker's office shortly after 1 pm on 7 November.

'I was taken to a room at the rear of the office, where I saw the body of Herbert Leigh Walker,' Dr Cook said.

'The deceased was lying on three pillows, which were on the floor. He had been dead for about one hour. The body was dark in colour and the top teeth had bitten into the lower lip, but there were no other signs of violence or injury.

'An almond-like odour was discernible around the body. A glass containing water and a white crystallised substance, which appeared to be cyanide, was alongside the body. There was a quantity of cyanide in a freshly opened tin nearby and some cyanide was spilled on the floor.'

Dr Cook described cyanide as a deadly poison, with five grains being a fatal dose.

'I estimate the deceased had about twenty-five grains,' he said.

After hearing medical and police evidence, Mr Hardwick found 71-year-old Herbert Leigh Walker died from 'the effects of a deadly poison, known as cyanide, wilfully administered by himself'.

William Boyd, the teenager who found James Smith's rotting remains on the banks of Narrabri Creek, stumbled across another gruesome discovery seven years later.

Boyd found human skeletal remains in the bole of a hollow tree when rabbit trapping at Oakey Creek, about five miles from Texas, just north of the Queensland border.

The bones were badly decayed and one of the thigh bones was severely broken and not properly reset.

Police estimated the bones were fifteen to twenty years old. Four large nails were embedded in the tree, as if bark or timber had been fixed across the opening at some point.

Local police said there was no record of any persons missing from the district during the previous twenty years. They theorised the discovery was an Aboriginal burial and did not suspect foul play.

The *Brisbane Truth* reported: 'Many Aborigines, according to men in the force with bush experience, were buried in this fashion many years ago, wherever a hollow tree could be found.'

However, the presence of nails cast doubt over the theory.

'The opening of the tree might have been closed up for the simple purpose of preventing crows from getting at the corpse, or for the more sinister purpose of further assuring it would remain hidden from possible discovery until, at least, identification of the dead man was beyond possibility.'

Harry Mullen was sentenced to ten years in gaol with hard labour for the manslaughter of his mate, Ernie Brown. Mullen steadfastly claimed Brown's death was an accident (Image credit: Brisbane Truth)

CHAPTER 3

EVEN HIS JEWELLERY AND DENTAL PLATES ARE MISSING

E rnie Brown and grog didn't mix.

The fifty-three-year-old former publican and wool-classer was fond of the bottle and liked starting blues when the mood took him.

After a night on the drink at a campsite on the edge of St George in south-west Queensland, an argument over missing liquor led to Brown's death.

His trussed body was found under the Millie Creek Bridge near Miltonville homestead, about fifteen miles north of Garah on Monday, 24 May 1937.

There was a single bullet wound to the head. Brown's legs were doubled back and the body rolled up in a tent-fly, with the head wrapped in a piece of woolpack.

The gruesome discovery was made by drovers Tom Pugsley and Les Hinch. They had rested near the bridge and made their way to the creek's edge to replenish their water supply.

The men, who were taking cattle from Queensland to Midkin station, south of Garah, immediately rode at full gallop to Garah police station and reported the finding.

Sgt Bill Robson and constables Ralph Whalen and Michael Keefe went to investigate.

District Coroner William Cole and Dr Ronald Hunter accompanied the police officers.

Although they were unable to identify the body, Coroner

Cole was confident attaching a toe-tag would be straightforward, given there were distinct features on the face and body, as well as physical evidence at the scene.

'The body has a pronounced receding chin line, which gives him an unusual appearance,' Cole said.

'There are also no teeth in the upper or lower jaw and the hands are small and the nails well-kempt. They are in such a state of preservation, it will be possible to obtain fingerprints and establish identification of the body.

'The presence of a wool sack and potato bag indicates the dead man was connected to shearing sheds somehow — maybe as a shearers' cook or cook's offsider,' the coroner continued.

'There is red dust in the deceased's hair. The evidence points to the fact the murder was most likely carried out in Queensland.'

Shoes and a hat were found on the Garah-Mungindi road, not far from the Millie Creek Bridge, by Weemelah resident Pearlie Porter. She handed them over to Garah police.

Tamworth Superintendent John Walsh and Sydney CIB detectives Tom McRae and Milner Calman, arrived the following day to assist with investigations.

Coroner Cole's observations were close to the mark.

Fingerprints were dispatched by overnight train to Sydney and within twenty-four hours the deceased was identified as wool-classer Ernest Harry Brown, who had been working the shearing sheds in Queensland.

On Wednesday 26 May, the deceased's estranged wife, Hilda Brown, arrived in Moree to formally identify her husband's body. With her was four-year-old daughter, Patricia, and Mrs Brown's sister, Mary Alexander.

Mrs Brown told police her husband had no enemies and believed the motive for the crime was robbery.

'Even his jewellery and dental plates are missing,' Mrs Brown said. 'He possessed a considerable amount of money when he left for the north, and since January he would have earned probably £200 as a wool-classer.'

A post-mortem examination conducted at Moree Hospital by doctors Harry Hollingworth and Ronald Hunter, found death was caused by a bullet wound from a .22 calibre pea rifle.

Det-Sgt McRae was present at the autopsy.

'The man had been dead for three days. He was about six-feet tall and well-built,' Dr Hollingworth said.

'There was a small circular wound in the left side of the head behind the tip of the left ear. A second wound was found in the cranium two-and-a-half inches above the right ear. The bullet dropped out of the second wound.

'All other organs were in a healthy condition. Death was due to a cerebral haemorrhage caused by a piece of lead, being a portion of a .22 calibre bullet, penetrating the brain. Death would have been practically instantaneous.'

A few months earlier, Brown was travelling with a mate, Harry Mullen, in search of work.

Brown was living at Marrickville in Sydney after pub ownership and management stints at Temora, about fifty miles north of Wagga Wagga, and Ulmarra in the Clarence Valley, a short distance north-east of Grafton.

Brown and Mullen found a few weeks' work at Scone then headed further north to Queensland for the shearing season.

In March, they were employed on the property Dongan Plains, about fifty miles from Dirranbandi. Brown was taken on as a wool-classer and Mullen as a piece-picker.

They had known each other for about three years; Mullen and his wife had worked for Brown at the Temora Hotel. Mullen, a small, wiry man and partly bald, worked behind the bar and his wife was employed as a housekeeper. There is evidence she also held the liquor licence while there. They were married in 1921.

Mullen, a former truck driver, left Temora because of Brown's drinking habits and returned to Sydney. Brown was always drunk, Mullen later told police.

Oddly, Mullen's wife stayed on and continued working for Brown at Temora and later at Ulmarra.

Despite their differences, Mullen and Brown teamed up in early 1937 to try their luck in the Queensland shearing sheds. The fact Mullen could not be found when police ramped up investigations made him a chief suspect.

Brown's motor car, a chocolate and cream, Auburn single-seat roadster with a dicky seat, was also missing.

Investigating officers firmly believed Mullen was behind the wheel — and heading somewhere in a hurry.

'We hope to make an early arrest,' Det-Sgt McRae told newspapers.

Within days of the discovery of Brown's body and after interviewing dozens of witnesses at St George, Mungindi and Moree, police had their suspect. A huge manhunt was launched and Mullen was tracked all the way to Sydney.

Around 10 am on Wednesday 19 May, five days before Brown's body was discovered and the day of the alleged murder, shearer George Munro observed Mullen in Brown's vehicle.

Munro was lodging at the Royal Hotel at St George and met Brown and Mullen the previous day. He told police he was relaxing on the hotel's front steps when Mullen drove past in an Auburn single-seater.

'The car stopped on the corner of the hotel,' Munro said. 'Mullen got out of the car and went into the hotel. The dicky seat of the car was up and what appeared to be a swag or mattress was in the back with a cover like a tent-fly over the top.'

Mullen stayed in the hotel briefly then returned to the vehicle and drove a short distance to the Metropolitan Hotel, where he again parked and went inside for a few minutes.

'When he came out, Mullen seemed unconcerned and quite normal. He got back in the vehicle and drove along the Thallon road, towards Mungindi,' Munro said.

A short while later Mullen was spotted on the side of the road by Constable Egmont Rackerman. The constable was heading north with Sgt Rob Carter and Bert Maher, a Mungindi mechanic.

Brown's two-tone Auburn roadster was facing Mungindi with Mullen tinkering under the bonnet.

He had one of the vehicle's number plates in one hand and tools in the other. There was a bulky package like a swag wrapped in tent material in the back and the dicky seat was ajar.

The party heading north stopped and offered help.

'No, everything is fine; it's all right,' Mullen told them.

At this time, it was unknown a crime as serious as murder had been committed, more than likely that very morning.

Sgt Carter and his party wished Mullen good luck and bid him farewell, blissfully unaware the bundle stashed in the back of the vehicle was more than likely the body of Ernest Harry Brown.

Meanwhile, Mullen completed his roadside repairs and continued his journey south, despite a loud knocking noise from the engine.

Just after 4 pm the same day, station hand Jim Robinson was walking along the Mungindi-Moree road, about ten miles from Mungindi, when Mullen pulled over and offered him a lift.

'I travelled about three miles with him and got out about twelve miles from the Millie Creek Bridge, and about three miles from where I live,' Robinson said. 'There appeared to be swags in the back of the car and the dicky seat was half-closed.'

Robinson had been at the Neeworra wine saloon, about six miles from Mungindi. Saloon owner Bob Cooper said he knew Brown from previous visits and last saw him about nine weeks earlier.

'The last time he was here, he had a yellow Auburn car,' Cooper said.

Closer to Moree, Mungindi schoolmaster Ivor Stanford and his family were returning home from Garah when they saw a single-seater Auburn motor car on the Moree side of the Millie Creek Bridge.

'There was only one person in the car,' Stanford said.

It was around this time that Mullen allegedly dumped Brown's body under the Millie Creek Bridge.

Mullen continued heading south and stayed at the Moree Hotel for two nights while waiting for repairs to be done to the vehicle.

By Friday 21 May he had made it to Wyong.

Torrential rain forced Mullen to stay overnight on the central coast and he arrived in Sydney the following morning where his first port of call was to an old friend, Norm Fletcher, a military pensioner living in Newtown.

They had known each other for about sixteen years.

Fletcher was aware Mullen and Brown had gone north for the shearing season.

'We came back to trade the car in for a utility truck and are going back in July,' Mullen told his mate.

Mullen left and returned a few hours later with travel bags and camping equipment, which were stored in the front bedroom and laundry of Fletcher's home.

Fletcher was suspicious. Mullen's story didn't ring true. In Mullen's absence, Fletcher rummaged through his mate's swag and found a Winchester repeating rifle. He handed the rifle over to police.

On Sunday 23 May Mullen approached garage attendant John Fuller at King Street Automotive Services in Newtown with a request to park a vehicle on the premises for a few days.

The vehicle was a two-tone Auburn single-seat roadster.

Mullen told Fuller he travelled from St George in Queensland and was on the lookout for a new vehicle, preferably a Chevrolet.

'Do you think I'd get £5 for the Auburn if I wanted to sell it?' Mullen asked Fuller.

'No question; you'd get that easily — probably more with a trade-in,' Fuller replied.

Mullen was given a gate key so he could access the vehicle at night, and signed for the key using the name Thomas Lee Mullen.

At about midday the following Tuesday, 25 May, Mullen returned to the Newtown garage and collected the vehicle. He left without returning the gate key.

Police tracked Mullen to Newtown but missed him by a matter of hours, and newspapers across the country tracked the police.

'The hunt for the man against whom detectives are building a case, is definitely concentrated on Sydney, and the trail has been followed right to the city,' said one report. 'Brown's car is believed to have been seen at Gunnedah and to have been parked in a garage at Newtown.'

CIB detectives appealed to private and public garage owners to keep an eye out for any two-tone Auburn roadsters frequenting their premises.

They dismissed reports a car similar to Mullen's was seen at Bourke in far-western NSW and concentrated their search in the greater Sydney area.

The police dragnet was closing in on Mullen, and took officers further west toward Penrith. Four detectives and more than twenty officers — on foot and in vehicles — were deployed to the Blue Mountains after detectives were tipped off the suspect had been seen in the area. Mullen had also been traced through a rail ticket he purchased for Glenbrook in the Blue Mountains.

Meanwhile, Brown's Auburn roadster was found in a garage at Stanmore, not far from Newtown.

At about midday on Saturday 29 May, exactly one week after arriving in Sydney, Mullen was found in a dazed state by Constables Sawtell and Engel under bushes on the banks of the Nepean River, about one-and-a-half miles from Penrith.

He was dragged from the scrub and revived with hot coffee.

Dr Fred Higgins treated Mullen, who said he had fallen from a tree.

'I am glad it is all over. He took to me with a rifle and it went off. I should have given myself up,' Mullen told arresting officers.

Mullen, half-starved and at times incoherent, was transported to Penrith police station, where he ate ravenously.

He was moved to CIB headquarters on Central Street, between George and Pitt Streets in the Sydney CBD and charged with the murder of Ernest Harry Brown.

Brown's Auburn roadster was driven to St George, Queensland, by detectives Oswald Milgate and Arthur Nye to be presented as evidence at St George courthouse.

The hearing of thirty-six-year-old Harold Thomas Mullen began on Monday 7 June 1937, at the St George police court before police magistrate Alfred Bernard Hansen.

Prosecution was handled by sub-inspector Aloysius Moloney.

Arnold Bennett, of Coutts and Bennett Solicitors, St George, appeared for the accused.

It was the first time in history the St George court sat at night.

Mullen was charged with wilfully murdering Ernest Harry Brown at a camping reserve three miles from St George on 19 May 1937.

Mullen steadfastly claimed the shooting was accidental, saying Brown aimed a rifle at him after accusing him of stealing liquor.

A struggle ensued and the gun went off, Mullen claimed.

'As far as doing it intentionally, I had no inclination to do that, because he was always a good cobber to me when he was sober, but a terrible man when he was drunk,' Mullen said.

Det-Sgt McRae told the court that on 24 May he went with detective Calman to the Millie Creek Bridge, on the Moree-Mungindi road.

'On the southern side of the bridge, near the eastern end, I saw the body of Brown. It was fully clothed, with the exception of the hat, coat, and boots. It was wrapped in a portion of a tent-fly, and a piece of wool pack was tied around the head. Both legs were trussed up in a flexed position with string and cord. Inside the tent-fly and around the body were a number of gum leaves,' McRae said.

The following day detectives McRae and Calman, in the company of Mungindi Sgt James Johansen and St George constables Harper and Bills, arrived at the reserve grounds near St George, where Brown and Mullen had camped, and collected evidence.

State health department assistant bacteriologist Hubert Edward Brown stated he was given a soil sample, small twig, piece of cork and a portion of burned material for forensic examination.

'Examination showed human blood in the soil and on the twig and blood on some cork, but not enough to say if it was human. There was no evidence of blood on the material,' Brown told the court.

Mungindi schoolmaster Ivor Stanford, who saw Mullen in Brown's vehicle near the Millie Creek Bridge, was asked by Insp Moloney if the person driving the vehicle that day was in the courtroom.

'If a certain person would turn his head to one side and ask a certain question I might be able to recognise him,' Stanford said.

Mullen was requested to turn his head to a particular angle, however, he didn't speak.

'I could say that is the man,' Stanford said.

'Are you able to swear the man you saw that night is in the court?' asked defence counsel Bennett.

'If he asks me the question which the man asked me that night I would be able to swear. Unless he asks the question I am unable to swear,' Stanford said, adding the man he saw in the car near the Mille Bridge spoke as if he were in a hurry.

It was revealed in court that when work finished at Dongan Plains, Brown and Mullen camped by the Balonne River, about three miles from St George.

On 17 May 1937, they stayed at the Royal Hotel in St George while waiting for repairs to be completed to Brown's vehicle. They spent most of the night breasting the bar, a marathon session that saw Brown in bed and crook most of the next day. Royal Hotel barman Frank Kentwell told the court Brown and Mullen were often at the watering hole.

'They would come into town to collect mail and inquire about work,' Kentwell said.

'On 17 May Mullen and Brown came to the hotel about dark and the remark was passed that they'd had a bit of bad luck and had broken an axle on their car.

'They wanted to be put up for the night and I showed them to a room. Later, they left the hotel and returned about 10 pm. Brown was sick and drunk; Mullen appeared quite okay,' Kentwell said. 'Brown at the latter part of his sojourn at the hotel drank OP rum. On the morning of 18 May Mullen came and got drink for his mate who, he said, was "pretty crook". I supplied him with rum.

'Later, Mullen came and asked me to try to keep his mate off the spirits but at about 10.15 am Mullen took another glass of rum upstairs.

'Both of them seemed tip-top mates and very decent chaps,' Kentwell said.

Around 7 pm on 18 May, Brown and Mullen headed back to their campsite on the Balonne River, despite Mullen pleading with Brown to stay in bed at the hotel until fully recovered.

'We were there (at the camp) for about an hour when Brown drove back to town on his own,' Mullen later told Det-Sgt McRae.

'He got back singing and I told him to shut up.'

Brown, still worse for wear after a two-day bender, finally

dozed off. But the following morning, when he awoke, all hell broke loose.

Tonguing for a hair of the dog, Brown went searching for a stash of "rot gut" he had at the campsite.

When Brown couldn't find the liquor, he allegedly grabbed a rifle he kept for shooting white cranes and threatened Mullen.

Brown also commented on Mullen's wife, who worked for him at Temora and Ulmarra.

'He started to abuse my wife. I told him "leave my wife out of this; I don't care what you say to me, but leave my wife out of it",' Mullen told the hearing.

'Brown used to shoot white cranes because he could get a pound a feather, and he brought the rifle into the tent. I didn't know what his intentions were. He said "if you don't find the whiskey there will be something doing" so I tried to take the gun off him. There was a bit of a struggle and he went down on his knees. The rifle went up over his head and went off,' Mullen said.

With his mate dead at his feet, Mullen went into panic mode.

He told detective McRae he planned to report the incident, but changed his mind when weighing up his panic-addled options.

'I thought they (the police) might not believe me so I wrapped him up and cleared out,' Mullen said.

'It was very early in the morning. After he was shot I wrapped up his body and packed up camp. I put him in the back of the car. I burned his Gladstone bag on the campfire. After that, I don't remember anything until I got into Mungindi and got some petrol, and a cup of tea and a sandwich.'

On 4 June, detectives McCrae and Calman escorted Mullen to the Millie Creek Bridge.

'It was dark when I got here. I can't make out how I got him here,' Brown told the officers.

On Thursday 10 June 1937, the hearing was transferred to Mungindi courthouse.

'A ninety-four-mile drive by all interested parties from St George, one car towing an Auburn single-seater which was out of commission, was undertaken so that the hearing might be resumed in Mungindi, the curious town on the Barwon River, half situated in NSW and half in Queensland,' newspapers reported.

A cavalcade of vehicles carrying the police magistrate, police officers and the accused and his solicitor made its way to the border town.

The tiny courthouse was jam-packed, with curious onlookers sitting on kerosene tins to be closer to the action.

More than thirty pieces of evidence were submitted, including soil and twig samples, gum leaves, pieces of cork and scraps of burnt material, a single .22 calibre spent cartridge, a tent-fly, cord and rope, woolpack, blanket, sheet and a flour sack.

Despite Mullen's claims that Brown was a terrible drunk, shearing contractor Charles Stewart, who employed both men at Dongan Plains as well as Woolerbilla, told a different story.

'Brown and Mullen were friendly at both sheds and I saw nothing to indicate they were other than good friends. Brown did not drink at either of the sheds,' Stewart said.

'When Brown commenced work, he was in a proper condition to do so. He was a good worker and knew his job. Brown had no drinking bouts while employed by me and, to my knowledge, neither did Mullen,' he said.

Conversely, Sarah Ann Yarrington, of Marrickville, told the court Brown and his wife had, at one time, boarded with her.

'Sometimes Brown was so drunk it was impossible for him to use a knife and fork. He would remain all night in that condition and, in the morning, would almost be the same,' she said.

On Wednesday 9 June, Mullen was committed for trial at Goondiwindi and, on 24 August, appeared before Justice Hugh Macrossan, charged with wilfully murdering Ernest Harry Brown.

Mullen pleaded not guilty, steadfastly claiming the rifle went off during a struggle to retrieve the weapon from Brown.

Witnesses included the deceased's estranged wife, Hilda, who said she had been married to Brown for six years and lived with him for three of those six years. During that time a daughter, Patricia, was born.

'He had been a model husband, but after a while he started to go out and seemed to neglect the family,' Mrs Brown told the court.

She had a maintenance order taken out against her husband and, at the time of his death, he was behind in payments. Hilda Brown testified her husband would occasionally get drunk and then become very sick.

'He would become so sick he could not hold up his head. He was never quarrelsome when drunk,' she said.

On 27 August Mullen was found guilty of murdering Brown near St George on 19 May.

In summing up, Justice Macrossan said the jury had three choices.

'The accused can be found guilty of wilful murder; guilty of murder; or guilty of manslaughter. The Crown has proved its case beyond reasonable doubt,' Justice Macrossan said. 'The prisoner could have gone into the box and given evidence or he could have made a statement from the dock, but he has done neither.

'If the prisoner had however gone into the witness box he would have been subjected to cross-examination, but if he had made a statement from the dock, he would not have been subject to cross-examination.

'By giving evidence, the prisoner might have been able to have thrown a good deal of light upon certain important matters in the case. However, the prisoner has not given statements, and these the jury could have weighed with the sworn evidence produced by the Crown,' the judge said.

'The test of a mate,' continued the judge, 'could only be gauged by an action which would cause people to say: "That was the action of a friend". Not from drinking in a bar, or working with him.'

'One could not know what was smouldering underneath the appearance of "hail-fellow-well-met".'

Justice Macrossan argued it was difficult to reconcile Mullen's methods of dealing with the body of his mate after the latter's death if the whole incident was indeed an accident, as the accused claimed.

'The most serious of crimes has been committed as a result of the flimsiest of motives,' Justice Macrossan said.

It was also conjectured Brown had, in some way, been associated with Mullen's wife.

'This might have caused a concealed feeling of hostility by Mullen towards Brown,' Justice Macrossan said.

'The other two motives advanced were those of money and Brown's car. There are unplumbed depths in every man's character, and one of them in Mullen's character was his capacity to deal with his dead mate. Did that show great determination, or that the accused was in a dazed condition after the alleged action?'

Justice Macrossan told the jury while it appeared Mullen was unsure what to do with Brown's body after the alleged accident he fully intended to destroy all means of identification. Had the body not been found when it was, there might never have been a trial. 'Before the body was discovered, Mullen, on his own admission, had gone for a drive around Sans Souci and other places with friends while Brown's body smelled to high heaven under the Millie Creek Bridge.

'Did that show Mullen was dazed or did it show he was callous? Once, however, it became known the body had been discovered, Mullen disappeared,' Justice Macrossan said.

He added Mullen was the only person to suggest Brown was "a terrible man on the drink" while other witnesses testified otherwise.

After the jury retired counsel William Mack for Mullen applied for a redirection of the jury on the ground that in summing up Justice Macrossan had misdirected the jury by stating the motive mattered very little.

Counsel Mack submitted that in such a charge, where intention was the element, the motive was material.

He also asked for redirection on a second matter — the disposal of the body.

Justice Macrossan said he believed the jury had been properly instructed.

The jury found Harold Thomas Mullen guilty of the wilful murder of Ernest Harry Brown at a public reserve known as Broadwater, near St George, on 19 May 1937.

Justice Hugh Macrossan sentenced Mullen to imprisonment for life.

The defendant received the verdict and sentence in silence.

Mullen's defence counsel lodged an appeal against the harsh

sentence, and, on Tuesday February 15, 1938, the conviction was quashed by the Queensland Court of Criminal Appeal.

An appeal by the Crown against the quashing of the conviction was then lodged.

However, the High Court of Australia, before Chief Justice John Latham, upheld the decision of the Queensland Court of Criminal Appeal and a new trial was ordered.

'Mullen's defence was that Brown was shot accidentally during a struggle. The defence of accident in a murder case was really a contention that the Crown had not proved the essential elements of intention in the crime charged,' Chief Justice Latham said.

'It was not a defence which excused killing on the ground of self-defence or sought to reduce it to manslaughter on the grounds of provocation. At the trial the jury was told the burden rested on Mullen to establish to the satisfaction of the jury any excuse for the killing of Brown and the defence of accident was one which fell under the heading "excuse".

'Thus, according to that direction, the accused could not properly be acquitted on the ground of accident unless he satisfied the jury the killing was accidental.

'That direction appeared to be wrong in law,' the chief justice said.

*   *   *

A new trial began on 29 March 1938, before Chief Justice James Blair and lasted four days.

After the jury deliberated for two-and-a-half hours, Harold Thomas Mullen was found guilty of manslaughter, with Chief Justice Blair remanding the defendant to Brisbane for sentencing.

On 7 April, Chief Justice Blair sentenced Mullen to ten years' imprisonment with hard labour.

'The Crown case had been put with exceptional fairness and Mr Mack had done everything possible to put Mullen's version of what happened to the jury,' Judge Blair said.

He said the jury had four verdicts open to it — wilful murder, murder, manslaughter or not guilty.

'The jury has found you guilty of manslaughter,' Judge Blair told Mullen. 'They made no recommendation on the grounds you received any provocation, nor did they make any recommendation to mercy.

'A judge's duty in sentencing is the most unpleasant in judicial life and I have given this case very anxious consideration. After full consideration of the circumstances, and treating your case with the utmost leniency I think it deserves, I have decided the sentence of the court should be that you be imprisoned with hard labour for ten years.'

Postscript:

During the trial, Ethel Mullen steadfastly claimed her husband was innocent, despite stories and innuendo she was romantically involved with the victim, Ernie Brown.

She told newspapers her relationship with Brown was purely platonic — merely 'a business partnership' — and that her husband was wrongly accused.

'I cannot see how my husband could have deliberately killed Brown,' she wept outside the Goondiwindi Court House.

'They were great pals. My husband is one of the purest men who ever lived — so kind and gentle he could never bring himself to kill a fowl for the dinner table. How could he be as heartless as the police make him out to be. Brown's death was accidental.'

Likewise, Mullen defended his wife.

'There is all this stuff about Brown and my wife. Various people have tried to throw mud at her because she and Brown kept a hotel at Ulmarra,' he told newspapers.

'I knew all about it, and my wife was Brown's partner with my full consent. It was purely a business proposition, nothing further. I did not object at any time to their being together in the hotel, because I knew there was nothing wrong.'

Three days after Ernie Brown's trussed body was found under the Millie Creek Bridge, he was named as the plaintiff in New South Wales Equity Court proceedings against Ethel Mullen.

Brown and Mrs Mullen had entered an agreement in 1935 when Brown purchased the leasehold of the Commercial Hotel at Ulmarra, near Grafton.

In the statement of claim filed by Brown, he declared that Ethel Mullen agreed, if he purchased the lease, goodwill and licence of the hotel, she would act as a salaried manager and would hold the hotel for him on trust without any right of ownership on her part.

The statement of claim set out that Mrs Mullen 'was to manage and conduct the hotel at a salary mutually agreed upon.'

After the agreement was struck, Brown purchased the premises in the name of Ethel Mary Mullen in August 1935. He borrowed money to make the purchase.

Registration and ownership of his motor vehicle, a chocolate and cream two-tone Auburn single-seat roadster, was also transferred to Mrs Mullen.

Less than twelve months after her shingle was nailed above the Commercial Hotel's main entrance, an application by Mrs

Mullen to transfer the hotel licence to former Hay butcher Bernard McKell was granted in June 1936.

The licence was transferred back to Mrs Mullen one month later and by May 1937 McKell was back at Hay in the western Riverina region cutting up carcases with his brother, Kevin.

Brown had obtained an interim injunction in early 1937 restraining Mrs Mullen from receiving any further monies from March 1 without his consent.

Mrs Mullen admitted the hotel was purchased in her name as a trustee, but she denied she had absolutely no right in the estate or title. She claimed she had not received all salaries due to her. She said money to purchase the hotel was provided jointly by herself and Brown.

However, Ernie Brown's lawyer, James Fitzpatrick, had a problem — his client was dead.

'This matter is complicated by the fact that Brown's body was found in the northern part of New South Wales. The only action we are proposing at present is to have the matter struck out,' Fitzpatrick told Justice Harold Nicholas.

'I don't know whether we are entitled to have it struck out, though. A settlement had been reached (prior to Brown's death) and the money handed over and accounted for.'

Justice Nicholas pondered the dilemma.

'Was any notification of the settlement sent to the office before Brown died,' he asked.

Fitzpatrick sighed. 'No, Your Honour. When the matter is again called, there will be no appearances as there are now no parties, and the case can be struck out.'

CHAPTER 4

THOMAS NEWMAN: THE FIRST MAN HANGED AT DUBBO GAOL

C onvicted murderer Thomas Newman sobbed hysterically. The thirty-year-old farm worker sat pitifully in a tiny cell at Dubbo Gaol. He was waiting to die.

Newman was thick set; a powerful, stocky man with a dark complexion, high cheekbones and deeply indented temples.

But as Newman sat in a cramped gaol cell awaiting death, he was a mere shell of a human being. His shoulders were slumped and his whiskered, weather-beaten face rested forlornly in the palms of his dirty, callused hands. Tears rolled down his cheeks. He was chained to the cell wall and allowed one hour's exercise each day.

Wesleyan ministers Joseph Mullens, Charles Graham and William Clarke consoled the prisoner.

When Newman was awaiting trial, warders found a knife blade in one of his boots, hidden between the inner lining and outer leather.

Newman's intention to commit suicide was patently clear and he was placed under constant watch.

On 5 April 1877 at Dubbo courthouse, Newman was found guilty of murdering and raping twelve-year-old schoolgirl Mary Ann McGregor near Ulamambri station, about nine miles east of Coonabarabran in central-western NSW.

Newman declared his innocence throughout the trial. However, one week before his scheduled execution — Tuesday

*Child-killer Thomas Newman was the first man
hanged at Dubbo Gaol after being found guilty of
murdering twelve-year-old Mary Ann McGregor
in 1877 (Image credit: Museums of History NSW —
State Archives Collection)*

29 May — he broke down and confessed to murdering the little girl.

He unconditionally denied raping Mary Ann. His denial, however, was in complete contrast to medical evidence supplied by Dr Charles Barnard and chemist Edward Purchase.

'As God is my judge I deny this. I do not plan to die with a guilty conscience,' Newman said.

Newman also confessed to being involved in two other murders, but gave few details of the crimes, believed to have been committed in Victoria.

For the next seven days he prayed continuously and penned letters to family and friends begging forgiveness.

But prayers and pleas for salvation could not deny, nor forgive, the pure evil Newman sadistically inflicted on little Mary Ann McGregor.

Newman also wrote an open letter to the people of NSW:

As I lay locked up in this condemned cell, I give you a little history of my life. I would give you a little more but I do not have much time left for myself. I have got to seek forgiveness from the Lord Jesus Christ and I hope a good many of the brethren will do the same outside. I forgive the judge and jury that tried me, and hope the Lord Jesus Christ will bless them all in everlasting life.

While awaiting the hangman's noose, Newman chronicled his life of crime. His lawless ways began in Victoria at sixteen years of age. During the next fourteen years there was prison time at Pentridge and Melbourne gaols as well as incarceration on floating prisons, known as convict hulks.

When not doing gaol time, Newman traipsed across Victoria,

South Australia, NSW and Queensland, thieving sheep and cattle or robbing innocent folk of cash and belongings. Newman tried to go straight a couple of times. He found work in hotels, on farms and with drovers, but invariably returned to his old ways.

In early 1877 he found work shepherding at Ulamambri station, near Coonabarabran.

'Coming to New South Wales was the ruination of me,' he said.

The ministers sat with Newman until midnight. When they left, the prisoner slept soundly until 4 am, when the cold night air stirred him.

Ministers Mullens and Clarke returned to Newman's cell door and stood watch. When Newman awoke, acting gaoler George Henry Bartlett allowed the clergymen entry.

The condemned man was to hang in a few hours.

'My sentence is a just one,' Newman whispered. 'I do not wish to live. I have tried in my heart and soul to make my peace with God and I believe the Lord has heard my prayers. It is better I should die now, for if I get out of gaol I am so weak minded I might afterwards turn again to my evil ways. Tell all I died a Christian.'

Newman started to cry. At 8 am Mullens and Clarke were relieved by Minister Graham, who stayed with Newman while he ate breakfast.

As Newman slowly consumed his last meal of salted meat, bread and black tea, Minister Graham sat by his side and prayed.

Around 8.30 am, ministers Mullens and Clarke returned to the cell and joined the prisoner and Minister Graham. They prayed together and sang hymns, ever so softly. Newman joined them in song.

* * *

Three months earlier, on Sunday 18 February, Newman was shepherding sheep on Ulamambri station, a vast grazing property owned by the Victorian pastoral company, Shanahan and Jennings. Newman had been in the Coonabarabran district less than a fortnight.

The same afternoon, Mary Ann McGregor left her home at nearby Hawthorne Hill to visit neighbours, John and Ann Field. The Fields lived about a mile away.

Mary Ann was dressed in one of her favourite frocks, with a pink ribbon around her neck and a blue ribbon in her hair. As she skipped along, she softly hummed one of her favourite hymns, *I Want to be an Angel*.

She was on her way to collect some eye ointment from Mrs Field. She arrived about 5 pm and stayed for about half an hour. She collected the ointment, as well as a small shirt made by Mrs Field to take to her mother.

'Thank you, Mrs Field,' she said politely.

Mrs Field bid Mary Ann farewell and watched the young girl walk across the paddock.

A short distance away, Thomas Newman was tending his sheep. Mary Ann's singing made him look up.

Mrs Field saw Newman in the distance and observed the shepherd jump a fence and head in the same direction as Mary Ann. She assumed Newman was bringing in the sheep for the evening and thought no more of it.

Her nephew, George Boyle, was also at the house. George

watched Mary Ann walk away. She seemed to quicken her pace. George also saw Newman leap the fence.

'Aunty Ann, look. Mary thinks the shepherd is following her,' he said.

The young girl was indeed aware of Newman's presence and quickened her steps. She walked rapidly along a well-worn track, but was accosted by Newman near Ulamambri station woolshed.

Mary Ann McGregor never made it home.

*   *   *

Meanwhile, Shanahan and Jennings' storekeeper, Theodore Russell, arrived at the woolshed and found the sheep penned much earlier than usual. Newman was nowhere to be found.

As the sun went down, Janet McGregor wondered what might be keeping her daughter. She sent her son, nine-year-old David, across to the neighbour's place to collect his sister.

When David arrived about 8 pm, Mrs Field told him Mary Ann left a good while earlier. 'It was about quarter-to-six when she left. She should be well and truly home by now,' she said.

John Field and David began searching for Mary Ann. Later that night, David rode to Coonabarabran to alert police and resumed the search for his sister when he returned.

He met Newman, who told him a young girl was lying on a ridge near the woolshed.

'Was she asleep?' David asked.

Newman seemed confused by the question.

'Maybe, but I don't think she's dead,' he stammered.

David went to the area indicated by Newman and found his

sister's rigid, battered body under a yellow-box tree. He fell to his knees, crying.

Mary Ann was laid out on her back, arms extended, a mangled mass of blood and bruises. She was partly covered over by branches and tree boughs. A rope was around her neck, tied so tightly it cut through her skin and was embedded in the flesh. Part of her nose was missing.

Mary Ann was less than three hundred yards from home.

Constable George Steele from Coonabarabran arrived at Ulamambri station woolshed and met John Field and district neighbours William Buckley and Thomas Deans. The men were out all night searching.

Steele was taken to Mary Ann's body. David McGregor was with his sister.

Janet McGregor sat with her son and daughter. Mrs McGregor's eyes were red from sobbing. Her body heaved. David held her tenderly.

Constable Steele had never seen a more sorrowful sight. Tears welled in his eyes. He studied Mary Ann's body and the immediate surrounds. There were torn shreds of clothing in a nearby bush and a single coat button close to the body.

He sent for a cart to take Mary Ann's bruised and battered body back to the McGregor home.

Thomas Newman was several hundred yards away, feeding sheep.

Steele mounted his horse and rode across to the shepherd.

'What happened last night is an awful affair,' the constable said.

'Yes; yes it is,' replied Newman.

Steele escorted Newman to a wool room, where the shepherd slept. Steele noted Newman's coat and shirt were torn and there were fresh abrasions on the shepherd's shoulder.

The torn fabric Steele found near Mary Ann's body matched Newman's coat which, Steele observed, was missing a button.

Steele looked suspiciously at Newman. 'You have blood on your coat.'

'Yes, I killed a sheep on Sunday night,' Newman replied.

The constable was not in full uniform.

'Do you know who I am?' he asked Newman.

'Yes, you're a trooper.'

Constable Steele looked Newman directly in the eye.

'Thomas Newman, I arrest you on suspicion of having murdered Mary Ann McGregor.'

Newman showed no emotion at all. His reply shocked the constable.

'Right you are, sir,' Newman said.

Steele manacled the suspect and escorted him to Coonabarabran lock-up.

Later that day, the constable returned to Newman's living quarters and noticed several floorboards were loose. He levered them easily from the joists below.

Steele found a blue ribbon and a pink ribbon as well as a brooch and a small white shirt in the cavity beneath the floor. There was also a length of rope very similar to the rope used to strangle the young girl.

Steele collected Newman's swag and returned to Coonabarabran lock-up. He searched the swag in the presence of Newman and Constable John O'Flaherty. Inside were a pair of drop earrings and a blue bead. There was also a piece of twisted wire and metal brooch leaf.

* * *

When news broke of the gruesome murder, the entire community was shocked and outraged. A pall hung over the tiny, pioneering district.

Angry residents organised lynching parties and marched on the Coonabarabran police station. They wanted answers — and blood.

Newman was kept under lock and key for his own safety.

'The awful crime which has been perpetrated in our midst has thrown the town and district into a state of gloom, indignation and intense excitement,' newspapers reported. 'The people are intensely incensed against Newman, and the police can only protect him from violence with difficulty.'

Freeman's Journal recorded: 'This horrid crime has cast a deep gloom over the entire district. The one feeling reigning supreme from the highest to the lowest, is a universal sympathy for the bereaved parents. Business has been almost entirely suspended by the paralysing sense of this great crime. The accused is a total stranger in this part of the country, having arrived here only eleven days before the murder, being employed as a shepherd with travelling sheep.'

A magisterial inquiry was initiated on Tuesday 20 February by Ulamambri station manager Hubert Hugh Kelly, a justice of the peace.

The NSW Government, however, ordered the facilitation of qualified medical testimony.

Coroner Thomas Alexander Browne and Dr Charles Barnard, both from Gulgong about a hundred miles away, arrived on Thursday 22 February.

Dr Barnard performed a post-mortem examination that evening at the McGregor residence.

At 7 am the following day a jury was sworn in. Jury members

were taken to view Mary Ann's body and a coronial inquest began at Coonabarabran courthouse at 9.30 am.

Evidence was given by police constables George Steele and John O'Flaherty.

Sgt John Ewing was away investigating a bank robbery at Coolah, about sixty miles south-east of Coonabarabran.

When informed of the grisly crime, Ewing rode all night to attend the magisterial inquiry the day after Mary Ann's mutilated body was found.

Dr Barnard's medical testimony showed death was caused by strangulation.

Coonabarabran chemist Edward Purchase deposed Mary Ann McGregor 'was outraged with brutal violence'.

The day-long inquest recorded damning evidence from numerous witnesses and police officers.

At 5.30 pm Coroner Browne summed up, and at 6 pm the twelve-man jury unanimously found Thomas Newman guilty of murdering Mary Ann McGregor.

Newman's response was incredulous.

'Very good,' he replied, and requested reading material 'to pass the time away'.

His cold-hearted indifference shocked the most hardened observers.

Mary Ann McGregor was buried that afternoon at Coonabarabran Cemetery.

The solemn service was delivered by Church of England minister, Henry Dicker.

As pallbearers lowered the coffin, a group of children sang *I Want to be an Angel*, the hymn Mary Ann hummed as she left home to visit neighbours, John and Ann Field.

*   *   *

Thomas Newman was ordered to stand trial at Dubbo Quarter Sessions on Wednesday 4 April before Justice Matthew Henry Stephen.

The Crown's case was led by 28-year-old prosecutor Edmund Barton who, twenty-four years later, would become Australia's first Prime Minister.

Newman was defended by barrister John Watkins, as instructed by court-appointed solicitor Charles Fitzgerald.

The accused was charged with 'having at Ulamambri, near Coonabarabran, on 18 February 1877, wilfully, feloniously, and of malice aforethought, killed and murdered one Mary Ann McGregor, a little girl, aged twelve years'.

Newman pleaded not guilty to the charge and sat expressionless in the dock. He was almost nonchalant and seemingly oblivious to the legal proceedings unfolding around him at Dubbo Court House.

The evidence was overwhelmingly conclusive.

It was proven beyond doubt jewellery and ribbons found in Newman's sleeping quarters belonged to the victim.

Mary Ann's siblings David and Catherine gave evidence.

Seventeen-year-old Catherine deposed: 'On Sunday, the eighteenth of February last, I saw my sister half an hour before she left the house. She wore a pink ribbon round her neck and a blue tie in her hair; the ribbons produced correspond exactly. I put the ribbon around her neck and she went to Mrs Field's with it. She had a brooch on at the same time nearly similar to the one produced, and a pair of earrings (produced) which I recognise by a flaw, like a crack, in one of them.'

David recalled finding the mutilated body of his sister:

'I found her there lying at the foot of the tree, near a log, her feet towards the south. She had one hand stretched out. Her nose was off, like as if bitten off. There were marks of teeth on her face, marks of blood about her face. A rope was tied round her neck, like the rope produced. There was blood on the rope. The rope was tied very tight, with the knot on one side; the flesh was swollen around it. I had difficulty untying the knot,' he told the court.

Constable Steele recalled the moment he arrived at Ulamambri station and saw Mary Ann's body. The rope around her neck had been removed by her brother, David.

'The body was lying on its back, covered over with some boughs. On the body was a female's hat and coloured handkerchief. The arms were extended and the face was very much disfigured. Part of the nose was absent and there were scratches all over the face. A piece of rope was lying underneath the little girl's neck; the neck was very much discoloured and there were stains of blood on the rope,' Steele deposed.

'Mrs McGregor, the mother of the child, was there. She lifted up the child's clothing and pointed out bruises on her knees and thighs.'

The constable gave a detailed account of his initial interview with Newman, and the evidence found afterwards at the suspect's living quarters.

'There was a button and torn clothing very close to the body, identical to the clothing worn by the suspect. There was a button missing from the suspect's coat,' Steele deposed.

It was also alleged Newman herded a flock of sheep around the body to cover up tracks and footprints.

Justice Stephen praised Constable Steele for his detailed, investigative work.

After a trial lasting two days, the jury, after much consideration, found Thomas Newman guilty of the wilful murder of twelve-year-old Mary Ann McGregor.

The sentence was death.

Before Justice Stephen handed down the death penalty, Newman addressed the court: 'I have nothing to say, only that I am perfectly innocent of the charge.'

*   *   *

Shortly before 9 am on Tuesday 29 May 1877, Under-Sheriff Joseph Giovani Thurlow arrived at Thomas Newman's cell door at Dubbo Gaol, accompanied by hangman Robert Howard and his assistant.

As they bound rope around Newman's arms, the condemned man sobbed.

'Please don't let them hurt me.'

Ministers Joseph Mullens, Charles Graham and William Clarke prayed and wept.

'We're ready,' the hangman said.

Gaoler George Bartlett, Under-Sheriff Thurlow and warder Michael Langley led the slow march to the scaffold.

Howard and his assistant flanked Newman. Ministers Mullens, Clarke and Graham fell in behind.

Newman halted for a moment and turned to the gaoler. 'Mr Bartlett, this button is too tight. Please loosen my collar, so the rope will go well around my neck.'

Gaoler Bartlett gently unclipped the top button on Newman's shirt.

The deathly procession continued along a darkened corridor to an open courtyard, where the recently erected gallows stood before a small gathering of witnesses.

About twenty people were present including Dubbo Sub-Insp Edward Grainger, Sgt Thomas Wallings, surgeon Edward Tennant, visiting police magistrate John Oxley Norton, *Dubbo Despatch* editor Will Morgan, hotelier James Yeo and saddler Alf Benton.

It was a glorious autumn morning.

Newman stared skyward. He slowly took in the imposing scaffold before him. Gradually, yet defiantly, Newman ascended the steps. There were twelve in all. The Rev Graham was at his side.

The condemned man, dressed in a prison suit, was pale and withdrawn. His eyes were vacant and his face expressionless.

Newman listened carefully as Mr Graham offered a final prayer.

When the minister finished, there was a pause. Newman cleared his throat.

'Amen,' he whispered hoarsely, then turned to Mr Graham and clasped his hands. There was just enough give in the prisoner's bound wrists to allow a brief embrace.

'Goodbye, Mr Graham. Please remember me to the congregation and let them know I died in peace with God.'

The Rev Graham fought back tears. He nodded grimly and offered one last farewell, then turned and softly descended the stairs.

Hangman Howard ascended the steps and placed the rope around Newman's neck.

'Please don't put it on too tight,' Newman asked.

A white hood was placed over Newman's head. He stood firmly over the drop.

Howard gave the noose a final adjustment. Satisfied, he

stepped aside and nodded. His assistant approached the scaffold and drew the bolt.

The drop snapped open and Newman fell to the void below. The rope tightened immediately.

Thomas Newman was the first man hanged at Dubbo Gaol. *Freeman's Journal* reported:

> The drop fell with a crash and with a dull, sickening thud the body of Thomas Newman hung stiff, still and rigid. Poor murdered Mary Ann McGregor was avenged, and the scaffold received its unhallowed baptism of blood. Death was wonderfully instantaneous, not a limb having quivered to denote he who stood a few short moments before, full of life and vigour, suffered a degrading and horrible death.

When Thomas Newman's lifeless body was cut down and the scaffold dismantled, Dr Walter Tibbits pronounced the death of a cold-blooded killer.

'I, Walter Hugh Tibbits, being the medical officer of the gaol of Dubbo, do hereby declare and certify I have this day witnessed the execution of Thomas Newman, lately convicted and duly sentenced to death at the Circuit Court, Dubbo; and I further certify the said Thomas Newman was, in pursuance of such sentence, hanged by the neck until his body was dead.'

Thomas Newman, the thirty-year-old habitual offender found guilty of raping and murdering twelve-year-old Mary Ann McGregor, was buried in an unmarked grave within the walls of Dubbo Gaol.

CHAPTER 5

IT'S OKAY; I KNOW WHAT I'M DOING

A reckless attempt to journey hundreds of miles in a tiny flat-bottomed boat led to the drowning deaths of a mother and her three young children in 1934.

How English immigrant Lilian Grace Gray, aged thirty-seven, and her children — nine-year-old Royston, eight-year-old Phyllis and sixteen-month-old Colin — became caught up in such a bizarre situation makes a profoundly tragic and truly intriguing story.

The sole survivor of the tragedy was Mrs Gray's young lover, twenty-seven-year-old Charles Arthur May, who had befriended the Gray family in Brisbane the previous year.

Lilian, her husband Fred, also thirty-seven, and their three young kids were a loving, close-knit family who, despite the Great Depression, lived fairly comfortably in Brisbane.

Everything changed when Charlie May entered their lives.

*   *   *

Fred, a popular and well-respected milk vendor, felt sorry for May, a young Englishman down on his luck and living rough. He extended the hand of friendship and welcomed May into the family home.

Fred was a hard worker, determined to succeed. He owned his own business and worked his fingers to the bone. The milk run demanded long, odd hours but he was driven by success.

Fred wanted nothing but the best for his family, and strove tirelessly to achieve his goals. As a result, the family did well despite the tough times, and lived blissfully on Anderson Street in Fortitude Valley.

Fred was born in Bristol, Gloucestershire, England in 1896, one of four children to Henry and Alice Gray. Lilian was born in 1897, in Leyton, Essex, to William and Annette Rogers.

Fred and Lilian were married in Bristol on 4 April 1920. Baby Roy arrived in 1925, followed by sister Phyllis in 1926.

When the children were old enough, Fred and Lilian made ambitious plans to move to Australia. On 7 January 1929, they arrived from London on the *Osterley*.

In 1932, Fred and Lilian welcomed a third child to the fold, a son they named Colin.

Life couldn't be happier for the family of 'new chums'.

Around the same time, Charlie May was experiencing hardship like he'd never known or seen. He was all but destitute. Like countless others across Australia in the early 1930s, he was on the breadline.

May arrived in Australia from London on 29 November 1926, aged eighteen, on the *Oronsay*, disembarking in Brisbane.

From there, May jumped the rattler south and worked his way around Victoria and NSW before making his way back to Queensland. He tramped his way up and down the coast, finally settling in Brisbane.

He lived in a flat on St Paul's Terrace for a while and picked up casual work where he could, spruiking himself as a labourer and sometimes as a painter, builder and decorator.

Life was hard for the young Englishman. He relied largely on his wits and gift of the gab to put food on the table. It was a means of support proving much more reliable than his stop-start income and government dole rations.

In September 1933, May moved into single-room accommodation on Brookes Street, not far from St Paul's Terrace.

A week or two after May settled into his one-bedder, the Gray family relocated to a dwelling across the street.

Fred Gray remembered May as a St Paul's Terrace customer on his milk run and was truly grateful when the friendly neighbour offered to help the family move in.

May lifted heavy furniture and carried luggage, boxes and belongings. He welcomed Fred and his family to Brookes Street with a hearty handshake and a big smile. He joked with Fred, teased the kids, and flirted with Lilian.

This fellow countryman from England with a devil-may-care attitude and magnetic personality was the perfect neighbour. Fred couldn't believe his luck.

And so the hard-working milkman from Bristol, and the down-and-out drifter from London, struck up an odd friendship. They were poles apart, but Fred took a shine to the young English redhead and offered him part-time work on the milk run.

A few weeks later, May moved his belongings into a spare room at the Gray family home.

'You are welcome to live with us until times get better,' Fred told his new friend.

The arrangement worked well — for a few weeks, anyway.

The older Gray children, freckle-faced Roy and little sister Phyllis, with her mop of tousled straw-coloured hair, adored the new lodger, who often helped with their schoolwork and education.

May paid weekly board and used his ration tickets to help with household costs and groceries.

However, the arrangement quickly soured.

Fred and Lilian frequently bickered and arguments often broke out between Fred and May, especially when May tried to tell Fred how to run his milk-vending business.

May, it seemed, was an expert, with no end of advice. It was a big call from a Johnny-come-lately who spent most of his life in Australia on skid row.

Tensions in the household flared. Fred also disliked the way his new-found friend connected with the children, who treated May as their uncle or much older big brother.

However, he was more concerned with the friendship developing between May and his wife, Lilian.

He became increasingly jealous. The situation was too close for comfort. It was untenable and the more Fred and Lilian argued, the closer Lilian and May became.

Fred felt he was on the outer. He felt threatened.

It was all too much for the hard-working milkman. After yet another heated argument, he demanded May leave the family home.

Surprisingly, May readily agreed. He packed his meagre belongings and returned to his old one-bedder across the street.

May had hardly moved out of their lives, but at least he wasn't under the same roof.

The eviction didn't last long as Fred's eight-year-old daughter Phyllis begged her father to allow "Uncle Charlie" to return.

Fred yielded to his daughter's pleas and within days May was again holding court in the family home.

Life in the Gray household seemed marginally better the second time around. Rules were set and adhered to. May was the perfect gentleman and doting "uncle".

Arguments were few and far between — almost non-existent — and May diligently helped Fred deliver milk across greater Brisbane. He never once told him how to run his business.

Fred was still concerned, however. The new arrangement seemed a little too perfect. To Fred it was as if May had cast a spell over the entire family.

* * *

Fred's gut-wrenching belief was spot on.

Talking his way out of tricky situations was Charlie May's stock in trade. He was a master craftsman and caught the Gray family hook, line and sinker.

And Lilian, who was becoming increasingly smitten by the smooth-talking lodger, was his biggest catch. Her impressionable children, Roy and Phyllis, were also captivated by May's carefree ways.

Even Fred couldn't help but like the confident young Londoner. However, his gut feeling told him time and again that things were simply not right. The warning signs were everywhere. Bells were ringing loud and clear.

Fred grew increasingly jealous and deeply anxious about the close relationship May was forming with Lilian right before his eyes.

There was no proof his wife was cheating, but Fred was suspicious. The thought gnawed at him constantly. Sadly, his fears were on the money.

Lilian was indeed having a torrid affair with the knockabout young Englishman, more than ten years her junior.

The passionate affair continued unbridled and, one afternoon while her husband was out delivering milk and the two older children were at school, Lilian told her young lover she was expecting his child.

The sharp-witted boarder, usually lightning fast on the uptake, was lost for words, possibly for the first time in his life.

Lilian gave May an ultimatum — start planning their escape or she would pack up the kids and leave him and her husband and go it alone.

Using savings her husband had squirreled away, Lilian gave May cash to buy a car.

On 31 October 1933, Fred came home for breakfast after his morning milk deliveries.

The children were dressed in their best clothes.

'I have to take them for their appointment this morning at the dental clinic,' Lilian told her husband.

Fred wished them luck and told the children not to be frightened of the dentist. He went back to work. When he returned for lunch, his family was gone. The house was cold and empty.

At first, Fred thought they were simply out for the afternoon, maybe shopping or playing in a nearby park, but as shadows lengthened he was increasingly worried.

Fred criss-crossed nearby streets and dropped by shops his wife often visited, but his search came to nothing.

When he returned home he discovered £34 in cash savings was missing. Some clothing and many of the children's toys were also gone. His gut feeling, the cause of so many sleepless nights in recent weeks, returned with a thudding vengeance.

Fred slumped down in his favourite easy chair, a broken-hearted man, and called the police.

He sobbed quietly as he reported that his wife, her lover and his three young children had disappeared.

*   *   *

Meanwhile, May, Lilian and the children were heading south-west towards the Queensland border east of Goondiwindi.

They hastily packed up a few belongings, bundled the kids into the backseat of the newly acquired vehicle, and fled Brisbane.

Knowing the police would soon be looking for them, May assumed the name of Fred Gray, his one-time benefactor.

They settled at Texas, and later Bonshaw, a small farming village about a hundred miles south-east of Goondiwindi on the NSW side of the border.

May sold the car at Texas and bought a horse and sulky, and for the next couple of months barely scraped by.

When he wasn't cadging or begging from charitable locals, he made a living trapping rabbits on properties and stock routes around the district.

Lilian and her three children had never known such poverty. Christmas and New Year were grim affairs, with little cause for celebration or good tidings.

Back in Brisbane, Fred Gray relentlessly searched the city for his wife and children. He spent the festive season alone in the family home. He, too, had no reason to celebrate.

In January 1934, Charlie May, by now a desperate man with a family to look after, suggested they sell the sulky, buy a boat and embark on a river voyage across three states.

The ambitious voyage would follow the Macintyre, Barwon, Darling and Murray River systems, starting at Goondiwindi in Queensland and finishing in South Australia at Adelaide.

The entire trip, estimated to cover more than 1100 miles, was likely to take several months.

May was possibly inspired by Dr George Clarke and his wife, who successfully completed the trip nearly forty years earlier. The Clarkes, however, sailed in a sixteen-foot canoe yawl, purposely fitted out for the voyage.

In subsequent years, the Clarke expedition was successfully replicated by numerous intrepid adventurers, the most recent a few weeks before Charlie May came up with the bizarre notion to attempt the same journey.

On 30 January, May sold the horse and sulky and the following day bought a tiny, flat-bottom boat — nothing more than a dilapidated dinghy — from Goondiwindi blacksmith and coachbuilder, Robert Cooke.

May paid £4 for the boat, optimistically named the *Phar Lap*.

Cooke used the craft for fishing trips along the Macintyre River and nearby creeks and lagoons.

When May revealed his plan to take his wife and three children from Goondiwindi to Adelaide in the tiny vessel, Cooke told the brash young Englishman he was stark-raving mad.

'That boat is not suitable for anything like that. It is only meant for two people. If you put your wife and kids in it, you are sure to have an accident. You're all likely to drown,' Cooke said.

'It's okay. I know what I'm doing; I understand boating. If there is any danger I will make the boat safer,' May replied.

May later confessed his only maritime experience, was the occasional fishing expedition at Yeppoon during his vagabond travels along the Queensland coast.

The *Phar Lap* was only ten-and-a-half-feet long, one foot deep and three feet, eight inches across at the beam.

There was barely room for food, personal items, clothing and camping equipment, let alone two adults and three children.

The party began the first leg of the epic voyage on 31 January 1934.

May was blasé to the fact the Macintyre River was in flood — running a half-banker when he pushed the *Phar Lap* away from the river's edge — or that the tiny vessel was utterly ill-equipped to undertake such a dangerous journey.

The dinghy averaged about four miles a day during the first few days before heavy rain forced the party to seek shelter.

May rummaged food and hand-outs from various properties along the way, including Bloomfield and Callandoon stations.

The children, exhausted beyond belief, traipsed alongside May as he begged for food and shelter at homesteads.

Boundary rider, Rod McDonald, came to their aid when the weather turned foul and Bloomfield station manager John Ross allowed May, Lilian and the children to stay on the property until the rain cleared.

'Be careful. The river is dangerous and can rise rapidly in weather like this,' Ross warned May.

About 9 am on 5 February they stopped at the property Stewartville, owned by the Carrigan family, about thirty miles from Boggabilla.

They obtained food and clothing from Allan and Mary Carrigan and resumed their journey.

Later that afternoon, tragedy struck when the *Phar Lap* became entangled in partly submerged ti-trees.

May attempted to navigate a narrow passage between fallen trees on the northern bank and a clump of ti-trees on the southern bank. The stemmed torrent was much stronger through the narrow gap and the *Phar Lap* was turned violently sideways. The craft struck a submerged tree trunk and flipped over before miraculously righting itself.

All occupants were flung from the boat like ragdolls. Baby Colin, sound asleep in a small wicker-basket, was swept away by the raging torrent. He was gone within seconds.

Lilian, pregnant with May's child, was quickly pulled under by the strong current and disappeared beneath the foamy surface.

May managed to clutch Roy and Phyllis by gripping their clothing and hoisting them on to the upturned boat. As they clung on for dear life, their mother suddenly emerged from the swirling waters, screeching and choking.

Completely panic-stricken, Lilian allegedly grasped the side of the boat and attempted to clamber back on board to safety.

However, the *Phar Lap* again flipped over and Lilian and her two children were dragged to the dark depths of the unforgiving Macintyre River.

May desperately attempted to rescue them but the fast-flowing torrent was simply too much for the slightly built Englishman.

He was the sole survivor.

*   *   *

May made it back to shore on the Queensland side of the river and returned to Stewartville station, a frantic, sodden, blubbering mess.

He told Allan and Mary Carrigan what unfolded on the raging Macintyre River.

Allan Carrigan immediately notified Boggabilla police station. Charlie May spoke at length with Sgt Charles Grimes.

Nearby neighbours were alerted and a grim search of the swollen river was launched.

Goondiwindi Sgt Stephen Meekin notified Toowoomba

police district inspector Robert Ferguson, who directed officers from neighbouring districts to assist in the search for Lilian Gray and her children.

Police arrived with grappling irons and ropes to search for the victims. Recent rains and a rising Macintyre River made the search risky.

Police officers consoled May, who told them the boat overturned several times. He had still not divulged that Lilian was his lover, not his wife.

'I saw my wife struggling in the water, holding one of the children (Roy) above her. I immediately went to her aid, but seeing one of the other children in difficulties I left my wife and tried to save the other child (Phyllis). Before I could reach the child, she was washed downstream, and my wife and other children also disappeared,' May said.

'I reached the bank in an exhausted state and immediately notified Mr Allan Carrigan, the owner of Stewartville station, who informed the police.'

Several boats were used to drag the river and a second tragedy was avoided when one of the craft carrying three officers overturned.

Constables Claude Wagner from Talwood, Norman Madsen (Goondiwindi) and Horace Johnson from Boomi were all strong swimmers, however, and safely made it to shore.

Stewartville station was used as ground-zero for the huge search operation as scores of police and volunteers from across the region scoured the area.

There was still hope the missing family members may have made it safely to shore.

Room was made in the Carrigan homestead to accommodate

parties of police and civilians as the huge search continued. Horses, motor cars and boats were at their disposal.

Back in Brisbane, distraught milkman Fred Gray learned of his family's death the worst possible way.

When newspapers broke the story, police were led to believe Lilian, Roy, Phyllis and Colin were Charlie May's wife and children, and reported the tragedy as such.

Fred Gray read about the accident in the *Courier Mail* as he sat down for breakfast after completing early morning milk deliveries.

He slumped down in his favourite easy chair, picked up the telephone, and called the police.

Around 11.30 am on Wednesday 7 February, the body of Lilian Gray was found entangled in tree roots on the NSW side of the Macintyre River, about one mile from Stewartville station.

Shortly afterwards, the body of baby Colin was recovered from the murky, dark brown water.

William Kent and his wife, relatives of Lilian Gray, arrived from Brisbane to formerly identify the bodies.

Newspapers reported Charlie May was 'ill and overcome with despair' as the search continued.

'His face, wan, thin and drawn, is covered by three days' growth of beard. Searchers relate that while he was assisting them, he would suddenly cover his face with his hands and cry out in anguish.'

Moree Coroner William Cole directed the bodies of Lilian and Colin Gray be laid to rest on the banks of the Macintyre River.

Members of the search party silently constructed a makeshift coffin and Dr Edward Perry travelled from Goondiwindi to conduct a post-mortem examination.

Mother and son were buried together, a few yards from where Lilian was found snagged in the angry torrent.

Sgt Charles Grimes solemnly conducted a service to a small group of mourners.

Charlie May, a broken-down wreck of a man, sat alone on a log about a hundred yards away, his face buried in his hands. He wept quietly as Sgt Grimes addressed the small gathering.

A few minutes after Grimes closed the riverside service and bowed his head to pray, Constable Claude Wagner and Sgt Edward Ayres arrived by boat with the body of eight-year-old Phyllis Gray.

They found the little girl midstream, not far from the NSW side of the river, attached to a clump of driftwood.

By now, the flood-swollen river had subsided considerably.

Phyllis was laid to rest with her mother and baby brother on the banks of the Macintyre River and the funeral service was resumed.

About 5.30 pm on Friday 9 February, the bloated body of nine-year-old Roy Gray was found wedged between two logs, about two hundred yards downstream from where the *Phar Lap* capsized.

The gruesome discovery was made by Sgt Ayres and Constable Wagner.

An oar belonging to the *Phar Lap* was found six miles downstream, further emphasising the overpowering force of the flooded Macintyre River when the dinghy overturned.

An atlas and several items of clothing were found strewn along the river's edge.

Sgt Ayres conducted a poignant service as Roy joined his mother and siblings in the lonely grave on the banks of the Macintyre River, less than a mile from where the boat overturned.

The following day at Stewartville station, Sgt Grimes arrested Charlie May on a charge of vagrancy.

May appeared before Justice of the Peace William Gow at Boggabilla courthouse and was found to have 'insufficient lawful means of support'.

'Do you have anything to say for yourself?' Justice Gow asked.

'Nothing,' replied May.

Sgt Grimes requested a remand of eight days, which Justice Gow granted. May did not apply for bail.

On Monday 12 March 1934 a magisterial inquiry into the deaths of Lilian Gray and her children Roy, Phyllis and Colin opened at Boggabilla courthouse before police magistrate George James Johnstone, who travelled from Narrabri to oversee proceedings.

Several witnesses were called to give evidence, including Lilian Gray's grieving husband, Fred.

The sad tale, described by newspapers as a "matrimonial shipwreck" and a "sordid, pathetic story", made headlines across Australia.

Charlie May, the only witness to the tragedy, more than once changed his version of events as the inquiry progressed.

Sgt Grimes referred to a statement made by May shortly after the deaths of Lilian Gray and her children.

'May said in his statement, he had never been too familiar with Gray's wife,' Grimes told the police magistrate.

However, May interjected: 'That is wrong. We were more than familiar. The reason I said in my statement I had not had relationships with Mrs Gray was because I did not want it to get into the newspapers.'

May said he and Lilian had no particular destination in mind when they left Brisbane. However, after barely surviving a long, hot summer in towns and villages along the Macintyre River, they decided to pack up camp and head to Adelaide.

'Mrs Gray was in a certain way and expected to be confined there,' May said.

They decided, for some bizarre reason, to attempt the trip by boat.

May denied telling Sgt Grimes he caught hold of the children and placed them in the *Phar Lap*, when describing what happened that steamy January afternoon.

May said 'everything seemed to go black' when the boat turned over.

'I came up underneath a tree on the Queensland bank of the river, seventy-five or a hundred yards away from the spot where the boat went down,' he said.

Sgt Grimes told the court May did not search the NSW side of the river.

'This is despite the fact the boat capsized seven yards from that side of the river,' Grimes said.

May shook his head. 'I have no recollection of swimming. When I came out of the river I looked along the Queensland side.'

Sgt Grimes grilled May relentlessly.

'I put it to you that this is what happened: The boat capsized and came up where you had it tied, but you continued to hang on to the boat until it came to the tree and then you swam to the bank,' Sgt Grimes said.

'No, that is not what happened,' replied May.

Sgt Edward Ayres supported his colleague's theory.

'In my opinion, May's statement that he grabbed Roy and Phyllis and put them in to the boat or on the side of the boat is utterly impossible,' Sgt Ayres said.

'It is almost as impossible as his statement that he remained under the water from where he let go his hold of the boat to where he says he reached the tree more than seventy yards distant.'

Sgt Ayres said the current was stronger on the NSW side of the river.

'I cannot understand how May came to be washed up on the Queensland side of the river. All the bodies were found on the NSW side.'

Sgt Grimes told the magistrate he organised a search party after May telephoned him from Stewartville station. 'May said, when the boat capsized it was six feet from the NSW bank. The river there was seven feet deep.'

'It must have been apparent to May that this tragedy was imminent. I cannot understand how he was washed out on the Queensland side of the river. He could not catch hold of the boat and at the same time hold up the two children as he said he did,' Sgt Grimes argued.

The sergeant then fired a barrage of questions at May.

'Have you had any experience with boats?'

'I used to do a bit of fishing around Yeppoon,' May replied.

May could not recall whether he caught hold of Roy and Phyllis when the boat capsized. He told Sgt Grimes he was under the impression he had.

'But you definitely say so in your statement. There is nothing about an impression you may have been under. Why did you put that in your statement?' Sgt Grimes argued.

'I don't know. In thinking it over, I believe we might all have seized hold of the boat.'

Sgt Grimes simply did not believe May's account of the tragedy.

'Why did you run along the Queensland side of the river, which is fifty to sixty yards wide, searching for people who could not swim and who disappeared thirteen or fourteen feet from the NSW bank?'

'I thought I might see Roy or Phyllis hanging on to the boat,' May replied.

May recanted everything he allegedly told Sgt Grimes when Allan Carrigan telephoned Boggabilla police station from Stewartville station.

'I think I was half-crazy at the time,' May said.

May denied Lilian and her children suffered months of hardship after leaving Brisbane.

'Did you not cadge food and other items around Texas and Bonshaw?' Sgt Grimes asked.

'No,' replied May.

'Day by day your condition became worse and you were living on charity all along the riverbank,' Sgt Grimes said.

'I intended to fish for food but rain prevented me and I had to get food from Stewartville station and Mr McDonald. I take full responsibility for what happened, but I was not responsible for us running short of food,' replied May.

Sgt Grimes questioned May at length about the time he lodged with Fred Gray and his family.

May was penniless and out of work when the Gray family became his neighbours.

'Gray took you into his home when you were in want,' Sgt Grimes said.

'I was never in want at any time,' May replied.

'Did you ask Gray to take you in?'

'No. I think it was a mutual arrangement. I gave him a hand to build up his home and went to auction sales, getting furniture for him,' May replied.

'Where did Mrs Gray get the £15 she gave you (to buy a vehicle)?'

'I don't know. I didn't ask her. The day before we left she told me she was in a certain condition and asked me to take her away. She said she could get the money and it was arranged I should take her away,' May replied.

'There was more than £15, was there not?'

'Yes, but I don't know how much. Mrs Gray always carried it. She gave me the money to buy the car, but I didn't know whether it was her husband's money. I did not worry about that aspect of it at the time.'

The young Englishman appeared at the inquiry in a dishevelled state. He was clad in nothing more than rags and his mental state was deteriorating quickly.

Midway through the inquiry, May delivered a rambling discourse about his philosophy on life and morals in general. He was at times incoherent and his words jumbled.

Magistrate Johnstone cut him short.

'None of your philosophy is evidence in this case,' he told May.

May denied he was told by Robert Cooke, the Goondiwindi blacksmith who sold him the boat, that attempting a voyage to Adelaide from Goondiwindi in such a small craft was foolhardy.

'Cooke said he had been fishing in the boat. He did not say it was unsafe. He did say the boat was "not too clever" when standing in it while fishing,' May said.

Sgt Grimes shook his head despairingly.

'Did Cooke say: "Why, man, that boat is not suitable for

anything like that (a voyage to Adelaide). It is only suitable for two persons. If ever you attempt to put three kids and a woman in that boat you are sure to have an accident, and probably the whole lot of you will be drowned".'

'No,' replied May.

Fred Gray told the inquiry his family lived in perfect harmony until Charlie May entered their lives.

'I have always been in steady work and my wife and I lived together contentedly for thirteen years,' Gray said. 'I treated my wife and my family with kindness. In fact, there was always money in the house, more than was necessary for immediate needs.'

May, infuriated by Gray's testimony, jumped angrily from his seat and cross-examined the milkman.

'Did you cause your wife to leave home?' May asked.

'No, no. She never left home on my account,' Gray replied.

'Will Mr Gray tell the court what state his home was in before he shifted to Brookes Street,' May sneered.

'I do not wish to answer the question. My wife is dead, but she is still my wife and dear to me. By answering the question I might put a blot on her name,' Gray said.

May was becoming increasingly agitated. He strutted back and forth as he threw questions at Gray.

Magistrate Johnstone demanded May compose himself.

In a fit of rage, May declared: 'I am ready to die if I have to, but before doing so I want to see if Gray has the guts to stand up like a man and tell this court how he made his wife's life a misery.'

Sgt Grimes arced up. He was outraged by May's outburst. 'In what way did Mrs Gray suggest her husband made her life a misery?'

'I would rather not answer that question in deference to the woman,' May replied.

May's implication that Fred Gray was not exactly a doting husband and father was considered a fabrication, especially by Sgt Grimes.

The sergeant gave damning evidence against May. He clearly wanted the Englishman's blood.

'May has been in custody since 9 February. Since he came over the NSW border he was rabbiting, but he left that simply because he would not work. He has been living with another man's wife and another man's family on another man's money,' Sgt Grimes said.

'At Goondiwindi he was begging from house to house and, according to his own statement, he was prepared to go on like that all the way to Adelaide.'

The sergeant said May's mantra was simple: 'A man is always sure of his tucker and in any country in the world I always cadge my tucker.'

The inquiry lasted two days.

One of the final witnesses to appear was Dr Edward Perry, from Goondiwindi. He said the cause of death was accidental drowning.

'None of the bodies showed any marks of violence,' he told Magistrate Johnstone.

When the inquiry closed about midnight on 13 March, the magistrate supported Dr Perry's findings and recorded the deaths of Lilian Gray and her three children, Roy, Colin and Phyllis, as accidental.

'This was caused by the upsetting of the boat in the Macintyre River,' he said.

The day following the inquiry, Magistrate Johnstone

sentenced May to twenty-one days' hard labour for the charge of vagrancy, with the stretch to be served at Narrabri Gaol.

The magistrate told May he considered the time already served in custody when handing down the three-week sentence.

According to several newspaper reports, May walked out of the tiny Boggabilla courthouse smiling.

*   *   *

Life went on for grief-stricken milkman Fred Gray. Working the milk run around the streets of Brisbane was the one constant keeping him going, he told newspapers.

The support from customers and friends was overwhelming, he said, and he never stopped thinking about what may have been had he found his wife and children in time.

'I treated Charlie as one of the family. I gave him a job on the milk run and took him into our home,' Gray said.

'The blow nearly killed me, and for months I searched Brisbane from end to end, but could find no trace of them.

'Had I found Lilian she would, perhaps, have let me have the children and the poor little things would be alive today.'

Postscript:
Nearly three years after losing his wife and three young children in the swirling waters of the Macintyre River near Boggabilla, Brisbane milkman Fred Gray's own life was sadly cut short.

About 4.15 am on 20 October 1936, Gray suffered shocking injuries when his milk van collided with a *Courier Mail* delivery truck at the intersection of Wickham and Constance Streets in Fortitude Valley.

Gray died in Brisbane General Hospital eight days later aged forty.

At an inquest into Gray's death before City Coroner John Leahy, it was found Gray failed to pull up at a stop sign on Constance Street. It was alleged the milk van's headlights were switched off.

Newspaper delivery driver Wally Lawrence told the inquest he was making his return trip from Cribb Island when the collision occurred.

'I was on the correct side of the road and did not notice any object ahead of me as I approached Constance Street,' Mr Lawrence said.

'I was on the Breakfast Creek side of the intersection when I saw a grey lorry. I'm sure it had no lights and it seemed to be going pretty fast.'

Mr Lawrence said he desperately tried to avoid hitting the milk van but the collision was unavoidable.

Constable Heinrich Carl Vonhoff was the first police officer at the scene.

'The front of the milk van was completely destroyed and there was a man lying unconscious in front of the vehicle,' he told coroner Leahy.

The coroner found the collision was accidental and that speed, on Gray's part, was a contributing factor.

'The milk van should have stopped as it entered Wickham Street,' Coroner Leahy concluded.

Dan Daley's 1935 Ford sedan struck a tree near Pallamallawa in north-western NSW, resulting in the deaths of five people (Image credit: Michael McNamara)

Daley's car was unrecognisable after hitting a tree at high speed (Image credit: Michael McNamara)

CHAPTER 6

I HAVE SOME TERRIBLE NEWS
ABOUT YOUR DAUGHTER

They were phone calls Bill McKechnie didn't want to make. Every time he went to pick up the telephone, he hesitated and found something else to occupy his mind.

Rather than ask the operator for a connection to New Zealand, McKechnie placed the handset back in its cradle and flicked through the latest edition of the *North West Champion* — again.

McKechnie re-read the story about Moree beating Inverell 15-3 in the Spicer Cup. He forced a smile. The fact he read the story at all was living proof he was dodging responsibility.

McKechnie hated football.

But he knew there was no time to dilly-dally or make excuses. He had to make these calls.

He looked at his watch. It was 9 am on Sunday 21 August 1949. Moree local time was a couple of hours behind New Zealand.

Kit McKechnie watched her husband struggle with his emotions. She glanced at the handset and nodded gently. 'You have to do this, love,' she whispered.

Earlier, McKechnie was called to Moree Hospital where he viewed the mangled bodies of five people killed the night before in a tragic single vehicle accident eleven miles east of Moree on the Gwydir Highway.

Two of the victims were from "The Land of the Long White

Cloud". They were nurses at Aubrey maternity unit and had been working in Moree for the past five months.

As Moree District Hospital Board president, McKechnie was obligated to make the calls across "the ditch" — and they were calls that would stay with him for the rest of his life.

He pushed the local paper to one side and again picked up the handset. The connection was swift — too bloody swift for McKechnie's liking.

He half hoped he wouldn't get through, or there would be no-one home to take the call.

McKechnie grimaced at the unmistakable click as the two countries connected. His heart skipped a beat.

'Hello? Mrs Archibald? My name is Bill McKechnie. I'm calling from Australia. I'm the president of the Moree Hospital Board . . . I have some terrible news about your daughter, Audrey,' he whispered.

He swallowed hard. There was another call to make after this one.

McKechnie was a tough as nails, lump of a man, a hugely successful shearing contractor. He employed dozens of hardened men in sheds across the north and north-west, but the calls he made that frosty August Sunday morning buckled him to his knees.

The night before, 24-year-old Gwendoline Dorothea Godber and 26-year-old Audrey Agnes Archibald enjoyed a few drinks at the Gravesend Hotel with well-known locals Dan Daley and Les McNamara.

Audrey was a native of Blenheim, in the heart of wine-growing country at the tip of New Zealand's south island; Gwendoline was from Te Puke, a town near the Bay of Plenty in the north island. The area was famous for growing kiwifruit.

Joyce Sutton, Les McNamara and driver Dan Daley were thrown from the vehicle when it hit a tree near Pallamallawa (Image credit: Bob McKechnie).

The parents and families of car accident victims Gwen Godber and Audrey Archibald are welcomed at Moree airport by hospital board president Bill McKechnie. The families were flown from New Zealand at the expense of Mr McKechnie (Image credit: Bob McKechnie)

Audrey and Gwendoline travelled from New Zealand to Moree on the first leg of a working holiday. They were trained in obstetrics and planned to travel the world to hone their craft.

Moree was their first port of call.

Gwendoline was that day released from Moree Hospital as a patient after having her appendix removed. She was due to return to work the following week.

A relaxing day out with friends was the perfect pick-me-up.

Also in the group were John and Joyce Sutton, former residents of Pallamallawa, a small rural community about nineteen miles from Moree.

John had established a butcher shop at Pallamallawa in January of that year but left the business in March and relocated to Bondi Junction in Sydney. He and his wife were back in the district for a few days and the trip home gave them a chance to catch up with family and friends.

They were lunching at the Astoria Café in Moree on Saturday 20 August, when they met old friends Les McNamara and Dan Daley.

The group strolled down Balo Street and called into the Imperial Hotel.

Around 2 pm they walked across the road to the Max Hotel and enjoyed a relaxing Saturday afternoon chatting and joking over a couple of drinks.

Joyce Sutton sipped a gin-squash and soda; the men each had two brandy and ginger ales.

Later in the afternoon, McNamara and Daley left the hotel. They returned about 4 pm with nurses Gwendoline Godber and Audrey Archibald.

After a while, the group returned to the café to buy

sandwiches. About 5.30 pm they jumped in Daley's 1935 black Ford sedan and headed east to Gravesend.

Midway to Gravesend the vehicle suffered a flat tyre and was stuck on the side of the road for more than an hour. The vehicle's jack malfunctioned and traffic on the highway was virtually non-existent.

Eventually, a truck driver pulled over and helped Daley change the wheel, using a different jack.

It was nearly 8 pm by the time the group arrived at the Gravesend Hotel, where licensee Ted Musk welcomed them heartily. Daley and McNamara were regulars at the hotel and well known to locals.

'G'day, Teddy. Is there any chance I can wash my hands somewhere? We got a flat tyre on the way here and my hands are covered in grease,' Daley said.

Musk smiled and directed Daley to a sink behind the bar before taking orders from the group.

Everyone, except Audrey Archibald, drank alcohol. She was due to start an overnight shift at the hospital and was concerned they wouldn't get back to Moree in time.

As the night wore on, Audrey and Gwendoline told their friends they had to be back in Moree by a certain time. They were boarders at Moree Hospital nurses' quarters and curfew times were strict. If they weren't back on time, there would be hell to pay with hospital matron Robina Lillicrap.

Audrey was also rostered to start work at 10 pm. She rang the nurse on duty and asked her to cover her shift until she arrived.

Dan Daley, whose family owned the properties Springfield and The Point, near Biniguy, offered to drive everyone back to Moree.

They bought four bottles of Sydney Bitter Ale and left the Gravesend Hotel about 9.30 pm.

The beer wasn't consumed on the way back.

Daley, 33, was a decorated war hero, a Tobruk Rat. He was awarded the Distinguished Conduct Medal for action taken at Tel el Eisa, north-west of Alamein, Egypt, on 17 July 1942.

He was a good boxer and an adroit horseman, widely known at show events and rodeos across north-western NSW and southern Queensland.

Daley was considered tall, dark and handsome, and an extremely popular member of the local community — a good bloke and a good catch.

Grazier Les McNamara also excelled in the saddle. Earlier in the year, at the Sydney Royal Easter Show, he won the Australian open camp drafting championship and in 1948 won the coveted Warwick Gold Cup on champion mare Flashlight.

His Warwick Gold Cup victory followed campdrafting championship wins at Warialda, Moree and Bingara and dual wins at Texas and Narrabri.

He was a prisoner of war for four years in Changi, in south-east Asia, and in 1942 worked on the Burma-Thailand Railway.

The notorious railway took twelve months to complete and later became a byword when describing the courage and resilience shown by thousands of men, women and children confronted with extreme hardship and brutality.

More than 100,000 people died building the railway, including 2800 Australian prisoners of war.

McNamara returned to a semblance of normal life at the family property, Riverside, at Pallamallawa. He also owned the property Lucksall at Toobeah, between Talwood and Goondiwindi, but signed it over to his father, John, when he enlisted. 'Just in case I don't come back,' he told his family.

McNamara married Kit Peachey at Inverell in 1934. They divorced twelve years later, not long after he came home from war.

The boisterous group bundled into Daley's 1935 black Ford sedan. The journey to Moree was about thirty-five miles.

Daley, laughing and joking, jumped behind the wheel, slammed the door shut and knocked the car into gear. 'I'll get you back in time,' he told the girls.

Car trouble, however, again caused a delay.

The Ford was recently fitted with a new, supercharged engine and began overheating. Daley called in to the property of his uncle, Colin McKenzie, near Yagobie, to top up the radiator.

McKenzie was awoken by his dogs barking.

'It's just me; we need some water for the radiator. The car's overheating,' Daley called out.

McKenzie gave his nephew a jug to collect water from a nearby tank and they chatted for a few minutes.

Daley filled the radiator and McKenzie returned to bed. As he dozed off, he heard his nephew's car cross the stock ramp as it left the property.

The powerful Ford lurched on to the Gwydir Highway and headed back to Moree, at times exceeding sixty miles an hour.

As the vehicle passed Gum Flat, John Sutton asked Daley to slow down.

'Can you break down the pace a bit,' he asked.

Daley obliged and took his foot off the accelerator. But he increased speed as they neared Mia Mia Creek Bridge.

The sweeping bend on the approach to the bridge — a notorious black spot well known to locals — was too much for the hulking black Ford. Daley tried desperately to control the car but it left the highway and went bush at breakneck speed.

Laughter and good-natured chatter quickly turned to horrific screams as the Ford roared through the scrub and struck a tree at high speed.

Dan Daley, Les McNamara, Gwendoline Godber, Audrey Archibald and Joyce Sutton were killed on impact.

John Sutton, a front-seat passenger, miraculously survived.

The Ford was smashed beyond recognition.

Sutton was pinned between the front seat and windshield, suffering broken ribs and internal injuries. His wife lay dead alongside the vehicle.

John and Joyce were the parents of two young daughters, three-year-old Carolyn and two-year-old Sandra. The children were in Sydney with Joyce's mother, Mary Gaudry.

Dan Daley and Les McNamara were also thrown from the vehicle; Gwendoline Godber lay across the front bench seat, partly wedged under the steering wheel; and Audrey Archibald was in the back seat in a sitting position.

Pallamallawa grazier Colin Burke discovered the grisly crash site about 4.30 the next morning, on his way to Moree. As he slowed down and cast his eye across the scene, he knew immediately the car belonged to Dan Daley.

Burke saw bodies strewn around the vehicle and found John Sutton barely alive on the front passenger seat.

'Please, please get me some water,' Sutton gasped.

Burke, numb with shock, raced back to his vehicle and returned with a canvas water bag.

Sutton was in incredible pain. He gulped down the refreshing liquid.

Burke jumped back in his vehicle and sped to the nearest

property, owned by the Lees family, and called Moree police station. Sgt Bill Forrest was manning the station when the phone rang at 4.50 am.

Burke was frantic as he told Sgt Forrest what had unfolded on the edge of town.

The sergeant immediately alerted Moree ambulance station. The early Sunday morning silence was shattered by the shrill sound of sirens as three ambulances and a police vehicle rushed to the scene.

Constables Bert Rizzi and Norm Marchant accompanied Sgt Forrest.

What they saw made their stomachs turn.

John Sutton was seriously injured, semi-conscious and barely able to speak. He told Sgt Forrest the accident happened about 10.15 the night before.

Sutton was pinned in the smoking vehicle for more than seven hours, surrounded by the bodies of his wife and friends.

* * *

Bill McKechnie was woken from his Sunday morning slumber and told the tragic news.

He rushed to the hospital where he met Dr Geoffrey Hunter.

The smashed, mangled bodies of Gwendoline Godber, Audrey Archibald, Dan Daley, Les McNamara, and Joyce Sutton were laid out side by side. It was a shocking sight.

McKechnie held his gaze for just a few seconds, before looking away. He fought back tears.

'My God, Geoff, this is terrible. What on earth happened?'

Dr Hunter explained: 'Dan's car hit a tree near Mia Mia Creek, about ten miles out of town. They were going very, very fast. Someone will have to tell the families of Gwen and Audrey. I was hoping you could.' He knew he could rely on his old friend to carry out such a thankless task.

The funerals of Daniel Alexander Daley and Leslie McNamara were held the next morning at the Moree Church of England. Mourners spilled from the church and lined footpaths along Albert and Chester Streets. Family members and friends stood shoulder to shoulder, heads solemnly bowed. The church's perfectly manicured garden was laden with floral tributes and heartbreaking mementos.

Les McNamara was born at Moree on 16 March 1913, one of eleven children to John and Mary McNamara. He enlisted at Tamworth with the Australian Army, 2nd AIF and was issued service number NX40513. He disembarked in Singapore on 18 February 1941.

He was promoted to lance-corporal on 27 September that year and promoted to corporal on 6 February the following year.

McNamara was incarcerated at Changi for nearly four years with more than twelve months of that spent on the Burma Railway.

He arrived home in October 1945 and spent the next seven months in various hospitals suffering malnutrition and a nervous disorder, as well as venous thrombosis and hook worm. At the time of his discharge, McNamara had ulcer scars on his right leg, with a twenty per cent degree of disability.

* * *

Dan Daley was born at Moree on 6 August 1916, the youngest of four children to James and Ethel Daley.

He was bred to be a horseman. His great-aunt, Alice Maud

138

Timmins (nee Daley), was the mother of champion horsemen Stumpy (Bruce), Buck (Noel) and Lance Timmins.

Daley also enlisted at Tamworth with the 2nd AIF. He was issued with service number NX40585 and reached the rank of lance-sergeant with the 2/3rd Anti-Tank Regiment.

Daley was wounded while fighting for Makh Khad Ridge, but not before putting six German tanks out of commission.

While recovering in hospital, Daley was awarded the Distinguished Conduct Medal. He re-joined his regiment during the historic battle of El Alamein.

Daley served in Papua and New Guinea in late 1943 and the following year was released from the AIF on compassionate grounds. He returned home and assumed management of Springfield and The Point for his seriously ill father, 65-year-old James.

More than two hundred former servicemen formed a guard of honour from the church steps to awaiting hearses. The funeral cortege was so large that vehicles were still leaving the church when the hearses crawled through the main gates of Moree Cemetery, more than a mile away.

* * *

Joyce Sutton's body was transferred to Sydney, where she was laid to rest in the Roman Catholic section of Eastern Suburbs Memorial Park at Randwick.

Her husband, John, lay injured and bandaged in Moree Hospital. His physical condition improved daily; the mental scars, however, would take many, many years to fade.

* * *

The funerals of Gwendoline Godber and Audrey Archibald were delayed until the arrival of the girls' parents from New Zealand.

Thomas and Ellen Archibald and widow Ruby Godber arrived at Mascot airport in Sydney on Tuesday 23 August and, through the generosity of Bill McKechnie, arrived in Moree the following day.

Gwendoline Godber's father, William, passed away ten years earlier, when Gwendoline was fifteen years old.

"A Moree resident, Mr Bill McKechnie, the Moree District Hospital Board president, chartered and paid for a special plane to bring the bereaved parents to Moree from Sydney," newspapers reported.

Moree residents, already deeply sadden by the deaths of two of the town's favourite sons of war, braced for another funeral, delayed until the arrival of immediate family members.

Both young women were Seventh Day Adventists. Because a pastor could not be procured in time to officiate, Presbyterian minister Carlyle McKenzie Moulton delivered a heart-wrenching service at Moree Methodist Church.

Members of Moree District Hospital nursing staff formed a guard of honour as pallbearers carried the coffins from the church.

Gwendoline Godber and Audrey Archibald were laid to rest together in the Presbyterian section at Moree Cemetery.

* * *

On Tuesday 4 October a coronial inquest into the deaths of Daniel Alexander Daley, Leslie McNamara, Gwendoline Dorothea Godber, Audrey Agnes Archibald and Joyce Barbara

Sutton opened at Moree courthouse before Coroner Henry Francis Brown.

Sgt Bill Forrest told the inquest Daley's black Ford was travelling at high speed when it left the highway and struck a tree. Forrest was regarded an expert in motor traffic accidents. He spent several years investigating road accidents when stationed in Sydney.

'Everything indicated to me the vehicle struck the tree with considerable force,' Sgt Forrest told the inquest.

'I have since travelled (the section of highway) in three different vehicles over the same route at fifty and sixty miles an hour and the effect of the turn in the road made no impression on the cars at all.

'I am regarded an expert in motor traffic and from that point of view I have seen many other impacts. It is in my opinion the car was travelling, at the time, at a speed not less than seventy miles an hour.

'At that speed the car would have travelled at 105 feet a second and covered the distance in a little less than four seconds from the time it left the road,' Sgt Forrest said.

A detailed map of the stretch of roadway approaching the Mia Mia Creek Bridge was presented as evidence.

'The bitumen is even where the car left the roadway and is good, firm bitumen,' Sgt Forrest said. 'The crown of the road was higher than the surrounding ground. The road is a main highway and is not well equipped with white guide posts. I do not know of any other turn as pronounced as this one that has no guide posts, and there are no guide posts at this turn.'

The sergeant told the court visibility on the night of the accident was good. 'There were no abnormal conditions.'

Sgt Forrest said the tyre tracks indicated the vehicle left the road in a straight line.

'I examined the tracks of the car very carefully and I could not say what the driver's intentions were,' he said.

'There was no sign of braking. The wheel tracks of the car were even and the weight of the car appeared to have been distributed over the wheels. There was no sign of braking of any description. A feathering to the right, and light stones, indicate the car resisted being turned from its original straight line. There was nothing to indicate a blowout or mishap occurred,' he said.

Constable Bert Rizzi agreed the black Ford was travelling at high speed when it left the highway.

'It was a powerful vehicle and capable of high speeds,' Constable Rizzi told Coroner Brown.

'I made an examination of the scene of the accident and followed the tracks back for a distance of four hundred and ten feet to the road from where it collided with the tree. I saw no signs of a blowout.'

The constable told the court he was familiar with the sweeping turn approaching Mia Mia Creek Bridge.

'It would be easy for a driver going at a reasonable speed to negotiate the curve, but it is dangerous to a person using the road at high speed,' he said.

Constable Rizzi said the speed of the vehicle on impact was hard to estimate.

'But I would say it would have been doing at least seventy miles an hour. The vehicle's speed was definitely very high.'

The constable told the inquest Dan Daley was known to drive above the speed limit, especially around the streets of Moree.

'I knew Mr Daley and knew he was a fast driver. I have

spoken to him about fast driving and the thirty mile an hour speed limit (in town). I have not seen him driving outside of town,' Constable Rizzi said.

Gravesend Hotel licensee Ted Musk told the coroner everyone in the group was sober when they arrived at the bush pub.

'They were all very sober, and I had a conversation with Mr Daley. He was perfectly sober and not affected by drink.

'He asked me if he could wash his hands. After he washed, the party had some drinks. They were only drinking beer,' Musk said.

Musk, a well-known picnic-racing jockey in the district, said all but one member of the group were drinking.

'The beers were in eight-ounce glasses and one of the ladies (Audrey Archibald) didn't drink at all,' Musk said.

Musk said the pub telephone was used to call Moree Hospital to notify the sister on duty that Audrey would be late starting her shift.

'One of the girls had to be on duty at 10 pm, but it was arranged for the nurse on duty to cover for her,' Musk said.

'The party left my hotel at 9.30 pm. They were quite sober and I do not know who was driving after they left. They bought four bottles of lager to take with them.'

Dan Daley's uncle, Colin McKenzie, told the inquest his nephew was sober when he called in to top up the car's radiator.

'When I was talking to him, he was strictly sober; I did not detect any liquor on him. We talked for about ten minutes. I never saw my nephew under the influence of liquor (that night).'

McKenzie said he knew Daley's black Ford and was doubtful it was capable of reaching seventy miles an hour.

'I have had a lot of experience with motor vehicles and

machinery (but) I did not know the car was supercharged or that it was fitted with a new engine,' he said.

Grazier Colin Burke said he was travelling to Moree when he saw the crumpled black Ford just off the highway as he approached the Mia Mia Creek Bridge.

'I knew the car belonged to Dan Daley,' Burke said.

'I saw a tree close by with some bark off it. The car was about three yards to the south. I saw the body of Dan Daley and Les McNamara and the bodies of three ladies. I know Daley and McNamara.'

Burke found John Sutton in the front seat of the vehicle.

'He was conscious and crying out for water and I went to my truck and got some water,' Burke said.

'I was talking to him but I cannot remember what was said. I have some slight recollection of having given him a draw of a cigarette. I am not trying to hide anything. I think I might have asked him what happened but I can't remember what his exact words were. I was too upset. I was in shock.'

Dr Geoffrey Hunter described in detail the injuries received by all five victims.

'I found no trace of alcohol in the bodies; there was no examination made for that purpose,' he said.

Sole survivor John Sutton suffered six fractured ribs, a pierced lung, vertebrae damage and a cut above the left eye. Speaking under incredible emotional strain, he gave the court a detailed account of the events leading up to the accident.

'We left Moree about 5.30 pm for Gravesend. On the way we had a puncture in the near-side back wheel,' Sutton recalled.

'We arrived at the hotel at Gravesend about 7.30 or 8 pm. When we got there I was sober, McNamara was sober and Daley was sober.

'We had no more than six beers. My wife had two drinks; one of the girls had none at all; and the other girl had two or three.

'We left the hotel about 9.30 pm and none of us were under the influence — we were all sober,' Sutton said.

'Dan bought four bottles of beer as we left the hotel but none of them were consumed on the road.

'I have no idea at what pace we were travelling and Daley did not have any difficulty controlling the car.

'We called into Mr McKenzie's place to get some water for the radiator and after we left I asked Dan to slow down. We continued towards Moree and it was then I told the driver to reduce his speed, which he did.

'It was obvious we were travelling at a fair pace. Dan increased the speed just before the crash, but I cannot estimate the speed the car was travelling,' Sutton said.

'I only asked him once to cut down the speed. I cannot remember much about the crash. I can remember the glass; there was glass flying over me when we crashed.

'After the crash I woke up and found myself lying in the front seat. I have no idea what the time was as I didn't have a watch but the crash would've been somewhere about 10.15 pm or 10.30 pm,' he said.

Sutton said the group consumed twelve brandies and six beers during the afternoon and evening.

'These were drunk over a period of seven hours. We were all sober when we left the hotel at Gravesend.'

At the conclusion of the inquest, Coroner Brown found 'the victims died from the effects of injuries accidentally received in a motor vehicle driven by Daniel Alexander Daley'.

'I further find the vehicle was driven in a dangerous and reckless manner by the said Daniel Alexander Daley.'

*   *   *

Months later, Sgt Bill Forrest recalled first meeting nurses Gwendoline Godber and Audrey Archibald at Moree police station about five months before the accident.

'They called into the station in search of directions to the hospital, where they were later employed,' Sgt Forrest said.

'During the course of our conversation that day, both ladies told me they completed their training in general and obstetric nursing in New Zealand and planned to travel to various countries and accept temporary appointments at various hospitals in the hope of broadening their knowledge in their profession.

'For various reasons Moree was included in their plans and as much assistance as possible was afforded them as visitors,' he said.

Sgt Forrest sadly remembered the morning of Sunday 21 August 1949, when Colin Burke alerted Moree police that Dan Daley's huge black sedan with "bodies everywhere" was smashed against a tree just out of town.

'I took charge of inquiries. I assisted in removing the bodies of both nurses from the wreckage of a motor car. I refer to that accident with the deepest respect and sympathy to those relatives of the other victims, only to relate the means by which these two unfortunate women lost their lives,' Sgt Forrest said.

'In other words, they were accidentally killed while enjoying a period of relaxation from their arduous duties in one of the most honourable professions known to man.

'One may doubt if there is a living woman who would not freely admit her appreciation for the science of obstetrics, and her admiration and affection for those who have devoted their lives to its study.

'Even more tragic is the fact both lives were lost in a land which is far separated from their native country, and thus isolating their resting place from those who would afford it their affectionate care and attention.'

In September 1951, Bill McKechnie, along with Dan Daley's father, James, and the Rev Moulton established an appeal for donations through a public subscription to erect headstones and plaques on the gravesites of both nurses at Moree Cemetery.

'I feel sure a lot of people and a lot of mothers remember their kindness at Moree District Hospital as well as Aubrey maternity unit,' McKechnie said.

McKechnie, Daley and Moulton opened the public subscription with a combined £30 donation.

'Should any others feel like adding to this amount, I will be pleased to receive their donations at my office. All donations will be acknowledged through the press,' McKechnie said.

Sgt Forrest made a formal application on 4 August 1951 — two months before McKechnie initiated a public plea for help — with the Commissioner of Police for permission to 'organise an appeal for money to assist the public of Moree to suitably mark the graves of Gwendoline Godber and Audrey Archibald'. Permission to organise a public meeting to discuss the matter was granted on 16 August.

'Upon permission to organise the public appeal being granted, I approached the North-Western Monumental and Terrazzo Company, of Moree, and received a quotation for the erection of a monument over the double grave at a cost of not less than £143. This cost, with the cost of a framed photograph of the monument for presentation by the public to the relatives in New Zealand, would make the total sum required amount to not less than £150,' Sgt Forrest said.

Moree mayor Reg Simpson applauded the memorial, with the headstone shaped to resemble an open book.

The inscription states: Erected by the people of Moree and District, in loving memory of Audrey Agnes Archibald, aged 26 years, and Gwendoline Dorothea Godber, aged 24 years.

'The memorial is a credit to the contractor and I think it is well in keeping with the desires of the people who subscribed to the fund,' Councillor Simpson said.

Postscript:

Les McNamara, one of the five people killed in the accident, was a returned soldier and Changi prisoner of war.

Historian Michael McNamara said his great-uncle was a champion horseman despite physical and mental illness, and partial disability.

'Les survived Changi, only to be killed a few years afterwards,' Michael said.

'He was a great rough-rider prior to the war, but after a spell as a PoW in the hands of the Japanese, he could not stand up to the strenuous side of rodeo events.

'After the war he concentrated on camp-drafting and won many events on horses Flashlight, Tarzan and Steel Dust.

'Flashlight was later sold at auction for £340 and went on to win another championship in Sydney, the Duke of Gloucester Cup at Tenterfield, a championship draft at Bundarra, and the Dave Sharp Memorial Cup at Stanthorpe. There were other camp-draft wins along the way,' Michael said.

'While a prisoner-of-war Les often said to himself, *I must get back home and win the Warwick Gold Cup.*'

And that's exactly what he did.

* * *

Hospital board chairman Bill McKechnie, who was tasked with informing families on both sides of the Tasman about the accident, was a tough man with a big heart, according to McKechnie's son, Bob.

The accident and circumstances surrounding the gut-wrenching telephone calls McKechnie reluctantly made that chilly August morning in 1949 left indelible scars on an entire community.

'I was only two years of age at the time of the accident but when I was older dad often talked about it,' Bob said.

'It was a terrible crash that shocked Moree and district. Years later, dad told me that when he went to view the bodies they were actually in a ward at the hospital, not at the morgue — simply because the morgue wasn't big enough to handle five bodies at once.

'Dad was asked to inform the families of the two nurses killed. That must have been very hard for him. He always remembered one thing the nurses' mothers said to him when they arrived in Moree and thanked him for providing a chartered flight from Sydney.

'They said they always knew Australians were generous people, and dad's generosity only proved that to be true,' Bob said.

In November 1949, a memorial trophy was unveiled to perpetuate the memories of car crash victims Dan Daley and Les McNamara. The trophy recognised their involvement with horse sports and rodeos across the district.

Dick Makim and his family, from the property Alma at Pallamallawa, donated the trophy to Moree P&A Society for competition at future equine events.

In subsequent years, competitors in open camp-drafts held at the Moree Show or district rodeos under the auspices of Moree P&A Society vied for the Daley and McNamara Memorial Cup.

The imposing trophy bore the inscription: 'In fond memory of Dan Daley and Les McNamara. Though time changes many things, memory forever like the ivy clings.'

Sadly, the trophy was destroyed in a fire at Moree Showground and never replaced.

CHAPTER 7

JUST A KID WORKING THE SHEDS

The going was tough but the money was good, especially for a sixteen-year-old lad from Liverpool, west of Sydney.

In early 1943 Mervyn Medley packed a few belongings, jumped on the red rattler, and headed to grazing country in north-western NSW.

Mervyn, tall, slim and good-looking with a shock of black hair, signed on as a roustabout and shed hand. He worked alongside seasoned, hardened shearers and discovered more about life in the first few months of 1943 than he did during all of his sixteen years in western Sydney.

His aim was to learn the game and travel the bush. Picking up after shearers in the sheds around Croppa Creek and North Star between Goondiwindi and Warialda during the war years was a good place to start.

Mervyn's father, Robert, was a World War 1 Digger granted a soldier settlement block in 1919 at Hillview, near Liverpool. Sgt Medley re-enlisted when war broke out in 1939 and was posted to Cowra prisoner of war camp.

Mervyn's eighteen-year-old brother, Jack, enlisted at Bonegilla, Victoria, in June 1943 and spent five months in the Citizen Military Forces before joining the AIF. Another brother, twenty-three-year-old Robert, enlisted two years earlier.

Mervyn was too young to wear a uniform. Instead, he pecked his mum, Catherine, on the cheek and went bush. He also said goodbye to his girlfriend, Mary Cameron,

Mervyn Medley was killed in a motorcycle accident on Christmas Eve, 1946, on busy Woodville Road, near Granville in western Sydney. Mervyn's girlfriend, Mary Cameron survived the accident (Image credit: Medley family)

a trainee hairdresser from Homebush he had known since childhood.

It has long been said Australia was built on the sheep's back. The wool industry found its roots in the late 1700s when John Macarthur arrived with several head of Spanish merino sheep, bred and reared in South Africa. Although the industry flourished in the 1940s widespread labour shortages placed shearing contractors at breaking point and Mervyn had little trouble getting a start.

After working a run of sheds around the Croppa Creek and North Star district, Mervyn's next stop was Frank King's property Yeral, near Delungra, a small village about seventeen miles east of Warialda.

On Saturday 28 August 1943 — two months after his sixteenth birthday — Mervyn took a ride from Croppa Creek to Moree with shearers Charlie Sutherland, Paul Liddy and Max Jones, all from Sydney.

Forty-one-year-old Sutherland, from inner-city suburb Newtown, owned the vehicle, an old Hudson Essex super six tourer. Sutherland was unlicensed, but that didn't stop him driving from shed to shed.

Fifty-two-year-old Liddy, born and bred in Broken Hill, lived in Kings Cross, and twenty-two-year-old Jones, originally from Tamworth, lived in Marrickville.

They stopped at Moree to have new tyres fitted at Roy Kempe Mechanical Repairs.

The shearers thought long and hard about spending the afternoon at the Moree Race Club's Diggers' Cup meeting, but knew they needed to be at Yeral the following day.

'The horse sports are on today, boys. It's a pity we'll miss them but we'd never find a bed in town and we'd be a day late for everything; we've got a new shed to start,' Sutherland despaired.

It was a pity. A shearing contractor Sutherland knew — Bill McKechnie — was likely to have runners.

'Big Bill will most likely win a race today, maybe two; he's got some handy horses,' Sutherland said.

Instead, the shearers drove to Gravesend, about sixteen miles west of Warialda, arriving shortly after 9 am. The sign of the Gravesend Hotel beckoned.

Sutherland checked his fob watch. 'We may as well have a couple of beers; we've got a bit of time up our sleeves and don't start the shed 'til Monday. Besides, we might cop a tip; the bloke that runs the pub is a jockey.'

Liddy and Jones nodded; Mervyn, still a kid but learning fast, smiled. A beer with the men sounded appealing.

The group sauntered into the pub where they were warmly greeted by Jessie Musk, who ran the hotel with her son, licensee Edmund Musk. Mrs Musk, a widow of more than thirty years, was polishing the bar.

Edmund, a well-known picnic jockey and racehorse trainer known widely as Teddy, was away riding at the Moree races.

Mrs Musk, 60, poured beers for Sutherland, Jones and Medley. Liddy preferred soft drink.

'My Teddy's at Moree today; I thought a group of chaps like you lot would be there, too,' Jessie said.

Sutherland smiled. 'We'd love to be there, Mrs Musk, but we're starting a new shed on Monday and thought better of it.'

Sutherland, Liddy, Jones and young Medley pulled up barstools. Max Jones flipped open a pack of Camels and offered his mates a cigarette — rationing was still in place but Max had a few fags to spare.

The hotel was quiet. It was still early. The shearers were Mrs Musk's only customers. She chuckled and plonked drinks on the bar. 'I think everyone must be at the races, except us.'

A battered old radio at the end of the bar crackled and spluttered. Naturally, being a Saturday, the talk turned to horse-racing.

'Any tips today, Mrs Musk?' Jones asked offhandedly.

'Sorry boys. Teddy's the person to talk to about racehorses. But, as I said, he's not here. Mind you, he trialled one yesterday called Widden; he likes it a lot and might be one to watch out for in the future — an ex-Sydney horse, apparently.'

The radio signal drifted in and out. The first at Rosehill was still a few hours away, according to Ken Howard's race day preview.

One beer led to another and the men settled in. Mervyn drank sparingly.

'You're still a kid, remember,' Liddy chided.

After a while, hunger overtook thirst.

'We might duck across the road and get a feed, and then get going,' suggested Sutherland.

They thanked Mrs Musk, downed their ales and walked across to Archie and Evanthia Gavrily's Greek Café, where Archie welcomed them warmly as they huddled into a four-seat cubicle.

Archie, a proud Kytherian, was in a good mood. In fact, he was beside himself. 'Our daughter, Golfa, is getting married,' he told anyone willing to listen. 'We'll have a big party at Barraba tomorrow. That's where her new husband, Peter Psaltis, lives.'

Sutherland shook Archie's hand and smiled. 'Well done, Archie. Now, make four hungry shearers some lunch — the bloody works, please.'

The group chatted as Archie flipped steaks and turned sausages. He hummed Wagner's *Here Comes the Bride* as he cooked. Evanthia shook her head and rolled her eyes.

A little while later, Archie helped his wife deliver four oval plates laden with food to four hungry shearers.

'There you go, boys,' he grinned.

After a feed of steak, eggs, snags and chips — a Greek café staple — the shearers made their way back to the old Essex. It was nearly 2 pm.

Sutherland steadied himself as he jumped behind the wheel. The men laughed and joked. A couple of miles out of Gravesend, Sutherland felt drowsy.

'I'm not sure I should be driving,' he said.

Liddy was sober but unwilling to drive. He reckoned he had the perfect solution, though.

'Why not let young Mervyn drive? He only had a couple of beers at the pub and this will be good experience for him.'

Sutherland nodded and pulled over to the side of the road.

As he stepped out, he smiled and threw the keys to Mervyn. 'There you go champ; jump behind the wheel and take us home.'

Mervyn snatched the keys mid-air and grinned. He was still grinning as he slid across to the driver's seat and knocked the car into gear.

Sutherland jumped back in and sat next to Mervyn; Paul Liddy claimed the window seat; and Max Jones, unlicensed and unable to drive a motor vehicle, stretched out on the back seat.

Sutherland gave Mervyn a friendly elbow jab. 'Off you go, young fella.'

Mervyn felt confident, but was nervous just the same. He crawled through Warialda, heading for Delungra. The streets of Warialda, once the business and legal hub of north-western NSW, lay empty.

'Looks like everyone here has gone to the races, too,' Liddy chuckled.

*   *   *

Conversation among the men turned to serious matters. They spoke about the war, shearing and their rights at work. The beers at the Gravesend pub ensured all subjects were fully covered.

A few weeks earlier a shearer named Watson had died in the sheds at Kooroogamma station, west of Moree. Watson was working for contractor Jack Jones, and died of a cerebral haemorrhage. At a subsequent inquiry, it was found Watson's death was a direct result of hard, excessive work while crutching.

'That was a terrible thing,' Liddy told his mates.

'According to the other blokes working the shed — there was only four of them — the sheep being crutched were very heavy in lamb and the chutes were way too small. Ray Robinson and Harry Wolfenden told me all about it. They were there when it happened and gave evidence at the inquiry.

'Charlie Sabine was there, too. Anyway, the bloody insurance company reckoned the work being done wasn't the cause of death. But a doctor from Moree, Hunter I think his name was, said otherwise and the poor bugger's wife — her name was Kate — was awarded eight hundred quid, and rightly bloody so,' Liddy said.

Mervyn listened to every word.

The road was rough. There were wide stretches of gravel either side of a narrow strip of bitumen, and the highway was winding and hilly as they approached Cranky Rock, a well-known landmark a couple of miles east of Warialda.

Mervyn's fingers gripped the steering wheel tightly. He felt a bead of sweat trickle across his brow but was too nervous to brush it away. He blinked a couple of times, hoping that might work.

Mervyn silently prayed the men didn't notice.

'The fact we had to get our own tyres earlier at Moree to get to work is wrong,' Liddy continued.

Sutherland nodded. 'Bloody oath it's wrong. If these cockies want us to drive from shed to shed in our own bloody cars, they can bloody well help with running costs and repairs.'

As the car approached a rough-looking section of gravel, Mervyn slowed to about twenty-five miles an hour.

The road was badly corrugated and the steering wheel rattled and shook with machinegun rapidity under Mervyn's tight grip.

'We just got new tyres; we'll probably need new suspension after this little trip,' Sutherland joked.

Suddenly, the vehicle hit a pothole and bounced hard.

Mervyn tried desperately to keep the old Essex under control, but the car started to drift towards a deep embankment on the edge of the road. He applied the brakes but it was too late. The Essex drifted slowly in the loose gravel and overturned as it slid down the embankment.

Mervyn was thrown clear and sat up dazed but unharmed. Sutherland was also uninjured. Jones — in the back seat — was struck by fallen luggage but otherwise okay.

Paul Liddy, however, was badly hurt. He suffered a gaping wound to the back of the head when the car tipped over. He lay in agony on the side of the road.

'Get the battery off my foot,' he screamed.

Mervyn scrambled across and freed Liddy's foot. Liddy, with blood pouring from the head wound, got to his feet and staggered a few yards before falling to his knees in agony.

Mervyn helped Jones crawl out from the back of the upturned vehicle; luggage and clothing was everywhere. Sutherland went to help Liddy. He wrapped the shearer's head with a coat and tried to make his mate as comfortable as possible.

Sutherland saw a truck approaching from the east and flagged it down. He asked the driver to get help at Warialda, about five miles down the road.

'We'll need a doctor and an ambulance most likely; our mate's knocked about pretty badly,' Sutherland said.

The driver nodded and the truck sped off. Sutherland and Jones went back to the overturned Essex and comforted Liddy.

'Hang in there Paul, help is on its way,' Jones said.

Sutherland rested his arm around Mervyn's shoulder. 'Don't worry, champ, this wasn't your fault; everything will be okay.'

Mervyn fought back tears as he watched Liddy lose consciousness. The teenager had never felt so alone or so far from home. He thought of his mum, Catherine, and his sweetheart, Mary.

* * *

Mervyn watched helplessly as Paul Liddy died alongside a lonely stretch of highway on a chilly August afternoon in 1943. He slumped against the overturned Essex, buried his face in his hands to stop the tears, and waited for help to arrive. There was little else he could do.

Around 3.30 pm Dr Arthur Wheatley arrived at the crash site. Warialda police Sgt John Fardy arrived minutes later.

Dr Wheatley examined Liddy's body. 'He's been dead for about an hour, I'd say. What in the hell happened here?'

Fardy established Mervyn was driving the vehicle when the accident happened and questioned the teenager. 'What happened to make the car go over the embankment?'

Mervyn wiped tears away. His eyes were red. 'When I came to this part of the road the car skidded and I must have lost control of it as I couldn't stop it before it went over the embankment. There were three of us sitting in the front seat. Paul was sitting on the outside and Charlie Sutherland — the owner of the car — was sitting in the middle. Max was in the back.'

Fardy studied Mervyn closely. Common sense told him the kid was too young to be driving a motor vehicle. 'Have you got a driver's licence?' he asked, knowing full well what Mervyn's answer would be.

'No, I'm only sixteen. I drove the car because the owner was under the influence of liquor after we left Gravesend. As I had some driving experience, Paul said I would be the best to drive the rest of the way. I drove the car from a few miles the Warialda side of Gravesend to where we are now.'

Sutherland, Jones and Mervyn were taken to Warialda police station, where they made full statements.

The following day Paul Liddy was given a quiet burial at Warialda Cemetery. The Rev Dean Healy conducted the service.

Two days after the fatal accident — Monday 30 August — an inquest into Liddy's death was held at Warialda courthouse before Coroner Andrew Stewart.

Stewart, 65, was owner-editor of the *Warialda Standard*, the local newspaper, and a highly respected public figure. He was appointed district coroner in 1932.

Sgt Fardy told the coroner he attended the accident site and interviewed Mervyn Medley, the alleged driver of the Essex tourer.

'The tourer was lying on its side and the body of Paul Liddy was lying about four yards to the front of the vehicle,' Fardy said.

'I examined the body in company with Dr Wheatley and noticed an injury to the back of the head. There were no other marks of violence on the body. Dr Wheatley informed me the injury to Paul Liddy's head was the cause of his death.

'I interviewed Mervyn Medley and he told me he was the driver of the car at the time of the accident.'

Dr Wheatley told the coroner he attended the accident about 3.40 pm and examined Paul Liddy's body.

'My examination revealed two skull fractures. In my opinion, death was due to cerebral haemorrhage, accompanying the fractures. The injuries were consistent with being caused by the overturning of the car in which the deceased was travelling. In my opinion, death occurred about half an hour prior to my arrival,' Dr Wheatley said.

Mervyn Medley nervously told the inquest how he lost control of the car on a badly rutted section of gravel road.

'When I was approaching the rough road the car seemed to bounce, and when it got to the culvert it seemed to skid and go over the embankment. I was thrown clear and not injured,' Mervyn told Coroner Stewart.

Mervyn supressed tears as he relived the moments before Liddy's death. 'I did all I could to avoid the accident, but I was unable to stop the car from going over the embankment after it skidded. I have had very little driving experience and was driving at about fifteen or twenty miles an hour when the accident occurred.'

He told the court the car was in good working order and

that he was not under the influence of intoxicating liquor at the time of the accident.

'I had two beers at the Gravesend Hotel,' he said.

Charlie Sutherland, the owner of the Essex tourer, told Coroner Stewart he was driving the car when they left Gravesend.

'A short distance from Gravesend I became sleepy, probably through the effects of the few drinks I had at the hotel. Paul Liddy suggested I let Mervyn drive. I let Mervyn into the driver's seat and he drove the car through Warialda to where the accident happened,' he said.

Sutherland supported Mervyn's testimony.

'When the car came on to the corrugated road it seemed to skid and turned off the road over the embankment before anything could be done. I think Mervyn applied the brakes, but the distance was so short Mervyn could not pull the car up before it went over the embankment and capsized,' Sutherland said.

'When I got out of the car Paul was lying alongside the embankment. I went over to him. He was moaning. I could see he had a cut on the back of his head. I put my coat under his head. Just at that time a lorry came along and I asked them to send the doctor out. A short time afterwards Dr Wheatley arrived and when he examined Paul he told us he was dead. The time of the accident was about three o'clock.'

Max Jones gave similar evidence to that of Sutherland and Mervyn.

After all witness accounts were recorded, Coroner Stewart addressed the courtroom.

'As coroner, I declare and find the deceased, Paul Aloysius Liddy, on 28 August 1943 on the Warialda to Inverell Road — five miles from Warialda — died from the effects of injuries accidentally received when a motor car in which he was riding overturned on that date. The cause of death was haemorrhage caused by injuries to the head accidentally sustained in said motor vehicle accident.'

Coroner Stewart found intemperance 'indirectly' contributed to the cause of death.

He reprimanded Sutherland, in particular, for his actions.

'Your decision to allow a young, unlicensed person — no more than a boy — to drive the vehicle was, in part, responsible for the accident.'

The same day, Sutherland fronted Justices of the Peace John Archibald McGregor and John Webb at Warialda police court and was fined £2/10/ on each of two charges of not being a licensed driver and allowing a minor to drive a motor vehicle.

Mervyn was charged with being an unlicensed driver and dealt with in the Warialda children's court. He was committed to the care of his mother, Catherine, on the condition he was of good behaviour for twelve months and did not drive a motor vehicle during that period.

Paul Liddy left £93 in cash and bank savings — nearly $7000 in new millennium dollars. His only will was dated 2 May 1917, made while on active service with the AIF.

Liddy's mother, Helen, was the sole beneficiary. However she had died on 7 November 1939.

* * *

Mervyn Medley went back to Liverpool with his mother. However, the collateral damage from the tragic events on that August afternoon in 1943 never really went away.

He found work at a western Sydney sawmill and reconnected with his childhood sweetheart, Mary.

Mervyn suffered further anguish when his father, Sgt Robert Dunn Medley, died at Cowra Military Hospital on 24 November 1945.

Medley, a machine-gunner in both world wars, was attached to the Garrison Battalion at Cowra. He was born near South Shields, Durham, England, in 1894 and arrived in Australia with his parents, James, a stonemason, and Jane, shortly before the outbreak of World War I.

He married Catherine Mulcahy at Liverpool, west of Sydney, and immediately enlisted. At age twenty-two he joined the 17th Australian Infantry Battalion and left for active service on HMAT *Themistocles*. Medley returned home injured on hospital ship TSS *Karoola* in December 1918 and applied for a soldier settler's block at Hillview, Liverpool.

He worked for a time for NSW Railways and later as a telephone linesman but re-enlisted when war broke out in 1939. His death in 1945 at age fifty-one was sudden. Newspapers reported:

Sgt Robert Dunn Medley was a former well-known resident of Hillview and his widow and family mourn their irreparable loss. A machine-gunner of both wars, the late Sgt Medley served for some time with the 13th Garrison Battalion of this war and was extremely popular with all ranks.

His headstone at Cowra War Cemetery reads: 'His duty nobly done; ever remembered by his wife.'

* * *

Mervyn grappled with his demons. He struggled to stay on the right side of the law and drank often, despite his young age.

On 6 May 1946, he fronted Liverpool police court, charged with riding a motorcycle while under the influence of alcohol.

Police stated Mervyn, just eighteen when arrested, was observed cutting a corner and 'swaying about'.

The motorcycle coughed and spluttered and came to a stop shortly afterwards because the reserve fuel switch had not been engaged. He was fined £5.

Mervyn's older brothers, Jack and Robert, found themselves in court a few months later.

Jack, thickset with chubby features and blue eyes, was discharged from the army in October that year and established a carrier business. Robert, also a former AIF serviceman, ran a garage at Hillview.

Both were charged with stealing wheat from Eulomogo siding near Dubbo on the main western railway line to Bourke and from Erigolia siding, near Carrathool in the western Riverina district.

They teamed up with a mate, labourer Keith Ford from Parramatta, and between 9 and 28 October allegedly knocked off large quantities of grain belonging to the Australian Wheat Board.

More than three hundred bags of wheat valued at £300 were taken. The haul was worth about $21,000 in new millennium dollars.

On Thursday 28 November the trio fronted police magistrate Martin Meagher at Liverpool Court to face eleven charges of theft. They were each remanded on £300 bail until 5 December.

Det-Constable John Renehan alleged the stolen wheat was being sold to poultry farmers in the Liverpool district. Police prosecutor Henry Taylor said the wheat was taken at night when the sidings were unattended.

Police said the Medley brothers were carting wool from Gilgandra to the city and helped themselves to the bags of wheat. They retagged the bags before offloading them.

After selling seventy-three bags from their initial heist, the Medleys enlisted Ford for subsequent forays. The three men stole more wheat from the same siding.

It was alleged Ford was paid £10 a trip as payment for his role in the theft.

Police conducted an early morning raid on Jack Medley's Green Valley home on Tuesday 26 November and later impounded a lorry found at Robert Medley's Hillview home.

Ford was arrested at his Parramatta workplace.

However, police magistrate Meagher went soft on the three offenders as they were all returned servicemen.

'It seems they travelled a hundred miles from Liverpool and at night, stole this wheat, and sold it to Liverpool poultry farmers. I will take into consideration the fact they are young men, all married and have all seen service overseas. I am going to extend leniency to the three of them but it depends on them whether that leniency is justified,' Mr Meagher said.

Jack and Robert Medley were fined £15 on each of four counts of theft and ordered to pay £97/10/- compensation to the Commonwealth. They were further required to enter into recognisances of £50 each to be of good behaviour for two years.

Ford was fined £8 on each of the three charges, ordered to pay £35 compensation and also placed on a £50 bond for two years.

* * *

Mervyn Medley was determined to celebrate the 1946 festive season in style.

The past twelve months had been hard, especially on his mum, Catherine.

Her husband died a month before Christmas the previous year and her two eldest sons were lucky to escape gaol a month before this Christmas for their theft of wheat. And then there was Mervyn's earlier conviction for riding a motorcycle under the influence and unlicensed.

'Things will be different this Christmas, I promise,' Mervyn told his mum. Catherine smiled, wiped away a tear and held her son tightly.

Sydney, like the rest of the country, was experiencing a postwar boom. The entire city was on a high. Prosperity and good times reigned.

During the first half of December, Sydneysiders withdrew more than £1.25 million from banks to cover celebrations — and that figure spiralled as Christmas Day drew closer.

The year also heralded the first *Carols by Candlelight* in Hyde Park, an event organised by the *Daily Telegraph* in conjunction with radio station 2UW. The newspaper proudly headlined the yuletide season as "Sydney's best Christmas since 1939".

Around 6.30 on Christmas Eve, Mervyn jumped on his motorbike and rode to Homebush to collect girlfriend Mary from her Underwood Road home.

Catherine waved her son goodbye and told him to be safe. 'It's Christmas Eve and the roads are busy; there are people everywhere. Please, Mervyn, be careful.'

Mervyn gave his mum a wink, smiled broadly, and roared off down Hillview Parade.

Just after seven o'clock, Mary climbed on the back of

Mervyn's motorbike and held on tightly. She rested her cheek against his back and locked her hands around his chest.

Mary had never ridden pillion before and was unaware Mervyn was unlicensed. Her heart beat loudly — a mixture of fear, love and excitement.

'Merry Christmas, honey,' Mervyn yelled above the roar of the engine.

He clicked the motorbike into gear, released the clutch and sped along Woodville Road.

Meanwhile, small goods salesman Reg Sly was heading home, driving his Chevrolet tourer along the same road, near Granville. He noticed the lights of a motorcycle in the rear-view mirror.

'You're getting along a bit,' he said out loud as he heard the roar of the motorbike behind him.

A little further up the road, approaching from the opposite direction, carpenter John Smith and asbestos cement contractor Kieran Stiff were heading to the city. Stiff was driving.

As the two vehicles climbed a rise up Woodville Road, Mervyn attempted to overtake Reg Sly's Chevrolet.

'Hang on, honey,' Mervyn yelled as he hooked the motorbike around the Chev — and straight into the path of Kieran Stiff's car.

Stiff slammed on the brakes but was too late. Sly also braked heavily as the wayward motorbike struck both vehicles.

Mervyn and Mary were thrown from the motorbike. Mary was dazed but otherwise okay.

Mervyn's leg was badly broken and blood poured from a gaping head wound. He was hurled more than forty feet when the motorbike bounced off both vehicles.

Constable James Parker from Granville police station arrived at the scene as medical officers treated Mervyn and Mary. He helped stretcher them to the back of a waiting ambulance.

He noted the mangled wreck of Mervyn's motorbike on the western side of busy Woodville Road as well as the damaged motor vehicles.

Constable Parker interviewed Kieran Stiff.

'How in God's name did this happen?'

Stiff was visibly shaken. 'I was driving north along Woodville Road up the hill at about 25 miles an hour when I saw the headlights of another car coming down the hill towards me. It was on the correct side of the road. When it was almost abreast of me I suddenly saw the glare of a single headlight come from behind the car and then something struck the front of my car — I now realise it was the motorbike that hit me.'

Mervyn died on Christmas Eve in the back of an ambulance as it raced to Parramatta District Hospital. He was nineteen years old.

Twenty-year-old Mary was treated for shock and a lacerated right foot and released from hospital at about 10 pm.

Dr Ariel Robey examined Mervyn's body that night. She gave the cause of death as a 'compound fracture to the right parietal region and a fractured base of the skull'.

Robert Medley identified his brother's body at 11 am the next day — the hottest Christmas Day seen in Sydney in ten years — in the company of Granville police Sgt Lionel Whitney.

'The deceased died in the ambulance between Woodville Road and the hospital,' Whitney told Coroner George William Richards at the subsequent inquest at Parramatta courthouse on Thursday 9 January 1947.

Mary Cameron remembered very little about the crash

— but she did claim there were two cars approaching from the opposite direction.

'I remember the deceased swinging to his right to overtake the car we were following. He was about three or four feet behind the car when he swung out,' Mary said.

'When we swung to the right I felt the motorcycle increase its speed. The deceased did not attempt to drop back, but continued on. The next thing I remember is waking up on the road. I am quite sure I saw two cars approaching.'

Constable James Parker told the inquest Woodville Road was well sealed with bitumen and in good condition.

'At the time of the accident, the weather was fine and the traffic fairly heavy. Where the collision occurred, there is a fairly steep, downward slope to the south,' Parker said.

'The point of impact, where the motorcycle struck the offside front portion of Kieran Stiff's car, was determined by me by a patch of broken glass on the roadway. There were also scratch marks made by the motorcycle and both drivers of the vehicles indicated to me where the accident took place.

'As a result of the collision, the nearside rear wheel of Edward Sly's car was smashed as that vehicle was still in motion at a stated speed of 20 miles an hour.'

Parker estimated Sly's car travelled out of control for nearly fifty yards before stopping on the eastern side of Woodville Road.

'In my opinion, the damage done to Edward Sly's car was caused by the motorcycle striking the offside rear mudguard after the motorcycle collided with Edward Stiff's car. This forced Sly's car to the nearside and caused the collapse of the wheel's wooden spokes.'

Edward Stiff said there was little he could do when the

motorcycle attempted to overtake Edward Sly's vehicle.

'I noticed two lamps of a vehicle approaching me from the north. It was on the correct side of the road. As I was nearly abreast of that vehicle, a headlight seemed to flash from behind that vehicle and something hit me on the offside front of my car. My car was stopped immediately by the impact,' Stiff said.

Reg Sly said he was driving to his Merrylands home when he saw a motorcycle behind him.

'I was coming down a rise and I noticed a light shining into my rear-view mirror. It was going up and down and I knew a motorcycle was coming down the hill behind me. I heard the engine of that motorcycle and it sounded as if it was moving fairly fast,' Sly said.

'Then I heard a crash and almost instantly felt a bump on the back of my car. I felt the car roll over to the eastern side of the road and then it rocked. The wheels of my car have wooden spokes and I subsequently discovered the wooden spokes of my rear, near wheel had been broken. At the time of the accident there were only the two motor cars and the motorcycle at that spot.'

Mary Cameron, however, maintained there were two cars approaching from the opposite direction.

'When we were about half a mile from the northern end of Woodville Road I saw a motor car travelling in the same direction, ahead of us. I noticed that our motorcycle was passing that car, and I then saw the headlights of two other cars coming from the south.

'When the deceased swung to the right to overtake and pass the car in front of us, the two cars proceeding in the opposite direction were fairly close to us.'

Mary said one of the vehicles was attempting to overtake

the other vehicle.

'I do not know for certain what happened after that, but if the motorcycle collided with one of those cars, it was the one which was attempting to pass the one in front of it,' she said.

'The next thing I knew, I was lying on the roadway. Shortly afterwards I was placed in an ambulance and taken to Parramatta District Hospital.'

Mary told Sgt Whitney that Mervyn collected her at 6.45 pm on Christmas Eve. She said she had known him for nine-and-a-half years and was "keeping company" with him. She said he was "perfectly sober" at the time of the accident. 'He was riding a motorcycle and this was the first time I had ridden pillion on this particular motorcycle. I had seen the deceased on numerous occasions and was not aware he was not a licensed rider.'

Edward Stiff's passenger, John Smith, said there was only one vehicle approaching.

'I saw the lights of a motor car coming toward us. There was only one car. It was about the middle of the hill when I first saw it, about a hundred feet away. It was travelling at about twenty to twenty-five miles an hour. That car and our car were passing one another when I heard a crash,' Smith said.

* * *

For Catherine Medley, Christmas would never be the same again.

Her husband died one month before Christmas in 1945 and twelve months later her son was killed on Christmas Eve. Twenty years earlier Catherine's fifteen-month-old daughter, Jean, accidently drowned when playing with an old oilcan filled with water.

Catherine's grief was palpable.

She last saw Mervyn about 4 pm on the day of the accident. Four hours later he was dead.

Catherine told the inquest her son was happy, eager to pick up Mary, and looking forward to festive celebrations with family and friends. 'Mervyn was in good health and spirits, and completely sober.'

Her son was laid to rest at Liverpool Cemetery on Friday 27 December 1946 after a funeral service at All Saints' Catholic Church, Liverpool.

On 2 November 1950, further tragedy consumed Catherine when her second-youngest son, Hilton, an apprentice welder, was rushed to Prince Henry Hospital near Randwick, suffering acute anterior poliomyelitis. Despite the efforts of doctors and medical staff, Hilton died the next day — seven weeks before Christmas — aged seventeen.

Within five years, Catherine lost her husband and two sons, all around Christmas time — and haunting memories of the drowning death of her baby daughter in 1925 were ever present.

Despite the sadness she shouldered, Catherine lived a full life and died at Liverpool on 7 June 1985 aged ninety-three.

Postscript:

Nine years after the accident that killed Paul Liddy, shearer Charlie Sutherland, the owner of the vehicle driven by Mervyn Medley, was charged with unlawfully killing seventy-two-year-old pensioner Dick Ellis near Warwick on Queensland's Darling Downs.

Ellis and Sutherland were good mates.

Sutherland was accused of reversing a truck over Ellis after an afternoon on the drink. Sutherland claimed to have no recollection of the accident, telling police he must have blacked out.

On the morning of 8 September 1952, Sutherland drove to Yelarbon to start a new shed, but fell ill. He returned to Inglewood about mid-morning and had a couple of brandies before driving to the Karara Hotel, about forty miles away and consuming two more brandies.

He chatted with publican Roy Forbes then drove a couple of miles up the road to Ellis's hut and ate lunch with his mate.

After lunch, Sutherland and Ellis drove back to the pub and settled in for the afternoon. Sutherland drank more brandy as well as beer.

'A brandy or two every now and again is the only relief I get from my ulcer,' he said.

Around 5.30 pm, they bought a half-bottle of rum and bid Forbes goodbye.

Forbes, 38, liked Sutherland and Ellis, and considered them mates. He was confident Sutherland was capable of driving the short distance to Ellis's home, but was worried about 'old Dick'. Just to be safe, he left his wife, Elva, in charge of the bar and followed them home.

'This won't take long, love. I'm just a bit worried about old Dick having an accident or falling out of the truck. I want to be sure he gets home safely.'

Sutherland and Ellis were unaware Forbes was tailing them.

Forbes watched Sutherland's truck pull up at Ellis's home. Satisfied they were both safe, he returned to the Karara Hotel.

Sutherland fell asleep in the truck and later that night rolled out his swag on the front veranda of Ellis's cottage. He awoke the next morning and looked around for his elderly mate. He assumed Ellis was inside.

A few minutes later Sutherland found the old man under the truck. Ellis was unresponsive.

Frantic, Sutherland thumbed a ride to the Karara Hotel and asked Forbes to contact police. 'I think Dick is dead under my truck,' he said.

Forbes and Sutherland returned to Ellis's home and waited for the police and ambulance to arrive.

Warwick Det-Sen-Constable Ron Trost and Sgt John Wade attended Ellis's property and observed a broken fence post near Sutherland's truck.

'It appears to me that when you reversed your truck last night you knocked over this post. Dick was either leaning against the post or lying behind the truck when you reversed over him,' Sgt Wade suggested.

'It looks like that, but I can't remember. I can remember going across the bridge, just up the road, but everything after that is blank,' Sutherland replied.

The truck was engaged in reverse gear and tyre marks indicated the wheels were spun at high speed. Dirt and grass were thrown back under the chassis.

'The engine of this truck must have been revved at high speed to cause that,' Trost observed.

'Yes, it looks that way,' Sutherland replied glumly.

Trost shook his head. 'Are you sure you don't remember parking the truck in this position? You remember coming to the bridge, which is only thirty yards away, but you don't remember pulling up?'

Sutherland was clearly distressed. 'Honestly, I can't remember.'

A tobacco tin, spectacles and loose coins were near Ellis's body. 'That all belongs to Dick,' Sutherland said.

The truck was removed from the property and impounded at Warwick police station. Sutherland was questioned further at the station. He again stated he did not remember anything about the accident and denied he was drunk when leaving the hotel at Karara.

Sutherland was charged with unlawfully killing Ellis and fronted stipendiary magistrate Charles Knowles at Warwick circuit sittings on Thursday 25 September 1952.

Sen-Sgt Austin Cooper handled the prosecution and Sutherland was represented by Warwick solicitor Richard Leeper.

Sutherland told the court he and Ellis left the Karara Hotel just after dusk and arrived at Ellis's home shortly afterwards.

'I do not remember anything after that; I must have had a blackout,' he said.

When questioned whether he remembered parking his truck, Sutherland replied: 'No, I don't remember a thing until I woke up behind the steering wheel at 10 o'clock. I know it was 10 o'clock because I looked at my watch.'

He told the magistrate he had no recollection of Ellis stepping down from the truck when they arrived home.

'I had a look around for Dick, but could not find him. I thought that as he had a few beers, he may have gone back to the hotel for more. I then got the swag out of my truck and threw it on the veranda, where I camped until daylight,' he said.

Sutherland said he searched for Ellis the next morning.

'He was not in his bed so I went out to the truck and saw the poor old fellow lying underneath. I felt him and he was cold, so I started to walk toward Karara to notify the police.'

When asked whether he often suffered blackouts, Sutherland replied: 'I had a blackout three months ago in Allora, but was not attended by a doctor.'

(There was also the incident nine years previously and recorded earlier in this chapter when he suffered a similar medical episode when driving a group of shearing mates and handed the keys to teenage shed hand Mervyn Medley, with deadly consequences).

Det Trost told the court Ellis's body was moved from under the truck and taken to Warwick Hospital morgue.

Dr Clyde Dent stated he made a superficial examination of Ellis's body and later conducted a post-mortem examination which revealed the fourth and fifth ribs on both the right and left side of the chest were fractured, the left collarbone was fractured and the chest pushed to the left side.

'The heart and lungs were normal and the pleural cavities were free of fluid and blood,' he said. 'There was also considerable damage to the skull.'

Dr Dent said the injuries were consistent with Ellis being dragged or crushed under a truck.

Publican Roy Forbes told the court how he followed Sutherland and Ellis home after their session at the pub because he was concerned about "old Dick" and wanted to make sure he got home safely without falling out of the truck or anything happening to him.

Forbes told the court Sutherland's truck never exceeded twenty miles an hour and was going quite straight and not zigzagging.

When cross-examined by Sutherland's defence counsel, Richard Leeper, Forbes said he was a little concerned about Ellis because he was an old man and short-sighted. 'I've taken him home on previous occasions when he'd had a few drinks. I was confident Charlie Sutherland was quite capable of looking after himself when he left the hotel and was satisfied he was capable of exercising control over his truck.'

Leeper submitted there was no case proven against Sutherland. 'The circumstances were most unfortunate and no-one regretted the incident more than the defendant. The mere fact of the occurrence of an accident is not evidence of negligence.'

He argued Sutherland had no case to answer.

Magistrate Knowles disagreed and committed Sutherland to stand trial at the next sitting of the circuit court in Warwick on 25 November. About two weeks before the trial, Leeper was advised by the Department of Justice that no true bill would be filed against his client.

The charge was dropped and Charlie Sutherland was cleared of any wrongdoing.

CHAPTER 8

GET UP! THERE'S BEEN A TRAIN SMASH!

The spring school holidays were over.

Teenagers Ada Fripp and Nancy Seccombe waited at Narrabri railway station for the North-West Mail to arrive from Moree.

It was late afternoon on Monday 13 September 1926. The girls, both aged fifteen, were on their way to Clifton Gardens Catholic Boarding School at Mosman after a two-week spring hiatus.

Ada's sister, nineteen-year-old Emily, was with them. An exceptional student she was returning to Sydney University to start her second term after passing every examination with credits during term one.

Ada and Nancy were friends. Their parents, Tom and Isabella Fripp and Les and Zara Seccombe, were well-known graziers in the Rowena district, about sixty-five miles north-west of Narrabri.

The girls' parents were there to bid them farewell, along with Nancy's cousin, twelve-year-old David Seccombe, who was returning to Beecroft Grammar School, near Pennant Hills.

Another cousin, Tom Scholefield, was going to Barker College, Hornsby.

The group of children chatted excitedly among themselves. Their parents talked about everything to do with farming, especially the weather. Winter refused to move on; a late frost looked likely.

Volunteers and survivors help the injured and begin cleaning up the carnage left by the Murulla train disaster in 1926 (Image credit: Museums of History NSW — State Archives Collection)

The train's brake van rests on its side after catapulting the North-West Mail's engine and deflecting off the train's first carriage (Image credit: Museums of History NSW — State Archives Collection)

A crane and winch were used to help clear the track (Image credit: Museums of History NSW — State Archives Collection)

The point of impact: twenty-seven people were killed when the North-West Mail from Moree to Sydney collided with a runaway goods train at Murulla, midway between Murrurundi and Scone (Image credit: Museums of History NSW — State Archives Collection)

Ahead lay thirteen long weeks of intense schooling before the children returned home to a hot, western summer.

Tom Fripp twirled his handlebar moustache and smiled. 'Don't worry kids, the Christmas holidays will be here before you know it.'

The children weren't convinced. Another three months at boarding school was in front of them, hundreds of miles from home.

There was also a twelve-hour train-trip to Sydney to endure — if the North-West Mail ran to schedule. It rarely did.

The children knew the journey would be cold, boring and uneventful; they knew the drill — they'd done it before.

Pilliga farmer Bill Wilson, sixty-seven, and his wife, Flora, forty-nine, waited on the platform. Their son, Ted, was there to see them off. The Wilsons, originally from the Hunter region, were travelling back to their roots for a Back to Singleton reunion.

Flora was the key driver of the bush nursing service in the Pilliga district. The movement, rolled out in 1910, provided nursing care to rural and remote townships across Australia.

Bill and Flora chatted with forty-one-year-old Azubah Anderton, from Narrabri, and her husband, David.

Nineteen-year-old Richard Bails, from Wee Waa, was ready to board. He planned to get off at Strathfield and make his way to Parramatta.

All agreed there wouldn't be much peace and quiet with so many children returning to school. 'Maybe we should've waited until tomorrow,' joked Mrs Anderton.

The growing crowd huddled against the late afternoon cold air and waited patiently for the North-West Mail to roll up to the station. Spring officially arrived two weeks earlier, but winter had a habit of hanging around like an overbearing house guest.

The P-Class steam engine, pulling two sleeping cars, two passenger carriages and a guard's van, left Moree at precisely 2.15 pm.

Passengers from Moree included fifteen-year-old Arthur Jurd.

Arthur worked at Lillyman's cordial factory in Moree but the ambitious young lad, son of racehorse trainer John Jurd, wanted more in life. He was on his way to Sydney to sit his final exam as a fitter's apprentice with NSW Railways.

Arthur felt uneasy. Twelve months earlier a younger cousin, Stanley Jurd, had been killed in an incredible accident on the North-West Mail.

Also waiting to board was Arthur Manchee, a well-known Biniguy grazier.

New Zealander John Mockridge, Stan Noller, Vaughan King, Clyde Kay, Owen McGrath and Alf Brush, a forty-two-year-old returned serviceman, boarded at Moree.

Brush, known as Stumpy, was a Moree taxi driver. He served as a sapper with the Imperial Army in World War I and was heading to Sydney. He carried war-related injuries and was plagued by ill health.

McGrath, forty-five, worked at the Criterion Hotel in Moree. He was returning to the city to see his wife, Ethel, at Bondi.

Kay, twenty-two, recently completed a six-year apprenticeship under newspaper proprietor Alf Handley at the *North-West Champion*, where he trained in handset and hot-metal typesetting.

Kay and his sister, Gladys Williams, were travelling to Sydney to visit relatives.

Mockridge, a 26-year-old accountant, was on the first leg of his journey back to Dunedin in New Zealand's south island. He'd been working in south-west Queensland, but needed to get home. His wife of three years, Mona, was seriously ill.

Stan Noller owned a garage at Parramatta and was in Moree on business, a regular visit. He recently opened a branch in the town. The twenty-six-year-old, an organist at St Barnabas' Church of England in Westmead, was from a well-connected Sydney family.

Noller was homeward bound to Parramatta, where his father, building contractor William, was highly regarded in political, social and business circles. He was Parramatta mayor, chairman of the Parramatta Park Trust and trustee, churchwarden and superintendent at St John's Anglican Cathedral.

Nurse Elsie Rankin, twenty-one, from Manly Cottage Hospital, was returning home from a holiday with her widowed aunt, Catherine Shepherd. They visited Elsie's father John — Catherine's brother — at Dirranbandi in western Queensland, then drove to Mungindi to catch a train to Moree and connect with the North-West Mail.

Also on the Mungindi train were James and Maria Taylor from Thirroul near Wollongong and their seven-month-old son, Sidney.

James, 27, was a fireman with NSW Railways. The young family holidayed at Mungindi with James' mother, Lila Dawes, and stepfather Matthew Dawes, the local saddler and mail contractor.

Maria, 34, held her baby tightly as they boarded the North-West Mail at Moree. They had a long journey ahead. From Sydney, James and Laura would board the Melbourne Express and disembark at Goulburn.

NSW Railway Department's southern area commissioner James Reid and his wife Laura were holidaying in Moree, where they enjoyed every spare moment relaxing at Moree Bore Baths. Now it was time to go home.

Reid joined the railways in 1881 as a telegraph probationer and worked his way through the ranks until appointed southern area commander in 1925.

The North-West Mail chugged through Gurley. A few miles later it stopped at Bellata and collected Andy Samios, a twenty-three-year-old Greek from the island of Kythera.

Samios and his brother, Nick, established a café and carrier business at Bellata in early 1926 after three years at Narrabri working for fellow Kytherian Archie Gavrili.

Samios's friends, twenty-seven-year-old Manuel Kepreotes and thirty-one-year-old Nick Zographos, were due to board the train at Gunnedah. They planned a two-week break in Sydney. With them was twenty-six-year-old Panagiotis Hadzevogiannis, a visitor from Sydney, who had been in Australia for only nine months.

Driver Bill Charlton and guard Jim Marx chatted as they took in the vast open spaces. Paddocks full of golden wheat were only weeks away from harvest.

'The last thing these poor, bloody farmers need is a late frost. The way the weather's been, that's more than likely,' Charlton said.

Fireman Horace Findlater checked the train's firebox. It was a cold, spring afternoon but the cool air made no difference to Findlater.

*   *   *

Passengers on the Narrabri platform peered anxiously down the tracks for a glimpse of the train and the sound of its tell-tale whistle.

The piercing toot was right on cue.

'Here it comes,' yelled David Seccombe.

Arthur Jurd peered out the window as the train pulled up. He saw Ada Fripp and Nancy Seccombe on the platform and smiled. The trip might not be so bad, after all.

Walter McMillan, twenty-six, climbed on board. He travelled more than two hundred and fifty miles from Bourke in far western NSW to catch the train to Sydney, where he worked at the Eveleigh railway depot.

McMillan, a returned officer awarded the Military Medal for gallant service during the war, had returned home to Bourke to visit parents Walter and Selina, and siblings Janet, David, Dolly and Grace.

Albert Jefferson, a twenty-six-year-old boilermaker at Werris Creek railway yards, couldn't wait to get home to see his parents, Bill and Agnes. He had finished six months' relief work at Narrabri railway yards and was heading to the Newcastle suburb of Merewether, where his father was an alderman on the local council. Waiting at the Pell Street family home were siblings James, Bill, Jack, Ted, Sara, Polly, Aggie and Edna.

Jefferson grinned broadly as the train hissed to a stop.

Conductor Tom Grant and guard Jim Marx marched along the platform, encouraging passengers to climb aboard.

'It's time to go; we can't be late,' Grant yelled above the din.

Ada and Emily Fripp hugged their parents and said goodbye. Isabella Fripp smiled and wiped away a tear. She was so proud of her two girls. Both were academically gifted with the world at their feet.

Zara Seccombe embraced daughter Nancy.

Tom Grant blew the whistle to alert driver Bill Charlton and, with an almighty grunt, the North-West Mail lurched forward.

The children pushed back windows and shutters and waved excitedly.

As the train began the sixty-mile leg to Gunnedah, Isabella Fripp swallowed hard and waved back. Ada's beautiful smile would haunt her for the rest of her life.

*   *   *

Celebrated judge, William Hugh Mocatta, and seasoned crown prosecutor, Robert Jardine Browning, waited on the Gunnedah platform.

Mocatta, sixty-four, and Browning, seventy-three, were returning to Sydney. They had wrapped up circuit court duties at Gunnedah and were looking forward to a few hours' downtime.

The law enforcers were a spirited team. Newspapers likened them to Sherlock Holmes and Dr Watson. Mocatta and Browning gelled and bounced off each other in courtrooms across NSW, and were loyal friends away from them.

Browning, a long-serving prosecutor with thirty-eight years' experience on the northern circuit, was accompanied by Department of Agriculture chief accountant Arthur Adams, known widely as Bill.

Adams was a key witness for the prosecution in a case before Judge Mocatta at Gunnedah courthouse that very morning.

Browning smiled. 'As soon as we get back, my friends and learned colleagues, I'm heading straight to Rose Bay for a round of golf. I think I've earned it.'

'I just might join you,' Mocatta smiled.

Also in the group were Percy Hunter and Phillip Akhurst.

Hunter, a former returned soldiers' settlement district officer at Murwillumbah, was Judge Mocatta's shorthand clerk. Akhurst, a brother of Australian lawn tennis champion Daphne Akhurst, was a solicitor attached to the Crown Law department.

Further down the platform were Percy and Annie Sampson, and their fifteen-year-old daughter, Clarice, known affectionately as Tally.

Percy Sampson was considered one of the biggest wheat growers in NSW.

Tally, an exceptional student, athlete and violinist, was returning to Presbyterian Ladies' College at Croydon. She wore the school hockey team's blazer and badge proudly and carried her valuable violin safely in its case. The instrument never left her side.

As night fell, the North-West Mail rolled into Gunnedah.

Nellie Walker, from Tambar Springs, and her six-year-old son John, known as Jack, stepped on board. They were on their way to Chatswood, in Sydney's lower north shore. Nellie clasped her son's hand tightly.

'You watch the gap, Jack,' she warned, with the hint of a smile.

Also needing help to board was sixty-three-year-old widower Frank Pelham, the Canterbury postmaster. The senior postal employee, eighteen months away from retirement, lost a leg in the 1870s in a riding accident.

His twenty-three-year-old son, Ted, a former A-grade soccer player in Sydney before a knee injury ended a promising career, helped his father on to the train. Frank and Ted spent the weekend at Gunnedah and were returning to Sydney.

Ted still shuddered about what might have been three months earlier. On 10 June he was a passenger on the last train to cross the Aberdeen viaduct before the next train on the line, the Brisbane Express, fell through the structure on the approach to a bridge across the Hunter River. Five passengers were killed and more than fifty people were injured.

Once on board, Frank and Ted were separated. Frank secured the last bunk on one of the sleeper carriages; Ted sat in the front carriage behind the engine.

The North-West Mail crept across the Liverpool Plains toward Werris Creek, an important railway junction widely recognised as Australia's first railway town.

Beekeeper Frank McKeown sat on the Werris Creek platform and watched the train edge closer.

The thirty-two-year-old returned Digger, born in Pymble and formerly of Coorabell near Byron Bay, established an apiary at Dungowan, near Tamworth, in 1924. He planned to build a home for his parents, Ebenezer and Eliza, and move them across.

McKeown was a deeply religious man and often contemplated joining the ministry. He was a trustee of the local Methodist church, Sunday school superintendent and congregational representative at quarterly circuit meetings. Right now he was on his way to the Singleton Show to exhibit his range of home-grown honey.

Show week incorporated Back to Singleton celebrations and many passengers were looking forward to a good, old-fashioned hometown reunion.

McKeown sat patiently with his Bible and luggage. His mother, Eliza, and older sister, Alice, would be waiting for him at Singleton railway station. He smiled the smile of a contented man; he was happy with his lot in life.

Emily McDonald, a forty-two-year-old mother of two teenage children, Ella and Keith, waited for the train to arrive.

Daughter, fourteen-year-old Ella, was schooling at Newcastle. Sixteen-year-old son, Keith, was supposed to be on the North-West Mail but convinced his mother to allow him to go on an earlier train with some friends. Keith had passed the entrance examination to the NSW Railways, and was offered employment in the city. He was going to work on the trains, just like his old man.

When he discovered some of his mates were heading to Sydney a couple of days earlier, he begged his mother to let him tag along.

Emily and her husband, Albert, a thirty-six-year-old railway worker, were married in Ryde in 1909 and relocated from Sydney to Werris Creek in 1924.

Emily peered over the top of her round-framed glasses and smiled. She would meet Keith on Tuesday morning to make sure his new accommodation was in order. She had toyed with the idea of motoring to Sydney in a new vehicle recently purchased by her husband. She was an excellent driver but thought the trip by train would be more relaxing.

John and Evelyn Rich and their children, three-year-old Alan, seven-year-old Howard and ten-year-old Eric waited on the Werris Creek platform. The family was returning home to the Newcastle suburb of Waratah.

Rich, a forty-five-year-old NSW Railways employee, was a key witness in the 10 June Aberdeen incident when a Brisbane-bound train fell through the Hunter River bridge. He was appointed an acting permanent way inspector on the Lismore line shortly afterwards.

John and Sarah Giles, from western Sydney, also boarded at Werris Creek.

John, sixty, and Sarah, sixty-five, married in 1887, and were closely connected with the Salvation Army. They were returning to Sydney, where John, an engine driver, worked at the Everleigh railway yards at Redfern. They were returning from holidays — John's last allocation of official leave before retirement.

At Quirindi railway station, Sydney Mallett waited on the platform. The American-born sixteen-year-old was on his way home to the Sydney suburb of Auburn, where his parents, George and Phillis, and brothers and sisters, waited anxiously. They hadn't seen Syd for more than six months. The adventurous teenager was working at Coomoo Coomoo station, a vast property on the Liverpool Plains, owned by Quirindi district pioneer James Allison.

The Mallett family was well travelled. Both parents were born in England. They married in 1902 and two years later landed at Ellis Island, New York, on the *Umbria*.

Syd was born in 1909 in Manhattan and his younger brother William came along in 1911. The young family returned to England in 1914 on the *Mauretania*. They set up home in South Shields, Durham, where siblings Hilda and George were born.

Six years later, the family was on the move again. They departed England on the *Beltana* and arrived in Australia in November 1920.

They settled in Stanley Street, North Auburn. In March 1926, Syd left the family nest to start work at Coomoo Coomoo. He smiled from ear to ear as he watched the North-West Mail pull its way up to the platform. He was heading home.

Janet and Margaret Doyle weren't quite as enthusiastic as

Syd. While he was heading home to family; the Doyle sisters were leaving family and moving to the Church of England Girls' School at Chatswood.

Margaret was sixteen, Janet a year younger. Parents George and Edith Doyle were emerging sheep breeders. They relocated from Wagga Wagga twelve months earlier and established Romney Vale, a vast sheep-breeding property on the edge of Quirindi.

George and Edith stood with their daughters on the platform and watched the train arrive.

'Don't worry girls, next year you'll be at school in Armidale and much closer to home,' George yelled above the hissing engine.

Elizabeth Martin-Templeton, forty-five, was also employed at Coomoo Coomoo station. Scottish-born, she was on her way to Sydney to meet up with her boyfriend of thirteen years, Frank Garland, a butcher employed at Berilda station, near Gilgandra.

Frank left for Sydney on an earlier train and was staying at the Town Hall Coffee Palace on George Street, not far from Central Station, where he would meet the auburn-haired love of his life.

For the sake of family harmony, Elizabeth adopted Frank's surname. Her kin back home in Scotland thought they were married, and Elizabeth preferred it that way. It was a little white lie of mammoth proportions, to be sure, but the last thing her family needed to know was that she and Frank were, in fact, unwed and living together under the same roof.

Such a relationship was frowned upon in 1920s Australia, and strictly taboo in Scotland.

* * *

Conductor Tom Grant, shivering from the cold night air, jumped from the train and ushered passengers on board. A full moon made the task easier.

John Dunbar stood back and allowed the women and children to board the train. That was just his way. The quietly spoken seventy-year-old from Scone was one of the town's most respected citizens. He smiled and watched as the children scrambled on to the North-West Mail.

Oh to be young again, he mused.

Dunbar, a recently retired dairy-farmer, fruit grower and confectioner, was returning home after visiting his thirty-eight-year-old son, Jack.

In a few weeks he would travel to Leeton, in the Riverina district, to live out retirement with another son, Donald.

Sixty miles down the line, sixty-two-year-old Bertha Dunbar was waiting for him. They'd been married forty-one years and were still very much in love. A new chapter beckoned at Leeton, a fruit- and rice-growing centre about eighty miles from Wagga Wagga.

Dunbar thought of his younger brother, Randolph, who died after a railway accident at Doughboy Hollow railway station thirty-five years earlier.

Randolph was stationmaster at Doughboy Hollow, renamed Ardglen in 1893. On 17 March 1891 he accidentally dropped the tablet passed by engine driver Sol Reuben as a goods train from Murrurundi crawled through the station.

Tablets, or tokens, are objects which a locomotive driver must have or see before entering a particular section of single track. Tablets, sometimes attached to a large ring, are clearly marked with the name of the section to which they belong and are exchanged with a designated station staff member, generally the station master.

The system is used for single railway tracks to ensure there is only one train on a particular block of line between two stations at any one time.

Randolph had leaned across from the platform to receive the tablet. He overbalanced and fell forward against the engine and was dragged more than twenty-five yards before the frantic engine driver could stop the train. Randolph was rushed to Murrurundi Hospital with serious injuries, including severe bruising, suspected internal injuries and a badly crushed foot, necessitating amputation.

He died six days later.

Randolph, born on 13 September 1863 was aged twenty-six at the time of his death.

'It's Randolph's birthday today. Your uncle would've been sixty-three,' Dunbar said. Jack smiled fondly, shook his dad's hand, and watched him board the train.

'Watch your step, pop.'

* * *

As the evening wore on, the North-West Mail ambled its way through Willow Tree. The next stop was Murrurundi at the foot of the Liverpool Ranges.

Reuben and Kate Ackland, and their three-year-old son, Kevin, were waiting at the station. They had recently moved from Wingen to Scone, twelve miles away, where Rueben worked on NSW Railways. He started with the railway in 1916 as a fettler but reverted to light duties after a workplace accident in December 1925.

He married Kate, a widow with five children, in 1918. Her previous husband, William Cox, passed away at Narrabri Hospital in 1916, aged thirty-nine.

Passengers loaded at Murrurundi and the train began plugging its way towards Sydney.

Andy Samios, Manuel Kepreotes, Nick Zographos and Panagiotis Hadzevogiannis chatted among themselves. Hadzevogiannis, also known as Peter Vagianis, had been in Australia since Christmas. He left the family village of Kato Tritos in Mytilini, the capital and main port of the Greek island Lesbos, in late 1925. He told his friends there was no real desire to return.

'I can make so much more money here in Australia — this is the lucky country. I may go back one day, but only to visit,' he said.

In another section of the train, the conversation wasn't so upbeat. Passengers spoke about the spate of recent railway accidents and derailments.

Garnet Wilson, a telegraphist from Auburn, was freezing cold. He tried for the umpteenth time to fully close a carriage window but the damn thing simply wouldn't budge. Wilson and fellow passengers discussed the rail disaster at Ardglen two months earlier. There was another disaster at Aberdeen a month before that.

The dark, depressing conversation wasn't exactly ideal fodder for a long and tiring rail trip. In the Aberdeen crash, a combined sitting and sleeping carriage was smashed to pieces, another carriage was snapped in half and a third carriage teetered over the bridge spanning the Hunter River. A twenty-berth sleeping car fell on its side and another carriage rolled more than sixty feet down an embankment.

Ted Pelham's ears pricked. 'I was on the train that went across the Aberdeen viaduct just before the Brisbane Express crashed through it. I read somewhere the viaduct was riddled with white ants. It's a wonder more people weren't killed.'

Gladys Williams listened intently. 'Don't you worry,' she said, 'the North-West Mail will be next.'

Arthur Jurd winced at the conversation. He swallowed hard. Only twelve months earlier, his younger cousin, Stanley, was killed when the North-West Mail stopped at a siding at Ardglen railway station to allow a southbound goods train to pass. The train was laden with wool bales from Moree.

Stanley and schoolmates Roy Ledingham, Matthew Hall and John Boland were on their way home from boarding school. Shortly after midnight, the boys watched through the carriage window as a goods train passed. A loose wool bale scraped the side of the North-West Mail, striking Stanley in the head. He died instantly.

It was nearly twelve months to the day since Stanley was killed. Arthur Jurd and his fellow passengers had rattled through Ardglen minutes earlier. Now, as they approached Blandford, everyone was discussing rail disasters and grisly deaths.

Arthur Jurd closed his eyes — and his ears.

*   *   *

More than a hundred and fifty people of all ages and backgrounds — many of them children returning to school — had that day, 13 September 1926, boarded the North-West Mail at stations and sidings between Moree and Murrurundi. Every carriage was full.

Around 11.15 pm, as the train trundled through Blandford towards Murulla, chugging along at thirty miles an hour, most of the passengers dozed. Children slowly stopped chatting. Sleep took over.

The night was cold and a fog slowly descended. The train's gentle rocking made slumber a little easier.

As the clock edged closer to midnight, the North-West Mail was deathly quiet.

At the next stop down the line, things were not so calm. The Murulla siding, straddling the Liverpool Ranges eight miles north of Wingen, consisted of two sets of points about 1250 feet apart, a signal box and signalman's hut, outhouse, level crossing and a loop line to allow trains to pass.

Around 11.15 pm, the crew on a south-bound goods train, No. 62, were in difficulty.

Murulla signal box operator, twenty-three-year-old Wally White, controlled the loop line for trains to pass on a single rail track. He was anxious to send the goods train to Wingen without delay as there were already three mail trains running late.

Number 62 was hauling thirty-four wagons, laden with wool bales and wheat, as well as a brake van. The train, fitted with Westinghouse airbrakes, was more than 950 feet long and carrying 746 tons.

Another goods train, No. 95, was heading north and entered the loop line to wait for No.62 to pass.

As the driver of No. 62, Ernie Turner, applied steam to allow the train to scale an incline, the bump forward caused a draw hook between wagons to disengage.

The last twelve wagons, more than three hundred feet in length and weighing 264 tons, were separated from the front section.

However, both sections of No. 62 were within clearance points of the loop line, opposite the signal box, which allowed No. 95 to exit and continue its northward journey.

As staff made several attempts to fit a tail rope and reconnect the two sections, the brake van was shunted back each time until it eventually crossed the clearance of the loop line.

Staff improvised. They jerry-rigged a wire rope and coupling to haul the wagons clear of the crossing point and further along the main line so the North-West Mail could pass safely on the loop.

The brake pipe hoses weren't connected to the train. They were shorter than the makeshift tail rope, about twenty feet in length, and therefore unable to charge up the brakes on the guard van.

At 11.30 pm, about the same time the North-West Mail was trudging through Blandford, four miles away, signalman Wally White yelled out to driver Ernie Turner to pull the train past the fouling point.

'Bring it forward! Bring it forward! Clear the point!'

White was unable to set the points for the passenger train from Moree to pass the loop line because the goods wagons were crossing them.

The North-West Mail was minutes away.

The handbrakes on the rear portion of No. 62 were released, leaving it unbraked and driver Ernie Turner climbed hurriedly up to the engine. When the locomotive thrust forward, the jolt caused the improvised tail rope to snap about a foot from the point of connection.

White jumped from his cabin. To his horror, he saw the unhitched wagons begin to roll and gather momentum.

White and train guard David Davies charged alongside

the carriages and tried desperately to manually engage the handbrakes.

They managed to apply the brakes on two wagons, but as the breakaway section increased speed, White and Davis were thrown to the ground.

The men watched helplessly as the unbraked rear section of No. 62, made up of the brake van and eleven wagons laden with wool bales, began a deathly roll down the incline towards Blandford — and the approaching North-West Mail.

The runaway wagons hurtled down the line for one-and-a-half miles, gaining tremendous pace.

North-West Mail fireman Horace Findlater glanced up and saw the red lights of the runaway brake van on the tracks ahead.

He yelled frantically to driver Bill Charlton.

'Whoa! Slam on the brakes, Bill! There's a runaway ahead!'

Charlton immediately wrenched back the emergency brake lever — a final, desperate attempt to avoid the unavoidable.

Seconds later, as the clock approached midnight, the North-West Mail and the runaway wagons from the No. 62 goods train collided.

The moment of impact was so great the brake van attached to the goods train leap-frogged the North-West Mail's engine and deflected off the train's first carriage.

It came to rest on the side of the tracks, a twisted, broken, smouldering wreck.

Miraculously, driver Bill Charlton and fireman Horace Findlater survived the head-on collision.

Findlater was flung into the coal-box and escaped with minor injuries.

Charlton, pinned in the engine cabin, was not so fortunate.

He received a number of cuts and bruises and suffered severe shock.

Ernie Taylor and David Davies, engine driver and guard from the stricken goods train, raced down the track to find a scene of utter devastation.

They helped Findlater rescue Charlton from the engine cabin.

Jim Marx, sitting in the guard's van when the collision occurred, was thrown across a bullion chest but escaped serious injury. He jumped from the van and staggered alongside the twisted carriages towards the front of the train. As the horror of what had happened sank in, he heard the painful, sobbing cries for help from the smashed carriages.

Both trains completely stopped on impact, throwing passengers from their seats and bunks with tremendous force. Many were killed instantly.

The wool wagons piled on top of each other over the train's engine. The North-West Mail's first carriage, a sleeper, was compressed like a concertina and the second carriage, constructed primarily of timber, was splintered and completely crushed.

The third carriage was telescoped by the rear sleeper carriage, which escaped major damage. However, it was the second carriage, a composite of first- and second-class compartments that was all but completely destroyed.

Dead bodies were scattered like discarded rag dolls. Injured men, women and children, wedged between wrecked, twisted seats and debris, screamed for help.

Nellie Walker cried uncontrollably as she nursed her dead son, Jack.

Garnet Wilson was thrown clear through an open window

— the very window he couldn't close fifteen minutes earlier.

The crushed body of schoolgirl Ada Fripp lay beside her injured older sister, Emily. Their friend, Nancy Seccombe, escaped serious injury.

Moments after the collision, woolpacks on the mangled goods trucks burst into flames, lighting up the night sky.

* * *

Grazier Max Wright, from the nearby property Bickham, was awake when he heard the North-West Mail trundle past. Wright's property adjoined the Murulla siding, half a mile away.

He looked at his watch. Running late again, he figured.

Seconds later he heard an ear-splitting explosion, followed by an eerie few seconds of complete and utter silence. Then the void was filled with piercing screams.

Wright realised exactly what had happened. He sprang from his bed, dressed quickly and ran from the homestead to alert a team of shearers working on the place. They were sound asleep when Wright started yelling and thumping on the corrugated tin walls of the shearers' huts.

'Quick, there's been a train smash! Get up! Get up!'

The shearers climbed aboard a lorry and Wright drove at speed to the crash site, just minutes away.

They could clearly see the bright red haze of burning wool packs through the cold, foggy darkness.

When they found the mangled North-West Mail, a mass of twisted ironwork, splintered wood and upturned wheels, they were speechless.

Dozens of dead, battered bodies were strewn throughout the wreckage. Injured, trapped passengers screamed for help.

The more fortunate were able to crawl through windows and doors to safety.

Max Wright spotted Garnet Wilson lying on the side of the tracks and rushed to help the stricken telegraphist from Auburn.

'I'll be fine; go help the others,' Wilson pleaded.

'An open window saved my life. I couldn't close the damn thing; not for the love of Mary could I close it. I was thrown clear through that window and got wedged halfway. I'm the luckiest man on the train.'

John Hutchinson, a passenger from Werris Creek, helped drag eight bodies from one of the carriages. The stench of burning wool was everywhere.

Judge Mocatta and crown prosecutor Robert Browning escaped injury and assisted with the rescue operation. Helping them was Dr Bill Sheehan, captain of the Sydney University Football Club, and Dr Robert Horniman. Sheehan and Horniman recently secured degrees in medicine at Sydney University.

Within thirty minutes, doctors, nurses and medical staff crossed paddocks and rough ground to reach the crash site. The blazing wool bales acted as beacons.

Among them was Dr Oswald Barton, the son of Australia's first Prime Minister, Sir Edmund Barton.

Dr Barton, from Scone, arrived at the devastating scene still dressed in his pyjamas.

Doctors Charles Scott and Keith Grieve, also from Scone, and doctors Bertram Middleton and John Beith, both from Murrurundi, attended the injured and helped identify the deceased.

Many of the casualties were taken to Scott Memorial Scone Hospital, named after Dr Scott's brother, the late Dr Charles Scott.

Robert Rogers and John Halliday, doctors from Muswellbrook, arrived well before dawn and treated survivors. They were joined by Dr Hessel Howell, from Quirindi.

Matron Olivia Lowrey and Sister Flora Parker from Scone attended dozens of casualties. Sister Parker began duties at Scott Memorial Hospital only five weeks earlier.

Scone chemist Keith Evans administered first-aid and supplied medication, bandages and splints. Evans had been called to recent rail crashes in the district twice in as many months.

Dead bodies, as well as survivors, were hauled from the wreckage, but many of the injured were trapped for hours.

Cousins David Seccombe and Tom Scholefield were thrown to the floor of the first carriage. Incredibly, both boys escaped serious injury. They crawled from the carriage and slid down the embankment, coming to a rest behind a clump of prickly pear.

They were quickly to their feet and began helping rescue the injured.

Ted Pelham was sound asleep when the trains collided.

He realised the extent of what had happened and immediately thought of his dad, Frank, who was in the last carriage.

Pelham tried to move but couldn't. He was pinned hard and fast under the twisted rubble. The pain in his legs and back was unbearable. The screams and cries for help were worse.

He could hear rescuers chopping overhead and the muffled, excited sound of voices. He prayed his father was safe.

Suddenly, an axe head came crashing through the wreckage, striking Pelham's ear. 'Stop, please stop, I'm underneath you,' he screamed.

After three hours of painstakingly removing splintered timber and blackened iron, Pelham was delicately lifted to safety and taken to Murrurundi Hospital, where he later spoke to reporters:

> The rescuers were chopping above my head, and at every blow I thought my head would come off. Then the axe blade came through and struck my ear, and I shouted so loudly the axeman stopped, and worked around me. Then I heard someone sawing a dead man's legs off to free his body and our fears were increased by the danger of the fire spreading towards us. I felt more dead than alive when I was finally released.

Pelham's father, Frank, was trapped in the sleeper compartment but relatively unharmed. He and fellow passengers scrambled through the carriage door to safety.

James and Maria Taylor, from Thirroul, were dozing lightly as the train approached Murulla. Maria held baby Sidney close to her chest. When the trains collided, Sidney fell between his mother's legs and the side of the carriage, and was completely shielded.

James and Maria weren't so fortunate. Maria suffered a broken pelvis and badly damaged right forearm. James' thigh, ribs, clavicle and sternum were fractured.

James was taken to Scone Hospital; Maria went to Prince Alfred Hospital in Sydney; and seven-month-old Sidney was cared for at Murrurundi until relatives arrived. The family was reunited in Sydney a few days later.

Andy Samios, Manuel Kepreotes and Nick Zographos survived. Samios and Kepreotes were in the second carriage — labelled the "death car" by newspapers — and crawled to safety after being trapped for more than an hour. The wooden carriage, splintered and twisted beyond recognition, bore the brunt of the smash.

Samios escaped with facial abrasions and bruising, as well as damage to his back.

'Everything seemed to come down on my head. I looked around for Manuel. A man was lying across his legs, but I got him out by levering up part of the roof,' Samios later told *The Sun*.

Samios and Kepreotes were taken to Scone Hospital, but Samios returned to the crash site to look for Nick Zographos and Peter Vagianis, and to help with salvage operations.

He found Zographos safe and well, suffering abrasions. Vagianis was dead.

'It was terrible getting out the injured,' Samios said. 'If we stood on the wreckage to remove a victim, people would cry out that we were standing on them, and if we used axes people would yell out to stop, because we were hitting them.'

James Rowan, who boarded at Murrurundi, was firmly pinned beneath the body of a dead man. Rowan's legs were broken and shattered. He lay trapped, wedged tightly by the rigid legs of the deceased and was fed morphine to ease the agony.

Doctors Scott and Grieve made the agonising decision to amputate both legs from the dead body to save Rowan. Chemist Keith Evans held a kerosene lamp and comforted Rowan as the doctors went about the gruesome task.

'Don't look,' Evans whispered and gently placed a shredded shirt across Rowan's eyes.

Evans later told the *Sun*: 'Rowan remained conscious as the doctors hacked at the dead person's legs. We got Rowan out. Both legs were smashed but his spirit was amazing. On the way to Scone he talked about taking a ticket in the Golden Casket.'

Elsie Rankin, the nurse from Manly Cottage Hospital, crawled from the wreckage unscathed and immediately sprang into action. She worked tirelessly, tending the injured with splints fashioned from train debris and bandages made from bedsheets. Pillows were shaped from seat padding.

As news spread, residents from the immediate area arrived with cars to ferry the injured to hospitals at Scone, Murrurundi, Quirindi and Muswellbrook. Later, several victims were transferred to Newcastle Hospital, including John and Evelyn Rich, and sons Alan and Eric. A third son, seven-year-old Howard, was killed.

The *Newcastle Sun* reported Scone residents were quick to act.

> The town awoke to pulsing life and the streets were filled with the screech of cars and the shouts of men. Breathlessly they dashed into the bush to succour the victims of the disaster. One soft goods firm had opened its store and heaped rugs and blankets into the departing cars. Through a tranquil night sown with stars this motor procession threaded its way over the winding road. Scone is 17 miles from the scene of the ghastly crash. They are 17 hard miles and the way is tortuous and not direct.

Max Wright's nearby homestead was thrown open to survivors and rescuers and served as an operations hub.

Fires were lit along either side of the railway track and the injured and shocked huddled together against the bitterly cold night air.

NSW Railways traffic inspector Eddy Heery, from

Muswellbrook, began investigating the disaster well before dawn.

The inspector arrived about 4 am and was joined soon afterwards by the district superintendent of the North and North-West Lines, Joseph Green, and his assistant Frederick Allen, both from Werris Creek.

Heery spoke at length with guard David Davies, who told him the Westinghouse brakes did not operate on the section of train that broke away.

'We tried to apply the handbrakes but the runaways were travelling too fast,' he said.

Heery asked Davies whether the brake housings were reconnected to the breakaway wagons.

'We couldn't get them close enough to apply the air and the trucks broke away too quickly to apply the handbrakes,' replied Davies. 'The train had been stationary for so long all the air had leaked out.'

Sgt James Grady from Scone and Sgt Bill Willard from Murrurundi headed preliminary police investigations. They interviewed dozens of people as well as railway staff and witnesses.

Bodies were laid out alongside the train line and later conveyed to Murrurundi in railway vans. They were placed in the former Murrurundi stationmaster's residence, about eight miles from Murulla.

The house was converted into a makeshift morgue, described by newspapers as a "chamber of horrors".

The injured, and there were many, were transported to numerous district hospitals in private vehicles. The *Newcastle Sun* reported:

Out there under the fading stars, clergymen knelt

beside battered men and women and spoke words of spiritual comfort as lives ebbed away. In the cold dawn, cars threaded their way back over the hills to Murrurundi, carrying smashed and broken men and women wrapped in rugs and blankets. It was a procession of tragedy.

*   *   *

When dawn broke, and the dust and smoke settled, Murulla siding resembled a war zone.

It was only in the light of day that rescuers and survivors could fully comprehend the magnitude of the disaster.

More than one-third of the hundred and fifty passengers on the North-West Mail were injured, many seriously, and twenty-six were dead.

Nellie Walker, whose son Jack died in her arms as rescuers tried to free them, passed away at Scone's Scott Memorial Hospital eight weeks after the crash.

She became the twenty-seventh and final fatality of the second-worst train disaster in Australian history to that time.

[Previously, forty-three people were killed when the Ballarat and Bendigo express trains collided in 1908 at Sunshine, seven miles west of Melbourne. Both disasters would be surpassed in 1977 when eighty-three people died and 213 were injured in the Granville train disaster].

A relief train laden with rail workers arrived at Murulla siding early on Tuesday morning to help with the clean-up. Men jumped from carriages as the engine rolled to a stop and began clearing the bloodied mess and sorting luggage and personal effects.

The task was enormous, and heartbreaking. Grown men

wept and held each other. The mental scars and grim memories of that terrible night would eventually fade, but not entirely.

The Glen Innes train carried survivors to Central Station in Sydney, going via Broadmeadow Station at Newcastle.

Frank Scott, who worked for more than seven hours helping medical staff and rescuers drag the dead and injured from the ruins, told the waiting media pack at Newcastle about the absolute carnage at Murulla:

> No words can describe the scene of horror. You simply could not realise what a frightful spectacle it was unless you actually saw it in the red glare of the burning wool. It is a scene that would make the strongest sick. The wonder to me was that the rescuers were able to continue so long with their heroic work without collapsing.

Passenger John Hutchinson had a similar story to tell:

> I was fortunate to be in the last carriage of the train, having travelled from my home at Werris Creek, where I found most of the carriages already occupied. The scene of the disaster was dreadful, and the smell of burning wool accentuated the awfulness of the surroundings.

Moree grazier Arthur Manchee was greeted at Central Station by anxious friends and family members. He told them the devastation he witnessed at Murulla was "indescribable":

> But the behaviour of people was wonderful, and there was an entire absence of panic. The conduct of the schoolchildren, in particular, was exemplary. They did

not scream or show excitement, but quietly did as they were told.

Richard Bails, from Wee Waa, a passenger in the "death carriage", somehow escaped serious injury:

I was asleep at the time and the suddenness of the jolt dazed me. The next moment I found myself being hurled towards the roof of the carriage, and instantly the roof was swept away as though by a windstorm. I clambered out through the roof.

Passenger James Saunders said uninjured passengers were quick to respond:

Our worst handicap was the absence of light. It was dreadful to hear the cries for help, and feel that we were almost powerless to assist. The passengers and train crew worked with superhuman strength, pulling tangled wreckage aside and extricating victims.

It seemed hours before the relief train arrived, but by this time we had undertaken many rescues. We had to lay out the dead and injured on the cold, damp grass. From the injured came cries for water, and with the glasses and water-bottles from the undamaged carriages we did our best for them, but in some cases they were too weak to drink.

One of the many pathetic sights was in a part of the wreckage where a mother and father were jammed so tightly that they could not move a limb, and in between them was their little child, crying to his mother to pull him away.

All the time there were the cries of the children, and the cries of mothers looking for their children. It was a terrible experience. We could work only from one end of the wreckage. We came upon one man who was dreadfully injured; he died in my arms as I was carrying him onto the grass. He had been crushed between the sleepers. The force of the impact was tremendous.

William Mocatta, the humble circuit court judge who helped rescue survivors despite his age, told pressmen the most tortuous part of the Murulla train disaster was listening to other people die:

It seems appallingly unjust that death should have passed over me, a man so old that he cannot hope, in the normal course of things, to live more than a few years longer, and snatched up young people whose lives before them promised achievement and success.

How it was that I escaped, I cannot explain, except to suggest that providence specially guarded me. I was in the first carriage, and of all places, one would think, the most dangerous in a head-on collision.

Judge Mocatta paused, seemingly lost for words. He continued:

Oh, that second carriage . . . I cannot bear to describe it, though the memory of it will haunt me for the rest of my life.

*   *   *

Sadness and profound grief cast a pall across the entire district as parents and family members arrived in Murrurundi to identify the dead.

Police officers gently escorted next of kin through the maze of bodies. Kerosene lamps, candles and matches were used until daylight filtered through the vacant building.

Tom and Isabella Fripp drove three hundred miles from their Rowena property, Beethoven, not knowing whether their daughters Ada and Emily were alive or dead. Police descriptions of the deceased made them fear the worst.

It was almost certain Ada was dead and the Fripps feared Emily was also killed. Their grief was palpable and the anxious drive across rough country from Rowena was unbearable. They drove in silence.

The news that Emily was safe at Quirindi Hospital, albeit injured and suffering shock, gave them some relief. Ada was dead.

Mrs Fripp, president of the Collarenebri branch of the Country Women's Association, bravely spoke to newspapers after identifying Ada's body and breaking the tragic news to Emily. 'Emily will recover. She knows that her sister is dead, and is heartbroken,' she said.

Tom Fripp comforted his wife. 'Our daughter is broken-hearted, and so are we. Emily and Ada were more than just sisters — they were best friends,' he said.

Peter Vagianis, 26, the Greek waiter from Lesbos who came to Australia seeking his fortune, was identified by Sydney hairdresser Anthony Janis. 'Peter was a resident of NSW for about nine months before his death,' Janis said.

'I had several conversations with him; he often called in to chat at my shop on Harris Street. He liked Australia and was able to earn a better living here. He did not at any time express any intentions of returning to Greece.'

Vagianis was well on his way to fulfilling dreams of success in his newly adopted country. After only nine months in Australia, he died with £34 in savings — the equivalent of nearly $3000 in new millennium dollars. His savings and personal effects were forwarded to his parents, Evastratios and Vlotiny Hadzevogiannis, in Greece.

Assistant railway superintendent Bill Kimber, stationed at Narrabri, was tasked with identifying the deceased. He had difficulty identifying one victim, thought to be a married woman named Elizabeth Garland. Elizabeth lived at Gilgandra, but was working at Coomoo Coomoo station, near Quirindi. A few days after the accident, Frank Garland arrived in Murrurundi and identified Elizabeth as his wife.

However, after returning home to Gilgandra a broken man, he was racked with guilt. Frank penned a letter to Murrurundi police, which was later read out at the inquest.

In my first distress, knowing her to have been identified as Mrs Elizabeth Garland, I stated that we were married in an endeavour to shield her. But this is untrue. We were not legally married, but were together thirteen years as man and wife. I can only plead my love for her. She was a good woman, respected wherever she went, and my agony of mind.

Garland returned to Murrurundi police station and spoke at length with sergeants Willard and Grady.

'Her name is Elizabeth Martin-Templeton. We have been living together at Gilgandra. She wanted her family back in

Scotland to think we were married. She took my surname as her own and told her family we were living as man and wife; she told them we were married,' he whispered.

Garland feared he had broken the law and was prepared to pay the penalty.

He wiped away tears. 'I will await the decision of the law as I am willing to meet any punishment. I recognise the law of man is the law of God, and it must be accepted and obeyed.'

Garland reached into his coat pocket and handed Sgt Willard a cheque for £44. 'This is the money Elizabeth earned at Coomoo Coomoo station. Please make sure it gets to her sister, Mrs Hatton, in Glasgow,' he said.

Two days after miraculously being thrown through a carriage window, Garnet Wilson was at his Auburn home recuperating from a dislocated shoulder and abrasions.

'I could not move and made frantic efforts to clutch the side of the carriage to pull myself up. As I did, I released myself and found that a woman had been hurled across my legs, which saved me from going headlong out the window. I was partially dazed, but as soon as I found I was free, I released the woman and jumped from the carriage. I must have been the first out, for there was not a soul about, but the cries of the injured were awful,' he said.

'In a few moments the wool trucks burst into flames, and with the others that had extricated themselves by this time, we gazed on an appalling scene.

'I did not feel my injury from then on, but with a man who came running along with a little flare light set about helping drag some of the others to safety. Our carriage was a heap of matchwood. As the helpers arrived, we worked to get the mangled remains out of the wreckage.

'Most of them, however, were dead. In other places, great work was done in hacking away the debris and lifting badly injured people to safety. The sights and sounds were awful. One woman was rushing up and down, crying frantically, "my baby has been killed" but fortunately the little one was found in the wreckage only slightly injured,' he recalled.

Albert McDonald was home at Werris Creek when news of the crash filtered through. His wife, Emily, was on the train after deciding not to drive to Sydney in the new family car.

McDonald drove at speed to Murulla, nearly an hour away. His heart raced as he searched the broken, twisted carriages. The longer he searched, however, the more he realised Emily wasn't among the injured. That left only one other possibility.

McDonald tried not to think about it.

People around him silently scoured the debris, collecting personal belongings and broken luggage. Doctors and nurses treated the injured.

'There are some bodies in the empty stationmaster's house at Murrurundi,' a stranger told him.

McDonald drove slowly to Murrurundi, about ten miles away. He found Emily's mutilated body amid a row of corpses. The room was dimly lit with candles and kerosene lamps. McDonald fell to his knees and sobbed.

Bill Kimber comforted him.

'Our boy Keith should've been on the train as well, but his mother gave in and let him go on Saturday with some of his mates,' McDonald.

*   *   *

The small, tightknit town of Scone was paralysed by grief and profound sadness.

Locals were still trying to get over the Aberdeen rail crash of three months earlier, when five people were killed, and the Ardglen tunnel tragedy in July.

The Murulla train crash transcended any disaster the townsfolk had dealt with in the past. It was beyond comprehension.

The day after the tragedy a preliminary inquiry was opened by Coroner George Boyle White at the improvised morgue at Murrurundi.

White, 56, known by contemporaries and close friends as 'GB', had headed the coronial inquiry into the Ardglen rail disaster, when engine driver Tom Holt and fireman Herbert Heffernan, known as Jack, were overcome by fumes in a rail tunnel near Ardglen allowing the goods train to career unmanned through Ardglen railway station before derailing.

White, admitted as a solicitor in 1899, was one of Murrurundi's most respected residents.

In 1926 he was midway through his thirteenth year as town mayor and twenty-seventh consecutive year as a sitting alderman. He was also president of Murrurundi Golf Club and chairman of the board of directors of Wilson Memorial Hospital.

There was arguably no finer citizen to lead the Murulla train crash inquiry.

The morning following the crash, White sat on an upturned fruit box on the veranda of the empty stationmaster's house. He used a larger, wooden crate for a table.

A sombre crowd of locals, medical staff and newspaper reporters gathered before the coroner.

A row of corpses, covered by sheets and tarps, were laid out behind him. Only five of the twenty-six bodies had been identified to that time.

The initial sitting lasted only a few minutes.

Coroner White addressed the gathering: 'The bodies of those poor souls that have been identified can be buried by their grieving families.'

He solemnly announced a full coronial inquest would open at Murrurundi Courthouse on 29 September.

Undertaker Andrew Fishburn began lining coffins brought in from Scone and Quirindi. He was helped by a team of carpenters, builders and volunteers. Flatbed trucks carried the caskets back to Murrurundi.

'It was impossible to get so many coffins from my firm in Sydney,' Fishburn told newspapers.

'The majority of the coffins were lined with iron in my shop and then sent to their destinations.'

One resident, numbed by grief, told the *Newcastle Sun*: 'It has been nothing but a depressing trail of coffins.'

Anguished locals lined the streets and watched the sorrowful parade pass by. They bowed their heads and prayed as a lorry laden with child-sized coffins crept through town.

Waiting at Murrurundi were the bodies of Sydney Mallett, 16, Arthur Jurd, 15, Janet Doyle, 15, Howard Rich, seven, Clarice Sampson, 15, Ada Fripp, 15, and six-year-old Jack Walker.

In adjoining rooms were the bodies of Kate Ackland, John and Sarah Giles, Alf Brush, Stan Noller, John Dunbar, Peter Vagianis, Owen McGrath, Emily McDonald, William and Flora Wilson, Albert Jefferson, Arthur Adams, Kathleen Malone, Azubah Anderton, Walter McMillan, Frank McKeown, Elizabeth Martin-Templeton and John Mockridge.

The *Newcastle Sun* reported:

They are crushed and battered — even relatives would not know them. Their faces have been ground by jagged timber and twisted steel. Faces that smiled and laughed five minutes before death leapt on them among those tree-clothed hills. Men walk on tiptoe into those rooms. The coverings are lifted for a second, a shudder of horror trembles through strong frames, the coverings are replaced, and pale-faced men glide stealthily out again. In the chamber of death, once more, reigns an eerie silence.

The railway commissioners of NSW, a three-man body responsible for railway staff appointments and all aspects of rail administration, issued a statement:

When an up goods train from Werris Creek was being drawn into the crossing loop at Murulla for the purpose of allowing No. 8 North-West Mail, Moree to Sydney, to pass, the draw-hook on a truck of the goods train broke. Subsequently, while endeavouring to remove this portion with an improvised coupling, the rear portion of the goods train ran back a mile-and-a-half into the section of Murulla-Blandford and collided with the mail train, damaging three cars and smashing one second-class car. The portion of the goods train which collided with the mail train took fire and a number of vehicles were destroyed. Driver Turner, fireman Lloyd and guard Davis were in charge of the goods train.

Letters and messages of hope and support flooded in from across the country.

The morning following the crash, acting Prime Minister Earle Page sent a telegram to NSW Premier Jack Lang.

'I desire to express through you, to the bereaved and injured, the sympathy of the Commonwealth Government in the dreadful train collision which occurred last night. Everyone will feel deeply for the sufferers in this unhappy occurrence.'

At the NSW Railway and Tramway Association's annual conference held in Sydney four days after the tragedy, association president Oscar Meyer said NSW Railways had failed the community.

'While we feel in common with the general community, sorrow at the happening, we have in addition a more personal feeling. We feel, as railway officers, the victims of this accident had confided themselves to the charge of the service and, however free from direct blame, the service has failed in a trust,' Meyer said.

'Our great pride in the almost absolute safety with which for many years we carried millions of passengers has received a rude shock, which I am sure, every railway and tramway officer will feel as a personal grief and sorrow.'

* * *

More than forty witnesses, many of them railway employees and departmental managers and inspectors, were called to give evidence when the coronial inquest into the Murulla train disaster was opened at 10 am at Murrurundi courthouse on Wednesday 29 September.

Newspapermen, family members of the deceased and injured,

and curious onlookers angled for room. The crowd spilled out between four imposing pillars on the building's forecourt and down the courthouse steps to the footpath.

Coroner White opened proceedings by expressing his deepest sympathy to 'the families of the victims who lost their lives in this terrible, terrible tragedy and to those victims who were injured.'

'I will not exclude any relevant evidence, as I believe this inquiry is of the greatest importance, not only to the relatives of the victims of the disaster, but to the general public and the railway commissioners.'

Senior crown prosecutor William Rogers appeared for the crown and Sgts Bill Willard and James Grady conducted proceedings for the NSW police.

Several solicitors were present in the interests of victims and survivors of the crash, and railway staff.

Richard O'Halloran appeared for North-West Mail engine driver Bill Charlton; goods train engine driver Ernie Turner; goods train fireman Geoff Lloyd; and North-West Mail fireman Horace Findlater.

Also present were northern area commissioner William Charles Quinton and his assistant, Denis Mulheron, district superintendent Joseph Green, divisional locomotive superintendent Henry Kirkby, Tamworth sub-inspector George Markham and vice-president the Australian Federated Union of Locomotive Enginemen (NSW division), George Skelton.

Dr Charles Scott said the cause of death in every case was 'external violence as a result of the collision'.

NSW Railways traffic inspector Eddy Heery spent more than eight hours in the witness box during the opening two days of the inquiry.

He explaining the correct safety measures used when part of a train broke free and referred to a large sheaf of departmental papers as he gave a detailed insight into the procedure.

'Immediately the guard of the goods train knew his train had parted, it was his duty to secure the detached portion with handbrakes and sprags, and it was then his duty to make good the air supply to the brakes,' he told Coroner White.

'This could have been done at Murulla. The driver and guard were both responsible for seeing that the Westinghouse brake was made continuous.'

Sprags were heavy gauge, U-shaped steel pins wedged in the wheels to stop carriages from rolling.

'These measures were not carried out by the train crew of the goods train,' Heery said.

'Had sprags been placed in the rear part of the goods train to hold it stationary, that section would not have travelled far when the front part was shunted heavily into it.'

The breakaway occurred at 11.34 pm, one minute after the North-West Mail train left Blandford, less than four miles away.

Heery told solicitor Bob Sproule, representing train guard David Davies, the Westinghouse airbrakes did not fail.

'The brakes could have been made effective after the breakaway instead of using the tail rope coupling. The guard could have used the three-link coupling left on the draw bar, the hook of which was broken. This would have been attached to the automatic coupling on the next truck with a pin provided for those purposes,' he said.

Heery told Sproule if there was no pin, the guard would need to resort to his own discretion.

'The pin should have been obtained at Werris Creek. If no pin was available at Werris Creek to supply Davies, he could have refused to take the train out until the equipment of the brake van was complete. The guard was entitled to insist on being provided with all equipment as provided in the regulations and appendices list.'

Equipment listed in the regulations manual did not include a pin; however the apparatus was noted in the appendices.

Heery said the stationmaster of the depot from which the goods train started was responsible for ensuring the brake van was properly equipped.

Sproule questioned Heery at length.

'If no pin was available at Werris Creek, could the guard have refused to go on duty?'

'Yes. He could have absolutely refused to take the train out.'

Sproule: 'So, if there were no pins, no trains would run?'

Heery: 'I don't say that, but the guards would be entitled to refuse to take the trains out.'

Sproule: 'Assuming there were fifty stations without pins, there should be fifty stations from which no trains should run?'

'That is a ridiculous question but, I suppose, it is possible,' replied Heery.

'When a chain of wagons or carriages is broken,' Heery said, 'the Westinghouse brake is applied to the section of train that breaks away. However, the air on the breakaway section at Murulla gradually leaked out as it sat on the tracks because it wasn't connected to the front section.

'When the two sections were connected with a tail rope, the air hoses feeding the brakes were not long enough to be applied.

'Regulations distinctly state that a brake under those conditions was not to be relied upon, and the breakaway section must be secured by handbrakes and sprags,' Heery said.

Heery said a wire tail rope would hold 110 tons on a grade of one in eighty.

'If it were bound round the hook three times it would hold 330 tons. The weight of the portion of the train that broke away was 264 tons,' he explained. 'I have never known the absolute failure of a Westinghouse brake.'

Travelling locomotive inspector George Elliott explained in detail the workings of the Westinghouse braking system.

'The brakes can be applied by the driver or guard in case of an emergency,' he said.

Elliott conducted a series of simulated tests at Clyde, in western Sydney, on 27 September with twelve vehicles and a van weighing 281 tons.

'The rail line grade was one in eighty,' he explained.

'No special preparations were made for these tests. In the final test the vehicles and van were allowed to move at three to four miles an hour. The handbrakes brought them to a standstill in 219 feet.'

Sproule asked Elliott whether he considered the test conditions were comparable with those at Murulla near midnight on 13 September.

'Yes, as to loads and braking facilities. The handbrakes should be used immediately the rear portion of a breakaway train comes to a standstill.'

Federation of Locomotive Enginemen secretary Bill Ainsworth questioned Elliott about the emergency air brake system.

'It would be almost impossible to keep all goods vehicles quite airtight. There is great variation in the length of time it takes for air in a breakaway portion of a train to be exhausted,' Elliott said.

Elliott said regulations required for a wire or other rope to be used in conjunction with a tail rope.

'None was provided by the department,' he said.

'That means that in the absence of a rope or an automatic pin, the guard would be thrown on his own resources,' Ainsworth suggested.

Elliott paused momentarily before responding.

'A guard is thrown on his own resources not once, but a hundred times,' he replied.

Coroner White asked Elliott about the failed draw hook, which ultimately allowed eleven fully laden wagons and a brake van to disengage from goods train No.62 and roll head-on into the North-West Mail.

'If the draw hook of an engine disclosed a flaw similar to that of the broken hook exhibited in court I would consider the engine unfit to go into traffic. I have never seen a goods train without a rope of some kind and I have only seen four or five broken draw hooks during the last five years,' Elliott said.

Goods train guard Enos John Scott was in charge of an empty stock train travelling from Muswellbrook to Werris on the night of 13 September.

'We ran on to the Murulla loop at 9.57 pm,' he said.

'The Brisbane Mail passed at 10.15 pm and the No.62 goods train ran in at 10.40 pm. I noticed the engine of No.62 was labouring under its load. After the draw hook broke I saw driver Turner of the goods train putting on the handbrakes of the front portion of the train. The end of the goods train appeared close to the down starting signal. As I was passing the end of the goods train I estimate it was three or four feet behind the clearance point and about half a truck distance from the rest of the train — about eight feet between the buffers.'

Sgt Willard told the enquiry he and Sgt Grady inspected the signal points on the northern end of the Murulla loop on the morning of 14 September.

'They appeared to be in perfect order,' Willard said.

Willard and Grady spoke with railway traffic inspector Eddy Heery as well as signalmen Clive Smith and Wally White.

Smith said the points and signals were in good working order when he went off duty at 7 am on 13 September.

'The loop and main line will each hold fifty-five vehicles, exclusive of the engine,' Smith explained.

'That leaves little room to spare, but gives full clearance. The grade on the Blandford side is one in eighty-one, and on the Wingen side, one in forty.'

Signalman George Constable, who relieved Smith, gave similar evidence. Constable was relieved by Wally White at 3.20 pm.

Relief porter Stanley Fuller was on duty at Blandford on 13 September when he exchanged tablets for the North-West Mail.

'The train was due at 11.08 pm but ran through at 11.33 pm,' Fuller said.

'I exchanged the tablet with the North-West Mail fireman and the ring I got from Murulla indicated the line was clear.'

Travelling locomotive inspector James Cummins told Frederick Bretnall, assistant solicitor for NSW Railways, he had witnessed many instances in the course of his duties when a tail rope was used under such circumstances.

'I cannot conceive any circumstances where it would not be possible to connect the air unless the air hose was carried away,' Cummins said. 'A pinch bar could be used as a substitute for a pin and several other things might be used as substitutes by persons of reasonable intelligence and experience with defective couplings.'

Bob Sproule, representing train guard David Davies, questioned Cummins.

'I suggest to you that in the event of an emergency, the use of a coupling pin would be far preferable,' he said.

'Yes; it should be part of the equipment,' replied Cummins.

Sproule: 'I am not flattering you, but is it not a fact that you are regarded as the greatest expert in the whole of the railway service in these matters?'

Cummins: 'You flatter me.'

Sproule: 'Do not the "heads" bow down to you when they want to know anything on these matters?'

Cummins: 'I have never seen them at it.'

Sproule: 'Well, they must do things behind your back.'

Cummins said the shackle of the engine drawbar could have been used to make an effective coupling without the use of a tail rope. 'Properly used, however, a tail rope would be perfectly safe but unskilled tying might cause breakage.'

Sproule asked Cummins the same question he asked traffic inspector Eddy Heery.

'If there is no pin available in the brake van, can a guard refuse to take a train out if ordered to do so?'

'Yes, he can refuse. If he did so, the responsibility would not be his,' replied Cummins. 'The training of railway officers is such that they obey their superior officers unless the latter are flagrantly breaking the regulations.'

Sproule alleged the Crown and railways commissioners were attempting to lay the blame on railway staff.

'The evidence shows that the pin necessary to make a secure coupling, which cost a pittance, was not available. Who was responsible for providing these pins which all the witnesses have said were vital? The persons responsible for such criminal negligence could not be traced. The guard and other members of the crew were thrown on their responsibility and had to look for a substitute, such as a pinch bar or piece of fencing wire.'

Sproule said the accident would not have happened had there been an automatic coupling next to the drawbar.

He added there was no evidence to show whether drawbars were ever tested for safety. 'Yet the whole safety of the travelling public depends on them.'

Sproule said the coronial inquiry had developed into a railway department versus railway employees blame game.

'An attempt has been made to make the train crew scapegoats for the lack of efficiency by higher officials in the railways department,' Sproule alleged.

Sproule said crew members of goods train No.62 were told "they should have done this" and "should have done that."

'They were expected to be as wise before the event as after the event,' he said.

Sproule was categorically critical of the NSW Railways hierarchy.

'Were the great railway authorities as wise before this tragedy as they were afterwards? No, they were not too wise before the accident — and none the wiser later. But they endeavoured to place the whole of the blame on the unfortunate employees,' he growled.

'High and mighty railway authorities claim the guard is responsible if a coupling pin is absent from his equipment, yet it was not included among the articles comprising the guard's equipment, nor were they made available when required.

'Railway experts have admitted that had a pin been available, the disaster would have been averted — a pin costing little more than a shilling. This accident was not the fault of guard Davies but the fault of someone higher up. There is criminal negligence in regard to the pins and the supply of the pins,' Sproule said.

He added there was also criminal negligence in regard to (the wording) of the general appendices of the NSW Railways' safety manual.

'The lack of efficient administration is appalling,' Sproule continued. 'Higher officials were primarily responsible for the conditions which brought about the disaster forming the subject of this inquest, and not the under-employees.'

Richard O'Halloran, representing No.62 engine-driver Ernie Turner, agreed wholeheartedly with Sproule.

'No evidence has been brought forward to show there has been criminal negligence, in which case my client cannot be committed for trial. Driver Turner openly and frankly made statements to his department and to the police and, although not in a fit state of health, withstood examination.

'Driver Turner gave his evidence coherently and was supported by the signalman and fireman of goods train No.62,' O'Halloran said.

The inquest lasted eight days. There were 205 pages of typewritten depositions from forty-six witnesses, totalling more than eighty thousand words.

Coroner White addressed the packed Murrurundi courtroom.

He stated the deaths of the twenty-six victims in the Murulla railway collision were caused by the negligence of Ernest Turner and David Thomas Davies, driver and guard respectively of No.62 goods train.

'I find that Turner and Davies did feloniously slay the

twenty-six persons,' he said.

Coroner White committed Turner and Davies to stand trial at Tamworth quarter sessions on Thursday 28 October 1926.

White added a rider to his judgement.

'I also find there was no automatic coupling pin in the brake van of the goods train and that if such an automatic coupling pin had been in the brake van and had been used, as officially suggested, such an accident and loss of life would have been avoided.

'I further find that on the evidence of the chief mechanical engineer for the railways department and other departmental experts, an omission of great importance occurs in the list of guards' equipment for goods trains, as no mention is made of the automatic coupling pin as part of such equipment.

'The grave consequence resulting therefrom is that departmentally no person is regarded as culpably responsible for the absence of such pin, and essential principles of safe working have been overlooked.'

Turner and Davies were each granted £50 bail.

Soon afterwards, NSW Attorney-General Edward McTiernan moved the trial to Sydney.

On Monday 6 December Turner and Davies were charged with manslaughter before Justice David Ferguson at the Central Criminal Court at Darlinghurst, Sydney.

The death of Nellie Walker on 12 November brought the total fatalities to twenty-seven.

However, Davies and Turner were charged only with the death of sixty-year-old John Giles, a NSW Railways engine driver on holidays at the time of the crash.

Sidney Mack appeared for Turner; Bob Sproule and Dr Bert Evatt appeared for Davies.

Sproule, a former NSW solicitor-general, fervently argued the accused men had no charges to answer. He said the case should be taken from the jury — a suggestion Justice Ferguson said was not at all possible.

'Guard Davies was surrounded by a set of circumstances which never in the history of the Australian railway industry had confronted a man before,' Sproule told the judge. 'The fault for this series of unfortunate circumstances cannot be laid on Mr Davies.'

Crown Prosecutor William Thomas Coyle fell short of agreeing with Sproule.

He said the accused were men of the most excellent character, against whom nothing could be said. 'They have been in the railway service for a considerable time and have risen to positions of trust,' Coyle told the jury.

He stressed the case was not to be viewed as a Royal Commission into the administration of the railway department, or whether the brakes were right up to date or whether there were defects in them.

'The question, pure and simple, is whether, after hearing the crown case, the jury are of the opinion the charge has been proved against these men who made a great mistake, one that is not likely to occur again. If the jury is of the opinion the men made an error of judgement, free from gross negligence, they are bound to acquit the accused of the charge,' Coyle said.

'Errors of judgement do not make these men criminals, but gross negligence makes them liable. If the accused failed to link up the airbrakes when the appliances were there, they are guilty of gross negligence.'

In summing up, Justice Ferguson made it clear to the jury that the trial was not an inquiry in to the management of NSW

Railways. He said the court had not the material available nor was it the proper tribunal to conduct such an inquiry.

'The only question the jury has to consider is whether the two men charged are guilty of the crime of manslaughter. To return a verdict of guilty, the jury must be satisfied that the negligence was criminal in character, and that it was gross negligence,' Justice Ferguson directed.

'It is a deplorable fact that many lives were lost in the accident, but it is not for the jury to be influenced by that. The person whose death was being investigated by the trial is John Giles and the charge of manslaughter can only be established if the crown proves gross negligence which was criminal in character and deserving of punishment. The jury is not to be swayed by the number of passengers killed.

'It is alleged the accused are responsible for the original breakaway of the trucks; that was possibly the result of a defect in the drawbar. It was admittedly impossible for them to make the connection as provided by the regulations, but they did the best they could,' the judge said.

'The night was dark and misty when they made the connection, which was stronger than the regulations provided. They did their best with a wire rope, but they did not couple up the air hoses and this is the negligence the crown has charged against them.'

The trial lasted four days.

The jury deliberated for fifteen minutes before returning a not guilty verdict for both men.

The courtroom erupted in a chorus of cheering — from both sides — when the foreman read out the judgement.

When the jubilation subsided, Justice Ferguson addressed Turner and Davies. 'It is not often that I comment on the verdict of a jury, but in this case I must say I entirely agree with it,' he said.

Justice Ferguson acknowledged signalman Wally White and guard David Davies risked their lives when desperately trying to engage handbrakes on the runaway wagons.

'It is not disputed that, at great risk to their lives, the guard and signalman did everything possible to stop the trucks, but unfortunately they did not succeed,' he said.

A few weeks after the men were acquitted, the NSW Railway commissioners stepped in and dished out their own form of punishment — the search for someone to blame was far from over, it seemed.

Train guard Davies was sacked.

Murulla signalman White was demoted to the rank of porter and not permitted to take part in safe-work practices.

Goods train engine-driver Ernie Turner was reduced to the rank of fireman for a set term.

The men appealed the decisions.

The Railways and Tramways Appeal Board, chaired by Ralph Vivian Hodgson, heard the appeals at the Newcastle council chambers in March 1927.

Tests were conducted at Newcastle railway shunting yards using tail ropes similar to those used at Murulla.

Railway wagons were coupled with wire ropes and sufficient strain applied to snap them. Particular attention was paid to the nature of the break.

The board found against guard Davies and his dismissal stood.

Although a draw pin had not been supplied by NSW Railways, there were other means available on the night of the Murulla disaster to secure the unhitched goods wagons, the board found.

'Davies failed to take proper precautions, as laid out in railway regulations.'

When Davies' appeal was dismissed, engine-driver Turner withdrew his appeal.

Turner had been reinstated to the rank of engine-driver two weeks earlier; his appeal concerned lost wages during the time of demotion.

Wally White's appeal was unanimously upheld by the three-man board on the grounds he could not, as the signalman on that ill-fated night, be held responsible for any neglect of duty. He was completely exonerated from any wrongdoing.

Southern area commissioner and crash survivor James Reid, never forgot the tragedy. He was aged sixty at the time of the crash. He told newspapers: 'Please do not ask me to give you my impressions of the catastrophe. The terrible scenes of that dreadful night of death were such that I prefer not to describe them. I can only hope that the horror of their memory will one day be vanquished from my mind.'

CHAPTER 9
THE RAILWAYS STILL KILLED HIM

It took Reuben Ackland more than two years to recover from the Murulla train disaster — if he really recovered at all.

His wife Kate was among the twenty-seven people killed in the 1926 tragedy and life thereafter was never the same for the NSW railways' fettler.

Ackland was thrown clear from the train in the Murulla pile-up but suffered terrible back injuries. Kate was killed and their three-year-old son, Kevin, was so badly injured he was completely dependent on his father for years afterwards.

Ackland was born in Coonabarabran in 1886. He was thirty-two when he and Kate married at Narrabri in 1918.

Kate, born at Goonoo Goonoo near Tamworth in 1873, was forty-five and already the mother of five children — Sarah, May, Violet, Cyril and Alfred — from a previous marriage to William Cox.

That first marriage was full of tragedy. Three other children — Harriet, Patrick and William — died young and Kate's husband, William, was only thirty-nine when he died in Narrabri Hospital in 1916.

Ackland worked intermittently for two-and-a-half years after the Murulla crash and from 1929 moved from town to town with NSW Railways.

He was a flagman at Fassifern, near Newcastle, and was later retained as a gatekeeper at Scone, Lithgow, Bathurst and Blayney.

In 1939 he settled in Dubbo, in central western NSW, and was given the overnight shift at the Bourke Hill crossing, about a mile from town, on the road to Narromine.

The position of railway gatekeeper was usually reserved for employees injured or debilitated in some way during their employment. They were responsible for manually operating level crossing gates as well as general maintenance and upkeep.

Ackland officially worked seventy-two hours and six nights a week — twelve-hour shifts from 6 pm until 6 am. His one day off was Sunday.

Very early one warm February morning in 1947, Ackland was struggling to keep his eyes open. He'd been officially on duty since 6 pm, when he took over duties from the day shift gatekeeper.

Ackland laid out a groundsheet close to the railway line to get some sleep before the next scheduled train was due to pass through.

He was kept informed of the daily schedules and knew what time each train was due.

By lying close to the tracks, Ackland could hear approaching trains and feel the ground rumble as they neared. He could also hear the trains' whistles as they approached. It was a primitive alarm clock, effective, but very unsafe.

Around 12.50 am on Tuesday 11 February 1947, Ackland was sound asleep and dangerously close to the lines when engine 3296 from Narromine, pulling thirty-three wagons loaded with 519 tons of goods, approached the Bourke Hill crossing.

About one and a half miles from the crossing, engine-driver Hugh McKie released the train's whistle. He repeated the procedure about 150 yards from the crossing. The train's headlight lit up the tracks ahead as it rolled through at about fifteen miles an hour.

The second whistle roused Ackland.

McKie saw Ackland sit up and attempt to dart across the tracks in front of the engine. Startled, he immediately applied the brakes and yelled out to fireman John McNamara.

'Did that man get across?'

'Who?' McNamara had seen nothing.

'An old chap; he ran across the front of the engine.'

It was too late.

Ackland was struck by the train and suffered horrific injuries. Both legs and an arm were severed, his jaw was smashed and the top of his head was scalped.

When the train screamed to a stop more than a hundred yards down the line, McKie and McNamara ran back and found Ackland.

McKie sent McNamara to the railway telephone at the gatekeeper's hut to get help and report the accident to the Dubbo stationmaster.

Incredibly, Ackland was still alive when Dr Patrick McCormack arrived. McCormack tried frantically to revive Ackland, but the gatekeeper died in the doctor's arms.

An ambulance was called and Ackland's mutilated body was taken to Dubbo Hospital.

Sgt John Wilson, from Dubbo police station, arrived shortly after the ambulance left.

Train driver McKie showed the sergeant a groundsheet and overcoat, found less than four feet from the railway line and about twenty feet from the level crossing's telephone hut.

There was blood and flesh on the tracks.

Wilson noticed all four crossing gates were swung open along either side of the road, indicating the crossing was accessible to both vehicular traffic and rail traffic.

The groundsheet and overcoat, as well as a grey blanket and a pair of shoes were collected as evidence.

The train was taken to Dubbo railway station and examined by Wilson and NSW Railways inspector Harold Helmkemp.

Wilson and Helmkemp also inspected the lights fixed to the crossing gates.

'A train driver approaching from Narromine wouldn't know whether the gates were open or closed by the way these lights are positioned,' Wilson speculated.

A coronial inquest into the death of Reuben Edward Ackland was held at Dubbo courthouse on Wednesday 26 February 1947, before deputy coroner Gordon John Christie.

Sgt Wilson told the coroner engine No.3296 and approximately twelve wagons passed over Ackland.

'On the engine I found marks which appeared to be clothing marks in the grease on the brake gear and a large spot of blood, flesh and hair just forward of the ash pan,' Wilson said.

'There were also blood marks on the ash pan which would indicate the bar and the ash pan were the first spots to actually make contact with the body. There were no marks on the front of the train whatsoever.

'I do not know whether the deceased was asleep or had been sleeping on the groundsheet,' he said.

Wilson said blood marks on the outside railway track, about seventy yards from where the groundsheet was found, indicated Ackland had been lifted over the rail from beneath the train, and carried along.

'The only indication as far as I could see as to where he was struck by the train was right under the train on the ash pan,' Wilson said.

'There were marks along the permanent way which indicated the body had been rolled or pulled along, but not to any great extent were the marks visible.'

The term "permanent way" is given to all fixed railway lines. The description came about during the pioneering days of railway construction when workers often used a temporary track to convey materials and waste as the new track was laid out. The temporary track would be dismantled and moved further along once the "permanent way" was completed.

'If the deceased was in fact lying on the groundsheet, I'm of the opinion that a train passing would only just clear him,' Wilson said.

Sgt Wilson explained how the level crossing gates operated.

'The gates at the crossing were not damaged by the engine but were open to both rail and car traffic. The gates can swing both across the line and the road to shut both traffics,' he said.

The gates were embedded with red and clear-white kerosene-fuelled lights.

'When I arrived the four gates were wide open along the road,' Wilson said.

'If the gate had been closed across the road the red light would shine to oncoming traffic on the road. If the gates were closed across the railway line, the red would show to oncoming rail traffic. The position the gates were in, the red light would only be visible to either traffic only if up very close or side-on.'

Dr Patrick McCormack told the inquiry he didn't know what section of the train struck Ackland.

'The injuries were multiple. The body was lying between the two rails under the train, under one of the trucks,' the doctor said.

Engine driver Hugh McKie gave a full account of the accident.

'I have driven on that particular line for about eight or nine years, with a good knowledge of the level crossing,' McKie said.

'As we were over the roadway I noticed a man sit up from a heap of gravel. He was covered with a light-coloured blanket. He looked towards the engine for a second and then tried to cross in front of the train.'

McKie indicated on a map exactly where Ackland was positioned when he darted across the railway line.

'He appeared to roll or crouch across the line as he moved. When I first saw him, my engine would have been about ten yards away. The man was lying on the same side of the engine as I was working. His head was towards me with a blanket over his face. At the time he moved, the fireman would have no chance of seeing him,' he said.

'I applied the brakes to an emergency position immediately. When I pulled up I saw a man under the twelfth truck.'

McKie said the engine was equipped with a headlight that gave visibility for two to three hundred yards.

'The light was on at the time and could be seen a considerable distance from the train. A person standing on the roadway would see my light coming over the hill from about two miles away,' McKie said.

McKie said engine-drivers must release the train's whistle approaching level crossings.

'My instructions are that we must whistle for the gates and, provided we have the white light, we may proceed,' he explained.

'I saw the white light on this night and gave the two usual long whistles.'

McKie told the inquiry engine No.3296 was also equipped with two smaller side lights.

'There is a slight right-hand curve approaching the crossing, giving me only about twenty yards clear vision at the crossing. An object lying still is very difficult to see under railway headlights. We make an extra good look-out when approaching crossings.'

McKie said the level crossing gates were wide open to rail and road traffic at the time of the accident.

NSW Railways traffic inspector Harold Helmkemp said Reuben Ackland's duties were to open and close the level-crossing gates at the Bourke Hill railway crossing on the Great Western Highway.

Helmkemp was also Ackland's supervisor.

'There is no provision made to lie down during the hours of duty. It is regarded as a light duty job,' Helmkemp said.

'In addition to opening and closing the gates, the gatekeeper must clean, fill and light the lamps provided on the gates and see that they are kept burning all night.

'The regulation position of the gates is closed for rail traffic when open for vehicular traffic and vice versa. It is possible for the gates to be opened for vehicular and rail traffic simultaneously, but that is contrary to railway instructions,' he said.

Helmkemp said a telephone was at hand to receive and transmit information, and converse with stationmasters at Dubbo and Narromine.

'The gatekeeper is supplied with a timetable and each night after commencing duties he communicates with the stationmaster at Dubbo. He is supplied with specific information concerning the running of trains during his hours of duty,' Helmkemp said.

The traffic inspector said Ackland had been employed at the Bourke Hill crossing for several years.

'He should have had good knowledge of the running of trains on that particular line. The train which arrived at the crossing about 1 am was a timetable train and runs every night except Sundays,' he said.

Deputy Coroner Christie found Ackland died 'from the effects of injuries accidentally received through falling or slumping in front of a goods train, and being run down by the train'.

However, NSW railway department's safety practices were brought into question by the coroner.

'I am of the opinion the railway department has shown some disregard for public safety at this crossing, keeping in mind, of course, the difficulties at all level crossings,' Coroner Christie said.

'I believe the gates and the lights affixed should be swung so that they cannot be opened back to be in any but two positions — either they must be closed to rail traffic or closed to vehicular traffic and never, as they were on the night in question, open to both cross traffics.

'Although the employee concerned has shown negligence, I feel our efforts should be directed towards the greatest public safety possible. That should not be in the hands of an employee only,' he said.

'By fixing the gates to always close in one direction of traffic only would halt this traffic irrespective of the actions of the employee.

'I suggest also that the railway department might consider some electrical system which would ring an alarm for the gatekeeper when the train crossed a switch at some given distance from the crossing as in the case of the electrical wiring of the wigwag road signal at crossings,' he said.

The coroner was referring to a type of signal which swung back and forth with a red light and bell. Wigwag signals were used in Victoria, South Australia and Western Australia.

'This alarm may assist alerting a gatekeeper who may have unfortunately dozed off contrary to instructions, and this is possible when an employee is on continuous night work or who may be ill or could be otherwise surprised by the appearance of the train,' he said.

'The department has engineers capable of evolving these accident-prevention measures. Though I attach no blame to the department for Ackland's death, I do feel that the fixing of the gates may one day save a life.

'Had the alarm been installed, perhaps the deceased may have been saved the apparent fright he got with the train right near and approaching him, despite that before this he had neglected his duty by lying down and failing to close the gates,' Coroner Christie said.

Reuben Edward Ackland is buried at Dubbo Cemetery.

His son, Kevin, aged three at the time of the Murulla train crash and twenty-four when his father was killed, was awarded £800 compensation after his father's death.

By consent of the railway commissioners, Judge Alf Rainbow awarded the compensation, stating Kevin was thoroughly dependent on his father.

The payout, equivalent to nearly $60,000 in new millennium dollars, was described by newspapers as an 'unusual compo claim'.

Kevin lived to the age of sixty-seven and is buried at New Dubbo Cemetery.

* * *

Travelling locomotive inspector James Cummins, who gave evidence at the Murulla coronial inquest, also suffered a horrible death while working for NSW Railways.

At Moss Vale on Saturday 20 December 1930, Cummins was killed when he fell from a section of a slow-moving train, the Melbourne Express. He was inspecting the train for heating problems.

Cummins lost his grip and struck the side of a small rocky outcrop adjacent to the railway line. When the train was pulled up, the crew found Cummins dead on the tracks.

He served NSW Railways for thirty-five years, starting as a shop-boy at Eveleigh railway yards in 1896 at age seventeen. He was fifty-one when killed and buried at Rookwood Cemetery.

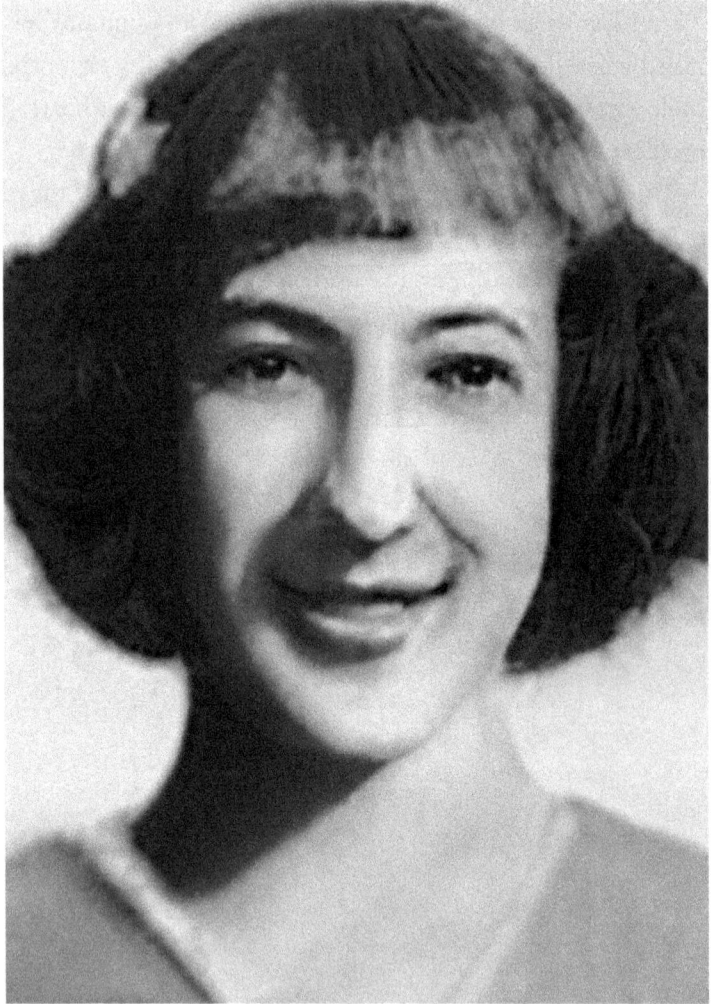

Minnie Jenkins was found bashed and dying in bed in her Royal Hotel quarters on 21 August 1944. She died the next day, less than a week after her twentieth birthday. Her killer was never found (Image credit: Sydney Truth)

CHAPTER 10

SHE LET OUT A BIT OF A GRUNT, SO I WHACKED HER AGAIN

Drifter Tommy Dowe was scared he'd be slotted for vagrancy when coppers hauled him in to Grenfell police station in November 1944.

They plonked him down on an office chair and questioned him relentlessly about a murder committed three months earlier at Moree, more than 350 miles away. They had apparently been tipped off, and Dowe was the man they'd been looking for.

Dowe quickly worked out that by cooperating with police, he would more than likely get a free ride out of Grenfell. The last thing the twenty-eight-year-old former AIF serviceman needed in this chapter of his life was another vagrancy charge.

To solve the problem, Dowe confessed to a brutal murder committed at the Royal Hotel in Moree — despite being more than four hundred miles away in Sydney the day the shocking crime was committed. He even detailed how he carried out the crime and described the murder weapon.

It was later alleged police coercion was used to elicit a confession from Dowe, a likeable drifter down on his luck.

When the thumbscrews were allegedly applied at Grenfell, Dowe confessed to bashing twenty-year-old hotel employee, Joan Jenkins, in the hotel's servants' quarters.

But when Joan, widely known as 'Minnie', was found barely alive about 7.30 am on Monday 21 August 1944, Dowe was preparing to head off to Homebush abattoirs, hoping to get a day's work.

Minnie was found battered and bashed in her blood-soaked bed by the hotel housekeeper, Margaretta Furney. Evidence showed she was viciously attacked as she slept by an intruder who gained access through an open window.

Minnie suffered a fracture to her left temple between the eye and the ear, an extensive wound to the left temple and a cut behind the left ear.

She was rushed to Moree Hospital in a critical condition and attended to by Dr Patrick McMahon, but died the following day without regaining consciousness, a few days after her twentieth birthday.

Four other employees occupied separate rooms in the servants' quarters, a bungalow-style structure about twenty yards from the hotel.

Moree residents were on high alert after the murder.

'Many people, who previously never bothered to lock their doors, are now placing wedges and temporary bolts on doors and windows,' newspapers widely reported.

'Although many hours were spent Wednesday and Thursday on a widespread search, which covered the drains, gutters and even open paddocks, no trace has yet been found by the police of the murder weapon, and none of the people so far questioned have been able to provide them with any clues.'

Around the time Minnie was being rushed to hospital, Tommy Dowe was working at Homebush abattoirs, an indisputable fact verified by several witnesses at the week-long coronial inquest at Moree courthouse three and a half months later.

About six weeks after the murder, Dowe was in Cowra, 150

miles south of Dubbo in the central west of NSW, where he struck up a friendship with eighteen-year-old Des Walsh.

Walsh later told police that Dowe told him he was in Moree at the time of Minnie Jenkins' murder and that he knew the victim.

Walsh further implied Dowe killed Minnie.

On October 27 the NSW Government offered a £200 reward for information regarding the murder.

In November, Dowe was traced to Grenfell, about forty miles west of Cowra, where he was questioned at length by police.

Dowe initially denied any knowledge of the crime but later made a full confession because, he claimed, he was threatened by police. He was also worried about being charged with vagrancy as a result of 'wandering around' Grenfell.

Dowe allegedly told police: 'I'll tell the truth. I was in Moree and I killed her. It has nearly driven me mad, and I have nearly given myself up a couple of times.'

*   *   *

Thomas Martin Dowe was described as five feet nine inches tall with a strong build, dark complexion, dark hair and brown eyes.

He gave a circumstantial account of what allegedly preceded the tragedy and the manner in which the crime was committed.

By signing the confession, Dowe figured he would be taken to Moree, where the charge of vagrancy would be dropped and the charge of murder annulled once he gave a full account of his actual movements on the night of the crime.

As far as Dowe was concerned, he'd signed up for a free

ride across half of NSW. He was remanded and transferred to Moree police station to be detained until the coronial inquest in December. What he didn't bank on is that he would be held there until his trial in Sydney in May the following year.

He was defended at the coronial inquest — and at the subsequent trial — by verbose solicitor George Roy William McDonald, known widely as Roy.

At the inquest, Dowe alleged he was pressured by police to make a full confession. 'I was frightened of being bashed. The police were standing over me with their coats off,' he said.

Dowe admitted he was in Moree — but left about three weeks before Minnie was murdered.

On 1 August ambulance officer Ivor Ernest Layton treated Dowe at Moree ambulance station for a large septic wound on his shin and put a splint on his left thumb, which carried a weak tendon because of a war injury.

A witness claimed she saw a young man, who looked like Dowe, talking to Minnie two days before she was murdered. However, the inquest was told the witness, Ada May Flanagan, couldn't identify Dowe in a police line-up because she 'didn't have her glasses on'.

Dowe back-flipped on his signed confession and produced an iron-clad alibi proving beyond any inkling of doubt he was in Sydney at the time of the murder.

Crown witness, Desmond Walsh, was brought to Moree under police escort from Goulburn reformatory, where he was serving a two-year slot for stealing bicycles. He claimed Dowe told him he was going with a 'nice little sort who worked at a Moree hotel', but while there, a girl was murdered so he left in case the police blamed him.

Walsh said when he and Dowe were at the Grenfell railway

station waiting rooms, Dowe made rude remarks about all the girls walking by.

Dowe's defence counsel, Roy McDonald, argued Walsh perjured himself with no reason other than to claim a reward.

'I will show that the evidence of this man is not worth a cracker,' McDonald told the inquest.

Walsh denied he was aware the state government offered a sizeable reward for information relating to the death of Minnie.

He also denied that while in the Moree police station lock-up waiting to give evidence at the coronial inquest, he called out to anyone within earshot: 'There's a £200 reward for the Moree murderer, and he's not in the race to get out of it!'

There was overwhelming evidence Dowe was indeed telling the truth about his whereabouts the night Minnie was bashed.

The assistant slaughtering inspector at Homebush abattoirs, Cecil Jack, immediately picked Dowe in a police line-up before the inquest.

Jack said Dowe was the same man employed at the abattoirs under the name of Dawe, or Dowe, on 18 August.

Marcus Meek, assistant foreman of the mutton slaughtering section at the abattoirs, told the inquest he was absolutely certain Dowe was the man who signed an employees' census form at the meatworks on 21 August, the day of the murder.

Meek said he remembered the incident because it was only the second time in twenty-five years he completed that particular form for an employee outside his department.

'I also saw Dowe dragging sheepskins to a conveyor several times during the day,' Meek said.

Thirty-four witnesses were called to give evidence at the inquest including Royal Hotel barmaid May Bondeson and pantry maid Lenora Mary Cox.

Miss Bondeson's room was two doors down from Minnie's bedroom.

She said she went to sleep about midnight, after she heard Minnie enter the staff quarters.

'Later in the night I was awakened by a scream. I could not say what time it was,' she said. 'I thought it was someone screaming in her sleep. I dropped off to sleep again.'

Mrs Cox, who occupied the room next door to Minnie, said she heard a noise from Minnie's room about 5 am. She entered the room by using the open window and found Minnie lying on her right side with her head near the window.

The room did not appear to have been disturbed and there was no sign of a struggle, she told the inquest.

Minnie's mother, Eva Jenkins, a widow from Narrabri, last saw her daughter on 13 August.

She told the inquest that a few months before the murder of her daughter, another girl, driven by jealously, threatened Minnie.

'The girl accused Minnie of taking her boyfriends,' Mrs Jenkins said.

'Minnie told me this girl chased her with a knife and threatened to have her run out of town. I know the name of the girl.

'Minnie was a lonely girl and used to tell me all her little worries. I worried over her sleeping in accommodation so far from the main hotel, but she assured me she always kept the door and window locked,' she said.

After giving evidence, Mrs Jenkins, a frail, ill woman, was helped from the courtroom by her daughters Florence and Grace, and Florence's husband, Jack Terbutt.

After a thorough investigation, police officers Sawyer,

Jardine and Barber dismissed the theory that jealously may have been a motive. They were satisfied the girl whom allegedly threatened Minnie had nothing to do with the murder.

Minnie's sister, Grace Jenkins, told the inquest an incident occurred between her sister and another girl. 'But they eventually became friends.'

'Minnie was always happy, fond of dancing, and got on well with other folks.'

She said she last saw her sister on Sunday 30 August about 9.30 pm.

'We used to go to dances together about twice a week. She had no worries and was always laughing.

'I can't imagine who did it. She was blond and slim, and had a number of boyfriends, but was not serious with any of them. She would make up parties to go to dances because she loved dancing,' Grace told the inquest.

Det-Sgt James Rogers, a handwriting expert attached to the CIB, gave detailed evidence.

He said pay receipts for casual labour at Homebush abattoirs on 18, 21 and 22 August bearing the signature of T Dowe were identical to Thomas Dowe's signature on fingerprint forms and military documents.

Det-Sgt Sawyer said Dowe first denied having attacked Minnie when interviewed, but later confessed to the crime.

Dowe told Sawyer he hit Minnie with a small leaf from a sulky spring.

In the statement read to the court Dowe was alleged to have said he was intimate with Minnie on two occasions — once in her quarters at the Royal Hotel and once in a railway carriage.

When Det-Sgt Sawyer asked why he attacked Minnie, Dowe said in a detailed confession: 'We had a bit of a row. I done my block and was half mad with grog. I went along to the veranda to her window. I got into the room. I went to get in to bed with her.'

When Minnie angrily told Dowe to leave or she would call the boss, Dowe said he 'got wild'.

'I pulled the sulky spring out of the top of my trousers and whacked her with it,' he said in his statement. 'She let out a bit of a grunt and I whacked her again. I got out of the window and went back to my camp.'

*   *   *

The week-long inquest made additional national news because of the bizarre behaviour of the coroner in charge, Trevelyan Guy Peter Nugent Oldham Doyle.

At times, Doyle created more headlines and column inches than the murder victim.

The inquest was labelled by some newspapers as 'a circus' and was underlined by a 'series of extraordinary departures from the usual solemn, impersonal legal practice in such proceedings'.

Bizarrely, a large pumpkin was used as a prop to demonstrate how a skull could be damaged when struck by a blunt instrument. The blade of a sulky spring, a tomahawk and a shingling hammer were used in the demonstration.

Coroner Doyle adjourned the inquest and the pumpkin was struck using the different instruments.

Counsel Roy McDonald, senior police prosecutor Ford and Dr McMahon, who treated Minnie at Moree Hospital, all took turns striking the pumpkin.

At some point during the gruesome demonstration, held in

the empty courtroom, Coroner Doyle left the bench to assist.

After an argument arose between McDonald and Ford, the coroner called a halt to the experiment.

Dr McMahon said the wounds inflicted on Minnie's left temple and ear were more likely to have been caused by a tomahawk, rather than a sulky spring.

During the inquest, spectators appeared more enthralled by the unorthodox behaviour of Coroner Doyle, who was made a minor celebrity by metropolitan newspapers for the duration of the inquiry.

Doyle, a justice of the peace, Moree alderman (elected a couple of weeks before the inquest), veterinary surgeon and unheralded poet, courted controversy and headlines.

When witness Ada May Flanagan explained her difficulty identifying the murder suspect because she didn't have her glasses, Doyle interjected: 'Hear! Hear!'

He then asked Mrs Flanagan whether she would notice a cow walking in a peculiar fashion among a herd of cows, which brought a roar of laughter from the packed courtroom.

Mrs Flanagan said she would.

'That's all I wanted to know,' the coroner replied tersely.

Another time, Doyle offered a seat at the end of the magisterial bench to a man standing in the courtroom. The grateful spectator, however, was ordered by a sergeant assisting the coroner to vacate the seat post-haste.

Dowe's defence counsel, Roy McDonald, was often rudely interrupted by Doyle.

It all became too much for McDonald.

'It is not quite right for Your Worship to carry on an argument while I am addressing,' he snapped.

Senior police prosecutor Ford asked one witness, John Noble, to be serious while taking the oath and to not wink at reporters in the press gallery.

Courtroom etiquette and decorum were frequently overruled by loud laughter, applause and good natured heckling during a series of three-way clashes between the coroner, police giving evidence and counsel.

The courtroom at times was so crowded spectators occupied seats in the jury box as well as the bench reserved for witnesses.

The coronial inquest into the death of Joan Minnie Jenkins was pure theatre — and for Moree residents, the best ticket in town. The *Daily Telegraph* reported:

Graziers and fashionably dressed women were among the people in the crowded public section of the court. Women sat fanning themselves during proceedings. Men were permitted to leave their coats off because of the heat. Some people who were swimming at the artesian baths carried their swim suits into the court.

Police officers called the court to order when a latecomer trod on the tail of a small black dog at the back of the gallery. The dog was removed, yelping.

When Roy McDonald said witness Desmond Walsh perjured himself for the sake of earning a fast buck, Coroner Doyle responded:

'I have no power to commit any person for perjury. That is too big a job for me to decide. Someone better learned in legal technicalities would have to decide. Someone in higher authority should take the responsibility whether they file a bill or not; I've got to finish my job.'

At the conclusion of the inquest on 15 December, Coroner

Doyle committed Thomas Martin Dowe for trial on a charge of having murdered Joan Minnie Jenkins.

Doyle concluded Minnie died, 'from the effects of a heavy blow to the head with some heavy instrument feloniously and maliciously inflicted upon her on the twenty-first day of August 1944 at Moree aforesaid by one Thomas Martin Dowe, and I further find that in the manner aforesaid the said Thomas Martin Dowe did feloniously and maliciously murder the said Joan Minnie Jenkins'.

Defence counsel Roy McDonald was absolutely flabbergasted.

'No jury on earth will convict Dowe,' he said. 'It is not humanly possible for Dowe to have killed the girl and then report for work at Homebush abattoirs in Sydney the next morning,' he argued.

McDonald also refuted Ada Flanagan's claim she saw Dowe with Minnie two days before the murder.

'You wouldn't hang the mangiest mongrel dog in Moree on evidence given by Flanagan,' McDonald roared.

He said the only evidence suggesting Dowe was guilty of murdering Joan Minnie Jenkins was his own statement, which Crown evidence showed was false.

'I submit it was based on suggestions given to him by police officers,' McDonald said, alluding to police coercion.

*   *   *

At the trial in Sydney in May the following year, Dowe's defence was a carbon copy of that presented at the Moree inquest five months earlier, when he claimed he was in Sydney at the time of the murder.

Dowe gave a detailed account of his movements during the weeks before Minnie's death.

He said he and a mate, Scotty Devine, left Moree on 3 August, on which day they were in Narrabri.

Doctor Robert Hughes said he treated Dowe for a leg injury at Narrabri on 5 August, possibly the same injury treated by ambulance officer Ivor Layton at Moree a few days earlier.

On 10 August they were in Boggabri and on 12 August he and Devine were on a southbound train held up because of a minor accident.

Soon after, Dowe and Devine went their separate ways and Dowe arrived in Sydney on 16 August.

Dowe applied for jobs with the railway and tramway departments and was medically tested the same day.

Dowe's timeline of travels across NSW was overwhelmingly supported by witnesses and documentation.

The day he arrived in Sydney, Dowe drew two weeks' sustenance from the army pay office.

An uncle, Alfred Haines, said Dowe was with him and other members of his family on 19, 20 and 21 August and stayed at his St Peters home in inner Sydney until 23 August.

On 19 August, referendum day, Haines and Dowe went to the polling booths to vote.

Dowe's cousin, Isabel May Smith, said Dowe played cards at her home until the early hours of 21 August — the day of the murder — before going to Homebush abattoirs hoping to get a day's work.

Handwriting expert Det-Sgt James Rogers examined pay dockets dated 18, 21, and 22 August, signed by Dowe at Homebush abattoirs.

'It is my opinion the signatures on the army discharge sheet, identity card, pay dockets and other papers shown to me (in court) were signed by one person,' Rogers said.

Dowe, who signed a written confession to the murder of Minnie, told the court: 'I made a statement to Det-Sgts Sawyer and Barber, admitting I killed the girl because I was frightened of being bashed.'

'I have been bashed before by police and after Barber hit me in the ribs I was prepared to say anything,' Dowe said.

'When I arrived at Grenfell, I got on the booze, and was locked up for twenty-four hours. When I was released a policeman picked me up and I was charged with vagrancy.

'I was kept in a cell until interviewed by Sydney police. Barber rushed at me and hit me in the ribs. Sawyer said, "Break it down; break it down. I'll handle it",' Dowe alleged.

'Sawyer asked me what I used to strike Minnie and I told him I used a piece of old iron. Sawyer asked me what sort of iron it was and finally asked me to draw it on a piece of paper.

'I drew a piece of iron like a sulky spring because there were sulky springs at the camp where I used to sleep in East Moree. I made the statement because I thought they would check up and let me go. I did not think it would go before the coroner's court. Now, it has got this far,' Dowe said.

Defence counsel Roy McDonald relentlessly pursued Det-Sgt Sawyer over Dowe's allegations of police brutality.

'Did you say to Dowe, "we will break it down to manslaughter"?' McDonald questioned.

'No,' replied Sawyer.

'Did you say a Labor Government was in power and they are not hanging people now?'

'No,' replied Sawyer.

'Did you say the girl had lived and was able to tell you something before she died?'

'No,' replied Sawyer.

'Were you all standing there with your coats off when Dowe came into the room?'

'Yes,' replied Sawyer.

'Did Det-Sgt Barber rush at Dowe and knock him in the ribs?'

'No,' replied Sawyer.

'Did he say "is this the cove? Let me at him"?'

'No,' replied Sawyer.

'Did you say, "we want a statement; be pretty quick about it"?'

'No,' replied Sawyer.

The trial's first day didn't go without controversy — a fresh trial was ordered by Justice Laurence Street because of "an error unprecedented in criminal jurisdiction in this state".

Jury members were permitted to go home after the first day's session. However, in murder cases, it was prohibited to allow jury members to be released overnight.

'The error made yesterday was discovered the moment the jury was released, but too late to stop them dispersing,' Justice Street said. 'Under the law the trial cannot go on. A fresh jury will have to be empanelled.'

A new jury, informed of the error, was empanelled and warned to forget anything they might have read about Monday's proceedings.

The fresh trial lasted four days.

In his address to the jury, McDonald asked for an acquittal on the grounds his client's alibi established beyond doubt he was in Sydney when Minnie was murdered.

In his summing up Justice Street asked the jury, 'How can

you escape that independent evidence?'

'Does it not show conclusively Dowe was in Sydney at the time of the murder, and it was physically impossible for him to have been in Moree?'

It took ten minutes for the jury to hand down an acquittal, a cut and dried verdict that brought loud cheers from Dowe's family and a gallery full of supporters.

On 4 May 1945 Justice Street acquitted Dowe of the charge of murdering Minnie Jenkins at Moree on 21 August the previous year.

Dowe was all but 'chaired' out of the court building.

The *Truth* newspaper reported: 'His reception was that of a movie star. Women rushed to kiss him; there was a struggle among men to shake his hand; Dowe, bewildered, accepted it all.'

Dowe told the newspaper: 'I want to forget it all just as quickly as I can. I want to get to work, get back to a normal life. There are a lot of movies I want to see. I want to start to live again.'

Roy McDonald told the media throng he would push for a full inquiry into Dowe's arrest.

'From the public standpoint, matters cannot be allowed to rest merely on the not-guilty verdict in favour of the accused,' McDonald said.

'The stark fact is, Dowe was falsely accused of the fiendish, brutal and purposeless murder of a sleeping woman, whom he had never met or seen.

'He was in prison for six months, awaiting trial,' he said.

'It was established he was not in Moree between 3 August and 14 November, when he was taken back to that town by the police.

'The question of what remedy, if any, is available to him, is now being examined.'

* * *

Two weeks after the acquittal, Dowe alleged he was assaulted by two men on Addison Road, Marrickville.

He claimed they were police officers and alleged he was struck in the face and kicked after being questioned about being out at 4 am.

An investigation by Newtown police failed to find any evidence of the alleged attack.

Joan Minnie Jenkins was born at Narrabri on 16 August 1924, one of seven children to Charles and Eva Jenkins.

She was buried at Narrabri Cemetery on Friday 25 August 1944, four days after her tragic death and less than a week after her twentieth birthday.

Thomas Martin Dowe was born in Dubbo on 24 November 1916, one of six children to Cecil and Isabel Dowe.

Dowe's mother Isabel died from septicaemia when he was sixteen.

Dowe served with the Australian Imperial Force for two years and was discharged one month before the murder of Minnie.

He married Lucy Violet Lillian Oldham at St Peters, NSW, in 1940.

They had a child together but separated about six months before Dowe was charged with Minnie's murder.

In the months before being remanded and dragged before the courts for a crime he didn't commit, Dowe worked in a textile factory but was laid off after two months. He told detectives he spent much of the time tramping the roads across NSW, 'jumping the rattler' and 'drinking a lot'.

'I worry about my wife and child,' he said during one police interview leading up to the trial.

In 1945, acting Premier Jack Baddeley ordered a thorough investigation into police coercion and 'standover tactics' allegedly used on Dowe to gain a signed confession for the murder of Minnie Jenkins.

Baddeley said investigations by the acting Attorney-General Robert Reginald Downing and NSW Police Commissioner William MacKay showed evidence for or against Dowe was made available to the Coroner by the police themselves, including evidence from a police department handwriting expert.

'The fairness of the police in producing a great volume of evidence in support of Dowe's alibi was the subject of favourable comment at the Coroner's Court,' Baddeley said.

MacKay's report said in part: 'From the transcript, Dowe appears to have been a most unimpressive witness, and one on whose uncorroborated story it would be most undesirable to rely.'

'From all the papers, I cannot find any good ground for finding improper conduct on the part of the police officers concerned in the case. On the contrary, they appear to have done everything to put the proper facts before the coroner and the trial judge.

'No relevant matter was withheld from the jury. I consider there is no need for further action,' MacKay said.

Postscript:
Trevelyan Guy Peter Nugent Oldham Doyle's career as Moree coroner came to a grinding halt when Acting Premier Joe Baddeley gazetted his removal from the office of Coroner at Moree.

He was also forbidden to sit as a coroner in any town or district in NSW.

The sacking came not long after Dowe's acquittal.

The Justice Department said in a statement the reason for the dismissal was because of Doyle's 'ill-health'.

Doyle was born in Hobart, Tasmania on 16 April 1886, one of nine children to John and Margaret Doyle.

He was a larger than life character with eccentric ways, an affable manner, and an odd take on life.

Doyle's humble maxims were many.

'When the outlook is black, try the uplook' was one of his favourites.

'When there's work to do, boys, do it with a will; those who reach the top, boys, must first climb the hill' was another.

'My mother, Maggie Doyle, taught me everything I wanted to know in life. She was educated at Oxford, in France and Germany, and spoke seven languages,' he said.

Doyle obviously enjoyed entertaining out of town journalists who came to Moree looking for headlines during the inquest into the murder of Joan Minnie Jenkins.

The *Sydney Truth* called Doyle 'the most discussed man in the district'.

In one interview the unconventional coroner said he owed his success as a veterinary surgeon to his photographic memory and his microscopic eye.

Doyle, known by Moree locals as 'Trilly', claimed one of his greatest surgical triumphs was extricating the eye of a laying hen, which 'laid two eggs in one sitting shortly afterwards'.

Doyle was a stock inspector in the 1920s but was dismissed in 1932 after a departmental inquiry found him temperamentally unfit to carry responsibility and that he lacked dignity as a stock inspector.

Doyle told one newspaper he once collected 3569 ticks from his fowl house.

'The fowl house is now tick-free,' he said proudly.

Doyle was appointed Moree coroner in 1939.

'There were no other applicants so I decided to take it on,' he told journalists.

'I get a pound an inquest, whether it lasts five minutes or five weeks.'

As a young boy, after his family relocated from Tasmania to NSW and settled at Whalan, north of Moree, he drove sheep and worked as a station hand.

Doyle's pioneering grandfather James Doyle and his brother John were early settlers of the Mungindi-Boomi district.

In the 1840s they took up the leasehold of Werrina, a 170,000-acre property on the Barwon River.

Doyle dreamed of one day becoming a barrister. However, he said his father once told him his 'brains were in his feet, not in his head'.

Doyle joined the AIF on 8 November 1915 and served in Egypt the following year. He told newspapers he went as a corporal but in an emergency he was made an acting-sergeant-major.

He claimed he taught many well-known Australians how to do the goose step.

In 1936 Doyle became a veterinary surgeon in Moree.

'I've been plugging along ever since, getting five bob for attending sick animals when I should get five guineas,' he said.

* * *

After giving false evidence at Tommy Dowe's trial for the sake of collaring a £200 reward, witness Desmond Bernard Walsh's life spiralled out of control.

Walsh was born at Moonee Ponds, Victoria, in 1925 and returned to Victoria when Dowe was declared a free man.

On 25 September 1951, Walsh was injured during a gangland-style hit that killed his younger brother, 23-year-old boxer Gavan Walsh, and seriously wounded Dulcie Markham, 41.

Ernest Alfred James Martin, 30, and Charles Henry Mills, 29, were charged with the murder. They were also charged with having wounded with intent to murder Desmond Walsh and Dulcie Markham.

'When you see your brother shot to the floor you would know who did it. Those two faces will stay in my mind for life,' Walsh testified at the coronial inquest into his brother's death.

He told the inquest he was tipped off someone offered £50 to have him and his brother 'done over'.

However, Walsh's reputation as an unreliable witness held fast.

When Dulcie Markham was called to give evidence she stated under oath that neither Martin nor Mills were present when the shooting occurred.

Both men provided rock solid alibis and were acquitted.

Three months after giving evidence at the inquest into the death of his brother, Walsh was charged with armed robbery. He allegedly threatened cashier Sophia Haslett at Hatcher's laundry depot on Flinders Street, Melbourne and stole £15.

While on £200 bail for the crime, Walsh was sentenced to two years' gaol — after four trials — for assaulting and robbing St Kilda shopkeeper John Ewing at his confectionery store on 9 February 1952.

Walsh admitted five prior convictions including illegally

using a car, hindering police, disorderly behaviour, larceny, and shop-breaking and stealing.

'You are a desperate and violent character, prepared to inflict injury to obtain a small gain with no regard for the law or the rights of others,' Justice Dean told Walsh.

In March 1953, Walsh was sentenced to five years' imprisonment.

Walsh's troubles didn't end in prison. In 1954 he was on a hit-list containing the names of eight men in Pentridge prison. The list included prisoners, warders and deputy-governor Ernest Fox.

The list was compiled by deranged gunman Robert Walker in an extensive diary, serialised in the Melbourne *Argus* after Walker committed suicide in prison in 1954.

'I do not know yet just which warder I shall hold as hostage while I am giving this little rub-out party,' Walker wrote.

'But I shall do everything possible to avoid hurting or killing any other warder or prisoner while the party is taking place.'

It is unclear why Walsh was one of the eight men Walker planned to kill.

Walsh died at Ballarat, Victoria, in 1985, aged 59.

*In 1894, John Cummings was sent to the gallows
for the murder of Barraba bank manager,
William McKay. Arguments continue about
Cummings' guilt (Image credit: Museums of
History NSW — State Archives Collection)*

CHAPTER 11

MY GOD, HE'S DEAD!

Trade at the Commercial Bank on Barraba's Queen Street was quiet.

It was shortly after 1 pm on Wednesday 18 April 1894 and the morning rush was over. The break gave manager William McKay, forty, and his wife Hannah, thirty-nine, time to retire to a dining room in the bank's adjoining residence and enjoy a meal together.

A few doors away twenty-three-year-old butcher Peter Sinclair was cleaning up after a flurry of mid-morning customers. Business was hectic and the break gave him a chance to sweep out the shop and to restock, salt and smoke his goods. He planned to duck across the street to catch up with saddler Elijah Turner once his chores were completed.

As Sinclair went about his business, perhaps whistling as he toiled, the McKays were dining and chatting. They were married eleven years earlier at Waverley, NSW, and moved to Barraba in 1893. William previously managed Commercial Bank branches at Candelo, about fifteen miles south-west of Bega and Cobar, in central-western NSW.

Barraba, with a population in the early 1890s of about five hundred, was built on the back of a gold rush in the 1850s.

By 1894, the town, nestled midway between Bingara and Tamworth, was an established cattle-growing and wheat-farming centre. A copper mine recently opened at nearby Gulf Creek, had given the region an additional economic safety-net.

William and Hannah were the parents of five young children: 10-year-old Isabel, seven-year-old George, six-year-old Mary, three-year-old William and two-year-old Marjorie.

As they ate, William heard people enter the bank chambers. He assumed they were customers as it was company policy to keep the bank open during the lunchbreak.

He left the table to attend to them, pulling the door closed as he went and unintentionally latching it.

Hannah remained in the dining room and continued eating. Her heart skipped a beat when she heard raised voices. William was clearly arguing with someone.

As Hannah's fears worsened and her stomach tightened, her husband's voice became louder and firmer.

Hannah was unaware that on the other side of the dining room door, two outlaws were threatening to kill her husband if he didn't hand over cash from the bank's safe and cash drawer.

She heard a scuffle as the voices became louder.

Although the voices were at times muffled, Hannah clearly heard her husband say, 'I will not; no, I will not; not if I die for it.'

Hannah's heart was racing. She ran to the door leading to the bank chambers but the door was locked.

She remembered hearing the door click when her husband pulled it closed, but thought no more of it at the time.

She heard William attempting to speak, so made her way back through the dining room and on to the veranda through a side door.

As Hannah ran out to Queen Street, a series of short, sharp pistol shots shattered the lunchtime silence. In all, four shots were fired.

Hannah screamed for help as she watched two men hurtle

from the bank's main entrance to horses tied to a fence alongside the bank.

Townsfolk emerged from shops, businesses and homes, startled by the shots and Hannah's screams for help.

Overhead, clouds grew thicker. The sky rumbled. It began to rain.

Peter Sinclair had by this time dropped in on his mate, saddler Elijah Turner. He and Turner heard the shots and raced outside as the two outlaws galloped past.

Sinclair stopped dead in his tracks when one of the outlaws reined his horse and raised his pistol. He aimed it directly at Sinclair.

As he trotted past, the outlaw kept the pistol levelled at the butcher, as if daring him to make a move.

Their eyes locked. Not a word was spoken. Words weren't needed. Sinclair stood stock still, yet defiant.

The gunman held his piercing stare, then clicked the reins, urged his mount forward and caught up with his mate.

Both men galloped out of Barraba along the Campo Santo road as rain set in.

* * *

The very moment Sinclair was seemingly seconds from being gunned down in the middle of Queen Street, Hannah McKay ran through the front doors of the bank in search of her husband.

She found William dead on the floor behind the main serving counter, blood seeping from a bullet wound behind his left ear.

Hannah slumped to the floor. She sobbed uncontrollably and held her husband tightly.

Her screams echoed through the streets of Barraba that wet, autumn afternoon. A crowd gathered and Barraba's main thoroughfare soon became a scene of panic.

Auctioneer Charles Williams was in his office penning a letter when he heard the commotion. He ran to the street and into the bank.

'My God, he's dead,' Williams yelled.

He raced back outside to alert residents and wire police.

Bernard Finkernagel, the local store owner who was also Barraba's police magistrate and justice of the peace, hurried to the bank and comforted Hannah.

The main banking chamber was a mess and Finkernagel immediately realised what had happened.

He secured all cash and valuables, some of which was still on the bank manager's desk and counter, and locked the bank.

The keys were later handed over to the Commercial Bank's Tamworth branch manager, William Robey, who arrived in Barraba at 2 am the following day to conduct a complete audit.

'I went through the books and cash and found everything in perfect order, so nothing could have been stolen,' Robey later told police.

Elijah Turner had watched the outlaws clamber on board two fine-looking horses. He noticed one of them had difficulty mounting his horse, as if injured in some way, and was given a leg up by his mate before they galloped out of town.

Meanwhile, Sgt Harrison and Constable Adams, Barraba's only police officers, were delivering electoral rights at Campo Santo station.

On their way back they passed the outlaws near a spot called Quelchy's Gate, unaware of what had unfolded in Barraba.

The outlaws were urging their horses along at a furious clip.

They passed Harrison and Adams, who thought the men were drovers working for local selector Alfred Blaxland, a grandson of early explorer Gregory Blaxland.

A couple of miles closer to Barraba, Harrison and Adams met Peter Sinclair and Springfield station manager Cyril Bloomfield, who gave chase.

They told the officers about the botched bank hold-up and the murder of McKay.

'Two men tried to stick up the bank. Mr McKay is dead. They came this way,' Sinclair told the officers.

Harrison and Adams were astonished.

'My God, we just passed them. They were on a chestnut horse and a black horse,' Sgt Harrison said.

Harrison sent Adams ahead with Sinclair and Bloomfield to search for the outlaws and returned to Barraba to collect evidence and witness accounts.

He wired police stations across the district, putting scores of officers on high alert.

The following day, Tamworth police magistrate William Corbett-Lawson arrived in Barraba to chair a coronial inquest into the death of William McKay.

Dr Loftus Campbell conducted a post-mortem examination the same morning. He said death would have been instantaneous.

'I found a wound through the brain which severed some of the large arteries and I found the bullet, which I now produce, embedded in the base of the skull on the right side,' Dr Campbell said.

'The wound inflicted would produce instant death as the bullet went through the most vital part of the brain.

'I do not think this wound could have been self-inflicted. The person firing would have to be over and in front of the victim to inflict such a wound. I would expect such a wound had the bullet been fired from the other side of the counter,' the doctor said.

Hannah McKay bravely retraced her steps. The inquest was only twenty-four hours after the brutal death of her husband.

'I heard two bullet shots in quick succession and something whizz past my ear. I have seen the bullet marks on the door; one near where I was standing. I ran out on to the veranda and screamed again,' she said.

'When I was on the veranda I saw two men run out of the front door of the bank towards their horses on the side street. They were a chestnut and a black horse. The black horse I believe was mounted first. The man had difficulty releasing the horse from the fence, and appeared to have difficulty getting on. The man on the chestnut horse faced me. I was very much excited at the time.

'After staying some seconds on the veranda, when I saw help coming, I went back to the bank office. Mr Williams was the first person I saw in the bank,' Hannah said. 'I found my husband lying behind the counter on his back, and saw blood coming from behind the left ear.'

Peter Sinclair said he witnessed two men emerge from the bank after hearing shouting, screaming and gunfire.

'I was at Elijah Turner's shop. The men mounted their horses and the man on the black horse appeared to be helped by the other man. They passed within twenty yards of me and the man on the black horse had a shiny pistol which he pointed at me. He had a black beard. I could not take my eyes off him while he pointed the pistol at me, so I had little time to observe the other man,' he told Coroner Corbett-Lawson.

Several witnesses conjectured one of the bandits may have

been wearing a fake beard. A tuft of black hair, consistent with a beard, was found in the bank chambers.

Bernard Finkernagel said the bank was a scene of mayhem and tragedy.

'The bank rapidly filled with people. I noticed a lot of banknotes, cheques and papers scattered all over the table and, as there was no-one to take charge of it, I gathered it all up and placed it in the safe with other valuables, which had been lying around the bank,' he said.

Finkernagel said he found a set of keys on McKay's body and locked the safe.

'I then requested the people who filled the bank to withdraw and locked up the premises for the inspection of the police,' he said.

'The great disorder about the place led me to believe a fierce struggle must have taken place.'

After a short retirement the jury's verdict was clear cut.

'We find that William Charles McKay, manager of the Commercial Bank, Barraba, died on 18 April 1894, from the effects of a pistol shot wound in his head, wilfully and feloniously inflicted by two men unknown to us who stuck up the bank and that they feloniously and wilfully did kill the aforesaid William Charles McKay. We are of the opinion that, but for the brave conduct of Mrs McKay in alarming the town, the bank would have suffered heavy loss.'

A huge manhunt for the killers was launched, with landholders, local residents and Aboriginal trackers joining police officers from across the district.

The search focused on the Horton and Mount Lindesay regions — Captain Thunderbolt territory — and the NSW Government offered a £400 reward for the capture of both men.

Several settlers in the district told police they saw two men on horseback. One of them appeared to be injured and bleeding.

A group of school children said they saw two men riding closely together. The bigger man, they said, appeared to be assisting the other man as they rode along.

'The injured man was bleeding and there was blood trickling down the horse's side,' they told officers.

Police from towns and villages across north-western NSW including Moree, Warialda, Narrabri, Tamworth, Gunnedah, Millie, Manilla, Bingara and Wee Waa joined the massive manhunt.

Heavy rain and muddy conditions hampered the Aboriginal trackers' progress but within days the net was closing in on the fugitives.

On Friday 20 April Wee Waa Sen-Constable Joseph Myers and Constable Rod Fraser, from Boggabri, met a man on foot about fifteen miles from Boggabri.

The man, known to Sen-Constable Myers, matched the description of one of the murderers, and was in a clearly distressed state.

He was John Cummings, 34, also spelt 'Cummins' in subsequent newspaper reports and court documents. He was known in the district as 'Jack'.

Cummings, clean-shaven with a moustache and sallow complexion, was dressed shabbily. He wore a faded, dirty, grey tweed suit, cape and slouch hat. He was stooped, exhausted and injured.

There were blood stains on the inside leg of his trousers, apparently caused by severe chafing.

'Good day; where are you going, Jack?' Myers asked.

Cummings replied: 'I am going to Boggabri to get a horse. I

lost mine in the mountains last night.'

He told the constables he was kangaroo shooting.

He said his gun was planted at his camp about ten miles away, but steadfastly refused to divulge the camp's location.

Myers had known Cummings for about four years. He noted the suspect was wet, excited and on foot.

Myers offered Cummings a horse to search for his own animal but he refused the offer.

Cummings was formerly arrested on suspicion of murdering William Charles McKay, to which he allegedly replied: 'All right.'

He was brought before the Barraba bench and remanded for eight days.

Cummings, born at Wallabadah near Quirindi on 2 June 1860, was well-known in the district as a shearers' union delegate and part-time jockey and horse-breaker.

He claimed the chafing on his inner-right leg was caused by a twist in the stirrup leather when he recently rode at Boggabri picnic races.

'In all the excitement, I did not notice it at the time,' Cummings said.

The sore had been aggravated since by frequent riding into Boggabri in wet clothes.

Cummings recently played a prominent role in the formation of a carriers' union and shearers' union across north-western NSW. He was at the head of the line for nomination as Moree's Labour interest at a coming election.

A search for the campsite was launched.

The party covered more than 150 miles of rough, strewn territory through Lindesay station and the Currangandi run, eventually bringing the group back to Campo Santo station.

Searchers found two sets of tracks on the Coolah run leading to Dripping Rock about eighteen miles east of Boggabri and forty miles south-east of Barraba.

The spot was widely known as one of Thunderbolt's old haunts.

Additional search parties, headed up by Constables Moroney, Dalton and King, scoured the almost impregnable territory but failed to find any sign of the camp.

On Saturday 21 April another camp was found near Hawkins' Creek about four miles west of Barraba, where it was believed the suspects took cover before the failed bank robbery.

Evidence gathered by Sen-Constable Myers included two pieces of hemp halter, a pint pot, sardine tin, three-bushel bag, a tin tag from a plug of tobacco and a scrap of a blue-coloured blanket.

William Taylor, who lived nearby, told police he saw a black horse and a chestnut horse in a reserve near Hawkins' Creek.

'Two men were camped not far off. One was standing up and the other was sitting down,' Taylor said.

Taylor also observed pint and quart pots, a piece of blanket and a sugar bag, similar to the evidence gathered by police.

After leaving the camp, Sen-Constable Myers, along with Constables Carvell, Adams, Fraser and two Aboriginal trackers, began searching mountainous country nearby.

'We made a diligent search in the mountains, but could find no trace of the camp alluded to by the accused (Cummings) on the day of his arrest,' Myers said.

On Tuesday 24 April a major breakthrough was made at Gunnedah when a man named Patrick McManus was arrested on suspicion of being involved in the murder.

McManus, well-known to police, allegedly told the arresting

officer: 'I expected this. Something in my mind told me I would be overhauled for this Barraba affair.'

Clothing resembling attire worn by the murderers was found at McManus's home.

'I can get the whole neighbourhood to verify my whereabouts if need be,' he said.

The following day, one week after the tragedy, two horses, believed to have been used by the murderers, were found dead in a spot called Myall paddock near Burindi station, about fourteen miles from Barraba.

Both horses' throats were slashed and their brands and manes badly mutilated.

Bingara police constable James Sommerville received a tip-off about a fence being cut at a spot on the Coolah run known as Mehi Paddock.

Sommerville and tracker Harry Tan followed three sets of tracks for about two miles and found the dead horses, as well as a razor with human hair on it, bridles, girths and a shingling hammer.

The chestnut horse was recognised as well-performed galloper, Derby, owned by Boggabri publican James Jones, who two weeks earlier gave the horse to Jack Cummings to take to Narrabri races to compete and possibly sell.

The black horse was identified as racehorse Tyson, owned by Boggabri farmer Fred Russell, who said he was unaware the horse was missing until shown its mutilated body.

Cummings rode Derby at Boggabri picnic races on Saturday 7 April.

Owner Jones, who had known Cummings casually for about four years, instructed Charlie Humphries, the trainer of Derby, to give the horse to Cummings to take to Narrabri races.

Cummings collected Derby from Humphries' stables on Wednesday 11 April.

'He was riding a bay horse, and rode away leading Derby,' Humphries said.

He gave Cummings a bushel of corn in a three-bushel bag and a rope halter.

Meanwhile, Sen-Constable John Mahon, in company with Constables Gardiner and Strachan, located a man boiling a billy at Burburgate, between Boggabri and Gunnedah.

The man was half-starved and appeared insane. He was short and stout, with a dark complexion and short black beard. He wore a faded, light-coloured tweed suit and a grey felt hat. He identified himself as Joseph Anderson.

'I have come from Narrabri and I have been about three weeks looking for work. I have been in the colony for about nine months,' he told Constable Mahon.

He was later identified as Alexander Lee, 28 — also known as Joseph Anderson and Alick Lee — and was taken to Boggabri police station shackled in leg-irons and handcuffs.

Lee was placed under arrest by first-class detective George Edwin Goulder, who travelled to Barraba from Sydney to head investigations.

Goulder, known in Sydney criminal circles as 'Little Billy', was a celebrated police officer.

'Detective Goulder has shown unusual shrewdness in unravelling the mysteries of this case. He has left no stone unturned to bring the guilty parties to justice, and has well-merited the praise of the community,' newspapers lauded.

The accused, Alexander Lee, was described by the *Scone Advocate* as 'a little man, very thin and very square-featured'. At first, it was thought he could not speak fluent English. It was also alleged he feigned insanity when captured.

Lee, a sailor believed to be of Swedish origin, claimed he arrived in Australia from Mauritius in August the previous year on the *Lysong*. He said he jumped ship and stayed at Newcastle for about seven months before working his way to Narrabri.

Lee's claims later proved to be an utter fabrication when it was established he and Cummings were long-time associates. They met in Berrima Gaol in 1885, and stayed in touch over the years.

* * *

On Friday 27 April, suspect Patrick McManus was brought before police magistrate William Corbett-Lawson at Barraba police court.

After evidence from police officers Harrison and Adams, as well as saddler Elijah Turner, McManus was cleared of any wrongdoing or involvement of the Barraba murder.

Turner emphatically stated McManus was not one of the men he witnessed running from the Commercial Bank on 18 April.

The bench expressed regret for the inconvenience caused and arrangements were made to pay McManus his coach and train expenses back to Gunnedah.

On the last day of the committal hearing Boggabri farmer John Lye told the court he had known John Cummings for more than ten years. Cummings had lived on Lye's 1000-acre dairy farm, about six miles from Boggabri, since late 1893.

'He was breaking in horses for me and is a very fair horseman,' Lye said.

Lye said he only knew the co-accused, Alexander Lee, for

about eighteen months.

'I know him as Alick and he came to my place on a creamy pony. Cummings did not say he was expecting Alick but I believe he came to see Cummings,' Lye said.

It was later established the creamy pony also belonged to Boggabri publican James Jones, who owned the racehorse, Derby.

'Alick stayed one or two nights. He came back the following Friday or Saturday week. He stayed till Sunday 8 April and left at dinner time. He was away for a few days. I saw him at the house with Cummings. I saw no strange horse after he came back. The two men seemed to be on friendly terms,' Lye told the court.

A subsequent search of Cummings' living quarters on Monday 23 April, conducted by Constables Adams and Carvell, unearthed a bag containing twenty-three revolver cartridges.

The search also uncovered a recently fired cartridge shell and a box containing a spent cartridge shell and a set of keys. The second shell was a different calibre from the cache of twenty-three cartridges.

There were also five pairs of tweed trousers, two of them almost worn out, a pair of moleskin trousers, a pair of pants, black coat and waistcoat, dark tweed overcoat, one striped blanket, a tent and fly, two pillows — one made of horsehair — and a pair of old shoes.

Lye said Lee stayed at his property until Sunday 15 April.

'I saw Alick go away that day at about midday, on foot, towards the gate leading to the main road, either to Boggabri or Gunnedah. Cummings stayed until the following Tuesday (the day before the murder) and I have not seen him since that morning until I saw him in custody here today,' he said.

Lye described Cummings as clean-shaven, except for a moustache. He said Lee had dark-brown whiskers about three-inches long.

Lye identified much of the evidence found at the Hawkins' Creek campsite as similar to property he kept at his farm.

'The tomahawk resembles one I had at my place. I saw it there about six weeks ago,' Lye told the court. 'I can't say if it is the same brand, but it is much the same shape; I kept it in my tool chest, but I do not know if it is there now.'

He identified a pint and quart pot and a bridle similar to those kept at his place. He kept the bridle to use only on young horses.

'Cummings used it when he broke in horses for me. I received a wire today to say the bridle is not there,' Lye said.

Cummings and Lee were committed for trial and were taken under heavy police guard by special coach to Tamworth.

A subscription among shearers raised £100 to help pay legal costs for Cummings, whose only previous charge was for horse-stealing in 1884, for which he received five years' imprisonment.

Lee, however, was well known to police as a 'cunning, dangerous and reckless criminal'. On 2 March 1885, shortly after arriving in the colony, he was tried in Sydney on a charge of shooting with intent and sentenced to five years in Darlinghurst Gaol. He was later moved to Trial Bay Prison and Berrima Gaol.

It was at Berrima Gaol he met Cummings, who was doing time for the horse-stealing charge.

On 27 March 1887, while incarcerated at Trial Bay, Lee was charged with making a frivolous complaint about prison conditions and sentenced to seven days' solitary confinement.

As he was escorted to the "dark cells" by chief warder

Rowley, Lee seized a knife as they passed the dining room and stabbed the warder in the abdomen.

Lee was immediately overpowered and subsequently charged at the Central Criminal Court on 24 March 1887 with inflicting grievous bodily harm with intent to murder, later reduced to malicious wounding with an extra five years added to his gaol time.

Judge Milner Stephen told him had the attempted murder charge stood, he would have been sentenced to death.

Lee was moved to Goulburn Gaol. On 15 March 1888, he attempted to escape and another six months was added to his sentence, which he successfully appealed against. He was released from prison in October 1892.

*   *   *

The trial of Alexander Lee and John Cummings, both charged with the wilful murder of William Charles McKay at Barraba on 18 April 1894, began at a special sitting of the circuit court at Tamworth Assises on 19 June before Judge George Innes.

When called to respond to their names, Cummings immediately answered. Lee, however, refused, saying his name was Joseph Anderson, not Alexander Lee. An alteration was made to the indictment and both men then entered not guilty pleas.

Throughout the trial, Cummings declared his innocence, saying he was not in Barraba on the day of the murder — or the day before, for that matter.

Peter John Sinclair, Bernard and Caroline Finkernagel, Charles Williams, Cyril Bloomfield, Elijah Turner, Edward White, James Moylan and Sen-Constable John Mahon were among more than thirty witnesses called for the Crown, led by prosecutor Francis Edward Rogers, assisted by Nugent Robertson.

Counsel for the defence Richard Denis Meagher and Gus Crowe appeared for Cummings, and Fred Tribe and Larry Armstrong for Lee.

Much of the evidence given at the coroner's inquest was revisited, including testimony from Caroline Finkernagel, wife of store owner Bernard Finkernagel.

She recalled the evening two days before the murder when two men she believed were the accused entered her store to buy tobacco and sundry items.

'We did not have the brand they wanted, so I sold them Sun tobacco,' Mrs Finkernagel said.

The taller man, allegedly Cummings, then enquired about purchasing firearms.

'He asked me if we had any cheap American pistols or revolvers. I said we had none. He asked me if we had a second-hand one or one in our own use I could sell. I told him I could sell him a second-hand Winchester but he said it would be too heavy,' Mrs Finkernagel said.

'He then asked me if I knew where firearms could be purchased in town. I said I did not know if any other stores kept them. He also asked me if I knew of anyone who might sell a firearm privately. I told him I didn't.'

Cummings' defence counsel, Richard Meagher, questioned Mrs Finkernagel's testimony, saying she could not say for certain whether it was Monday night or Tuesday night before the murder the two men visited the store.

'Surely, it was very rare for customers to come into the store and ask for pistols. The man who asked for a pistol seemed very anxious to procure one,' Meagher said.

'On the day of the murder Mrs Finkernagel heard one of the murderers held a revolver but she did not tell anyone two men tried to buy a revolver on the Monday before, although she could not swear it was Monday.'

The defence counsel told the court Mrs Finkernagel did not tell her husband about the incident until Thursday, the day after the murder.

'She was not in Barraba Court when Lye swore Cummings was at his place until Tuesday. She would swear no-one told her Cummings was sixty miles away from Barraba on the night she swore he was in her store. Mrs Finkernagel heard Cummings was at Lye's that night, but what she heard did not induce her to alter the day in her evidence. She did not remember if she had ever been asked for firearms before the evening of the day in question,' Meagher argued.

Cyril Bloomfield unmistakably identified the two slaughtered horses found at Myall paddock as the horses used by the accused. He also saw the men and the horses as he rode into Barraba about midday on the day of the murder.

'They were going towards the river,' Bloomfield told the court. 'I did not take much notice of them but I noticed their horses, particularly.'

Bloomfield was lunching at Wilkinson's Hotel when he heard gunshots and screams.

'I ran out into the street, and as I got to the middle of the road I saw a man on a black horse appear round the corner of the bank,' Bloomfield said.

'Immediately behind him I saw the rider of the chestnut horse getting into the saddle. He was about 250 yards away. They rode off in the direction of Campo Santo, from where I had seen them coming. I have no doubt whatsoever they were the same two horses I saw when coming into town. I've been around horses all my life.'

Bloomfield said he and Peter Sinclair then mounted their own horses and gave chase.

Saddler Elijah Turner and auctioneer Charles Williams firmly identified Lee as the man riding the black horse and Hannah McKay identified Lee as the man who confronted her moments after her husband was murdered.

Sinclair said he believed the man on the black horse was Lee. 'He pointed a pistol at me as he rode past.'

Mount Erin selector James Moylan identified Lee from a police line-up as the man riding the black horse and Sen-Constable Harrison identified Lee as one of the riders he saw when delivering electoral rights at Camp Santo station but could not identify the other man.

'I did not have the opportunity to see him as they passed on the day of the murder,' he said.

*   *   *

The trial took a complete about-face when the accused men were given their chance to address the court.

Not only did Cummings claim he was not in Barraba the day of the murder but co-accused Alexander Lee completely corroborated his account of events before and after the crime — a story which implicated a third man, known only as Jim.

As fantastic as this sounded, there was a ring of truth to it.

Cummings began his solemn address to the court with a protestation of innocence: 'Your Honour and gentlemen, if I had to meet my maker this moment I could faithfully say I had nothing whatever to do with the murder of Mr McKay, nor was I in Barraba on the day of the murder or the day previous.'

He continued with an account 'that I have not hitherto revealed.'

He said, 'A few days before the Boggabri races a man came to me and asked me to lend him a horse, a saddle and bridle. I said he could have the bay horse I was then riding and asked him what he wanted the horse for.'

The man told him he planned to hold up the Barraba bank with a mate and they needed horses.

Cummings claimed he was offered a quarter share of all proceeds from the robbery if he came on board, implying there may have been four people involved in the crime.

'All I had to do was plant the money or notes and send them to Sydney to the men after the whole affair had blown over,' Cummings said. 'On 13 April I saw this man again and we agreed to meet later at a certain spot eighteen miles from Barraba, at the foot of a steep ridge on the Barraba side of the range.'

In the meantime, Cummings said, he offered the man a bay horse and instructed him to get the horse from one of John Lye's paddocks the following Sunday, 15 April.

On Monday 16 April, Cummings saw the bay horse still in the paddock, but the racehorse, Derby, was missing.

'It then flashed across my mind that the man had taken, either by mistake or intention, Derby instead of the other horse,' Cummings told the court.

Cummings said he met the man and his alleged accomplice two days later, on the afternoon of the murder, at the designated spot eighteen miles from Barraba, where they were to divvy up the loot.

'That was a nice trick you served me — that horse (Derby) is known all over the district,' Cummings claimed he told the two men.

Cummings said the men told him the bank hold-up was a complete and utter failure. 'What is worse, the banker has been shot and has lost his life,' the shorter man allegedly told Cummings.

'The other, a tall man, taller than me with a full black beard, told me to lead them to the roughest country I could find,' Cummings told the deathly-quiet Tamworth Court House.

'They cut the fence, and after we rode for two or three miles we came to a rough mountain. Here, it was decided to kill Derby and the black horse. They killed them, and to secure myself I cut off the brands. When these were disposed of, the man who rode Derby took my bay horse and, believing I could get along better on foot than horseback, I let him have the horse.

'He rode away, and I have never seen him since,' Cummings said.

'The other man and I went in the direction of Boggabri. We wandered over the mountains all night and about noon the next day we got near the track, so exhausted we camped and ate the last bit of bread we had.'

It was here, Cummings said, he and the other man parted company.

'I had not gone far when I saw some shod horse tracks, which I thought were the tracks of the police search party,' he said.

'I camped that night away from the track and decided to start for home next day. As I was making for home I met the police and told them I was going to Boggabri.'

At this point Sen-Constable Joseph Myers and Constable

Rod Fraser arrested Cummings on suspicion of the murder of William McKay.

Cummings said he concocted the story about kangaroo shooting, a missing bay mare and the campsite he said was 'about ten miles away'.

'The reason I told them it was a bay mare was because if they found the other horse it could be traced to me,' Cummings said. 'I refused to show them my camp because I had no camp to show them.'

Cummings told Judge Innes the entire incident was a case of mistaken identity.

'I do not resemble the other man in the least. He is taller than me, and has a full black beard,' Cummings said.

'The reason I told the police all the falsehoods was because I saw the men who committed the murder and knew all about it, and I did not wish to give any information that might incriminate me. I knew I was likely to be arrested for the robbery.

'These are the facts. I was not one of the men in Barraba that day. I was at Lye's on the Tuesday. I was fixing the fence on the Monday. Since I have been arrested I have told many untruths, but what I have just said is true in every particular,' Cummings said.

Alexander Lee addressed the judge with a strong foreign accent, at times dropping his voice to an almost inaudible tone.

'Gentlemen of the jury, you have heard Cummings' statement and the fact he is innocent. As I have knowledge of the death of one man, I do not wish to have the knowledge of a second,' he told the hushed courtroom, referring to the fact both men would hang if found guilty.

'I solemnly declare the man John Cummings is innocent in

act and part whatsoever of the crime. He is not the second man who rode Derby. It is a case of mistaken identity.'

Lee corroborated Cummings' account of what happened at Boggabri races when a man approached him about borrowing a horse and saddle.

'Gentlemen, I am that man,' Lee said. 'I knew Cummings and knew if I went to him and wanted a horse he would lend me one.'

Lee said Cummings' statement to the court earlier was true and correct in every utterance.

'On the afternoon of April 18 at 3 pm we met on the ranges going towards Millanroy station, about twenty-five miles from Barraba and told Cummings what happened,' he said. 'I told him to leave the road and go into the thick country because I knew I had done him an injury by taking Derby instead of the other horse.

'We went into the country until we arrived on the brow of a big gorge. I shot Derby and the other man killed the black horse. We did so to save the man who I had done a terrible injury to by taking Derby without his consent. I did not want to do him another injury, so we took all chance of discovery away.'

Lee said Caroline Finkernagel swore two men came into her store and asked for firearms.

'Two men may have gone into her store, but not the two men who stuck up the bank,' he said.

'Neither my mate, nor me, were ever in Mrs Finkernagel's shop. On Tuesday, we rode into Barraba and met a young fellow, who afterwards could not identify me. I do not think he has been called as a witness because he could prove Mrs Finkernagel's statement incorrect.'

Lee said he and his accomplice saw police officers Harrison and Adams as they made their escape along Santo Campo road.

'Harrison saw the revolver in my hand and pointed it out to Adams, who was wearing a policeman's cap. They did not follow us, then.

'This statement is true in every particular and I make it to clear an innocent man,' Lee said.

* * *

In a powerful speech to the jury counsel for the defence Richard Meagher, pointed out inconsistencies in the Crown's case, especially conflicting accounts of Cummings' whereabouts the day before the murder.

Whereas witness William Taylor said about 8.30 am on April 17 he saw Cummings and Lee and the two horses used in the crime near Hawkins' Creek, John Lye swore that at 8 am Cummings was at his place, forty-six miles away.

'Was it possible Cummings could have been in two spots forty-six miles apart at or about the same time? This is what two Crown witnesses have sworn,' Meagher said

Constable Sommerville had previously testified he saw three sets of tracks leading through the fence at Mehi Paddock. 'This seems to point conclusively to the fact the prisoners' story is true, and that three men rode into the paddock,' Meagher said.

Meagher even suggested the outlaws could have been unarmed when they entered the bank and the gun used actually belonged to the victim, William McKay.

Meagher's address to the jury lasted more than two hours. He claimed some of the evidence presented by the Crown would 'not bear the light of day'.

'This case bristles with chaotic facts and doubts, and if a doubt exists in your minds, I ask the jury to give Cummings the benefit of the doubt,' he implored.

* * *

Crown prosecutor Francis Rogers debunked the incredible story put forward by Lee.

'The admission by Lee that he was one of the men who stuck up the bank and that Cummings was not there at the time was more or less a chivalrous act, but the jury must not attach too much importance to the statement,' Rogers said.

'As to what the learned counsel for the defence had to say about who actually held the revolver, the assumption it was the bank manager, Mr McKay, is absurd.'

In summing up, Judge Innes said he had never adjudicated over such a trial.

'I have spent forty-three years in the study, practice and administration of the law, and for sixteen years been a judge, but have never before heard a case which presented features similar to those which occurred in this court,' Judge Innes said.

'One of the men actually confessed his guilt and it was clear the other was an accessory, both before and after the fact. The circumstances of the prisoners' statements are unique in my experience; nor do I remember having read of a case presenting features similar to those before me.

'The law now allows a prisoner to enter the witness box and perhaps a man charged with such a serious crime would perhaps not hesitate to commit perjury,' Judge Innes conjectured.

'Mrs Finkernagel held a long conversation with the taller man and she swore positively it was Cummings who was in her shop. Lye stood alone in saying Cummings was at his place on Tuesday. Without imputing any intention of perjury to Lye it is reasonable to suppose he was mistaken as to the day,' Judge Innes suggested.

The trial concluded on Friday 22 June.

After nearly three hours' deliberation, the jury found both men guilty of the wilful murder of William James McKay.

Judge Innes unwaveringly passed the death penalty.

'May the Lord have mercy on your soul,' he addressed Cummings.

Cummings replied: 'And may the Lord have mercy on your soul for passing the sentence of death on an innocent man.'

The judge told Lee he could not hold any hope of mercy.

Lee accepted the sentence in the same poker-faced manner displayed throughout the trial.

When the trial jury at Tamworth retired, Meagher requested Judge Innes recall the panel and redirect them on several points.

Judge Innes declined to comply with Meagher's request.

The following Friday Supreme Court Justices William Windeyer, Milner Stephen and William Foster heard an appeal on behalf of John Cummings.

Meagher reasoned Judge Innes was wrong in directing the jury in that there was insufficient evidence or statements by the accused to make Cummings an accessory before or after the fact.

He argued there was no evidence to show Cummings, even if present at the bank for the purpose of committing the robbery, either 'aided, abetted, or was ready to render assistance in the commission of another felony, namely murder'.

Bernard Ringrose Wise, instructed by Meagher and Crick, asked leave to withdraw proceedings.

'The points reserved were points which could not be argued in view of the fact the jury found by their verdict that the prisoner was present and assisted at the murder,' Wise said.

Judge Windeyer agreed. 'You have taken the only proper course open under the circumstances, for it was quite clear on the finding of the jury that Cummings was actually present at the murder. The points reserved were unarguable, and it was therefore unnecessary for the court to go further into the case. The direction of Judge Innes was altogether correct,' he said.

The conviction was confirmed.

* * *

Shortly after midnight on the morning of his execution, Cummings used the broken blade of a penknife to gouge a vein in his left arm just above the elbow. He said the blade, about half-an-inch long, was planted between his gums and cheek since the trial.

'I would rather do away with myself than die at the hands of the hangman,' he told Warder Darcy, who stopped the bleeding by placing a ligature above the wound.

The blood was quickly staunched and the wound stitched and bandaged by visiting gaol surgeon Dr Walter Eli Harris, from Armidale.

When Archdeacon William Piddington visited Cummings' cell, the prisoner pointed to three spots of fresh blood on the wall. 'Those three marks indicate three men were implicated in the Barraba murder,' Cummings told the archdeacon.

* * *

At 9 am on Friday 20 July 1894 Lee and Cummings were led to the gallows by hangman Robert Howard and his assistant, Mr Goldrick. The hangman was known throughout the colony as

'Nosey Bob' having lost part of his nose when kicked by a horse while working as a hansom cab driver.

Cummings was so weak from the suicide attempt that a wheelchair was needed to convey him to the gallows. He was supported by hangman Howard and Archdeacon Piddington as he struggled up the steps of the scaffold. Once in position above the drop, he was strapped to a chair and given a shot of whiskey.

Lee, however, ascended the steps defiantly, at times stooping down to comfort Cummings. He carried a sheaf of documents.

'Where is the sheriff?' he asked the hangman. 'I want to hand him a bundle of papers and I want him to faithfully promise me he will hand them to Mr Piddington.'

Under-Sheriff Charles Maybury accepted the paperwork to pass on to Sheriff Charles Cowper.

Gaol officials, invited members of the public and several newspapermen stood silently before the gallows. Incredibly, a group of young boys scaled a tree outside the prison wall and watched proceedings.

Lee was given permission to speak. Even though he was minutes from execution, Lee resolutely declared his companion's innocence.

'To all those present here today, I declare John Cummings innocent of the crime for which he this day suffers. He was not the man with me in the Barraba bank. I myself am innocent of the crime of murder,' he said to the group of police officers, officials and witnesses.

Men watched and listened intently to Lee's parting words; others grimaced and looked away.

Lee turned to Cummings and said: 'Are you ready, Jack? We will meet once more in some other place.'

Cummings was clearly a defeated man. 'Silence is the

language of the dead,' he replied hoarsely.

At precisely 9.30 am, nooses were placed around the necks of the condemned men. White, hooded veils were pulled down over their faces.

Lee, defiant as ever, arched his neck to accommodate the noose. Cummings groaned. His head fell forward as if on the threshold of fainting.

The bolt was drawn. The bodies dropped — one strapped to a chair. It was over within seconds.

The lifeless bodies of Cummings and Lees swayed lightly, almost gracefully. The thick ropes were pulled taut.

The journey, and torment, was over.

*   *   *

Newspapers held little sympathy for Cummings and Lee.

'Each man was given a drop of eight feet and death was instantaneous,' they reported. 'There was not the movement of a muscle, and a moment afterwards both bodies were hanging perfectly motionless. The arrangements could not have been conducted more satisfactorily.'

Before his execution, Cummings penned a compassionate letter to counsel Richard Meagher. The correspondence, including a poem, was written on 10 July at Tamworth Gaol. It said in part:

> Our acquaintance was but brief, and is not likely to be renewed, and although formed under unhappy circumstances, particularly so to me, it afforded me an opportunity of spending a few happy moments in the company of a man whose ability as an advocate is, I

believe, second to none; and attributes as a man, and sympathies as a friend would require some abler pen than mine to adequately portray. Be that as it may, you want no references from such as me to commend you either as a counsellor or as a man.

They know, and you know, the jury arrived at a wrong verdict. I may say, although I suppose you know, Lee has offered to tell the name of the man who was at the bank with him on condition I be liberated.

So far, I believe no notice has been taken of his offer and, I suppose, will not. Justice, so-called, will not brook correction.

Let me thank you for what you have done for me. I do not claim to be a paragon of virtue; far from it. I have done many things I ought not have done, and left undone many things I ought to have done. I know I am a sad sinner.

Myriad newspaper reports and countless court documents spell the accused's surname either 'Cummings' or 'Cummins', however he signed 'J.T. Cummings' when penning his heartfelt letter of gratitude to Meagher.

He was also referred to as 'John Cummings' on the inquest journal entry, with the cause of death 'asphyxia by hanging in accordance with the death sentence passed on him'.

Lee was buried within the gaol grounds. Cummings' family requested he be buried in the Anglican section of the West Tamworth Cemetery.

* * *

Solicitors Fred Tribe and Gus Crowe documented a second confession from Lee, the day before the double execution. It was witnessed by first-class detective George Goulder, the case's chief investigating officer.

Lee implicated a man named Jimmy Campbell, a felon who also went by the name, Alf Johnson.

Lee said he met Campbell at Flanagan's billiard room on Oxford Street, Sydney, on or about 28 March 1894 — three weeks before McKay was murdered.

Campbell claimed he knew Lee from Goulburn Gaol, but Lee could not remember him.

It wasn't long before Lee and Campbell were talking shop.

'Do you know of any jobs we could do together,' Campbell allegedly asked Lee.

According to Lee's written confession, Lee and Campbell agreed to meet the following day in front of Sydney Town Hall with a plan to case the Union Bank branch at St Peters.

However, they decided the job was too risky and began looking elsewhere.

'I said, I know of two banks, one at Deepwater and the other at Barraba, but we would require horses and arms,' Lee told Tribe, Crowe and Goulder.

'As I didn't know anyone at Deepwater it would be difficult to get horses but if we decided doing Barraba I knew someone we could get horses from.'

Lee said he and Campbell left Sydney two days later, travelling by train from Redfern to Gunnedah.

'Campbell had two rifles and a revolver in his swag,' Lee said.

'We arrived in Gunnedah next morning and arranged for Campbell to walk to Boggabri and for me to go by rail.

'We were seen together at Bowen's hotel by the publican's

son, and then we parted. I stayed at Bowen's on Tuesday night and left by train for Boggabri the next morning.

'On arrival, I went straight to Jack Lye's place. The next day I saw Campbell at a hut about four miles from Boggabri, where I previously directed him.

'I told him Jack Cummings would lend me a horse and saddle.'

Lee said he and Campbell rode to the Commercial Bank at Barraba and entered the premises.

'I called to the banker: "bail up!"' Lee said.

'The banker held his hands up over his head and I jumped over the counter, my mate having him covered with a revolver. I went towards the safe, when the banker ran towards me, crying, "no, no". I then fired over his head, and he ran back to the dining room door. I then put out the money from the safe on to the table, when he came towards me again, and I again fired over his head.

'He then rushed me and forced me over the counter, with his right hand at my throat and with his left clutched at my revolver, which caused it to go off and shoot him dead.'

Lee said they fled the bank and met up with Cummings about twenty miles away.

Campbell, he said, left on a bay horse belonging to Cummings.

'I stayed with Cummings until the next day, when we parted. On the following Saturday I met Campbell in the bush between Boggabri and Narrabri. He was lying on the ground with his rifle and saddle. He said he let his horse go.'

The pair then parted ways.

'Campbell took the main road over the bridge after planting the saddle and rifles under the roots of a fallen tree,' Lee said.

The confession was forwarded to the Executive Council, which found it to be 'principally a tissue of falsehoods strung together with the object of clearing Cummings from the charge of murder'.

*   *   *

Even an inmate in Melbourne's Pentridge Prison, Bertie Osborne, sensationally laid claim to killing McKay, further adding to Cummings' cause celebre.

On 6 July, two weeks before the execution of Lees and Cummings, Osborne said he was McKay's killer. Osborne had started an eight-year stretch in Pentridge for house-breaking and robbery under arms.

He was released from the same gaol on 27 March for similar crimes and made his way to Sydney, where he fell in with a stranger named O'Neill. He said they headed north, met up with Lee, and planned the Barraba bank robbery.

Osborne bizarrely claimed he was the person who pulled the trigger and murdered McKay, before fleeing to Melbourne.

In late April, Osborne was convicted of robbery under arms and sent back to Pentridge, a place he liked to call 'home'.

Osborne's bold confession, possibly an attempt to ensure he would remain in prison, was documented and sent to colonial secretary George Dibbs for consideration.

Investigating detectives quickly dismissed Osborne's claims, saying the prisoner's conduct would be reviewed and suitable punishment handed out.

Dibbs said he saw nothing in the document to justify reopening the case.

Many questions remain.

Was Alexander Lee telling the truth or was he simply a pathological storyteller capable of creating incredible tales?

* * *

Misgivings about the guilt of John Cummings have lingered for many years — and still linger.

In 1936, journalist Allan Brennan penned a feature story in *The World's News*, theorising Cummings was wrongfully executed.

'The trial was a desperate and relentless scuffle for a second neck,' Brennan wrote.

'By his ceaseless efforts to save Cummings, Lee literally noosed his own neck beyond any chance of redemption but Justice Innes was clearly determined to similarly encircle Cummings.

'To his very last breath, Lee tried to save Cummings. It certainly seems if hanging was proper for Lee, then something less than the rope was sufficient punishment for Cummings.'

* * *

The board of the Commercial Banking Company of Sydney awarded Hannah McKay a pension of £100 a year for fifteen years and £20 to each of her five children.
Hannah left Barraba immediately after the tragedy and relocated to Orange, where her husband was laid to rest in the Presbyterian section of Orange Cemetery. William McKay left an estate valued at £1645.

At the coronial inquest, Hannah told police magistrate William Corbett-Lawson how she and her husband frequently discussed the possibility of the bank being robbed.

'My husband and I often talked about the bank being stuck up. I felt very uneasy about it for quite some time,' she said.

Every so often Hannah prompted discussions with her husband about bank security.

'I often asked William what he would do if robbers came and stuck us up with firearms, and demanded the keys and cash,' she said.

'William said he would do his duty and not give them anything. He also said robbers would not come at night but would come in the daytime when he had the keys and few people were about.

'I told him, if they do, I will take the keys from you and give them to the robbers, rather than see you forfeit your life,' she said.

Tragically, because of a door latched unintentionally, Hannah was denied that opportunity.

Postscript:

Racehorse trainer Peter Sinclair is always cautious when considering 'what could have been' on the streets of Barraba that bleak autumn afternoon in 1894.

Sinclair's great-grandfather, Barraba butcher Peter John Sinclair, was a key witness — and was also seconds away from being gunned down as the robbers jumped on their horses and fled the town.

'If the bank robber that day was a little bit too trigger-happy, a little bit too keen, and shot my great-grandfather, the Sinclair family tree stops growing right there on that street in Barraba in 1894 — our branch of the family tree, anyway. It's a pretty frightening thought,' Sinclair said.

Bingara historian Rod King says it's quite possible an innocent man was executed.

'What disturbs me about this gruesome, brutal affair is one

of those hanged for the murder could have been innocent,' King said. 'As one stumbles on events of historical importance, those rarely told after many decades, occasionally it's difficult to remain emotionally independent as the details unfold.

'The Barraba murder is one such case. The judge left no doubt he felt Cummings was guilty and the jury would have been clearly guided by this. In today's world, such summing up by a judge would demand a retrial.

'Also, with competent legal assistance, the possibility of others being involved would be subject to critical analysis of police evidence and the new trial would tease out all possibilities,' King said.

Assistant Tamworth police magistrate Dr Eustace Pratt was present at the double hanging in his official role as magistrate and medical consultant.

Dr Pratt's son and nephew also witnessed the executions — from a distance.

The doctor's grandson, retired Judge Eric Pratt QC, wrote in his 2013 book *Witnesses to History* that a group of children scaled a white box tree just outside the gaol wall.

Dr Pratt's nine-year-old son Clement and eleven-year-old nephew Basil watched proceedings with six of their mates.

The Commercial Bank building in Barraba was a single-storey structure built in the mid-1870s. Initial intentions were to use the building as a hotel.

Once completed, however, the building was leased to the Commercial Banking Company of Sydney and traded as a financial institution until 1898.

When the bank acquired freehold land nearby, new premises, with an adjoining residence, were constructed and officially opened in 1899. The same year, the existing building became the Victoria Hotel. A second floor was added ten years later.

Rod Fraser, the 26-year-old police constable who arrested Cummings days after McKay was murdered, spent his entire working life in the police force.

During a career spanning thirty-six years he was stationed at Parkes, Boggabri, Swamp Oak, Narrabri, Manilla, Somerton, Tamworth, Attunga, Warialda and Inverell.

Fraser died in 1940 and among his possessions was a ghoulish curiosity — the preserved hoof of stolen racehorse Derby, owned by Boggabri publican James Jones.

Cummings, a one-time jockey, rode Derby at Boggabri picnic races a couple of weeks before McKay was murdered. Derby was stolen from a paddock, used in the bank robbery, and callously destroyed afterwards.

After Cummings' and Lee's double execution, Jones presented Fraser with Derby's hoof — a macabre memento of the crime Constable Frazer helped solve.

CHAPTER 12

I'M GOING OUTSIDE TO GET SOME FRESH AIR

When stock agent Huntley James Forrester and grazier John Hubert McDonald were charged with conspiring to defraud the National Bank of Australia, their day in court was overshadowed by the sudden death of a key witness in the front yard of Moree courthouse.

Forrester was a larger than life character well known across the north-west of NSW. He was familiar with bush law courts, especially when money and matters of finance were chief concerns.

His sister, Agnes 'Topsy' Cornish, the wife of chemist Harold Cornish, was implicated in the crime as well.

Several other graziers charged with stealing sheep and altering brands, were also due to have appeals heard.

On the morning of Saturday 3 February 1934, Constable John Thomas Nolan, a key witness in all trials, boarded the train at Garah. There were a few loose ends to tie up at Moree courthouse before he gave evidence in several trials set down for the following week.

The journey was a perfect opportunity to relax and flick through his voluminous notes.

Nolan, forty-three, felt slightly off-colour and had been that way for a couple of days. Known widely as Jack, he joined the NSW police on 5 July 1917. He was appointed officer-in-charge at Garah police station in the mid-1920s after transferring from Gunnedah.

Back at Garah was Evelyn, his wife of eleven years, and their four young children.

Jack and Evelyn were married at Gunnedah in 1922. They relocated to Garah four years later where they soon became an integral part of the community.

Constable Nolan was president of the Garah Parents' and Citizens' Association and sat on the committees of numerous organisations in the district.

He was well known for his unfailing courtesy and participation in the development of the community.

For the past six months, he had worked closely with Sydney inspector Alf Small on a number of cases involving the theft of thousands of sheep across the region.

During the latter half of 1933, Nolan and Small formed a strong friendship as they trekked across north-western NSW and into Queensland, investigating large-scale stock theft.

Insp Small was called in to oversee inquiries by NSW police commissioner Walter Henry Childs.

Small, born in 1874, grew up on his family's farm at Gooloogong, between Cowra and Forbes in central NSW, where he earned a reputation as a recognised expert on livestock and horses. He possessed a remarkable knowledge of earmarks and brands.

Small was well known for his incredible memory and ability to store and recall evidence without needing notes or referring to documents.

After taking shipments of horses to Bombay and Cape Town in the late 1890s, Small served in the Boer War. He enlisted with the Natal Police Regiment as a trooper and was later awarded the Queen Victoria Medal.

He returned home at war's end and in 1902 joined the NSW police.

His first posting was Sunny Corner, between Lithgow and Bathurst in central-western NSW. Over the years he served at Molong, Windeyer, Hargraves, Trangie, Berrima and Narromine.

Small was the go-to man when livestock went missing, especially on a grand scale, and quickly rose to the rank of inspector, stationed at Clarence Street, Sydney.

Constable Nolan, too, was regarded an accomplished stockman and celebrated bushman. Garah locals claimed Nolan could tell a stolen wether simply by its gait.

Nolan and Small's collective knowledge and bush smarts made them a formidable team as they travelled thousands of miles in search of stolen sheep — and the thieves who took them.

In July 1933, they established a prolonged investigation at Welbondongah Station, near Garah, where 8000 head of sheep went missing. Graziers on both sides of the border emerged with stories to tell of stolen livestock.

The problem was so bad in southern Queensland, the Waggamba Shire Council on the Darling Downs pleaded with Queensland police commissioner William Ryan to increase police numbers to help combat rural crime.

They asked for at least one officer to be appointed full-time to investigate rampant stock theft.

Small and Nolan also discovered sheep-stealing had taken a new turn. The unlawful act, once romanticised by bush poets and fanciful storytellers, was now modernised.

In past years, sheep and cattle were rounded up by duffers on horseback and herded away. However, by the early 1930s, motor-lorries were the preferred mode of transport.

The trucks were quick, efficient and capable of accommodating several hundred head in a single hit.

For the next three months Insp Small and Constable Nolan recovered pilfered stock at Moree, Yetman, Hebel, Boggabilla, Inverell and Boomi in NSW, and Goondiwindi, Thallon and Nindigully in Queensland.

To underline the vast number of stock in the district at the time, no fewer than 872,548 sheep officially crossed the border bridge at Goondiwindi in either direction in the twelve months to 31 August 1933.

There were also 12,493 horses and 99,277 head of cattle recorded.

Constant vigilance on both sides of the border was necessary to prevent stolen livestock slipping through undetected.

By November 1933, Small and Nolan had recovered thousands of stolen sheep across a wide area, covering both states. They also unearthed cases where sheep of inferior breeding were being substituted with valuable pure-breds — woolly deceptions that could go undetected for months. Unregistered and crudely altered earmarks were being used to conceal true ownership.

But the biggest discovery was those allegedly responsible for at least some of the thefts were not the usual suspects in such crimes. Several graziers, one a justice of the peace, were dragged before the courts.

*   *   *

It is often jokingly said that the only time sheep-farmers eat their own mutton is when they dine at a neighbour's table.

The cheeky aphorism rang true in 1933 as Small and Nolan cast their net across the black soil plains, rounding up some unlikely suspects along the way.

In August, sixty-three-year-old George Allan Byron, from the property Watervale, near Moppin, was committed for trial at a special sitting of Moree petty sessions. He was charged with stealing fifty sheep from Midkin station. The sheep belonged to the New Zealand and Australian Land Company.

Police magistrate Arthur George Hardwick handled the case for the Crown.

Byron pleaded not guilty and reserved his defence.

However, he was sentenced to three months' hard labour on a charge of being in possession of a sheep carcase reasonably suspected of being stolen.

A charge of using unregistered premises as a slaughterhouse was dismissed and police withdrew charges of stealing sheep from graziers Allan Carrigan and Sidney Pitman. A charge of wilfully using his own brand to mark sheep not his own was also withdrawn.

Grazier Arthur Maurice Boulton pleaded guilty to a charge of using another person's earmark on his own sheep. He was fined £10.

Insp Small told Moree court, Boulton, an apparent repeat offender, claimed a thousand sheep on the property Wilby bearing his Tuncooey property earmark.

Small alleged the sheep belonged to Midkin station.

'I told the defendant it was not his earmark and that it was an easy matter to alter the Midkin earmark to his own,' Small said.

The inspector also located about two thousand sheep on Boulton's property bearing the Daley Estate earmark.

'The sheep were marked with the registered earmark of

John Thomas Daley, of Gravesend,' Insp Small said. 'The only difference between Boulton's and Daley's earmark is the latter is a notch and Boulton's is a slash. Daley's property is forty miles from Boulton's.'

Boulton was remanded on two charges of sheep-stealing — four being the property of the New Zealand and Australian Land Company and forty being the property of Edwin Jurd.

'We are undergoing further enquiries in the Boggabilla district that may implicate the defendant further,' Insp Small said.

On Tuesday 22 August, Boulton fronted Moree police court to face the sheep-stealing charges.

Insp Small told the court he had no evidence to offer and the charges were dismissed.

On Monday 11 September George Allan Byron appeared before Judge John Sydney James Clancy at Moree Quarter Sessions to answer sheep-stealing charges.

Byron, represented by Sydney barrister James Kinkead, was accused by police prosecutor Vernon Treatt of stealing thirty-six wethers and fourteen ewes from Midkin station.

The sheep at the centre of the allegation were yarded at the front of Moree courthouse and inspected closely by the twelve person jury.

The trial lasted two days. After retiring after lunch on 12 September and deliberating for nearly one-and-a-half hours, the jury returned a guilty verdict.

'However, we recommend mercy because of the accused's age,' jury foreman Percy Mellor told Judge Clancy.

Byron was called for sentencing the next morning, when a list of previous convictions was read to the court.

'I have decided to take into consideration the recommendation of the jury in fixing this sentence, otherwise I would deal more severely with the accused,' Judge Clancy said.

'However, the accused cannot put forward the plea the crime was committed through poverty or hunger. In view of the circumstances of this case, I cannot help but feel the stealing of sheep had been going on for a number of years.'

Judge Clancy convicted Byron to nine months' imprisonment with hard labour.

He also dismissed Byron's appeal against the three-month sentence handed down a few weeks earlier for being in possession of a sheep carcase reasonably suspected of being stolen.

'Both sentences will be served concurrently,' Judge Clancy ordered.

Two charges against grazier Carl Humphries for having in his possession sheep bearing unrecorded earmarks and sheep with altered earmarks were dismissed.

Charges of having an unrecorded earmark and failing to notify a wrongly branded sheep were withdrawn.

Small and Nolan also found eight sheep, allegedly stolen, on the property Glendello, near Millie.

The sheep belonged to grazier John Campbell, of Dunda-Lear station, near Wee Waa.

Gurley grazier Charles Edward Brazier was convicted of theft and placed on a twelve-month good behaviour bond.

Brazier's defence counsel, Richard John O'Halloran, appealed the decision, with an appeal hearing set for Moree Quarter Sessions on 5 February 1934.

John Hubert McDonald was charged with being in possession of 460 sheep bearing the earmark of Huntley James Forrester. McDonald was also charged with failing to notify the Pastures Protection Board or local police of the fact.

'When I went to the defendant's property he admitted the sheep were mortgaged to Dalgety and he intended swapping them for some merino sheep belonging to his son, John,' Insp Small told the court.

He alleged the earmarks were altered to make disposal easier and to stop Dalgety claiming them.

However, evidence proving the claim was not strong — a fact not lost on Insp Small.

The sheep were believed to be part of 8000 head stolen from Welbondongah Station.

During their investigation, Small and Nolan visited McDonald's property, Bonnie Doon, on the Moree-Boggabilla Road, and questioned him about the sheep.

Shearing was in full swing.

'Where did your son get these sheep?' Small asked.

McDonald refused to answer a policeman he barely knew. He'd heard a lot about Small, however. The bush telegraph travelled fast out Moppin way.

McDonald turned to Constable Nolan, the local officer trusted by the entire Garah community, and said: 'I am in trouble Jack. Shall I tell the truth?'

'Please do,' replied Nolan.

McDonald faced Small and said: 'My son got the sheep from Huntley Forrester.'

Small considered McDonald's response.

'I have been told Forrester has been trying to get his sisters and others to make a statutory declaration saying they sold you these sheep, but they refused to do so,' Small said.

'Evidently, Forrester is trying to do for you the same as you did for him in the cattle case at Boggabilla, when you gave him a crooked receipt for a carcase.'

About six months earlier, at Boggabilla police court, Forrester was charged with stealing a cow and calf belonging to Bill and Charles Thompson.

He was also charged with being in possession of five head of cattle reasonably suspected of being stolen.

Forrester was subsequently found not guilty of both charges after producing a bill of sale stating he purchased the cattle from John Hubert McDonald.

Insp Small clearly believed it was a case of mates looking after mates.

He alleged Forrester was now returning the favour after McDonald helped him beat the cattle-stealing rap six months earlier.

Small and Nolan stayed with the sheep overnight. Early the next morning McDonald arrived at their camp.

'I'm sorry; I told you a deliberate lie yesterday. My son did not get any sheep from Forrester. They were bred here on the place,' he told the inspector.

McDonald produced a document from his top pocket and handed it to Small.

'This is the earmark and brand of my sheep. These sheep were bred on the place. I gave my son some old ewes and he bred them up,' McDonald said.

The inspector shook his head.

McDonald was obviously unaware of Small's incredible eye for detail and vast experience with sheep, cattle and horses.

After all, McDonald smugly assumed, this was a Sydney copper standing before him.

Insp Small looked McDonald squarely in the eye.

'That is not right,' he said sternly.

'There are 250 two-tooth sheep and 250 four-tooth sheep

here. That is two drops, and they are ewes. You would require 500-600 ewes to produce 250 ewe lambs in one year. The wether section of the drop is missing, and there are some dry ewes and dead lambs. I would advise you to say no more for I now have decided to prosecute you for having sheep in your possession which might reasonably be suspected of having been stolen,' Small said. He didn't draw breath.

When Small finished his rapid-fire response, McDonald was speechless. He was flyblown.

Later at court, Insp Small detailed at great length the earmarks on the alleged stolen sheep and how such earmarks could be made.

'The earmarks on the sheep were not made with the pliers registered by John William McDonald,' Small said.

'His earmark is two parallelograms in the back of the registered ear, and is known as No.1303 on the list of authorised owners of sheep earmarks.'

Insp Small showed the court a card bearing the exact dimensions of the parallelograms.

'The defendant told me the sheep in the yard bore his brand and earmark and were all marked at Bonnie Doon, however every sheep in the yard bore an unrecorded earmark and, in some instances, an altered mark,' Small said.

'The marks were not all made with the pliers handed to me by John Hubert McDonald. At the same time, he told me the pliers belonged to his son.'

Small, an expert who wrote and delivered lectures on earmarking and branding, backed up his argument by demonstrating how the earmarks could have been made with two sets of pliers, both of which were produced as evidence.

'In some instances on some sheep, the earmark is like a fork at the back of the ear and an 'L' nearer the point of the ear,' Small said.

'At the time I inspected the sheep, John Hubert McDonald told me the pliers were given to him by Huntley James Forrester, the registered owner of earmark No.800, which is two Ls on the back of the registered ear.

'The fork pliers are capable of removing one of the Ls, leaving an altered earmark. In some cases, there appears to be two forks in the back of the ear but one of the forks is larger than the other. As the larger mark could not be made with the No.2 pliers, I consider that an alteration also,' Small said.

Counsel for the defence, Frederick Webb, disputed Small's allegations.

'Are you suggesting Huntley James Forrester's mark was on the sheep,' he asked the inspector.

'That is my suspicion,' Small replied.

'What is your suspicion worth?' asked Webb.

'It is worth a good deal when I am under oath,' Small responded.

'Did the woolly sheep have the defendant's tar brand?'

'Yes. Some of the sheep were shorn that day and many of them bore the tar brand of John William McDonald,' Small replied.

Webb challenged the evidence presented by the Crown, saying it did not prove the charge.

'There is no proof any sheep have been stolen from anywhere,' he said.

'Before my client is called upon to answer such a charge, there should be some proof sheep were actually stolen.'

McDonald, a justice of the peace and member of the local land board, maintained his stance the sheep were bred on his property. He repeated the claim he lied to Insp Small about his son, John, obtaining the sheep from Huntley Forrester.

'Those ewes were reared on the place and were the progeny of 350 ewes I gave my son,' he said.

'The reason I told the inspector the sheep were obtained from Forrester was because I did not want Dalgety's to think their mortgaged stock was being sold.'

McDonald said the sheep were, at the time, under offer to the Farmers' Relief Board.

The aim of the board, set up in 1932, was to provide assistance and relief to impoverished farmers.

The board's chief objective was to prevent creditors taking action against farmers on debts by means of stay orders. When such orders were issued, the board appointed a supervisor to administer farmers' affairs. The board was also empowered to provide carry-on finance to farmers.

McDonald's property was, at the time of going to court, placed under the Relief Act.

'I thought it better to lie to the board,' McDonald said.

He said he knew Huntley Forrester was an uncertificated bankrupt 'with not a feather to fly with'.

'It is not true Forrester received those sheep, or that they were stolen,' McDonald said.

McDonald also denied taking the sheep because Forrester could not hold them at his own place or because the sheep were obtained by Forrester 'under the lap' and being fed by McDonald.

It was also alleged McDonald's son, William, applied to register an earmark, with the registration papers witnessed by Forrester.

Another son, nineteen-year-old Alexander Charles

McDonald, said he helped his father mark the lambs with the pliers produced in court.

'These were the progeny of the ewes my father gave my brother. We marked them in about January 1931,' he said.

Insp Small questioned him about sheep movements and transportation.

'Had any sheep ever been taken away?' Small asked.

'Yes. I took some in a lorry to Camurra siding and put them on a train.'

Small asked where the truckload of sheep were sent, once loaded at Camurra siding.

'I do not know where they were going,' replied McDonald.

At this point, Magistrate Hardwick interrupted. He couldn't believe what he was hearing.

'Do you mean to tell me, you took sheep to Camurra, put them on a train and you did not know, or question, where they were going?' queried the magistrate.

'I do not know where they were going,' repeated McDonald's son.

Hardwick was flabbergasted. 'I put it to the witness that you never took sheep in a lorry anywhere at any time in your life.'

Alex McDonald was clearly anxious and undoubtedly nervous as he gave evidence. It all became too much for the teenager and he collapsed in the witness box.

Proceedings were adjourned for a few minutes to allow the witness to recover and compose himself.

'The witness is not well. I will not continue any further with his cross-examination,' Insp Small said.

When the court resumed on Thursday 24 August, Webb reiterated his argument there was not a shred of evidence to suggest the sheep were stolen.

'It is ridiculous to suggest the defendant should alter Forrester's mark to his son's when he could have disposed of the sheep quite easily while they were marked with Forrester's mark,' Webb said.

'My client is a man of good character, a Justice of the Peace, and a member of the local land board. He is one of the pioneers of the wheat-growing industry in the north-west.

'Mr McDonald's explanation about giving the sheep to his son is feasible. It is only the fact he is in financial difficulties. This caused him to tell an untruth to the police. The sheep belonged to his son and the fact the son's stock return showed no sheep was a mistake made when filling in the form,' Webb told the court.

Insp Small reiterated his belief McDonald and Forrester concocted the entire, elaborate story to dupe Dalgety &Co.

Magistrate Hardwick agreed.

'I am not satisfied the defendants came into the possession of the sheep in an honest manner,' he said.

'The elder McDonald admitted saying to Constable Nolan, who knew him well, "I'm in trouble Jack; should I tell the truth?" Would any man of intelligence say something like that?

'The next morning he said he told a deliberate lie. Does the defendant now expect me to accept him as a liar, or as a truthful man?'

The magistrate cast doubt on McDonald's claim he gave the sheep to his son.

'If he gave him old ewes when he said he did, I am satisfied they would not be living today. Further, I don't believe they could have given as progeny the number of ewes he said they did,' he said.

Magistrate Hardwick was convinced Huntley James

Forrester supplied the sheep.

'Why would he bring in Forrester's name, otherwise? He could have said he got them from Smith, Jones or Robinson, or any Tom, Dick or Harry,' he argued.

'I have no doubt Forrester's pliers made the marks on the sheep. Why were they used? Was it part of a scheme to prevent identification?

'I am satisfied the sheep were stolen and John Hubert McDonald was indeed the receiver, or 'fence'.

'I am not impressed by the evidence of the defendants and I cannot come to any other conclusion other than they failed to satisfy me as to how the sheep came into their possession.

'I consider the father the principal offender and he brought his two sons here to bolster up his cock-and-bull story.'

Hardwick sentenced McDonald to three months' hard labour.

'That is the maximum penalty I can hand down, but quite insufficient for such an offence,' he said.

McDonald's son, John William, was sentenced to one month in gaol, but released on a twelve-month good behaviour bond.

John Hubert McDonald was also fined £25 for having twenty sheep in his possession with unrecorded earmarks.

He appealed both decisions.

'I should have charged the defendant with five hundred sheep instead of twenty. There is no doubt the earmarks have been altered. There is no doubt they have been stolen,' Insp Small said.

Charges against McDonald for having in his possession sheep bearing defaced earmarks and failing to notify the proper authorities of the fact were withdrawn.

At the same sitting, grazier Jim Strang, of Mookoo station,

Garah, pleaded guilty to using an earmark registered to his father, Robert Strang, of Collareen Pastoral Company.

He told the court he planned to place the sheep with a mob belonging to his father and sell them as one lot.

Insp Small interjected.

'Graziers have been placing earmarks on the progeny of mortgaged sheep and selling such progeny secretly. That is what you were going to do, is it not?' Small suggested.

Strang's defence told the court their client wrote to Farmers' and Graziers' Company, outlining his intentions.

'I want to see that letter,' Magistrate Hardwick requested.

The letter, when produced, did not shed any light, nor add weight to Strang's argument.

He was fined £3.

William Taylor was fined £2 for using a brand not belonging to him as well as using an unrecorded earmark.

Ashley sheep owner and carrier Joseph William Morris was charged with being in possession of the carcase of a sheep reasonably suspected of being stolen.

Insp Small told the court he and Constable Nolan were in the Ashley district on another matter when they noticed smoke coming from the property of the accused.

'It was about five o'clock in the morning. When we saw the smoke, we rode over to investigate,' Small said.

It was alleged Morris scampered to his hut and locked himself inside when he saw Small and Nolan approaching.

'He refused to come out until a window was smashed. He then told me he was only just out of bed and dressing himself,' Small said.

The smoke spotted earlier was a sheep carcase burning in a fire near the accused's hut.

Morris was fined £5.

Proceedings against grazier and stock agent Huntley James Forrester were also commenced for aiding and abetting with regard to the earmarking of sheep mortgaged by John Hubert McDonald to Dalgety & Co.

He was remanded on £20 bail.

Further proceedings against Forrester were lodged by stock agent Thomas Elliott for obtaining £73 10s credit while an undischarged bankrupt.

John Hubert McDonald's appeal against a three months' gaol sentence was heard on Tuesday 12 September before Judge Clancy.

The mob of sheep were trotted out and yarded at the front of Moree Court House.

Defence lawyer, James Kinkead, as instructed by solicitor Frederick Webb, disputed Insp Small's claim the alleged sheep belonged to Welbondongah Station.

Small conceded Kinkead's claim held some credibility, casting question marks over the mob's true ownership.

Grazier Fred Kirkby and Moree Mayor Percy Mellor — the jury foreman in the case against grazier George Allan Byron the day before — submitted glowing references on behalf of McDonald.

'I have known Mr McDonald and his family for many years. His reputation in the district is very good and he has always been borne of excellent character,' Kirkby said.

Kirkby examined the sheep, yarded outside Moree courthouse, and was asked his expert opinion by Magistrate Hardwick.

'The sheep have been marked okay, but some of the marks were a little faulty,' Kirkby said.

Hardwick: 'Would you say the large mark could be made with one cut?'

Kirkby: 'I would say it could be done.'

Kinkead asked Kirkby about the sheep-breeding season and lambing.

'Is it extraordinary for a man to get 150 per cent of lambs in twelve months?'

'I do not think it would be extraordinary. No, not at all,' replied Kirkby.

Insp Small's case fell apart when Bill Bryant, Welbondongah station manager since the late 1800s, deposed the sheep grazing outside the courthouse were merinos and not the property of Welbondongah.

'Merino sheep have not been bred at Welbondongah for at least fourteen or fifteen years,' Bryant told the court.

Welbondongah station hand Jim Bateman corroborated Bryant's evidence.

'The sheep outside are not the property of Welbondongah,' he said.

Kinkead argued Crown evidence was not strong, which prompted Magistrate Hardwick's refusal in the lower court to issue an order for the return of the sheep.

Kinkead told Judge Clancy the only proof the sheep could have been stolen was because of 'certain marks' that had been explained by the McDonalds.

'Insp Small has admitted the sheep may not have been stolen from Welbondongah, and in support of that, there is the magistrate's refusal to make an order for the return of the sheep.'

Judge Clancy addressed defence counsel Kinkead.

'I agree with you the sheep have not been stolen from

Welbondongah, but how is that going to affect the case?' he
asked.

Kinkead pondered the question.

'Who are the sheep going to be returned to?' he asked the
judge.

'I do not know whether I will make an order at all,' Judge
Clancy told the court.

Kinkead stressed it was proven the sheep did not belong to
Welbondongah Station.

'This must go a long way to prove they belong to my clients,
the McDonald family,' Kinkead told Judge Clancy.

'There is not a tittle of evidence to say the sheep have been
stolen. Forrester was McDonald's agent, and he said he got
the sheep from Forrester simply because the stock was under
mortgage to Dalgety.'

Kinkead argued the altered earmarks had no bearing on
the case.

'Defaced or altered earmarks are a matter for prosecution
under the Pastures Protection Act,' he said.

'Having heard all the evidence, I would ask your Honour to
find there is no case to answer.'

Judge Clancy reserved his verdict until the following day. He
said additional evidence presented at the appeal hearing wasn't
presented at the lower court before Police Magistrate Hardwick.

'As a consequence, there were certain aspects of the case not
been placed before the magistrate,' Judge Clancy said.

'Having considered all the circumstances, I consider the
explanation in regard to the ownership of the sheep to be an
honest one.'

The judge said he was satisfied the earmarks were altered at
'some time by someone'.

'I am convinced of that — not only by Insp Small's evidence, but what I have seen myself.

'I take everything into consideration and accept the appellant's honesty.'

Judge Clancy refrained from elaborating further because charges of conspiracy against John Hubert McDonald and Huntley James Forrester were pending.

'I uphold the appeal and order the conviction be quashed.'

McDonald's appeal against the severity of a £25 fine for having a number of sheep in his possession with unrecorded earmarks — a charge to which he pleaded guilty — was held over until Moree Quarter Sessions on 5 February 1934.

On Wednesday 20 September 1933, McDonald and Forrester, and Forrester's sister Agnes Edith Cornish, were charged at Moree police court with having conspired together to defraud the National Bank of Australia of large sums of money.

Insp Small requested a remand until 4 October, on which date the accused were committed for trial.

Small gave detailed evidence regarding the sale of sheep earlier in the year to the Farmers' and Graziers' Co-Op as well as agents Badgery and Lumby.

'The sheep were consigned from Camurra station to Flemington on account of Agnes Edith Cornish (Forrester's sister) and were signed for at Camurra by Alexander McDonald, a son of one of the defendants here today,' Insp Small said.

When asked if the sheep in question were mortgaged to the National Bank of Australia and Dalgety & Co, McDonald, on the advice of his solicitor, remained silent.

The manager of the Moree branch of the National Bank, Ernest Marwood, said some of McDonald's sheep were under mortgage.

'There was no authority given for their disposal,' he told the court.

Dalgety & Co stock inspector Theodore Broughton gave similar evidence.

'My company held a mortgage over some of McDonald's sheep, and no authority was given for their disposal or sale,' he said.

The defendants pleaded not guilty and reserved their defence.

Counsel for the defence, Frederick Webb contended there was no evidence to connect Agnes Cornish with the charge.

'There is nothing to show she met McDonald or came in contact with him at all,' Webb argued.

McDonald and Forrester were each granted £80 bail and Cornish £40 bail.

*　*　*

On Saturday 3 February 1934, the train rattled its way from Garah to Moree.

Constable Nolan relaxed and reflected on the police work completed by himself and Insp Small during the previous six months.

The investigation had produced mixed results. Nolan and Small collected plenty of scalps, but only a few convictions.

They rounded up some improbable suspects and made numerous arrests. However, despite thoroughly investigating stock theft and suspected fraud across the black-soil plains of northern NSW and southern Queensland, only a handful of convictions stuck.

Again, Constable Nolan shifted in his seat. A bit of

indigestion, he figured, as he re-read his notes on the pending conspiracy trial of Huntley Forrester and John McDonald.

Nolan was collected at Moree railway station by Sgt Pat McGrath and taken to Moree courthouse for a pre-arranged meeting with relieving clerk of petty sessions, Harold Pelham.

However, when Nolan and McGrath arrived, Pelham was absent.

'We'll wait here for a little while. He can't be too far away,' McGrath told Nolan, who was still feeling ill.

'I'm going outside to get some fresh air. I'm not feeling well,' Nolan replied.

Nolan made his way to the rear of the courthouse, where he sat and rested for a few minutes.

Sgt McGrath returned to Moree police station, about half a block away on Frome Street.

At the rear of the courthouse, Nolan was feeling seriously ill.

He leaned forward and clutched his chest. The pain was sharp and spasms were frequent. They extended to his arm, neck and jaw.

The constable was nauseous and perspiring freely; a cold, clammy sweat stung his face and neck.

He could feel his heart beating rapidly — almost hear it — as the pressure against his chest and upper arm tightened. He knew exactly what was happening.

Nolan struggled to his feet and staggered to the front yard of the courthouse in search of help.

He fell to his knees in excruciating agony as the western sun bore down.

Passers-by rushed to his aid. Others hurried to the police station to alert officers and get medical help. A doctor was called and Sgt McGrath and Constable Lockhart sprinted up

Frome Street to the courthouse.

They were too late. Constable Nolan clutched his chest one last time as his heart gave out and he died in the arms of his colleagues.

Nolan's funeral was held two days later at St Francis Xavier's Catholic Church in west Moree, where members of the NSW police formed a guard of honour.

Uniformed policemen also acted as pallbearers and members of the legal fraternity, as well as representatives of local business houses and public bodies, joined hundreds of mourners from across the district.

The same day, John Hubert McDonald and Huntley James Forrester appeared at Moree Quarter Sessions before Judge John Clancy.

At 11 am the court was adjourned to allow police, court officials and the legal fraternity to attend Constable Nolan's funeral.

When the court resumed, Crown Prosecutor Vernon Treatt said the defendants were charged with conspiring to defraud the National Bank of Australia of large sums of money between 1 February and 31 March 1933.

'It is alleged McDonald mortgaged some sheep to the National Bank and then he and Forrester put their heads together and sold the sheep, despite the fact McDonald was not given permission to sell,' Treatt said.

Insp Small was cross-examined at length by defence counsel James Kinkead, who questioned the inspector's ability to commit vast amounts of information to memory.

'Have you told the court everything in connection with this case?' asked Kinkead.

'I cannot remember anything I have not told the court.'

'Did you request the National Bank to prosecute?' asked Kinkead.

'No.'

'Did you make a note of any conversations with McDonald?' asked Kinkead.

'No.'

'You have entrusted entirely to memory your conversations with McDonald,' probed Kinkead.

'Yes.'

'You have had many conversations with McDonald in connection with the sheep,' stated Kinkead.

'No, I would not say that,' Insp Small replied.

Kinkead asked Small whether he prosecuted McDonald and Forrester in connection with 150 head of Dorset Horn cross lambs.

'No, but I did in connection with 130 lambs,' replied Small.

Kinkead then implied Insp Small 'had it in' for James Hubert McDonald.

'How many times did you have McDonald appear at the court?' he asked the inspector.

'Three times,' Small replied.

'And now, this is the fourth time?'

'Yes,' Small replied.

'Did you take a statement from McDonald?'

'No, I am relying entirely on my memory as to what transpired between McDonald and me,' answered Small.

Further evidence was taken from stock and station agent Alexander Kimmorley, Farmers' and Graziers' Co-operative employees Charles Capper and Bertie Herrick, rail inspector Roger Sparkes, Badgery and Lumby employees Albert Morath and Reg Gordon, and National Bank Moree branch manager

Ernest Marwood.

After hearing lengthy arguments from crown prosecutor Vernon Treatt and defence lawyer James Kinkead, Judge Clancy held there was no case to answer.

'I direct the jury to acquit the accused,' he stated.

The jury formally returned a verdict of not guilty and McDonald and Forrester walked free.

At the same session, Charles Edgar Brazier appealed a 12-month good behaviour bond handed down the previous year and John Hubert McDonald appealed the £25 fine he copped for having a number of sheep in his possession with unrecorded earmarks.

McDonald pleaded guilty to the charge but appealed the severity of the fine.

Defence counsel James Kinkead argued his client already met considerable expense in respect to the same sheep.

'Under the circumstances, all of which are in regard to the same sheep, I believe a nominal fine would suffice,' he said.

After reviewing the evidence, Judge Clancy disagreed.

'The circumstances are not the same,' said the judge, and dismissed the appeal.

Richard John O'Halloran appeared for Charles Edgar Brazier, who appealed against a 12-month good behaviour bond.

O'Halloran cross-examined Insp Small at length.

'You are aware Mr Brazier is sixty-one years of age and bears an excellent character?' O'Halloran asked.

'Yes,' replied the inspector.

'Did Mr Brazier cause any trouble during the course of your investigation?' O'Halloran asked.

'No, he was very decent to me,' Small replied.

Again, Insp Small's testimony was given from evidence and

interviews committed to memory.

'Don't you ever take statements from people?' O'Halloran asked.

'Never in stock cases,' Small replied.

Brazier told the court at no stage did he claim the sheep as his own.

'They could have strayed on to my place, or drovers could have put them there. My neighbour, Henry Kempe, said there were some stragglers, seventeen in all. He said he mustered them and put them into the horse paddock with twenty-seven of his own sheep,' Brazier said.

Glowing character references from neighbours Glenn Cousins, Henry Kempe, Guy Wilson and Alf Campbell were given under oath.

'Mr Brazier is a man of excellent character and he has always handed back any of my sheep that stray on to his place,' Henry Kempe said.

Judge Clancy dismissed Brazier's appeal and the twelve-month good behaviour bond stood. However, the judge altered recognizance conditions from £60 to £30.

A few days later, a testimonial fund was opened for Constable Nolan's widow and four young children.

Garah locals attended a large public meeting in the village on 13 February to support the cause.

The *North West Champion* reported:

A largely attended meeting was held at Garah on Tuesday night, and it was decided, in recognition of the valuable services rendered by the late Constable Nolan to the town and district, to open a testimonial fund for his widow and children. Regret was expressed at the

sudden passing of this capable and popular officer, and
many eulogistic references were made to his unfailing
courtesy and consideration, and to the keen and active
part taken by him in all matters pertaining to the welfare
and advancement of the district.

Postscript:

The year after winding up investigations into stock theft across
north-western NSW and southern Queensland, celebrated
policeman Alf Small retired from the NSW police force to head
a private investigation unit for a group of farmers, graziers and
land-holders.

The former police inspector was given a roving commission
across a large area of NSW.

Small served in the police force for thirty-two years. During
that time, he received five meritorious service awards.

In 1906 he was lauded for saving wheat crops worth
thousands of pounds at Molong after digging a fire-break to
hold back a massive bushfire.

About ten years later, while still a constable stationed in
Sydney, he chased notorious stock and horse thief Jack Timmins
around the NSW countryside as well as other criminals, crooks
and reprobates.

Small was also responsible for finding controversial
racehorse Simba, a former New Zealand galloper used as the
pea in a failed ring-in scam at Flemington racecourse on 8 June
1931.

Simba, trained in Sydney, raced in the Rothsay Trial Stakes
at Flemington under the name Gagoola. However, the horse
was beaten a head by Stephanite when sensationally backed
from 20-1 into 7-4 favouritism.

Had Simba won, racing as Gagoola, the estimated collect was £15,000 — the equivalent of $1.4 million in new millennium dollars.

After a joint investigation by the Victorian Racing Club and Australian Jockey Club, Simba was disqualified from racing for life. The horse's owner, Sydney identity George Guest, was warned off for five years.

Afterwards, stewards were told the real Gagoola broke a leg and was subsequently destroyed. Stewards were shown a pile of burnt remains as evidence.

Meanwhile, Simba simply disappeared. The gelding was allegedly stolen from a set of Hyle Street stables at Sydney suburb Alexandria about five months after racing at Flemington.

Small, at the time a sergeant stationed at Redfern, was aware of the case but not assigned to it.

While driving through suburban Sydney to his home at Enfield late on 23 March 1932, he noticed a horse peering inquisitively over a fence near the corner of Rawson Street and George's River Road at Mascot.

The horse looked familiar. *Could it be?* he wondered.

Small stopped for a closer inspection and immediately recognised the horse as Simba.

He contacted owner George Guest and during the night they crept into the yard to confirm the horse's identity.

Simba, valued at £1500, was seized and forty-one-year-old horse-dealer Albert McCoy was charged with theft.

Privately, Alfred Robert Small was a troubled man harbouring deep-seated demons.

On 9 August 1938, four years after investigating one of the biggest stock theft cases seen in Australia, the highly-decorated former police inspector was found dead in his vehicle on a vacant block of land adjacent to Liverpool Road, near the Bankstown suburb of Lansdowne.

A garden hose, attached to the vehicle's exhaust pipe, was fed through the driver's side window.

Small, sixty-three, was found unconscious, slumped over the steering wheel.

Canterbury ambulance officers applied artificial respiration for nearly an hour but attempts to revive the celebrated former police officer failed.

Small left behind Kate, his wife of thirty-four years; daughter Beatrice and son Reg; and siblings John, Elizabeth, Charlotte, Rachel, Ruth, Thomas, Blanche and William, the latter an inspector at Burwood police division.

Newspapers reported Small was "deeply worried by ill-health".

Parramatta district coroner George Richard Williams found death was wilfully caused by "carbon monoxide poisoning by way of a garden hose from the exhaust of the motor car in which he was seated".

CHAPTER 13

YOU SHORT-CHANGED THE BOY!

Hot-headed black American Louis Williams had a habit of finding trouble wherever he went.

His short fuse and violent ways could ignite arguments and fights from seemingly trivial matters; he flew off the handle at the slightest provocation.

Numerous scars on his short, stocky body all had stories to tell. There was a long scar between his thumb and forefinger, another inside the corner of his left eye, others on his forearm, thigh and scalp, at least five across his back and a cluster of small scars below his chest.

Williams was born on 29 June 1862 in St Louis, Missouri, one year after the onset of the American Civil War — a time when four million of 32 million Americans were black slaves.

The war between the Union and Confederacy raged for more than four years until Confederate General Robert E Lee surrendered to Union General Ulysses S Grant at Appomattox Court House, Virginia, on 9 April 1865.

Slavery was effectively abolished and a new dawn beckoned. Louis Williams was then three years of age. But life wasn't easy by any stretch of the imagination.

From their early years, he and his brothers Lucas and Walter and their sister Belle worked on farms across Missouri alongside their father, Bill.

In 1880, when he was eighteen, Williams was employed by Missouri farmers Bill and Mary Foreman at Marion County,

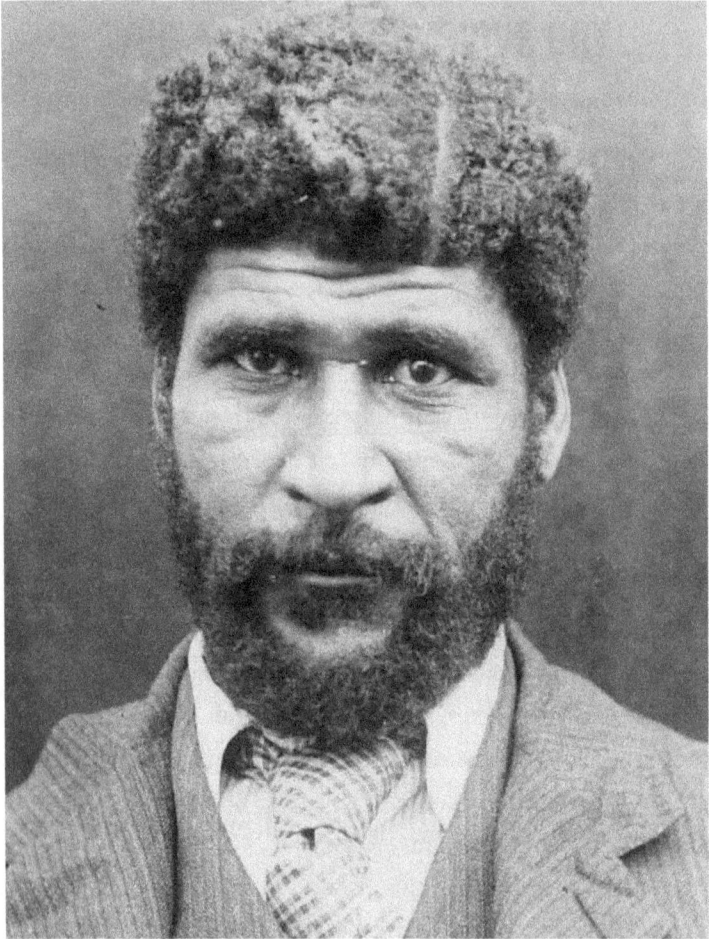

Louis Williams spent sixteen years behind bars for murdering Afghan hawker Abdullah 'Mullah' Mahomet at Berrigal Creek, near Terry Hie Hie, in 1904 (Image credit: Museums of History NSW — State Archives Collection)

known at the time as the 'breadbasket of Florida'.

Fruit, vegetables, cotton, rye, tobacco and forage crops were grown in abundance. And at some point, Williams fathered two children.

A few years later, Williams made the transition from land to ocean. He found work with the George E Plummer Shipping Company and began a new life on the high seas.

On 1 May 1898, he arrived in Australia on the clipper *John A Briggs* from Chemainus, British Columbia. The ship was loaded with Oregon timber.

Williams, aged thirty-five at the time, was an ordinary seaman and one of twenty crew members on board.

It is unclear whether he arrived with the intention of legally remaining in Australia, or jumped ship when the vessel dropped anchor off Mosman's Point.

The *John A Briggs* endured a rough, three-month voyage across the Pacific.

Midway through the trip the vessel encountered five days of treacherous storms. Thanks to skillful seamanship from Captain John Balch, and first and second mates Charles Johnson and George Stephenson, the vessel weathered the storms and arrived in Sydney mostly undamaged.

Captain Balch reported ship and crew encountered a violent cyclonic storm about a month into the voyage.

'The ship took a lot of water across the decks, but it was not sufficient enough to wash off the deck cargo,' Captain Balch said.

Maybe the rough weather and prospect of being shipwrecked or drowned was enough to convince Williams to remain in Australia, rather than risk the return voyage to the United States.

Regardless of his reasons for staying, Williams was on Australian soil when the *John A Briggs* left Sydney in July for Honolulu with more than 3000 tons of Wallarah coal on board.

* * *

Williams subsequently worked around NSW, generally as a labourer or farmhand.

On 30 December 1899, he appeared before police magistrate Joseph Francis Makinson at Dubbo police court, arrested for maliciously wounding a Chinese gardener, Chow Hing.

He had spent Christmas on remand following his arrest two weeks after an earlier violent altercation with Chow Hing at a market garden owned by Chinese immigrant, Jimmy Ah See.

Williams accused Chow Hing of telling lies about him and allegedly stabbed the gardener after challenging him to a fight and threatening to 'do for him, and every other Chinaman'.

Dr Edward Cuthbertson Hope told the court Chow Hing was hospitalised for four days after the attack.

'There was a wound to the abdomen and a second, more serious wound about half an inch deep under the lowest rib. The other wound was shallow and both wounds might have been made by a pocket knife. Both were true wounds,' Dr Hope told magistrate Makinson.

Ah See's twelve-year-old son, George, told the court he saw Williams on the street about half an hour after the alleged incident.

'I saw him (Williams) on the Commercial Bank corner about 8 pm and he told me he had had a fight down at the garden,' George Ah See said. 'He did not say with whom. He started sharpening a knife and said he would go down and kill the man when the knife was sharp enough. He said the knife was not sharp enough before, or he would have ripped the man open.'

Williams was committed for trial at the Dubbo quarter sessions, with bail set at £200.

* * *

He appeared before acting Justice Harris at Dubbo courthouse on 31 January 1900 when much of the evidence given at the police hearing was again presented.

After eighty minutes' deliberation, the jury found Williams guilty of maliciously wounding Chow Hing.

Judge Harris said he believed Williams was a hard-working man and generally inoffensive, especially when not under the influence of drink.

He then added, 'But I advise you to be more careful and, in particular, to get rid of your automatic knife which has a habit of going off and sticking in people. It might have stuck the Chinaman in the heart and killed him.'

Williams was sentenced to two months' hard labour in Dubbo Gaol.

* * *

By 1903 Williams was in north-western NSW and still in trouble with the law.

He was found guilty of false pretences at Boggabri in August and October of that year and sentenced to a month in gaol for each offence.

In June the following year Williams was camped along

Berrigal Creek, near Terry Hie Hie, about forty-five miles south-west of Warialda.

He had been in the area for about three weeks, making a living trapping and shooting possums for their fur.

Not far away, a group of Afghans had established a camp and trading store along the banks of Berrigal Creek. The store primarily serviced a nearby Aboriginal settlement and other smaller camps along the creek, as well as residents and landholders in Terry Hie Hie and surrounding districts.

The Afghans also trapped possums for additional income, as did others in the area.

Late on Sunday 12 June 1904, Williams sent twelve-year-old John Dillon across the creek to the Afghan camp to buy tobacco and matches from hawker Abdullah Mahomet, 25, widely known as 'Mullah'.

Williams gave Dillon instructions to buy sixpence worth of tobacco. However, the boy returned with a packet of matches and a half-cake of Yankee Doodle tobacco, valued at threepence, and one penny change.

Williams was furious. He took the tobacco and matches back to the Afghan camp and threw them at Mahomet.

'You short-changed the boy,' he accused.

'What is wrong? I gave the child what he asked for. I will not give you any more,' Mahomet replied.

A scuffle followed. Mahomet struck Williams with a tanning board but the stocky American overpowered the hawker, slamming him in the shoulder from behind and pushing him to the ground. Williams' hat was dislodged during the fracas.

Onlookers joined in, including hawkers Sedder Dene and Jokul Chung. The brawlers were quickly separated by Afghan community leader John Mahomet, Mullah Mahomet's cousin and employer.

A crowd gathered as calm was restored.

Sarah Harris, Maggie Williams, Henry Lock and Kate Cutmore, all from nearby settlements, were at the hawkers' camp buying goods and supplies, or simply socialising.

John Mahomet, better known as Charlie, admonished Williams.

'What do you want to row for?'

'That's my business. I will go fetch my gun,' threatened Williams. He quickly retreated to his camp on the opposite bank.

As the group dispersed, Mahomet resumed cleaning, tanning and packing possum skins.

Mahomet arrived in Australia from Afghanistan's capital Kabul about 1893 and worked for his cousin John, chiefly as a hawker.

Terry Hie Hie, and particularly tracts of land along Berrigal Creek, was a melting pot of cultures at the turn of the twentieth century. Camps dotted the landscape. An Aboriginal settlement on 120 acres was established by the Aboriginal Protection Board in the late 1880s and other micro-communities, made up of Afghan, Chinese and Indian immigrants, were nearby.

Williams was relatively new to the area. He was stopping at a camp set up by a fellow named George Hazzard. Part-Aboriginal Billy Buchan also lived at the camp.

Williams, with blood on his face from being struck with the tanning board, slumped down and stewed over what had happened.

Buchan, who witnessed the altercation across the creek minutes earlier, was washing clothes when Williams arrived.

A short while later Williams made his way back across

Berrigal Creek and hid behind an ironbark stump, about twenty yards from the hawkers' camp. He was armed with a double-barrelled shotgun; his short fuse primed and ready to again ignite.

John Mahomet noticed Williams and cautiously approached him.

'Don't shoot him; don't you be foolish,' he told Williams.

'I won't be foolish. All I want is my hat. Don't you come near me,' Williams replied.

Mahomet was about twenty-five yards away, kneeling over possum skins he had pegged out. He stood up as Williams approached.

Williams levelled the shotgun and blasted the Afghan hawker to the ground.

Mahomet buckled backwards in agony, clenching his stomach.

It was later claimed Mahomet was armed with a revolver and Williams acted in self-defence.

John Mahomet rushed to his badly injured cousin as Williams scampered back across Berrigal Creek.

'Lay me down on my side,' Mahomet whispered.

* * *

Meanwhile, Williams took flight. He jumped a fence near the Terry Hie Hie homestead and headed north-west towards the Queensland border, armed, dangerous and a wanted man.

A messenger was hastily sent to Terry Hie Hie police station and Constable John Moran arrived shortly afterwards.

Moran quickly assessed the situation. He instructed Sedder Dene and Jokul Chung to take Mahomet to Moree Hospital.

The only means of transport was a spring cart. Mahomet, badly wounded by shotgun blasts to the stomach and thighs, was delicately stretchered on to the cart and made as comfortable as possible.

The two hawkers and their seriously injured mate embarked on the thirty-five-mile journey to Moree, across rough ground and roadways. After about nine miles, Sedder Dene left Mahomet in the care of Chung and continued to Moree alone, arriving about 10.30 pm.

He went straight to Moree police station and informed Sgt William McCabe, who informed Dr Martin Magill.

Sedder Dene, Sgt McCabe and Dr Magill returned to Mahomet and Chung, meeting them about midnight.

Mahomet was in great pain. He was laid out on a spring cart on the side of the road in the middle of winter, vomiting and haemorrhaging.

Dr Magill stayed with Mahomet until dawn and, with Chung and Sedder Dene, conveyed the badly wounded Afghan to the hospital.

Mullah Mahomet clung to life for six days. However, at 2 pm on 18 June he succumbed to peritonitis caused by the shotgun wounds allegedly inflicted by Louis Williams.

A coronial inquest into the death of Mullah Mahomet was opened at Moree courthouse on 20 June before coroner Walterus Brown and a twelve-man jury.

John Mahomet told the inquest his cousin was shot by Williams after an argument over the purchase of tobacco and matches.

'Williams swore at Mullah. He rolled up his sleeves and punched Mullah on the back of the shoulder. Sedder Dene and some Chinamen were there as well,' Mahomet said.

'Mullah stooped down and picked up a piece of a box he was using for nailing skins on and hit the American. They got hold of one another and were struggling, about twenty-five yards away from my wagonette.

'Williams caught Mullah by the throat and threw him on the ground. The American got hold of the wood and hit Mullah with it three times on the shoulder while he was on the ground.'

Mahomet said he summoned Sedder Dene to help break up the fight and restore calm.

'I caught Mullah and Sedder Dene caught hold of the American from behind, and we parted them,' Mahomet said.

'I, or my countrymen, did not take any part in the fight. I am quite sure of that.'

Mahomet told the inquest Williams retreated to his camp but returned about ten minutes later, armed with a double-barrelled shotgun.

'He shot Mullah. I saw him fire the gun. He was about twenty-five yards away and brought the gun up quickly to his shoulder and fired. Mullah was standing up near the skins when he was shot,' Mahomet said.

'I never saw Williams again after that.'

Mahomet rushed to help his stricken cousin.

'I saw blood coming from Mullah; he was kneeling on one knee and was shot all around the stomach,' he told Coroner Brown.

Mahomet told the inquest he had known Williams for about two weeks. The American drifted between the Aboriginal settlement and camps along Berrigal Creek. 'He had no food and I fed him,' Mahomet said.

Jokul Chung, sworn in by the Hindu custom of kissing water,

corroborated John Mahomet's evidence.

Dr Magill deposed Mullah Mahomet was in a great deal of pain when he and Sedder Dene arrived.

'He was vomiting and there was some external haemorrhaging. The haemorrhaging had stopped when I arrived,' Dr Magill said.

'I waited there until daylight and then sent him on to Moree, where he was admitted to hospital.'

Hospital matron Trader stated Mahomet was admitted on Monday 13 June, the day after being shot.

'He was brought by two of his countrymen and was suffering from a severe wound.'

Mahomet was examined and treated by Dr William Tomlinson, who found eight puncture wounds on the left thigh, four on the right thigh and six on the wall of the stomach.

'Peritonitis set in,' Dr Tomlinson said.

'After admission, when the bowel was washed out in order to give a nutrient enema, some excrement was passed and in it was found one pellet of shot.

'He seemed to be doing pretty well until 16 June on which day his condition was not so good. After consultation with Dr Magill we informed the police he was probably in a dying condition. He sank further on 17 June and died on 18 June at 2 pm,' Dr Tomlinson said.

Dr Magill and Dr Tomlinson performed an autopsy that found numerous wounds over the abdomen, groin and thighs.

'There were seventeen or eighteen punctured perforations,' Dr Magill said.

An internal inspection revealed extensive leakage of blood into the abdominal cavity. The intestines were congested and showed signs of acute peritonitis. All other organs were in a healthy condition with the exception of the exterior portion of both lungs, which were adhering to the chest walls.

'In my opinion, death resulted from exhaustion and peritonitis caused by gunshot wounds,' Dr Magill said.

Billy Buchan told the inquest Williams returned to George Hazzard's camp after fighting with Mahomet.

'He got two cartridges and his gun and returned to Mullah's camp,' Buchan said.

'I went over to the Cutmore's place and we watched Williams shoot Mullah. He did not say he was going to shoot anyone when he was putting the cartridges in the gun.'

After a day and a half of evidence, the jury returned a verdict of wilful murder against Louis Williams, who remained at large. A warrant was issued for his arrest.

* * *

Williams didn't get far. On 24 June, less than a fortnight after fleeing Terry Hie Hie, he was arrested by Constable William Zendler on the Goodar Road near the property Welltown, just over the Queensland border, about twenty-five miles north-west of Goondiwindi.

He was taken to Goondiwindi police station and charged with the wilful murder of Abdullah 'Mullah' Mahomet at Berrigal Creek, Terry Hie Hie.

While held at Goondiwindi lock-up, Williams made a full confession.

However, he strenuously argued provocation and self-defence were the chief reasons he shot the Afghan hawker.

He claimed Mahomet was armed with a pistol — a claim later refuted by several witnesses.

Williams told Goondiwindi police Mahomet struck him with a board when he questioned the hawker about short-changing John Dillon.

'He grabbed a stick and hit me. He hit me three times and I ran. He threw the stick at me and hit me on the back,' Williams said.

'Then another Indian hawker (Sedder Dene) came running up and hit me. He caught me by my legs and they both threw me down. The one that had me down choked me until my tongue was out.

'Charlie (John Mahomet) told him to let me loose. Then I went over to my camp and came back with my gun, the one the constable found with me when arrested,' he told police.

He claimed the Afghan hawker was armed with a revolver.

Williams said Mullah Mahomet was kneeling down, cleaning possum skins when he returned to collect his hat, dislodged during the affray.

'He got up with a revolver in his left hand and pointed it towards me,' Williams claimed.

'I raised my gun and shot him.'

Constable John Moran was sent to Goondiwindi to formally identify Williams and escort the accused murderer back to Moree.

Williams was remanded at Moree police station and faced a committal hearing at Moree courthouse on 5 July before police magistrate Walterus Brown.

Williams repeated the confession he made at Goondiwindi lock-up and gave a detailed version of events leading up to the shooting.

He said Mullah Mahomet struck him with a stick 'as round as my wrist'.

'I threw up my left hand and ran, then went to my camp at Hazzard's. I stopped there a few minutes then went back to the Indians' camp. Charlie (John Mahomet) caught me by the right arm and was talking to me. He said something in his own language to the others and then Mullah Mahomet got a stick and hit me three times.

'Sedder Dene hit me in the face with his fist, grabbed me by my legs, and the two of them threw me down,' Williams claimed.

'Mullah was holding me and choking me, and Sedder Dene kicked me, once on the left side and once on my hip. Mullah choked me and hit me in the face. I wrestled until I got up on my feet. Charlie and another Indian came down and they made Sedder Dene turn me loose.'

Despite Williams' hot-tempered ways and short fuse, there was arguably an element of truth to his version of events.

Sarah Harris, Maggie Williams, John Dillon, Kate Cutmore and Henry Lock were called to give evidence. Harris was at the hawkers' camp when the melee occurred. She told the court Mahomet hit Williams with a stick after they argued about the tobacco.

'He flung (the stick) at him, but Williams ducked and it missed him,' Harris said.

'Sedder Dene came up and caught Williams around the legs and threw him; they all fell down. Two of them had him on the ground and jumped on him and kicked him.'

Williams, Dillon and Cutmore corroborated Harris's evidence.

Henry Lock's recollection of events was very similar to the previous witnesses. He added, 'Sedder Dene hit Williams two or three times with his fist and stood up and jobbed his foot on

Williams' face and neck two or three times. Charlie ran up and parted them.'

Lock said Williams went to his camp and fetched a gun then returned to the hawkers' camp.

'He stood talking to Charlie for a couple of minutes. Mullah was getting up and Williams fired at him very quickly. I saw Mullah fall, but I was too far away to see if he had anything in his hand,' Lock said.

Lock's testimony strengthened John Mahomet's claim Mullah was unarmed when shot by Williams.

Mahomet told the court there was only one revolver and two rifles at the hawkers' camp. He said the only time the firearms were produced was when a group of unarmed men suggested tracking Williams.

'They had no firearms to follow Williams. I showed them the revolver and guns but put them back immediately,' Mahomet said.

'Mullah had no revolver in his hand when he was shot. There was only one revolver in the camp and that was mine. It was in a box in the wagon.'

However, one of John Mahomet's workers, Ernie Duke, testified he saw a revolver at the camp on the afternoon of the shooting. 'It was lying alongside Mullah on some bags,' he said.

Jokul Chung told a different story. He said Mullah Mahomet was unarmed when shot by Williams.

'When the people came over after the shooting and asked for firearms, John Mahomet went to the wagon and brought out the guns and revolver and showed them. That was the first time they saw the revolver. John Mahomet put the revolver back again,' Chung testified.

The six-chambered revolver was presented as evidence.

Louis Williams was formally charged with murder and committed to stand trial at Tamworth Circuit Court before Justice Robert Darlow Pring on 11 October 1904.

* * *

Williams was defended by Alex Thompson, as instructed by Tamworth lawyer Fred Tribe.

In his opening address, crown prosecutor Cecil Alban White told jury members they should consider whether Williams was provoked and acted in self-defence. If so, this would reduce the charge to manslaughter.

Evidence from the coronial inquest and committal hearing was revisited.

Williams repeated his claim Mullah Mahomet was armed with a revolver when he returned to the hawkers' camp. Billy Buchan, also known as William Brennan, echoed his testimony regarding Williams' initial confrontation with Mahomet.

'Williams came running back to the camp; his face covered in blood. He got his shotgun and went in the direction of the Indian camp, putting a cartridge in the gun as he went along. When he got there he appeared to say something to Mullah Mahomet. When Mullah went to go in to his tent, Williams fired at him,' Buchan said.

Williams then raced back to his own camp.

'I suppose you'll be at my trial,' he said to Buchan.

'Maybe,' Buchan replied.

Debate, doubt and conflicting evidence over claims Mullah Mahomet was armed when shot by Williams hung heavily. Williams claimed Mahomet aimed a pistol at him in his left hand, yet John Mahomet and Jokul Chung claimed the hawker was right-handed.

'I've known Mullah Mahomet for three years. He is a right-handed man,' Chung said.

For Williams, his day in court was exactly that — one day.

After a trial lasting only a few hours, the jury found the black American guilty of the wilful murder of Afghan hawker Mullah Mahomet at Berrigal Creek, Terry Hie Hie, on Sunday 12 June 1904.

Justice Pring unhesitatingly handed down the death sentence.

The *Moree Gwydir Examiner and General Advertiser* reported: 'This will be a surprise to many in Moree as it was generally expected Williams would have been convicted of manslaughter or justifiable homicide.'

However, in a letter to the editor, a correspondent using the pseudonym Justitia, begged to differ:

I don't see how anyone acquainted with the particulars of the case could have been surprised. For my part, I should have been very much surprised had the jury brought in any other verdict. It was as clear a case as possibly could be of cold-blooded, premeditated murder.

Before the guilty verdict, a correspondent for the *Maitland Weekly Mercury* wrote:

From what I can gather, I think the evidence (is) very weak. I am informed the hawkers treated the accused very roughly.

349

Williams' protests that justice had not been served didn't fall on deaf ears. Two weeks later, the sentence was reconsidered at a meeting of the state executive council. NSW Premier Joseph Carruthers, acting on the recommendations of the council, commuted the sentence to penal servitude for life.

'Under the new prison regulations, this means the prisoner will have to serve a term of twenty years,' Premier Carruthers said.

The council adopted new regulations earlier in the year after reviewing a proposal by NSW Attorney-General Bernhard Ringrose Wise.

'It is unfair a 'life' prisoner with influential friends can get a portion of his sentence remitted, while the man without friends remains in gaol to the end of his days,' the Attorney-General told the council.

'It is also cruel when a man is sentenced to life he knows he is going to a living tomb.'

On 23 February 1904, the council adopted the new regulations, based on the English system. The new regulation stated:

> A life sentence, or a death sentence commuted to one of life, shall not be defined to mean a fixed period, but after serving twenty years the prisoner will be allowed to petition, upon the understanding this permission gives no promise of release at that date.
>
> If, at the date of conviction, the prisoner's expectation of life is less than twenty-two years, according to the Australian tables of mortality, the date when the prisoner may petition shall be fixed according to the scale given.
>
> In dealing with the petition the greatest weight will

be given to prisoner's conduct and industry in gaol, and for this purpose all marks and remissions should be credited to them in the gaol records. Any subsequent sentence imposed on the prisoner by any other court than the visiting justices of the gaol shall begin to take effect after the date at which the right is given to petition.

This regulation will not involve a limitation of, but will be an addition to, the right of a prisoner to petition under present regulations.

Williams was sent to Maitland Gaol and later transferred to Long Bay Gaol. He was released on 11 May 1920 and three days later applied for a new passport.

On 28 June, on the eve of his fifty-eighth birthday and nearly sixteen years to the day Mullah Mahomet was shot, Williams was granted new travel documents at the American Consulate in Sydney.

On 24 November 1920 he left Circular Quay on the SS *Ventura*, bound for the United States. He was one of five men listed on the ship's passenger manifest as 'held as aliens', strongly suggesting they were deportees.

Williams and fellow aliens Earl Cooke, William Furlong, Victor Kustel and Hyalmar Wigston arrived in San Francisco on 13 December.

Of the twenty-two years Williams was in Australia at least sixteen were spent behind bars for murdering Afghan hawker Abdullah 'Mullah' Mahomet at Berrigal Creek in 1904.

CHAPTER 14

I'VE GOT YOU NOW, YOU BASTARD

On a bright, sunny Saturday morning, Alf Merritt stepped out from the veranda of the Royal Hotel in Warialda and strolled nonchalantly down Hope Street.

He peered skyward. It was a beautiful day. Merritt was on his way to the nearby Lawson and Campbell's general store. He was pretty sure Messrs Lawson and Campbell would have what he needed.

Merritt was after a butcher's knife. He was told by Royal Hotel kitchenhand Martha Flannigan there were none on the premises when he went snooping around the pub kitchen earlier that morning.

'You'll have to go and buy one,' she told Merritt.

Hope Street was bustling with shoppers, in town for weekly supplies and convivial catchups and pop-ins. Merritt smiled at the men and tipped his hat to the women as he strolled along. He was known as 'Happy Jack' and it wasn't hard to figure out why.

It was 3 March 1888 and autumn had arrived on schedule and given the pioneering town an early blast of radiance. Nearly an inch of rain fell the previous week and there had been more than nine inches of rain so far that year; the district was waterlogged and wealthy.

Merritt, 31, strutted past the post office, bakery, the Bank of NSW, School of Arts, Commercial Bank and police station and stopped in front of Lawson and Campbell's store. He hitched his strides, adjusted his sleeves, and marched through the front door.

Tom Lawson peered up from the cash drawer. He looked Merritt up and down and stifled a frown. Lawson knew the type. This bloke was brash and full of confidence — a typical mug lair. Lawson's business partner, Bill Campbell, nodded accordingly.

Merritt, tall, tanned and rakish with short-cropped hair, well-trimmed beard and sharp hazel eyes, smiled at Lawson and Campbell.

'I'm looking at buying a knife; what do you have?'

Lawson forced a smile. 'We have several; exactly what type of knife are you looking for?'

'Something sharp,' replied Merritt.

Campbell sighed resignedly and left Lawson to deal with the newcomer.

Lawson opened a drawer from under the counter and showed Merritt a selection of knives and blades, including a carving knife and a table knife.

Merritt finally settled on a sheath knife. He ran his thumb along the blade but complained it was dull.

'It's not very sharp,' he said.

Campbell tersely offered to sharpen the blade on a stone.

Merritt watched closely as Campbell slowly ran the blade back and forth over the stone. After a few minutes, Campbell raised the knife and rotated it slowly. The blade glinted as it turned.

'Is that better?' There was a hint of irritation in his voice.

Merritt nodded. He paid for the knife and left the store.

Lawson and Campbell both frowned. They were glad to see the back of him. The stranger, a spiv good and proper, had been spotted about town over the past few days.

He and a mate, a young jockey that went by the name of James Osborne, were often seen walking the streets or regaling locals at the Royal Hotel, and sometimes at Tommy Howe's White Swan Hotel, where Osborne had enquired about work.

He made it known he was a horse trainer of considerable note. So far, no-one had rushed forward with a team of horses.

Osborne, also known as 'Jimmy the Stepper' or 'Fisk', lobbed in town with Merritt in late February. They had made their way over from Tamworth, stopping at Armidale and Inverell along the way.

They weren't exactly on the lam, but police had shown keen interest in the pair.

Newspapers later described Merritt as:

> A frequenter of race meetings and popular sports with those enticing little games to extract coins from the pockets of the unwary. He is fairly educated, but by no means an intelligent man, and used to pick up a living by attending race meetings as a spieler. He is naturally a quick-tempered man, and used to be a good-hearted one, who spent his money freely when he had any, but was not particular as to the means by which it was obtained.

Osborne was described as a 'somewhat unprincipled, roving youth, who used to drink and gamble as heavily as his means would permit'.

There was a matter of some counterfeit banknotes being passed around the district and the police at Tamworth reckoned Merritt and Osborne might know a thing or two about the matter.

They were seen cashing notes at George Pullman's Moonbi Inn, near Tamworth, but the money was clean.

In modern times, Merritt and Osborne would be 'persons of interest'. In outback NSW in the 1880s, they were two drifters under the watchful eye of the law.

They managed to stay one step ahead and made their way on foot to Warialda, nestled on Reedy Creek about fifteen miles from the Gwydir River, fifty-odd miles west of Inverell.

Warialda was gazetted as a town in 1855 and quickly became the business, legal and political hub of north-western NSW.

The Gwydir district, like the rest of Australia, experienced a boom during the 1880s. Stock returns in 1887 showed 7983 horses, 49,300 head of cattle and more than 890,000 sheep were in the region.

There was money to be had for a couple of silver-tongued sharpshooters like Merritt and Osborne.

* * *

Merritt lodged at the Royal Hotel, owned by Marion Horne, and Osborne found a room at the White Swan Hotel, where he made it known he knew a thing or two about racehorses.

They quickly ingratiated themselves in the community and came across as a likable pair, especially to the gullible and unwary.

Merritt was a racetrack urger and coat-tugger. He relied solely on his wits to make a living, by foul means or fair. Money meant nothing to him. One day he could be loaded with coin; the next, he might be penniless, destitute and wondering where his next meal was coming from.

He used the aliases John Key and John Darlington when a

quick name-change was needed — and that was often.

Merritt mixed with the rough end of society. Ten years earlier he was the victim of an attempted act of sodomy. The offender, Denis Connelly, 65, was sent to Berrima Gaol for twelve months.

Osborne, born in Maitland in 1863, was a disgraced jockey, barred from riding for allegedly pulling a horse called Nepicallina, a handy galloper on its day.

In his prime, Osborne, who also went by the name James Doherty, rode for some of the leading stables in Sydney and Melbourne including noted Randwick trainer Bill Forrester, who later trained Gaulus and The Grafter to finish first and second in the 1897 Melbourne Cup.

Osborne's time in the saddle was brief — increasing weight didn't help — but he rode his share of winners and was 'noticed' by owners and trainers.

At some point during his teens, Osborne served part of a boot-making apprenticeship under George Walmsley at Maitland and it was rumoured his father was a retired police officer living at Forest Lodge, in Sydney.

Now, at twenty-five, Osborne found himself in Warialda living a day-to-day existence with a like-minded rolling stone he hadn't known for very long.

Exactly when Jimmy the Stepper and Happy Jack teamed up is unclear, but they more than likely found each other on a racecourse. It was later established they operated a tipcart at Tamworth before making their way to Warialda. They also found something at Warialda that was right up their alley — a race meeting.

They missed the January races, but were sure there would be easy pickings at a double-header planned for April 4-5, especially now they had a couple of weeks up their sleeves to grease up the locals. After all, there was no shortage of hostelries in the district for Merritt and Osborne to 'work'.

Alex Allison ran the Stockman's Arms Hotel at Gunyerwarildi, about seventeen miles from Warialda; John Brodie had the Royal Oak Hotel; Bill Crane ran the Gwydir Arms Hotel; and Frank Leonard served weary travellers at the Little Plains Hotel on the Bingara Road, only a few miles out of Warialda.

* * *

Merritt and Osborne often quarrelled, sometimes violently, suggesting they hadn't known each other all that long. However, these blues, more than likely over money, were quickly resolved, or so it seemed.

It is unclear whether Merritt purchased the sheath knife because of a falling out with Osborne. He may have had revenge in mind — or self-preservation, perhaps.

It is patently clear however, he was armed with the knife when Osborne dropped by to see him at the Royal Hotel late on Saturday afternoon, 3 March, the same day Merritt bought the knife at Lawson and Campbell's general store.

Warialda locals told newspapers Merritt and Osborne were mates, but often argued. Journalists, using this local knowledge, speculated the pair were not cogging — hence Merritt's need to buy the knife. However, it is more than likely Merritt and Osborne hardly knew each other. They were probably drawn together by circumstances, rather than mateship.

About 5.30 pm, Osborne found Merritt on the hotel's upstairs veranda, playing with a caged parrot, the hotel pet. Merritt was

357

a little worse for wear as he had spent most of the afternoon downstairs in the saloon bar.

Maybe Osborne hoped to patch things up with his mate. He walked straight in to Merritt's quarters and made himself at home. Merritt turned and followed Osborne into the room. He pulled the door shut and calmly removed a piece of timber that propped up a sash window overlooking Hope Street. The window slid closed silently.

This seemingly harmless act suggested what happened next was premeditated.

Within seconds Merritt pounced. He violently pushed Osborne to the bed and straddled the much-smaller man.

'I've got you now, you bastard,' Merritt growled.

'Jack, don't,' pleaded Osborne.

Hotel employee Minnie Jenner was in the room next door, half-dressed. She heard a struggle and muffled voices through the paper-thin wall. She quickly finished dressing and raced to the hallway as Merritt plunged the sheath knife through Osborne's heart, killing him instantly.

The extra sharpening earlier that day at Lawson and Campbell's wasn't really necessary.

Jenner peered through the unlocked door and witnessed Merritt reef the knife from Osborne's heaving chest. The blade was embedded to the hilt. There was blood everywhere. Osborne's lifeless, piercing eyes stared at the ceiling. His arms lay limp by his side.

'I've got you at last, you little bastard, you're done for,' Merritt snarled again.

A blood-curdling scream poured from Jenner's lungs as she charged downstairs to raise the alarm.

By this time a crowd had gathered at the front of the hotel.

Merritt emerged from the building and threw the knife at the feet of Royal Hotel licensee Marion Horne.

'I've done for him; I've killed him,' Merritt told the crowd.

He slumped to his knees and waited for the law to arrive.

Warialda police were alerted and Inverell doctor, Thomas Lane, summoned.

Sgt Tom Clarke arrested Merritt and dragged him away. Later that evening Dr Lane conducted a post-mortem examination on Osborne's body.

'A single blow of the knife deeply penetrated the left ventricle of the heart. Death was instantaneous,' Dr Lane concluded.

Osborne had only two shillings to his name when murdered.

On the following Monday, 5 March, a coronial inquest was conducted in front of a big crowd of curious locals at Warialda Court House before William Vaughan May Cooke.

Police magistrate Cooke, appointed district coroner in 1886, found Osborne died from the 'effects of a wound unlawfully inflicted by one Alfred Merritt' and committed the accused to stand trial for wilful murder.

Merritt showed no sign of emotion throughout the inquest. However, he broke down and sobbed when Cooke announced his findings.

* * *

On Wednesday 12 April, Merritt faced Justice James Stephen at Tamworth circuit court. The case was adjourned until defence counsel could be arranged for the accused.

The following day Alexander Gordon arrived from Armidale to defend Merritt.

Crown prosecutor William Halse Rogers presented

cut-and-dried evidence, including testimony from Royal Hotel employees Martha Flannigan and Minnie Jenner as well as storekeeper Tom Lawson.

Flannigan testified that on the morning of the murder, Merritt asked to borrow a butcher's knife from the hotel kitchen. When told there were none on the premises, he went to Lawson and Campbell's store and bought a sheath knife. Lawson described Merritt as a fastidious customer who complained the knife wasn't sharp enough, so Campbell sharpened it on a rag-stone for him.

Minnie Jenner's damning evidence sealed Merritt's fate. She described how she witnessed Merritt extract the sheath knife from Osborne's chest. Newspapers reported:

> The chain of evidence establishing Merritt's guilt was so strong that his subsequent confession was not needed. The horrible fastidiousness the prisoner displayed in the selection of a suitable weapon, according to the evidence of the storekeeper Thomas Lawson, proves only too strongly the malicious aforethought of the cold-blooded murderer. Minnie Jenner heard the words and saw the deed. According to the evidence of this witness also, the removal of the stick from under the window in order to close it for the purpose of hiding his acts from prying eyes, also shows the premeditation of the deed.

Merritt remained calm throughout the day-long trial.

After hearing the evidence, including the fact Merritt had no prior convictions despite his alleged shady past, the jury found him guilty of wilful murder, adding a recommendation for mercy.

Justice Stephen addressed the accused: 'Is there any reason I should not pass the death sentence for this heinous crime?'

Merritt looked forlornly at the judge. His lips trembled.

'Drink was the cause of it all, Your Honour. But, as had been said in the past, there is no excuse for drink. I must have been literally mad to commit such a deed on a boy against whom I had no grudge,' Merritt whispered.

'Therefore, I ask for no mercy. I would willingly part with my own life if it could bring back the other. I am quite satisfied with the way I have been defended.'

Justice Stephen peered down at the accused. 'Alfred Merritt, I sentence you to be hanged by the neck until dead. May God have mercy on your soul.'

A single tear trickled down Merritt's cheek.

'I will try manfully to meet my God, Your Honour.'

Justice Stephen replied: 'I am sure you are regretful for what has happened and the crime you have been found guilty of committing. But in your case, repentance has come too late. In saying that, I will duly forward the recommendation of mercy to the right quarter.'

* * *

Merritt was placed in Darlinghurst Gaol to await the hangman's noose. Luck, however, was on his side.

On 8 May, the NSW Executive Council, under the presidency of Lieutenant-Governor Alfred Stephen, a cousin of Justice Stephen, commuted Merritt's death sentence to fourteen years' imprisonment.

Merritt was taken from Darlinghurst Gaol and placed in Berrima Gaol.

In 1892 he was moved to Goulburn Gaol and the following year transferred to Maitland Gaol. By September 1897 he was in Armidale Gaol.

Merritt was a model prisoner. He played by the rules and kept his nose clean and mouth shut.

NSW prisons' comptroller-general Frederick Neitenstein discharged Merritt from Armidale Gaol on 13 April 1898, adopting an early release scheme for good behaviour he developed the previous year.

Neitenstein was regarded as prudish and stand-offish, but his prison reforms were ground-breaking, if not unorthodox. He cultivated many ideas from juvenile reform policies he established when captain of the nautical school ship, *Vernon*, a floating prison for destitute and wayward children established under the Reformatory Schools Act.

Neitenstein's reforms included marking and grading systems, and physical exercise programmes. His changes, considered radical by some observers, aimed to reduce inmate populations across gaols in NSW.

Merritt was discharged by special remission — ten years to the day the one-time racetrack spiv was convicted of murdering former jockey James Osborne at the Royal Hotel in Warialda in 1888.

Osborne is buried at Warialda's Pioneer Cemetery.

CHAPTER 15

THE LIFE AND TIMES OF JACK TIMMINS

Jack Timmins had a knack for racking up acquittals.

It seems nothing ever stuck when the grandson of convicts James Timmins and Ann Baldwin was dragged before the courts.

Had he been around in the twenty-first century, the moniker 'Teflon Jack' would've suited nicely.

Timmins was a notorious sheep, cattle and horse thief. He terrorised stockowners and landholders across north-western NSW and southern Queensland during the late 1800s and well into the 1900s.

But despite a wing of charges against him over six or seven decades, including one of attempted murder, very few convictions were handed down.

During his ninety years, Timmins served a total of eighteen years behind bars for various crimes and bad behaviour, yet he also logged at least eight acquittals.

Even at age seventy-one, he was found guilty of stealing cattle in Queensland. However, a kindly judge at Dalby courthouse refused to slot him.

Timmins, a slightly built man standing a tick over five feet six inches, was born at Richmond, NSW, on 18 May 1863, one of ten children to Jack Timmins the elder and Elizabeth Scott.

Jack Snr passed away in 1911 at the age of ninety-five. He was a pioneer of the Windsor district and widely recognised as the first drover to take cattle across the Blue Mountains.

Jack Timmins served a total of eighteen years behind bars for various crimes, yet also racked up at least eight acquittals during his ninety years (Image credit: Museums of History NSW — State Archives Collection)

Like his old man, Jack Jnr was an exceptional horseman but his skills were generally used for all the wrong reasons.

At the crack of dawn on Saturday 29 December 1917, Constable Alf Small, from Sydney, and Constable Denis Hayes, 34, from Goodooga, arrived at Timmins' Scrubby Park home, a couple of miles from Collarenebri.

They had a warrant to search the property for a mob of rams allegedly stolen from brothers John and Colin Sinclair at Collymongle station.

Timmins, 54, was polite and obliging when questioned by Small.

'Are you busy today, Jack?' Small asked.

'No, not at all, officer. We've got some fencing planned for later but that's about it,' Timmins smiled.

'I have a warrant authorising us to search your paddock for stolen sheep.'

Constable Small read the warrant. Timmins listened offhandedly. This wasn't the first time he'd heard such a decree. When Small finished, Timmins remained silent. There was the hint of an eye-roll. He watched the constable fold the warrant — known as a 'blue paper' — and tuck it inside his coat pocket.

'Have you any sheep in your paddock that do not belong to you?' asked Small.

'I might have . . . some rams, maybe. Wait 'til I get my horse and I'll be with you,' Timmins replied.

Timmins' nephew, Jack Lawler, and Paddy Stafford, a local carrier and tank sinker, were a distance away chopping firewood. They watched intently; they were camped at Scrubby Park ready to start fencing with Timmins that day.

Timmins instructed Lawler to collect his horse. He then

returned to the house to retrieve an oil can from the kitchen and check on the breakfast his wife Alice was preparing.

They would be away fencing for a few days and Timmins wanted to oil his rifle in case they saw a rabbit. There were also foxes getting among the sheep and it would pay to be armed if they chanced upon any.

Constable Small also reckoned there was a fox among the sheep — a fox bearing the surname of Timmins.

Jack looked grimly at Alice.

'We might have some trouble on our hands. It's that bloody Small, the bastard from Sydney,' he said.

Alice, 34, harrumphed as she flipped eggs on the fuel stove. Police drop-ins were nothing new. The moment a crime was committed within fifty miles of Collarenebri or stock went missing, the local troopers would invariably drop by Scrubby Park for a look-see.

Alice married Jack in 1912. They had seven children during the course of their marriage: sons George (1910), John (1912), James (1914) and David (1917), and daughters Jessie (1916), Bessie (1919) and May (1924).

Long-suffering Alice thought her husband would've — or should've — grown up by now.

'You can bloody well deal with them,' she said angrily. A sweltering kitchen in the middle of a western NSW summer didn't help matters. Alice was livid.

* * *

Outside, Small and Hayes were talking to Stafford at the wood heap.

Small had dismounted; Hayes was still in the saddle. They

watched Timmins leave the house and amble over to a nearby shed. He was carrying a small, square-shaped object.

Hayes clicked the reins and trotted towards the shed. A few seconds later all hell broke loose.

Witness accounts of what happened next varied. According to police testimony, Timmins emerged from the shed armed with a .32-calibre Winchester repeating rifle.

He allegedly raised the weapon to his shoulder and pointed it directly at Hayes, who was less than twenty feet away.

The shocked constable dropped the reins and covered his face. A single gunshot rang through the morning stillness.

The bullet allegedly pierced Hayes' helmet. He fell from the saddle, unaware the bullet passed so dangerously close. Dazed and bewildered, he scrambled to his feet and rushed at Timmins.

Small raced across to help the constable. Hayes grabbed Timmins by the throat as Small crash-tackled him. The rifle was knocked from Timmins' hand and went flying.

All three fell to the ground in a screaming, punching, kicking heap. Small and Hayes towered over Timmins, who weighed in at around nine stone.

Timmins struggled violently. He bit, kicked and swore at Small and Hayes. They tried desperately to restrain him. For a little bloke, Timmins put up one hell of a fight.

Paddy Stafford and Jack Lawler cautiously approached the three men. They weren't quite sure what to do. If they interfered, they'd be in just as much strife as Timmins.

'Paddy, Jack, shoot the mongrels; kill them,' roared Timmins.

Stafford pleaded with Small. 'Don't hurt him; let me take him; I'll take him away.'

'Help me hold him,' Small retorted.

Stafford shook his head despairingly. 'No, I can't do that. I'll not interfere.'

Alice Timmins ran from the kitchen. All thoughts of a pleasant Saturday morning breakfast were long forgotten.

'Don't hurt him; don't shoot,' she screamed.

The rifle was lying on the ground a few yards away.

Stafford pointed to the rifle. 'Take the rifle away, Mrs Timmins.'

Hayes beat her to it, however. He snatched the rifle from the ground and slogged Timmins across the back of the head with it.

'Now, stay back the lot of you,' Hayes yelled.

The whack to the head dazed Timmins. The wound seeped blood. His struggles slowed somewhat and he slumped to the ground. Hayes retrieved a stirrup leather from his saddle and began tying Timmins' legs together.

Timmins slowly calmed down. Hayes relaxed the stirrup leather. He and Small helped Timmins to his feet.

'Why did you shoot at Hayes?' Small asked.

'You two drove me to it,' replied Timmins.

'We have no choice but to charge you with attempted murder.'

Timmins opened his waistcoat. 'Why don't you shoot me now and get it over and done with.'

His head was bleeding, but not badly. Small told Alice a doctor would attend to her husband once they got back to Collarenebri.

Small and Hayes handcuffed Timmins and made their way on foot to Collarenebri, leading their horses.

As they walked along, Small noticed what appeared to be a bullet hole in the constable's helmet.

'My God, Hayes, the bullet went through your hat,' he said.

Hayes removed the helmet and stared at it. He showed

Timmins the headpiece. 'How in the hell did you miss me,' he asked.

'I'll tell you that in court,' Timmins replied.

The trio arrived at Collarenebri and Timmins was thrown in the lock-up. A doctor was summoned to treat his wounds.

Small joined the NSW police force in 1902. He'd been a first -class constable for the past eight years but was earmarked for promotion to the rank of sergeant in three days' time.

Small closely studied the rifle Timmins used in the attack. The firearm was quite old but recently oiled.

'This must have been oiled this morning; the oil is quite fresh,' he remarked.

Around 3.30 pm Small and Hayes returned to Scrubby Park to gather more evidence.

They found a spent cartridge near the shed. Small sniffed the shell.

'It's obvious this was recently discharged; I can still smell the powder,' Small said.

Small and Hayes entered the shed and found more spent cartridges as well as ammunition in an old tin can.

Timmins was kept at Collarenebri lock-up for the next fortnight and was attended to daily by a doctor.

An application for bail at Narrabri police court on Monday 14 January 1918, was refused by police magistrate George Meeson. Timmins was remanded for a further eight days.

Bail was again refused by Supreme Court Judge Phillip Street.

On Saturday 2 March 1918, Timmins appeared before Judge Hugh Montgomerie Hamilton at Gunnedah quarter sessions, charged with 'that he did on 29 December 1917, at Scrubby Park, shoot at Denis Hayes, with intent to murder'.

The case for the Crown was handled by prosecutor Wilfred Blackett, assisted by Robert Jardine Browning. Timmins was defended by James Conley Gannon and Sidney Mack, as instructed by Narrabri solicitor John McDonald.

Timmins claimed the rifle 'went off' when he accidentally dropped it as he exited the shed.

'I'd just given it a quick clean with some oil,' he told prosecutor Browning.

Timmins claimed a similar accident happened the previous week when he and Paddy Stafford were preparing to go fox shooting.

'When I went to put the rifle down it went off and nearly shot Paddy in the leg,' Timmins said.

Alice Timmins claimed Constable Hayes levelled the rifle at her when she begged the officer not to shoot her husband.

'Before he raised the rifle he was doing something with the lever,' Alice deposed.

'I asked both officers to let me bathe my husband's wounds but they refused. When they took my husband away, they were dragging him along. His elbows were strapped behind his back, but his hands were free.'

Jack Lawler corroborated Alice's evidence.

'Hayes worked the rifle lever and pointed the rifle at Mrs Timmins. She came out of the kitchen at about the same time as Paddy Stafford came from the wood heap. Mrs Timmins cried out, "don't shoot me",' Lawler said.

Lawler claimed Hayes then said to Stafford: 'Help me, or I'll shoot you down.'

Lawler said he saw the rifle fall before discharging.

'When the rifle was falling to the ground Timmins was standing alongside a meat block, close to the door of the shed.

The rifle must have fired itself; it must have fallen outside the store door. I don't know how the rifle went off, but I don't think Timmins had anything to do with it. He did not pick up the rifle and point it,' Lawler said.

Sgt Small and Constable Hayes refuted the evidence given by Alice Timmins and Jack Lawler.

'I did not see Hayes point a rifle at Mrs Timmins, nor did he point the rifle at Stafford and threaten to shoot him,' Small told defence counsel Gannon.

Hayes gave similar evidence. 'I did not point the rifle at Mrs Timmins or Stafford; I only asked Mrs Timmins to stay back.'

Evidence given by both police officers was at complete odds with sworn testimony given by Jack and Alice Timmins, and Paddy Stafford and Jack Lawler.

The jury retired at 5 pm and did not reach a verdict by 10 pm. They were sequestered overnight and detained the following day, Sunday. On Monday, jury foreman George Bussell told Judge Hamilton the jury could not agree.

'And there is no chance of everyone agreeing any time soon,' Bussell said.

Judge Hamilton had no choice but to dismiss the jury and commit Timmins for retrial at a court determined by NSW Attorney General David Hall.

*   *   *

Timmins reappeared at Maitland circuit court on 26 April before Justice Robert Darlow Pring — the same judge that slotted Timmins for seven years in 1905.

Timmins was defended by Richard Windeyer and Sidney

Mack as instructed by Narrabri solicitor John McDonald and Walter Enright, from Maitland.

Not surprisingly, the accused pleaded not guilty.

Francis Stewart Boyce, famous for appearing as defence counsel for convicted murderer Jimmy Governor eighteen years earlier, appeared for the Crown.

Timmins didn't falter from the evidence he gave at the first trial.

'My missus was setting the table. I reached up to the shelf to get a tin of oil to clean the rifle so I would not keep him (Sgt Small) after breakfast,' Timmins told the court.

After chatting with his wife, Timmins left the house and made his way to a nearby shed.

Sgt Small deposed: 'I walked to where Paddy Stafford was cutting wood at the wood heap. Constable Hayes rode to the same spot with me. I entered into a conversation with Stafford. I saw the accused coming from the residence to a shed behind it.'

Small said Timmins was carrying a small article. He could not quite make out what it was. However, it 'was not a gun' but possibly the oil can Timmins collected from the house.

Constable Hayes rode to the north-eastern corner of the shed. Sgt Small was speaking with Stafford when a rifle shot rang out.

'I heard the report of the rifle and I immediately looked round and saw Constable Hayes falling from his horse on the off side,' Small said.

Small testified he witnessed Timmins come forward with 'one hand on the lever and the other on the rifle'.

The rifle was produced in court. 'It is a repeating rifle,' Small said. 'The barrel was facing downwards. When I saw him (Timmins), he was about five or six feet from Hayes, a very short distance.'

Although dazed from the fall and near-miss, Hayes sprang to his feet. With Small's help, he restrained Timmins.

'Hayes fell from his horse and rushed at me; he got me by the throat,' Timmins claimed.

The rifle was knocked from Timmins' hands in the struggle and quickly retrieved by Hayes.

'He continued to struggle and bit my arms and kicked. He drew blood from both my arms. I had my coat and shirt on,' Small told the court.

Hayes struck Timmins with the butt of the rifle. 'I thought it was necessary to club the accused with the rifle. I hit him only once.'

Timmins testified the rifle accidentally discharged when he fetched it from a high shelf in order to oil it. 'It went off. The shooting was accidental,' he said.

The bullet allegedly hit Constable Hayes' helmet, dislodging him from his horse.

The accused's nephew, Jack Lawler, stated when he heard the report of the rifle and looked round, he noticed his uncle entering the shed door, with the rifle falling to the ground.

Paddy Stafford said Constable Hayes threatened to shoot him if he didn't help restrain Timmins.

'I was an onlooker. I did not see that it was necessary for me to help. I reckon two police officers ought to have been quite capable of handling the accused,' Stafford said. 'I was standing by when Hayes put the rifle on me and said, "If you don't help, I will shoot you down". Hayes also pointed the rifle at Mrs Timmins and told her he would shoot her down as well. I am quite certain of that.'

Alice Timmins and Jack Lawler corroborated Stafford's testimony.

Timmins alleged he was treated poorly by Small and Hayes. 'My missus came out with a dish of water to wash my head but Small would not let her. He made me walk a mile and a half to town. I wanted to lie down on the road half a dozen or a dozen times but they would not let me. They never spoke about the hat being shot at, as we went along, or anything like that.'

The prosecution's case was thrown on its ear when defence counsel Windeyer and Mack called in expert witness, Lieutenant James Forbes Fletcher.

Fletcher was regarded an expert in musketry and had recently returned from active duty in France and Gallipoli.

'I looked at the cut in that helmet carefully. From my experience in musketry I would say that cut was not caused by a bullet, certainly not,' Fletcher told the court.

'It would not be caused by a bullet — not a direct bullet. It could not be hit by a bullet at all. I could understand that kind of thing in the western front with little bits of shrapnel flying about.'

Fletcher also debunked Sgt Small's claim he could tell how long a shell had been fired simply by its smell. 'It is perfectly ludicrous to say you would notice any smell afterwards. You might two or three seconds afterwards, but not after a time,' he said.

The prosecution was left scrambling. Timmins held back a smile.

At 10 am the following day, 27 April the jury returned a verdict of not guilty. Timmins, grinning from ear to ear, walked free.

The following month Timmins was also found not guilty of

stealing the mob of rams belonging to the Sinclair brothers —
seventeen in total — from Collymongle station.

*   *   *

Jack Timmins celebrated a similar, not-guilty incident thirty-
odd years earlier.

On 8 May 1885 Jack and his sister, Laura, fronted Judge
Charles Murray at Moree Quarter Sessions.

They were charged with stealing 150 head of cattle belonging
to Pitt, Son and Badgery from Benaba station, about twenty
miles from Mungindi, in September the previous year.

A Benaba station stockman was riding the plains on the
lookout for stray horses when he spotted a mob of cattle being
herded toward Mogil Mogil.

Police were alerted and Mungindi constable John Crawley,
assisted by three stockmen and two trackers, followed the cattle
tracks for forty miles to Collymongle station, where Jack and
Laura's father, also named Jack, had a selection.

Police told the court eight wire fences were cut along the
way.

The tracking party found the missing mob of cattle about
two miles from Collymongle.

When Jack and Laura realised police were hot on their tail,
they took off. After a three-mile chase, the Timmins siblings
were rounded up and arrested.

'It's a hard thing and a sad state of affairs when a man
and his sister can't go out for a ride on a Sunday without
being arrested for cattle stealing,' Jack allegedly muttered
to Constable Crawley.

Jack denied all knowledge of the cattle. He and his sister,

both represented by solicitor David Buchanan, pleaded not guilty.

The trial lasted nearly two days. After six hours' deliberation, the jury acquitted Laura Timmins.

They failed to agree on a verdict for Jack and he was discharged. He was also acquitted of stealing the horse his sister was riding when both were arrested.

*　*　*

Jack, his brother Henry and accomplices John Cameron and Charles Perry were not so lucky two years later at Walgett quarter sessions before Judge Alfred Paxton Backhouse when charged with cattle-stealing.

Henry was charged with receiving stolen cattle and copped three years and six months at Maitland Gaol.

Jack, only twenty-four at the time, was sent to Goulburn Gaol for seven years for the theft of the cattle.

Cameron was found guilty of larceny — he stole a saddle — and given eighteen months in Walgett Gaol. Perry was acquitted of horse-stealing.

An extra six months was tacked on to Jack's sentence when he was caught trying to file through bars on his prison cell window.

Walgett Court was told: 'These men and some other associates have been the terror of the countryside around the upper Barwon and Moree districts. John (Jack) Timmins is said to have been eight times before a jury and never before convicted.'

This time, however, the evidence supporting the Crown was overwhelming. Newspapers reported:

The unassailable manner in which Sub-Insp Cameron supported the charge, left the jury no alternative but to convict. Magistrates, managers, stockmen, free selectors, and police were all marshalled to tell a plain and unvarnished tale, and as each witness wove the web of evidence around the misguided and unhappy-looking man as he stood in the dock, his face became the picture of despair, while hope seemed to sink within him.

Timmins was transferred to Trial Bay Prison and walked free on 1 April 1893. He managed to keep his nose clean for a few years but by 1896 was wanted in two colonies on suspicion of cattle stealing.

An accomplice, James Read, was quickly rounded up by troopers but Timmins proved elusive.

Newspapers widely reported Timmins was 'splendidly mounted':

Timmins is armed with a sixteen-chamber Winchester rifle and two first-class revolvers. He has let it be known his motto is 'no surrender'. As the bushranger has (already) served seven years in Goulburn gaol and has a reputation to sustain amongst his criminal associates, a new menace to travellers by the highway has risen. As yet, since Timmins has not shed human blood, he is not a positively desperate man, but we doubt not that travellers up Moree way would rather be well-pleased to hear a dangerous character is once more safe and snug under lock and key.

Timmins was eventually captured. In November 1899 at Forbes

Quarter Sessions, under the alias William O'Donnell, he was found guilty of two counts of larceny (wool- and skin-stealing), one count of horse-stealing and one count of receiving.

Acting Judge Herbert Harris sentenced Timmins to two and a half years' imprisonment on each charge, to be served concurrently.

Timmins was released from Bathurst Gaol on 17 December 1901 just in time for Christmas.

*   *   *

On 26 May 1902 Timmins escaped from police at Young while under arrest for stealing a horse belonging to John Farrell at Burrowa. Timmins was on the run for nearly three years.

Aged thirty-nine at the time, Timmins was described as five feet, six-and-a-half inches tall, with dark-brown hair, dark moustache, short side-whiskers, light brown eyes, crooked nose, sallow complexion and sharp features.

He was dressed in a dark suit, dirty brown soft felt hat and lace-up boots 'burst at the toes'.

Timmins was rounded up on 19 March 1905 by Constable John Sheridan at Mogil Mogil, twenty miles from Collarenebri.

He told Sheridan he escaped custody while helping a constable feed horses. He explained: 'When the constable went into the feed room, he left the key hanging on the wall near the door. What is a man supposed to do in a situation like that?'

Timmins simply couldn't help himself. He locked the door, left the constable a prisoner in the feed room, and took off.

He appeared before Justice Robert Pring at Goulburn on 19 April charged with stealing John Farrell's chestnut mare in 1902.

Timmins was defended by Goulburn solicitor Augustine Betts and pleaded not guilty — despite the fact he'd been on the lam for three years.

It took the jury thirty minutes to find him guilty.

'The accused is obviously a very bad man. His previous sentences for similar offences have had no effect on him. I have no choice but to pass a heavy sentence,' Justice Pring said — and sent him down for seven years' penal servitude.

*   *   *

In May 1932, Timmins fronted the Dalby circuit court charged with stealing a bridle, saddle and saddlecloth on 21 December the previous year from Thomas Aisbett's selection, Beltana, between Warra and Dalby on the Darling Downs in Queensland.

Timmins, sixty-nine at the time of his arrest, was also charged with receiving stolen goods.

Crown prosecutor Henry O'Driscoll told the court Aisbett's son stored the riding gear in a shed after a day's mustering.

'Next day, when going to the shed, Mr Aisbett's son noticed the property missing,' O'Driscoll said. 'The matter was reported to the police, and on 24 December Constable Harley, with a Aboriginal tracker and Mr Aisbett, followed tracks from the shed across a paddock to a fence and there saw signs two horses had been tied up.'

The tracks were further followed and eventually led to Jack Timmins' property.

When questioned, Timmins denied any knowledge of the property, but when police searched a loft above a shed, the missing property was found.

Timmins told police he had no idea how the stolen riding gear found its way on to his property, let alone to the loft.

After half an hour, the jury returned a verdict of not guilty on both charges. Even after sixty-nine years, Timmins' apparent Teflon coating was showing no signs of wear and tear.

* * *

On 22 August 1934, at the ripe old age of seventy-four, Timmins was again before the beak.

Listed as residing at Braemar, Kogan, he appeared at Chinchilla police court, charged with stealing six cows and three calves from a paddock owned by George Armstrong. The cattle belonged to the Agricultural Bank of Australia.

Warra police constable James Hogan stated that on the night of 21 June he followed Timmins for some distance along the Tara-Kogan road behind a mob of cattle.

'I challenged the defendant. He made no reply,' Hogan said.

Scalper John Butterfield told the court he saw Timmins take a mob of nine cattle towards Kogan on 21 June.

Timmins was aware Butterfield had previously served six months behind bars and, assuming there was still honour among thieves, confided to Butterfield the cattle had been lifted from George Armstrong's block.

'You are a crook and I am a crook. I live by stealing cattle, but I never let a straight man see me doing anything,' Timmins allegedly told the scalper.

Butterfield, however, sang like a canary. He gave Chinchilla police a full account of the conversation.

Tara police constable Bill Hibbert stated he followed the cattle tracks on the morning of 22 June for about five miles to a gate. On the other side of the gate were a great number of cattle tracks.

Timmins was committed for trial at the circuit sittings of the Supreme Court in Dalby on 1 October, charged with stealing cattle as well as receiving.

Damning evidence against Timmins gave the jury no option but to hand down a guilty verdict. However Chief Justice James Blair threw the deceitful old septuagenarian a lifeline.

'I do not care to send a man of your age to gaol. But I want to warn you, if you are acting in concert with other people, or other people are using you, you had better refrain from having any further dealings with them. Try to keep your hands from other people's property in future,' Judge Blair warned Timmins.

Judge Blair discharged Timmins on the proviso he enter a two-year good behaviour bond with £50 recognisance.

*   *   *

After a week-long illness, Timmins passed away at his daughter Bessie McDonald's home in Dalby, Queensland, on 4 February 1954.

His obituary in the *Dalby Herald* the following day somewhat amusingly said:

> After spending a good deal of his younger life in western NSW, Jack Timmins became well known in the Dalby district over the last twenty years.

It has often been said that old age and treachery make perfect bedfellows.

Even up until his death at 90, Jack Timmins still had a sharp eye for a good bullock and a sixth sense for a good horse — especially those belonging to other people.

Postscript:

Denis Hayes, the young constable Jack Timmins allegedly tried to shoot in 1917, tragically committed suicide five years after the Scrubby Park incident.

Hayes was a well-travelled policeman born at Yackandandah in Victoria in 1884. He was stationed at the border town of Wentworth in the NSW far south-west and later at Louth, Mogil Mogil, Goodooga and Collarenenbri in the state's far north-west. Midway through 1922 he was transferred to Bulahdelah, about forty-five miles south of Taree on the mid-north coast.

In 1915, when posted at Louth, Hayes married nineteen-year-old Beatrice Mary Morrison at Cobar.

Three days before Christmas 1922, Hayes shot himself through the head while on duty at Bulahdelah police station.

Beatrice, at home in the adjoining residence, heard the gunshot and rushed to the station. Hayes was still alive, but died shortly afterwards. He was slated for transfer to Raymond Terrace the same day.

District Coroner Frederick James Callow found Hayes died 'from the effects of a revolver shot wound, wilfully self-inflicted'.

Newspapers reported he suffered from acute insomnia and had been melancholy for some time.

Hayes, 39, left behind three young children: six-year-old Sheila, four-year-old Eileen and twenty-three-month-old Kevin.

Beatrice was pregnant — and most likely unaware she was expecting — when her husband committed suicide.

On 3 September, nearly nine months after her husband's

suicide, Beatrice gave birth to a boy she named Neil Denis
Hayes.

*   *   *

Jack Timmins was a ne'er-do-well worthy of a Banjo Paterson
epic and also this writer's great-great-uncle.

Great-nephew, Warren Thatcher, said his mother, Stella,
often spoke of Jack's unsavoury past.

'I always knew a bit about Jack from my mother, who was
the granddaughter of his sister, Emily,' Thatcher said. 'Mum
remembered Jack when she was a child in about 1923 arriving
at her family's Caidmurra station on the Barwon River near
Mungindi. Jack arrived on horseback after dark and left fully
supplied early next morning headed for Queensland. He
eventually arrived at Roma.'

He said Jack was regarded as a stock thief by the grazing
community and his extended family. 'He ranged over a large
area that we know about and probably as much area we don't
know about. His early years were spent around Warialda,
Coolatai and Yetman on and near the big stations of Bogamildi,
Yallaroi, Yetman, Gunyerwarildi, Coolatai, Myall Creek and
Coppymurrimbilla. Stock was moved from these and other
stations legally and illegally to Toowoomba and south as far
as Homebush.'

Thatcher said, including the time on remand during the
attempted murder case, Timmins spent eighteen years in gaol.

When on the run, one of Timmins' preferred hideouts was
Mount Kaputar, near Narrabri. It is likely a cache of saddles
and riding gear found in a cave at the foot of the mountain
in the 1980s was part of his ill-gotten gains before doing time

in Maitland Gaol a hundred years earlier.

Timmins' criminal ways eventually became too much for his wife, Alice. She left the family home when the children were small.

Great-niece, Gene Makim, said Alice was a good woman. 'It was a case of not being able to teach an old dog, new tricks,' Gene wrote in her book, *The Tail Goes with the Hide.*

Alice got sick and tired of waiting for Jack to reform his ways. She spent most of her married life watching up the road for a posse of mounted police. When they did appear, although she was usually nervous and frightened, she managed to spin a good yarn and save his hide.

As Jack gained more experience, he became wily and elusive like a dingo, and almost impossible to catch out. Jack was a smart-talking conman and, when caught, he usually talked his way out of the dragnet.

CHAPTER 16

DOUBLE TRAGEDY SHOCKS A TOWN

Amy Freeman peered out the kitchen window of her Dover Street home and cautiously watched a wall of dust creep in from the west.

It was late afternoon on Tuesday, 19 January 1926 and the town of Moree was blanketed by a thick canopy of dust.

An unnerving, clammy stillness hung in the air.

As dusk fell, the wind increased and vast pockets of dust created an eerie, amber glow.

The sinking sun struggled to farewell the day and a strange darkness shrouded streets, laneways and parklands.

As the wind intensified, thirty-two-year-old Amy knew the washing on the line wouldn't survive such a lashing. She figured she still had time to drag it all inside before the dust and wind ruined everything.

Extreme weather patterns in this neck of the woods were nothing new, especially at this time of year; it was not uncommon for temperatures to soar past 100 degrees Fahrenheit for days on end. And when summer squalls arrived, they arrived with a vengeance.

Heavy downpours and storms in the weeks since Christmas created plenty of havoc and damage, but this dust storm was different — very different.

Amy's husband Edgar, a jeweller and watchmaker, would be home soon. The thought gave her comfort. Amy toyed with the idea of calling Edgar, but knew there was simply not enough time.

Instead, she raced outside and frantically began tugging washing from the line. Wooden pegs were flung aside as she bundled clothes and sheets under her arm.

Despite the incredible heat, Amy felt a chill surge through her body as she watched the wall of dust gather momentum. The intense wind stung her face and her eyes watered.

As she anxiously retrieved the washing, a fierce gust caused the house chimney to lurch and sway.

The chimney tended to be unsteady on windy days and was stabilised by a guywire tied to a nearby tree. But the wire wasn't strong enough, and it snapped under the weight of the chimney.

Amy saw the wire dangling in the wind. She looked up, terrified, as the chimney began to list dangerously.

Loose bricks broke away and dropped to the ground. Amy quickly sought shelter under the side veranda as the chimney buckled and fell.

The wind howled and roared as more bricks tumbled down, crushing the veranda's bullnose roofing and a nearby grapevine trellis.

Rafters and a section of wall-plate broke away. Within seconds, Amy was crushed by a torrent of bricks, mortar and splintered timber, and buried under a pile of rubble.

Carpenter George Mawkes was at his Alice Street home, which backed on to the Freeman residence. He was hastily closing up his house, trying to beat the storm. Windows had been left open all day to let the air circulate — the last thing he needed now was a house full of dust.

As he closed windows and shutters, Mawkes glanced over the back fence and saw the chimney start to collapse. He saw Amy directly below, struggling with an armful of washing. In a split second she was gone, buried alive under the collapsed chimney.

'Oh, dear Jesus,' Mawkes whispered.

The windows were quickly forgotten and Mawkes rushed across to assist his stricken neighbour.

Several other neighbours emerged from backyards and houses to help Mawkes rescue Amy from the pile.

They hastily dragged away bricks, timber and sheets of corrugated iron and delicately lifted Amy to safety.

She was laid out on a mattress on the front veranda and doctor Ronald Hunter was sent for.

He rushed to the Dover Street address and found Amy being comforted by neighbours. She was unconscious, seriously injured and barely alive.

Across town in Balo Street, Edgar Freeman was getting ready to lock up for the day.

Business had been slow the past couple of weeks, but Edgar, 35, fully expected the downturn after such a strong Christmas trade. Everything would be back to normal by February, or March at the latest.

The wind howled and the sky darkened. Late afternoon shoppers darted under awnings, huddled in doorways and ran into shops to escape the approaching dust storm.

This is probably a waste of time, Edgar frowned, as he swept out the store — the last chore for the day.

Edgar and Amy were married at Newcastle in 1921. They moved to Moree from Singleton, in the Hunter Valley, the following year.

Amy lost her father, well-known Singleton store-owner George Halter, in 1923. Her mother died in 1919 and a younger sister, Florence Lancaster, died in 1917. Florence was twenty-three and married for only two years.

Edgar, the son of Bathurst plumber William Freeman,

previously owned a watchmaking and jewellery store at Singleton. He was certain relocating to Moree was the right choice. The shift was a fresh start for both of them, especially Amy.

Moree was dirt-rich in wheat, sheep and cattle and an emerging agricultural hub situated on the rich black-soil plains in north-western NSW. There was an abundance of cash in the town and locals spent freely, especially when the seasons were good.

As Edgar was about to flick off the lights and call it a day, the telephone rang. The shrill startled him.

'Hello? Mr Freeman? This is Dr Hunter. You need to get home as soon as you can. Your wife has had a terrible accident and we have to get her to hospital. I've arranged an ambulance. We'll take her to Fairview.'

Edgar slumped on a stool behind the counter. His heart raced. 'My God, what happened?'

'The house chimney, Mr Freeman; the chimney collapsed. It looks like she was trying to get the washing off the line before the storm hit and she's been badly injured. Come as quickly as you can.'

'Yes, yes, I'm on my way, I just need to lock up the store,' he replied anxiously.

As Edgar drove across town to Dover Street, Dr Hunter treated Amy. An ambulance was ready to take her to Fairview Private Hospital, a short distance away at the eastern end of Albert Street. Edgar, frantic with worry, arrived home. He watched hopelessly as Amy was gently stretchered into the ambulance and taken away. Dr Hunter drove ahead.

Edgar looked around the yard and saw the pile of bricks and rubble. He looked up to where the chimney used to be. Washing was strewn everywhere.

'My dear Amy, what in God's name has happened,' he sobbed. George Mawkes and neighbours comforted him.

'She's in safe hands, Mr Freeman. Let me take you to the hospital,' offered Mawkes.

At about the same time, around the corner in Warialda Street, near the southern end of Moree Showground, two young boys were playing on the edge of the road.

Charlie Finn and Norman Hall were a couple of young larrikins prone to a bit of schoolboy mischief. The storm didn't worry them one little bit. They noticed Dr Hunter's car approaching and decided to have some fun.

'It won't get me,' shouted nine-year-old Charlie, as he ran laughing alongside Dr Hunter's car.

Norman held back, though. He saw the ambulance behind the car. Both vehicles were travelling swiftly.

But Charlie had other ideas. He darted across the front of Dr Hunter's car. Dr Hunter saw the boys spring from nowhere. He sounded the car horn and braked heavily, but it was too late.

Tragically, Charlie wasn't fast enough.

Car yard owner Harry Jones was pulling into his Warialda Street driveway about 150 yards away. As he opened his driveway gate he looked along the street and saw Dr Hunter's vehicle brake suddenly and skid to a stop. The ambulance carrying Amy Freeman continued to Fairview Private Hospital.

Jones saw Charlie Finn lying on the street, not far from Dr Hunter's car. He jumped back in his vehicle and drove the short distance to offer assistance.

Charlie was unconscious. Jones and Dr Hunter delicately bundled the young boy into Jones' car and both vehicles made their way to the hospital.

Charlie was treated by Dr Edward Parry and diagnosed with concussion, a fracture to the right thigh and right arm as well as abrasions about the face and right hip. He was in a bad way.

In the ward next door, Dr Hunter tried frantically to save Amy Freeman. Husband Edgar sat by her side. He clutched her hand tightly. Tears rolled down his cheeks as he watched Dr Hunter treat his wife.

'Please, doctor, bring her back,' he pleaded.

Amy Ann Freeman died about 7 pm without regaining consciousness.

The *Singleton Argus*, from Amy's hometown, reported she was 'very highly esteemed by a large circle of friends in Singleton, and her shocking death will be deeply regretted. She leaves no children.'

Magistrate Alf Chapman conducted a coronial inquest into Amy's death immediately after the accident.

At the same time, Charlie Finn was at Fairview Private Hospital fighting for his life under the watchful eye of Dr Parry.

Dr Hunter told the coroner Amy suffered wounds to the scalp and left side. 'Her pelvis was crushed and there was internal bleeding,' he said.

Edgar Freeman, told the coroner he received an urgent call at his jewellery shop about 5.30 pm.

'I left my business and went home immediately. When I arrived my wife was on a mattress on the front veranda. She never regained consciousness. There was an exceptionally heavy wind blowing and about eight feet of the chimney fell. The full height of the chimney is about seventeen feet.'

George Mawkes told the inquest he saw Mrs Freeman in her backyard about 5 pm.

'There was a heavy wind blowing at the time,' he said. 'I saw the top of a brick chimney falling past the roof of the house and then heard a crash. I went across to the Freeman house and saw Mrs Freeman lying under a heap of bricks on the ground just off the back veranda. Her head and shoulders were almost covered with the bricks and parts of her body were showing. I removed the bricks and noticed a scalp wound and a wound on the arm. Her clothing was torn.'

Mawkes added that Amy was unconscious. Other people came to help and together they lifted Amy from the bricks, procured a mattress and placed her on the front veranda.

Dr Hunter said when he arrived Mrs Freeman was lying on a mattress on the veranda. 'She was unconscious and bleeding from a wound on the scalp, and a perforating wound on the left side, just above the hip bone. Her clothing was torn at the back and there were abrasions on the left arm and left side of the body.'

He said there was also an extensive laceration of the rectum and a further examination at the hospital showed the pelvis had been crushed and internal bleeding was occurring.

'The deceased gradually sank and died without regaining consciousness,' said Dr Hunter. 'In my opinion, death was due to haemorrhage directly resulting from her injuries and the falling of the chimney was the cause of the injuries.'

Magistrate Chapman found Amy Ann Freeman 'died from haemorrhage directly resulting from injuries accidentally received by the falling of a brick chimney on her'.

Amy was laid to rest in the Church of England section of Moree Cemetery on 21 January less than forty-eight hours after her death.

The Freemans were new to the district. They arrived in Moree in 1922 and were warmly welcomed by the tightknit community.

Amy was an exceptional tennis player. She was an associate member of the Moree Girls' Friendly Society and a member of that organisation's tennis club, as well as the Presbyterian Tennis Club.

Hundreds of mourners gathered at the Moree Church of England on Albert Street to say their final goodbyes, including family and friends from Singleton.

*　　*　　*

Charlie Finn passed away eight days after Amy's funeral.

The two fatalities, accidental and tragically intertwined under extraordinary circumstances, shrouded Moree in grief and profound sadness.

Charlie, also known as 'Paddy', was like any other adventurous kid in the 1920s. But what started out as an apparent game of 'chicken' with Dr Hunter's car ended in the little boy's death.

On 2 February 1926, at Moree courthouse, Magistrate Alf Chapman conducted a coronial inquest into the accident.

Dr Hunter, represented by Moree solicitor Arthur Smith, told the enquiry he saw two boys running towards the road as he approached the northern corner of Warialda Street near Moree Showground.

He sounded the car horn and, as the boys continued to run toward the road, braked to avoid hitting them.

Both boys stopped running, so Dr Hunter accelerated, expecting to see the boys waiting on the left-hand side of the road.

'They suddenly ran across the road in front of me so I applied the foot brake and hand brake at the same time and the car skidded,' Dr Hunter told the inquiry.

Charlie was struck by the vehicle's mudguard and thrown to the ground.

Norman Hall told the inquiry he and Charlie were running along the side of the road when Charlie yelled out: 'I'm not going to let it bluff me!'

Dr Hunter's car was about fifteen feet away.

'Paddy ran across in front of it,' Norman said.

'He jumped on to the side of the road. The car caught him on his side and knocked him over and pushed him along. The wheels did not go over him.

'If Paddy stayed on the side of the road with me, the car would not have hit him,' he told the coroner.

Moree police Sgt Jim Deane told the inquiry he and Constable Tom Parmenter attended the accident scene about 7 pm, where they found a pool of blood and vehicle skid marks.

Sgt Deane estimated the skid marks to be about twenty feet long.

'The car then appeared to have rolled a further distance of about seven or eight feet where we located the pool of blood, then continued for about fifteen feet, veering toward the left-hand side,' he said.

'The tracks of the car showed it was being driven on the proper side of the road.'

Sgt Deane told the inquiry the brakes on Dr Hunter's vehicle were later tested and found to be in perfect working order.

The car was driven in a simulated test at twenty-three miles an hour and stopped just short of fifteen feet when both brakes were applied.

The sergeant said a car travelling at ten miles an hour could be pulled up in nine feet, seven inches and one travelling at twenty miles an hour could be pulled up in about fifteen feet.

'If the ground was slippery, it would skid further,' he said.

'I have always recognised Dr Hunter as one of the most careful drivers in Moree. I have never seen him drink and have never known him to take alcohol.'

Dr Parry said he treated Charlie Finn at Fairview Private Hospital on the night of the accident, at the request of Dr Hunter, who attended to Amy Freeman.

'The deceased was then unconscious, and had many abrasions about the face and nose, and a lacerated wound on the left eyebrow, left temple and bridge of the nose,' Dr Parry said.

He told Coroner Chapman there were no signs of a fractured skull.

'Unconsciousness was due to concussion and bruising of the brain. There were some bruises on the left side of the chest, but no ribs were broken,' Dr Parry said.

The right arm was fractured near the elbow joint and there was a contused wound near the thigh and hip, the inquest heard.

'The right femur was fractured and he was showing considerable signs of shock,' Dr Parry said.

In the days following the accident Charlie responded well to treatment.

However, the boy's condition worsened on 25 January, six days after being struck by Dr Hunter's vehicle.

'He began to run a septic temperature and developed definite heart murmurs, which I diagnosed as septic endocarditis,' Dr Parry said.

Charlie Finn did not regain consciousness and died on 29 January, ten days after being struck by the vehicle.

'In my opinion, the cause of death was septic endocarditis,' Dr Parry said.

The doctor told the inquest he thought Charlie had every chance of recovery, had there not been complications.

'This condition might arise from any septic focus through the septic matter entering the bloodstream and causing vegetation, as found in the deceased's heart,' Dr Parry said.

'It was a very fatal type of blood poisoning and might arise from any small blow on the nose if the right type of germ was present,' he said.

In layman's terms, Charlie Finn died from blood poisoning caused by germs entering his body through cuts on his face and nose.

His parents, Charles and Kate, held each other tightly as Magistrate Chapman addressed the courtroom.

'Charles Andrew Finn died from septic endocarditis originating from septic focus in the frontal sinus and behind the nose following injuries accidentally received when being knocked down by a motor car driven by Dr Ronald Hunter,' Chapman said.

Charlie Finn was buried on 30 January 1926 in the Roman Catholic section of Moree Cemetery.

Townsfolk were still numb with grief after the death of Amy Freeman nine days earlier.

Father Canice Donleavy delivered a solemn service in front of hundreds of mourners, including scores of children and school mates.

*   *   *

Edgar Freeman returned to his Balo Street jewellery store

— hard work was the one constant helping him overcome the tragic death of his beautiful young wife, Amy.

He struggled with more family tragedy the year following Amy's death when a brother, William, 43, died after a car accident in Newcastle.

On 23 March 1927, William was a passenger in a car allegedly being driven dangerously by Christopher William Duck. The vehicle collided with a horse-drawn brewery cart and William suffered severe spinal injuries. He died twelve days later.

Duck was charged with manslaughter but later found not guilty and subsequently acquitted.

In about 1937, Edgar Freeman relocated his jewellery store around the corner to the rebuilt Imperial Hotel building on Heber Street. The hotel was completely gutted by fire in 1928, when more than twenty businesses along Balo and Heber Streets were destroyed.

The Royal Hotel and five homes in Auburn Street were also lost in the blaze, with damage estimated at more than £250,000.

From the ashes emerged a new shopping precinct comprising rows of art-deco buildings including Freeman's Treasure Store, where Edgar's incredible award-winning window displays were the talk of the district.

At some point a business partnership was formed with John Norman Wallis.

Edgar Jaye Freeman never remarried and died a widower on 17 December 1972. He was 82.

Fond memories of Amy were never far away.

CHAPTER 17

I COULD NOT LET A MADMAN DO FOR THE CHILDREN

Myra Crowther couldn't take it anymore.

She thought life might get better when the family packed up and moved to Gilgandra from Forbes; hoped a fresh start in a new town might be a gateway to happiness.

But it wasn't — far from it.

Myra, a small woman with sharp features, knew that was always going to be the case. She knew she was kidding herself. Life was never going to get better, not while her depraved, abusive husband was around.

Ted Crowther was a sadistic maniac, a madman, and ruled the family home with an iron fist — and a loaded gun.

'While ever you live with me and I see a smile on your face, I will wipe it off,' he once told his wife.

Myra and the children lived in abject fear every day of their lives.

It was a living hell and Myra, 45, simply couldn't take it anymore. She was sick of all the running away, sick of the constant threats and violence. All she wanted was for her children to be safe and happy. All she wanted was a normal life.

On the morning of Thursday 11 October 1945 Myra walked purposefully into Forbes police station and told officers she had killed her fifty-year-old husband on a property near Gilgandra in central-western NSW, about 135 miles north of Forbes.

With the help of her eighteen-year-old son Teddie, she

buried Ted Crowther's body near Marthaguy Creek on the property Bungie, five miles from Gilgandra.

Sen-Constable John Scott and Det-Constable Sam Dunn were huddled around the wireless when Myra walked in.

World War II was finally over and newly elected Prime Minister Ben Chifley was assuring Australia the United Nations charter was days away from being ratified.

Scott and Dunn looked up and saw a frail, tired-looking woman at the front counter. She was clearly distressed.

Myra looked at the two officers and took a deep breath.

'My husband is a crank on racehorses, women and drink and I have shot him dead; I have murdered him.'

Scott and Dunn looked at each other, and looked back at Myra.

'I think you better come and take a seat and tell us exactly what happened,' Dunn said.

Two days before presenting herself at the police station, Myra sat at the kitchen table in an eight-room house at the property, Bundie. The family moved there for work about six months earlier. The clock on the wall approached 8 pm.

Myra's tyrannical husband, Ted, was lying in bed reading a newspaper.

Their older children, Kathie, 14, and Lachlan, 16, were in a garage next to the main house. Toddler Dawn was with her mother. She was sound asleep.

Lachlan worked as a farm labourer at a neighbouring Balladoran property, Woodlea, owned by Bill Law.

Myra had deliberately sent them to the garage. She didn't want the children to see what was about to unfold.

Her eldest son, Teddie, 18, also lived and worked on the Collie Road property, owned by Hector Wilson. He was asleep in a workers' hut some distance away.

Another daughter, Jessie, 19, lived at Forbes with her husband, Neil Duckworth, and their two young children, Elaine and Brenda.

Myra held back tears as she contemplated the future. The past could never be changed. She knew that.

But the future could. Not just her own future, but that of the children. And her children meant everything. They were her life. And if it meant going to gaol for them, so be it.

Life simply couldn't go on like this. Earlier that day her husband had charged through the house with a loaded pea rifle, threatening to shoot anyone who stepped out of line. The night before, he approached one of his daughters with a razor. He was known to throttle the kids with a belt buckle wrapped around a clenched fist. During an earlier incident at Forbes, Lachlan fearfully watched his father sharpen a carving knife and slowly run the blade across his mother's bare neck as he held her back by the hair.

'You had better look out or I'll put you all in the cemetery,' Crowther told his family.

He repeatedly accused Myra of infidelity and once tried to force her to blackmail a stranger for £500. She point-blank refused and the consequences were devastating.

Crowther was also obsessed with a pack of playing cards. He genuinely believed he could 'read' them and work out what Myra had been doing behind his back.

It's now or never, Myra told herself. The house was deathly quiet. Only the faint sound of crickets chirping in the distance and baby Dawn's soft breathing could be heard.

Myra rose slowly from the table and walked silently, yet purposefully, to her son's bedroom. She quietly slid open a dresser drawer and found a solitary cartridge. Her son's .303 calibre bolt-action rifle was on top of the dresser.

Myra loaded the rifle and stepped outside. She crept across the back veranda and peered through an open bedroom window. The bed she shared with her husband was less than three feet away, facing away from the window.

Ted was dozing. Myra aimed the rifle at the back of his head and looked away. Tears trickled down her cheeks. She squeezed the trigger.

A single gunshot blast shattered the stillness. He husband was dead. The back of his head was blown apart. The newspaper, now splattered with blood and brain fragments, lay across his chest.

Baby Dawn started to cry.

In that split second, a huge weight was lifted from Myra Crowther's mind and body. Her thinking was crystal clear, despite what had happened. She was fully aware of what she had done, and the likely consequences, but the moment was still very surreal.

As far as Myra was concerned, the consequences didn't matter. The evil bastard was dead. That was all that mattered. She swallowed hard and calmly walked back inside.

Kathie and Lachlan were startled by the gunshot. Myra called them to the kitchen. They were relieved to hear their mother's voice, not their father's.

'I have done it; I have killed him. We are free,' she told them.

'Is Dawn okay?' Kathie asked.

'Yes, she is fine.'

Myra told Kathie to stay with Dawn. She went across to where son Teddie lived and told him what had happened. He was not surprised.

'I was waiting for something like this to happen but I honestly thought it would be us at the hands of him, not the other way around,' Teddie said.

Together they wrapped Ted Crowther's body in an old tarpaulin and bedding. They lifted the gruesome, makeshift body-bag on to a pushcart and dragged it away from the house.

Myra watched her son dig a shallow grave on the sandy banks of Marthaguy Creek.

They buried Ted Crowther's body under a moonlit, autumn sky and returned to the house to figure out what to do next. Myra arranged a taxi and the family arrived at Jessie Duckworth's Forbes home around 1 am. Jessie was sound asleep when the taxi pulled up. She met them at the front door.

'I have a great shock for you,' Myra said.

Somehow, Jessie knew what her mother had done. The blank look on Myra's face told a grim story. The children's eyes were red from crying. Jessie knew, and she was relieved.

'Have you done it; did you fix him?'

Myra nodded as fresh tears trickled down her cheeks. 'Yes. He's gone. It was either him, or me and the kids. I'll tell the police everything.'

Jessie hugged her mother tightly and shared her tears.

'We'll work out what to do; it's okay; everything will be okay,' she whispered.

Myra slept very little that night. But she was at peace.

About 10 am the next day, Myra sat down at a desk at Forbes police station and poured out her sad, incredible story to Sen-Constable Scott and Det-Constable Dunn.

She told the officers everything. With her was a cousin, Alex Morton.

'At about eight o'clock on Tuesday night my husband went

to bed and was reading the paper. Something seemed to tell me it was now or never. It was either the family or him,' Myra said.

'I went to the top room, picked up the lad's rifle and took the last cartridge from the drawer. I pulled the bolt back and loaded the rifle. I walked to the back veranda where the window is at the head of the bed. I lifted the rifle and the barrel would have been about two or three feet from the back of my husband's head. I looked away and pulled the trigger. My baby was asleep in bed and the other children were doing their homework.'

Scott and Dunn hung on every word.

'I decided to hide the body until I could get the children safely to Forbes and then come here and give myself up. I could not leave the body in the house and have the flies crawling all over it. I helped Teddie put the body in the cart and we took it down to the creek bed about a quarter of a mile from the house. Teddie would not let me dig the hole. He dug it. We put the body in the hole and covered it up. I came back to the house and cleaned up the mess.'

She told the officers about the living hell she and her children suffered at the hands of her husband.

'For years my husband has been stealing. I was afraid he would lead the children to crime. I have begged and prayed of him to give up stealing for the kiddies' sake. I warned the children not to take anything, and not to go out with him when he went stealing.'

Myra alleged her husband was sexually abusive, intimating she had been raped by the man she fell in love with. They were married at Cobar twenty years earlier. Allegations of sexual advances towards daughter Jessie were also lodged.

'He got sort of sexually cranky and made demands which were unreasonable. He accused me of being with men of all types. He would walk around the house with a loaded pea rifle.'

Sen-Constable Scott and Det-Constable Dunn recorded Myra's full statement.

She told the officers about an alarming incident the night before she killed her husband. She said he'd awoken about midnight and crept towards their daughters' bedroom. 'He had an open razor in his hand. I called out to him to get me a glass of water. He dropped the razor, and came back to bed and assaulted me. Because of that incident, I could not let a madman do for the children,' Myra told Scott and Dunn. 'I decided it would be better to kill him and spend my whole life behind walls rather than let him kill my family.'

Myra and Teddie accompanied a team of police officers to the Gilgandra property and showed them where Ted Crowther's body was buried. They fully co-operated with police.

The remains, crudely wrapped in a tarpaulin and bits and pieces of kapok bedding, were exhumed and taken to Gilgandra Hospital for a post-mortem examination by Dr Julian Alexander.

Crowther's body, clad in a blue flannel singlet and underpants, was badly mutilated about the face and neck.

* * *

Dubbo police superintendent Jim Sweeney took control of the investigation.

Sweeney, born in Walcha in the NSW New England district, joined the police in 1911 and was considered one of the region's most accomplished criminal investigators.

He knew the central-western districts like the back of his hand and had returned to Dubbo three months earlier.

He was a sergeant at Dubbo from 1925 until 1935 before postings at Wellington, Yass and Goulburn. In 1939 he was promoted to assistant officer at Darlinghurst police station in Sydney, and in 1941 became officer-in-charge of No. 9 division at Burwood and was later officer-in-charge of No. 4 division in Phillip Street, Sydney.

But the bush was where he belonged and Sweeney welcomed the return to his old stomping grounds in the state's central west.

He read Myra's confession several times.

During more than thirty years in the force, Sweeney had never seen a case quite like this. The stories he was hearing about the deceased were absolutely appalling.

Sweeney was assisted by Det-Sgt John Burke and Constable Athol Vale, both from Dubbo. The Dubbo team joined Gilgandra officers John Scott and Sam Dunn and a full investigation was launched.

* * *

On Friday 12 October 1945, at Gilgandra courthouse, Myra Tenandra Crowther was charged with the murder of her husband, Edward James Crowther. Her son, Edward Neil James Crowther, was charged with being an accessory after the fact.

A post-mortem examination on Crowther's body by Dr Julian Alexander revealed a gaping hole in the back of his neck at the base of the skull, caused by a bullet. The upper and lower jaws were fractured and there was a wound in the chest where the bullet exited the body.

Dr Alexander also examined Myra Crowther at Gilgandra police station and found her to be 'of sound mind and body' and 'not unduly agitated'.

'Her manner was that of a normal person,' he stated.

Det-Sgt Burke opposed bail.

'Mrs Crowther, herself, informed Constable Scott of the facts of her husband's death,' he told the court.

Myra was refused bail and remanded until 30 October. Teddie was granted £200 bail.

Two weeks later an inquest into the death of Edward James Crowther was opened at Gilgandra courthouse by district coroner Edwin Townsend. He was assisted by police prosecutor, Sgt George Lithgow.

The co-accused were represented by Gilgandra solicitor Frank Astill.

Myra, withdrawn and tired, sat impassively in the dock. She was dressed in black and wearing an outdated, hooded hat. Teddie sat beside his mother.

Myra's cousin, Forbes gardener Alex Morton, told the inquest Myra came to him on 11 October and said: 'My God, I've shot Ted. I really didn't know until afterwards that I had done it.'

'She said her husband had threatened to kill her and the children. In the past I have witnessed Crowther flog his children with a buckled belt,' Morton said. 'I have known Crowther for about fourteen years and in my opinion he was a complete lunatic.'

Myra's daughter, Jessie Duckworth, said her father was a dangerous man. 'He once came to my bedroom when I was a schoolgirl and made improper suggestions to me,' she told the court.

Daughter Kathie, told how her father came to her bedroom with a razor. 'I pretended I was asleep. He left when I heard mum call out to him,' she said.

Kathie said her father once offered to pay her to spy on her mother and report back to him.

'I thought that was wrong and I told mum. He also told me that I had better learn to cook, in case something should happen to mum.'

Crowther's jealously and suspicious nature was maniacal, it was alleged.

Kathie said her father once shovelled dirt around sections of the house and kept it watered and damp. 'Dad reckoned someone was coming to the house to see mum and by doing this, he would see the tracks.'

She said the family relocated to Bungie in early May, five months before her father's death.

'For the first few days, dad seemed all right but soon started going off again,' she said.

She described an argument between her parents — one of many.

'Dad went into the bedroom and yelled at mum: "I will smack you across the face and put your kids in a state school — separate schools where they won't be able to talk to each other".'

'He once held up a sharpened knife and said to mum, "This would be a good thing to cut your throat with". He pulled her head back by the hair at the same time.'

Kathie looked directly at Sgt Lithgow. 'Dad seemed to mean what he said when he put the knife to mum's throat. Dad threatened to kill mum many times.'

She told Coroner Townsend a similar incident happened at Forbes months earlier. 'He said to me "don't be surprised if you come home one day and find your mother with her throat cut".' On another occasion, testified Kathie, her older sister Jessie tried to protect their mother when their parents were fighting.

'Dad was going to take to Jessie with a broken bottle. He once hit her with a strap and cut her lip,' Kathie said.

Kathie recalled the day of her father's death. She arrived home from school and did various chores around the house. After dinner, she began doing homework in the dining room.

'My brother Lachlan was with me. Dad was reading a newspaper and afterwards went to bed. I never saw him come out. Mum told us to go to a garage next to the house,' she said. 'A little bit later I heard a rifle shot. It seemed to come from the back of the house. I thought dad had shot mum.'

Son Lachlan told the inquest he arrived in the Gilgandra district about one month after the rest of the family. He found work at nearby Woodlea station.

Lachlan said there were constant arguments between his parents. 'Dad kept saying mum was carrying on with other men and there were terrible quarrels about it in front of us kids,' he said.

He said once in Forbes, when he and his mother arrived home from a night out at the movies, they found strands of barbed wire stretched across the laneway to the house.

Lachlan told solicitor Frank Astill the wire was strategically pegged out.

'One piece was low down to trip us and the other was higher up. If we had tripped on the first piece, we would have caught our faces on the second piece,' he said.

'When we got to the house the door was locked. Dad yelled out, "Did you enjoy the movie?" When we said we did, he said: "Well, now you can enjoy sleeping outside for the night". We went to a friend's house and stayed there.'

Lachlan said he saw his father physically assault his mother numerous times and recalled the night in Forbes when his father held his mother by the hair and slid a sharpened carving knife across her throat.

'Don't think I wouldn't do that to you,' Crowther allegedly snarled.

Collie Road farmer Sam Keen told the coroner he worked with Crowther on 8 October, the day before the murder. Keen said Crowther was a heavy drinker.

'We were stacking hay. The next day, he seemed a little different in his manner and went off working by himself. We had lunch together and he told me all about his domestic affairs, which I didn't want to hear about. He said his wife was untrue. He didn't mention his children. I last saw him about 6 pm when we finished for the day. He said he wouldn't be at work the next day because he planned to slaughter some beasts,' Keen said.

Sen-Constable Scott recalled the morning Myra Crowther handed herself in at Gilgandra police station.

'She gave a detailed statement and told me her husband once threatened to cut her throat when she refused to have anything to do with his stealing,' he said.

Dr Alexander confirmed he had conducted a full post-mortem on the body on 12 October. Also present were detectives Burke and Dunn and Sen-Constable Scott.

'The cause of death was the wound in the heart,' said Dr Alexander. 'Death would have been instantaneous.' The wounds were consistent with having been made by a .303 rifle bullet. 'The place of entry of the missile was the top of the head. There were no other marks or injuries other than those described.'

* * *

The rifle used to kill Crowther was bought by Teddie Crowther in early August from Bob Hunt, a farm worker at Gowang station, near Coonabarabran.

'Ted said he wanted the rifle to shoot kangaroos in season as well as foxes. Eight to twelve rounds of Mark V ammunition went with the sale,' Hunt said.

The inquest heard about Crowther's bizarre behaviour with a regular pack of playing cards.

Witnesses said he genuinely believed he could read the cards as if they were a tarot deck. He also believed he could pick horse-racing winners by reading the cards.

'As soon as dad got home from work he would get out the pack of cards and say he could tell what mum had been doing,' daughter Kathie said.

'He used the cards frequently and I told him a couple of times he was being silly; I told him he couldn't read fortunes with them.'

Crowther's employer, Hector Wilson, corroborated Kathie's evidence.

'Crowther had peculiar characteristics and thought he could tell what was going to happen by using a pack of cards,' said Wilson, who had employed Crowther seventeen years earlier during shearing season.

'On the Sunday before he died, he told me he had filled two writing pads trying to work out winners for the races. On another occasion, when we were shearing, he walked to the shed door and looked across at the cottage where he and his family were living. He was a nervous wreck. He said he had a feeling something was going to happen and if he had his pack of cards, he could work it out.'

At the end of the two-day inquest, Coroner Townsend

committed Myra Crowther to stand trial on one count of murder. In formal legal parlance he said, 'I declare and find Edward Crowther died on 9 October 1945 at Bungie, near Gilgandra, from the effects of a shot from a .303 rifle through the head and heart and other parts of the body, feloniously inflicted on him on the same day at the same place by Myra Tenandra Crowther. I further find the aforesaid Myra Tenandra Crowther did feloniously and maliciously murder the aforesaid Edward Crowther.'

* * *

The trial before Justice William Owen was transferred from Dubbo courthouse to the Central Criminal Court in Sydney on 10 December 1945.

More than fifteen witnesses for the Crown were subpoenaed, including Myra's children Jessie, Lachlan and Kathie.

Myra squared her shoulders resolutely and stared directly at Justice Owen.

'I plead guilty to murder, but I acted in self-defence,' she said clearly.

Evidence given at the inquest was revisited and Myra wept as stories of her husband's cruelty towards herself and the children were retold to a packed courtroom.

Edward Crowther terrorised his family for years. The night before his death, when he approached his daughter's bedroom with an open razor, was the turning point for Myra. The desperate decision to murder her husband was made at that very moment, the jury was told.

'I decided then and there that I could not let a madman kill my children,' Myra said.

The jury wasted little time finding her not guilty. Evidence from the defence was not required. Instead, a verdict of justifiable homicide was returned.

Myra broke down and cried when the jury foreman read out the verdict.

'You are free to go, Mrs Crowther; the law does not require you anymore,' Justice Owen said.

As Myra stepped from the dock, a broken but relieved woman, she collapsed in the arms of her daughter, Jessie.

Amid scenes not usually seen in a court of law, Crown prosecutor Charles Rooney defended Myra's actions. Had she killed her husband the night he approached their daughter with an open razor, Rooney said, she would not have been charged.

'It is unlikely she would have stood trial had she murdered her husband the night before,' he said.

Rooney conceded the Crown freely admitted Myra had complete justification in killing her husband. He said Myra's confession was the most frank and sincere statement he had read during a legal career spanning decades.

'This unfortunate woman put up with a life of terror,' Rooney said. 'She was a widely respected woman and a devoted wife and mother but the deceased was always threatening to kill her and the children or put the children in a state home.

'The Crown also admits Crowther was a persistent thief and that his wife was afraid he would influence the children to adopt a similar mode of life.

'For years, he was a drunkard, a gambler, a thief and a bully who terrorised his wife and family. It is unpleasant to speak ill of the dead, but Crowther was so depraved he once made unnatural overtures towards one of his own daughters,' he said.

Rooney praised Myra's absolute love and strong-willed devotion for her children.

'She is a decent, respectable, loyal and brave woman. I pay tribute to her steadfastness of purpose in concealing the body to give sufficient time to take her children to her married daughter in Forbes, rather than see them placed in a state institution after her arrest.'

Family, friends and supporters embraced Myra as she left the court a free woman.

'These last couple of months (since Crowther's death) are probably the most peaceful months this unfortunate woman has known for many years,' Rooney said.

Postscript:

Myra Crowther and her family started a new life at Shepparton on the Goulburn River in rural Victoria, about 120 miles north of Melbourne.

Myra's older brother, Alex, lived at sister-town Mooroopna, on the north-western side of the river. The move south was a fresh beginning after more than twenty years of pure hell.

But tragedy tracked Myra over the border.

On 11 March 1952 her oldest daughter, Jessie Duckworth, was found floating face down in Backwash Creek, an irrigation channel about two miles from Cobram, forty-one miles north of Shepparton.

Jessie was in Cobram working the tomato-picking season. Three days earlier she was seen in a Cobram hotel drinking and arguing with a man later identified as Frank O'Callaghan, a co-worker.

Coroner George Catlow reached an open finding at the subsequent inquest at Cobram courthouse on 23 April.

He concluded there was insufficient evidence to determine when, and by what means, Jessie ended up in the water.

'However, there is a good deal of suspicion concerning the means by which the deceased came to die. She and others had been drinking heavily on the banks of the river on the night of her death,' he said.

O'Callaghan told police he awoke about 3 am on Sunday and realised Jessie was missing. Her body was found three days later.

Jessie was twenty-six and the mother of five young children — eight-year-old Elaine, seven-year-old Brenda, five-year-old Neil, three-year-old Denis and toddler Allan.

Myra died in 1980, aged eighty-one, and is buried alongside her daughter at Shepparton Cemetery.

CHAPTER 18

WHERE ARE THE CHILDREN?

Inverell dairy farmers Tom and Ellen Fleming were finally seeing some light at the end of a very long tunnel.

By 1935, a chain of tragedies and heartache over the course of a decade all but broke their spirit.

On Sunday 10 May 1931, when the Great Depression was arguably at its worst, the Flemings lost everything in a house fire at Ross Hill, on the edge of Inverell, a bustling gem-mining centre on the western slopes of the NSW Northern Tablelands.

Tom and Ellen, known as Nellie, and their children — seven-year-old Florence, five-year-old Ronald, three-year-old Patricia and baby Darrell — were away at the time.

They were visiting Tom's older brother, Jim, at the property Stock Yard, at nearby Copeton, when their bungalow-style family home at Inverell went up in flames.

All contents and keepsakes were lost, including furniture stored in a bedroom belonging to Tom's brother, Ted, and a valuable violin belonging to a nephew, Gordon.

Tom, one of nineteen children to district pioneers Richard and Mary Fleming, was a well-known stock and station agent and auctioneer at the time of the blaze.

* * *

The fire was yet another heartbreaking setback for the family.

A sister, Bridget Bevin, died in 1926 after a long illness, aged forty-four. Earlier the same year, Jim Fleming's brother-in-law, Jack Heffernan, died in a rail disaster near Ardglen in the Hunter Valley.

Heffernan and engine driver Tom Holt were overcome by carbon monoxide fumes in a railway tunnel as they approached Ardglen. Both men collapsed and died as the goods train careered through Ardglen railway station and derailed.

Two months before losing their home and possessions, Tom and Nellie's daughter Florence — affectionately known as Flo — escaped death when a pair of scissors fell from a sewing table and stabbed her thigh, piercing a vein. The wound was staunched and the bleeding stopped. However, later that night the bandage worked loose as Flo slept.

Tom found his daughter semi-conscious in a pool of blood. Flo, named after an aunty who died as a baby in 1900, was rushed to Innishowen Private Hospital at Inverell, where doctors performed emergency surgery.

They stopped the bleeding — and saved her life.

About two months earlier, Tom's cousin, twenty-four-year-old Joseph Fleming, was killed in a shooting accident at Texas, north of Inverell, and an uncle, John Fleming — Joseph's father — died in September 1933.

After the blaze that destroyed everything they had, Tom and Nellie returned to Lilydale, the Gum Flat property near Staggy Creek he leased from Donald Cameron and began putting the broken pieces of their lives back together.

Tom's older brother, Ted, and his family — wife Margaret and son Gordon — lived nearby on Wiltshire Road.

Tom, an avid cricketer and exceptional tennis player, was a returned soldier who fought in World War I. He enlisted on 2 October 1916 and joined the 54th Australian Infantry

Battalion at the age of twenty-three. Tom left Sydney on the HMAT *Suevic* on 11 November and served for ten months. He was invalided back to Australian shores on 22 July 1917.

In 1914, at age twenty-one, he became the youngest person in NSW to be appointed a justice of the peace.

Tom and Nellie, devoutly religious, were married at Condobolin in 1923 — Tom's twin brother Patrick was best man — and returned to the Inverell district shortly afterwards.

Life was by no means easy for Tom and Nellie, but they remained upbeat. They were resilient and worked hard — resilience and stoicism were qualities typical of Depression-ravaged farm life in the early 1930s.

A son, Noel, was born in 1932 and a daughter, Colleen, arrived in 1933.

When times were good, Tom helped others in need; he was always the first to lend a hand. Sadly, the tide turned and by 1934 Tom was on the edge — financially, emotionally and mentally. He desperately needed help to keep his mixed-farming enterprise afloat and sought assistance under the Farmers' Relief Act.

This was granted and Lilydale was placed under the supervision of Wallace Kinross.

Later that year it all became too much. Tom suffered a nervous breakdown and his health deteriorated.

By now he felt there wasn't much more life could throw at him. Nonetheless he began to draw on the pioneering spirit so typical of the era and steadily recovered. Sooner or later, he figured, circumstances would surely change for the better. The Great Depression was all but over and the future looked bright.

Sadly, in the autumn of 1935, the shimmer of light at the end of Tom and Nellie Fleming's long, dark tunnel turned pitch black.

Tuesday 2 April started in the usual way for Tom. He was up well before dawn and planned to plough some paddocks and clear some scrub later in the day.

Nellie was away in Sydney overseeing medical appointments for Tom's 83-year-old mother, Mary.

Tom and Nellie's birthdays were fast approaching and celebrations were planned, despite the dire times.

Tom would turn forty-two on 6 April — four days away — and five days later, Nellie would be thirty, the day of the Inverell picnic races.

Tom planned to take Nellie to the races to meet Australia's youngest pilot, nineteen-year-old Nancy Bird. The aviatrix and her co-pilot, Peggy McKillop, were on a goodwill tour of NSW country centres and were invited to attend the two-day picnic racing carnival on 10 and 11 April.

Tom figured a joy flight in Bird's new Gypsy Moth would be the perfect present for Nellie.

Ivy Dixon, from the nearby village of Ashford, was also at the homestead. Ivy was housekeeping while Nellie was away, and babysitting the Fleming children as well as her own daughter, two-year-old Melba.

On the morning of 2 April 1935, Ivy was preparing breakfast while Tom was out milking the cows.

When milking was completed, Tom returned to a kitchen full of boisterous children and the smell of porridge and fresh toast. He read the latest edition of the *Inverell Times* as he ate.

'There's a new Shirley Temple movie coming to the Capitol Theatre. *Bright Eyes* it's called. Between that and a joy flight with Nancy Bird at the races, Nellie's birthday will be her best yet,' Tom told Ivy with a smile.

When Tom returned from war, Capitol Theatre management presented him with a lifetime free pass to the movies. Although greatly honoured by the thoughtful bequest, Tom never used the pass; he preferred to pay his own way.

The children were proving a handful for twenty-one-year-old Ivy; there seemed no end of farm adventures for the group of inquisitive, spirited toddlers.

'I'll take them out for a ride in the hay cart later, probably after lunch,' said Tom. 'That'll get them out of your hair for a while at least.'

The older Fleming children, Ronald, nine, and Yvonne, seven, also known as Pat, were leaving for school at Gum Flat, three miles away. Their sister, eleven-year-old Flo, was ill in bed.

Tom gave the older kids instructions as they headed out the door.

'Make sure to tell the teacher Flo is sick and won't be at school today, and get home as early as you can. There'll be plenty to do around here with your mother away in Sydney.'

After breakfast, Tom left to start clearing paddocks for ploughing while Ivy cleaned and scrubbed the kitchen. Meanwhile, the children played "soldiers" outside. Darrell, using a tin dish as a drum, led the charge with Noel, Colleen and Melba marching along behind.

Around 1 pm, Ivy rounded up the children for lunch. Tom arrived soon afterwards and checked in on Flo. She was feeling a little better, but her appetite had not returned.

After lunch, Tom stood up and stretched. He checked his fob watch. It was almost 2.30. 'Sitting here won't get that paddock ploughed,' he said. 'All you kids can come with me for a ride in the hay cart and we can give poor Ivy a break.'

Darrell, however, wanted to stay home and play and Ivy's daughter, Melba, could hardly keep her eyes open. Nap time beckoned, much to her young mother's relief.

Tom lifted Noel and Colleen into the cart and made his way to the paddock he had begun clearing earlier that morning. The children giggled as he belted out *On the Good Ship Lollypop*, the hit song from Shirley Temple's new movie he planned to take Nellie to for her birthday.

Tom smiled. Life on Lilydale was finally getting back on track.

*   *   *

Back at the homestead, Ivy lay Melba down for an afternoon nap while Darrell made a racket outside with an old oil drum he'd found near the dairy barn.

With her daughter sound asleep and Darrell happily keeping his own company, Ivy darted across to the home of Ted Fleming, less than a hundred yards away.

Meanwhile, Tom had only gone a short distance when he had second thoughts about taking Noel and Colleen on a hayride without Darrell and Melba. It seemed unfair to separate the children considering how well they all got along.

Unaware Ivy was visiting his brother, Tom sent Noel and Colleen back to the family home to play with Darrell and Melba.

'You two go straight home; it's not far,' he told them.

Noel and Colleen ran home as fast as their legs could carry them. For that few minutes, the three Fleming children and their mate, Melba Dixon, were alone, unsupervised and left to their own devices.

Older sister, Flo, was still feeling unwell. She was sound asleep on the front veranda when the four children began exploring the house.

Darrell's inquisitive eyes darted around the dining room. He pulled out a chair and climbed up and found a box of matches hidden high on a dresser.

They were put there for a reason; to be well away from prying fingers.

There had been minor problems in the past with Darrell's apparent fascination with matches and his mother thought it much safer to keep the fire-starters out of reach. Nellie's philosophy was simple: out of sight, out of mind.

Darrell often found dead matches around the house when playing and collected them in a box. To his credit, if he came across any unused matches he took them to his parents.

On this particular day, however, curiosity got the better of him. His younger siblings, and their friend, Melba, were equally as curious.

The children ventured outside and resumed playing soldiers. Again, Darrell was in charge as he led his unit around the house yard. He beat the old oil can he found earlier and fired off orders as they marched in single file away from the house.

Shouting and chortling, the children marched to a hay shed, seventy yards away that was laden with chaff and hay bales.

The children were armed with a box of matches.

Alice Dodd was at home, feeling ill. She and husband Claude lived in a cottage forty yards from the hay shed. Claude and fellow worker Bill Lowrey were bringing the cows in.

Alice heard the children laughing and shouting as they played. She was unaware they were unsupervised.

As Claude and Bill approached, they looked across at the hay shed. Bill noticed smoke coming from the adjoining chaff room. Flames were licking the shed's outer walls. Within minutes the old, timber structure was a flaming fireball.

'Oh, dear Jesus,' Claude whispered.

The men raced across to Ted Fleming's house, about a hundred yards away.

'Ted, come quickly, the hay shed's on fire. I'm worried about the children,' Bill yelled.

Ted, his son Gordon, and Ivy Dixon ran out to meet Claude.

'My God, where are the children?' Claude asked.

'Noel and Colleen are with their father; Darrell and Melba are back at the house with Flo — Melba is sound asleep,' Ivy replied frantically.

She had been away for only ten or 15 minutes. Surely, the kids were with Flo back at the main house. But she was horribly wrong.

Ivy ran back to make sure the children were safe, but they were nowhere to be seen. She remembered looking for matches on the kitchen dresser earlier in the day and realised they were now missing.

'Oh, dear God,' she whispered.

Ivy roused Flo and they raced back to the hay shed to help control the blaze.

'The children aren't there; I can't find them,' Ivy gasped.

Off in the distance, Tom Fleming saw smoke billowing from the hay shed. He rode at full gallop back to the house. Ivy and Flo met him at the house-yard gate.

'Where are the children?' he asked anxiously.

'Two of them are missing; I thought the other two were with you,' Ivy replied.

Tom handed Flo the reins and ran to the hay shed, where he

found Claude, Alice Dodd, Ted and Gordon, desperately trying to control the flames. There was little they could do but make sure the inferno didn't spread further.

A nephew, Jim Fleming, arrived with farm worker Clarrie Golledge and helped fight the fire.

Flames had spread across the grass and ignited a haystack and there were more haystacks and outbuildings nearby. Tom fretfully wondered where the children were. He swallowed hard. Surely, they weren't in the hay shed, for the love of God, surely not.

As Tom watched helplessly, the outer stringybark wall of the north-western corner of the hay shed, now fully alight and throwing off incredible plumes of heat, fell away from the main structure.

Inside, tucked away in a corner of the chaff room, were the blackened, charred bodies of four tiny children. They were huddled tightly together in one final embrace.

The bodies were burned so badly, they were unrecognisable. But Tom Fleming knew who they were.

His screams of despair, sadness and rage echoed across the vast, open paddocks of Lilydale. Tom fell to his knees and clenched his fists. Tears rolled down his cheeks. He was an utterly broken man.

Ivy Dixon collapsed in a crumpled, crying heap. She fainted from the sheer shock of seeing the smouldering remains of her daughter, Melba, clutching her dead playmates.

Claude Dodd and Ted and Gordon Fleming tried wildly to take control of the situation. But the terrifying trauma unfolding before their eyes was beyond comprehension.

The nearest telephone was three miles away at Gum Flat post office. Jim Fleming jumped on his uncle's horse and galloped off to get help. Claude and Gordon, with the help of Clarrie Golledge and Bill Lowrey, tried bravely to keep the flames at bay.

Alice Dodd and Flo Fleming, both sobbing with despair and coughing, choking and gasping from the rising smoke and flames, tried to comfort Tom and Ivy.

Flo was only eleven years of age and had just witnessed her two brothers and sister burn to death.

She stared helplessly at the smouldering remains of the children, only a few yards away. The lifeless, blistered, distorted faces of Darrell Fleming, Noel Fleming, Colleen Fleming and Melba Dixon stared back at her.

Inverell firefighters were at Lilydale within twenty minutes. Soon afterwards, station captain Tom Jacobs, rostered off on annual leave, arrived by motorcycle and assumed control of the operation.

More than 1500 feet of fire hose was rolled out to a dam and pumped back to the burning shed.

When the fire was under control and all but extinguished, firefighter Val Solomon crawled through the debris and retrieved the remains of the children.

Using a long-handled shovel, Solomon delicately removed the bodies, which were partially covered by a sheet of fallen corrugated iron.

One newspaper reported: 'Their heads and arms had practically been burnt from their bodies, and they were terribly charred. However, they had tried to bury themselves down in the chaff, which was nearly three-feet thick where they were lying. They had been unable to cover their bodies, but they had dug their legs into the chaff, which burned slowly and protected their limbs to some extent.'

Despite their best efforts, Jacobs and his men could not save the building, which had burned relentlessly for more than half an hour before they arrived.

The shed, a chaff cutter and most of the contents were completely destroyed — and so were the lives of the Fleming and Dixon families.

Inverell police sergeant Will Robson and Dr Murray Vernon arrived at Lilydale about 3.45 pm.

Robson saw the charred remains of the children laid out near the smouldering hay shed.

One of Darrell Fleming's legs was completely burnt off. His younger brother Noel's skull and body were severely disfigured and their little sister, Colleen, was missing both arms.

Melba Dixon was severely burned and barely recognisable.

Robson wiped a tear from his cheek and looked away.

With the help of firefighters, he carefully moved the bodies to the Fleming home.

* * *

Back at the house, Ivy Dixon sat at the kitchen table, numb from shock. She wept as she told Sgt Robson about Darrell Fleming's fascination with matches.

'There were matches on top of this dresser, but now they're missing,' Ivy said.

'Darrell had a habit of playing with matches so they were always kept out of reach.'

Claude Dodd told Robson he saw smoke as he returned from bringing in the cows for milking.

'Had we known the children were in the hay shed, every one of us would've risked our lives to save them,' he said.

An urgent message was sent to Nellie Fleming, in Sydney with Tom's mother Mary. She was told there was an accident but was unaware her children were dead. She returned to Inverell by rail, and broke down when told the tragic news. She clutched her rosary beads and wept a thousand tears.

Tom Fleming's soul was completely destroyed. 'The shock almost destroyed his reason, and for hours he was hardly able to describe what had happened,' newspapers reported.

Sgt Robson concluded the children were playing with matches, and accidentally set fire to the hay shed.

'As the fire worsened, the children became terror-stricken and huddled together in a corner of the chaff-room until the flames reached them,' he said.

The next day, Darrell Fleming, Noel Fleming, Colleen Fleming and Melba Dixon were laid to rest at Gum Flat Cemetery.

The *Inverell Times* reported:

> Mourners and sympathisers from all parts of the district followed the remains of the unfortunate Gum Flat fire victims to the village cemetery on Wednesday afternoon. The funeral cortege followed two vehicles carrying four tiny coffins. Both vehicles were laden with wreaths. The motorcade was more than a mile long. There was a mound of flowers on both vehicles, and two cars were requisitioned to carry the remaining floral tributes to the gravesides. There was not a dry eye in the peaceful rustic cemetery as the remains of the little ones were lowered to their last resting place.

Tom and Nellie Fleming found it impossible to return to

Lilydale. They stayed in Inverell, comforted by family and friends. Newspapers reported:

> The Flemings have remained in Inverell since the tragedy, for they are unable to face the Gum Flat farm. There is no rest from sorrow for the mother and father, for everywhere they look there is a reminder of their lost children. Friends of the couple are afraid for Mrs Fleming's health should she be forced to live again on the property, and are endeavouring to help them get away from the scene of their loss.

Inverell and Gum Flat Parents' and Citizens' Associations, in conjunction with Inverell Municipal Council, led by Mayor Spencer Butler, initiated fundraising events and subscriptions to help the stricken families.

'Our local picture show proprietor is arranging a benefit performance and other organisations in the district are helping out. Much sympathy is felt for the families, and it is hoped others will assist as well,' Mayor Butler said.

Apart from various fundraising endeavours, including a dance and euchre night at Gum Flat Hall, hundreds of pounds were directly donated by district families.

* * *

An inquest into the deaths of Melba Dixon, and Darrell, Noel and Colleen Fleming, was opened by district coroner Jim McIlveen at Inverell courthouse on 14 April.

McIlveen, a long-serving former Inverell mayor and highly respected public figure, solemnly addressed the inquiry: 'In all my twenty-seven years as district coroner, this is the most distressing and appalling case I've ever had to deal with,' he said.

Tom Fleming told the inquiry his son, Darrell, had been mildly infatuated with fire and matches.

He said a bag of kapok, a naturally grown fibre very similar to cotton, was once found alight in the Fleming home. 'No-one knew how it caught on fire,' Tom said.

Tom and Nellie Fleming insisted they always kept matches out of reach of the children.

'I am very particular about matches. I don't smoke but always carry them with me and never leave them lying around. Nellie, my wife, always kept them high up on a ledge or a piece of furniture, at least six feet off the ground. I told Ivy to do the same,' Tom explained.

Tom relived the terrible moments leading up to the discovery of the tiny bodies — everybody that tragic afternoon were focused on putting out the fire; no-one realised the children were in the chaff room, adjoining the hay shed.

'The flames leapt out some distance on the east and north-east side of the shed, and not on the chaff room side,' Tom said.

'There was a good breeze blowing from the west and the fire had burned the grass on that side of the shed before I reached it. The chaff room could have been approached from the west or south-western side in the early stages of the fire,' Tom said.

Sgt Robson theorised Darrell Fleming took the matches from the dining room dresser and, with the other three children, went to the chaff room.

'It is likely Darrell struck a match, which ignited the hay and started the fire,' Sgt Robson said. 'When the fire started to blaze, the children got entrapped in the chaff room and were unable to get out of the burning building.'

Sgt Robson believed the children were overcome by smoke before the flames reached them — or their rescuers.

'There were no suspicious circumstances surrounding the cause of the fire,' he said.

Coroner McIlveen summed up the day's proceedings:

'There is no doubt, in my mind, as to what has caused the death of these children, but there is a doubt as to the origin of the fire. I am quite satisfied, however, that the fire did not originate in the chaff room,' he said.

'It must have been burning for some time before it reached the chaff shed.'

He questioned Sgt Robson's theory the fire was started by Darrell Fleming: 'There was no evidence that Darrell had matches; no-one saw him with them and no-one saw him take the missing box from the dresser in the dining room. The children may have gone into the chaff shed to play and it is possible the fire may have been started by spontaneous combustion and trapped them there,' he said.

The coroner referred to a hay shed fire a few weeks earlier at nearby Swanbrook.

'No-one was near the shed (at Swanbrook), nor had been for some time, but a fire started, more than likely by spontaneous combustion,' he said.

Coroner McIlveen found, 'The children succumbed from burning as a result of a fire which destroyed a hay and chaff shed and contents on 2 April 1935 but the evidence does not enable me to say what caused the conflagration.'

* * *

Six months after the tragedy, Tom and Nellie penned a letter to the *Inverell Times*, thanking district residents for their unshakable support, friendship and financial assistance. The newspaper reported:

> Mr and Mrs Fleming express sincere appreciation of the Inverell people's tangible indication of their sympathy in connection with the blazing barn tragedy at Gum Flat in which three of their children perished in flames.
>
> Tom and Nellie wrote: 'We particularly wish to thank the residents of Gum Flat and Beaulieu and all others who assisted in any way whatsoever to help us recover our material losses.'

Sadly, there was absolutely nothing the generous townsfolk of Inverell and Gum Flat could do to bring back the four tiny children killed that horrifying April afternoon in 1935.

Postscript:
The Inverell fire tragedy left lasting scars.

Bill Lowrey was one of many frantic, shocked witnesses who tried bravely to put out the blaze. As the inferno intensified, he and the others scrambled to stop the flames spreading to nearby paddocks and outbuildings. Even then, they were unsure whether the children were inside the barn.

Bill's daughter, Gloria Baldwin, said her father and Claude Dodd were bringing the cows in for milking when they saw the smoke.

'They raced to the barn but could not control the flames. My aunty told me they watched the wall collapse and saw the children huddled together, but they could do nothing.'

Tom Fleming's nephew, Jim Fleming, jumped on his uncle's horse and galloped to the nearest telephone at Gum Flat to alert the fire brigade. His crucial ride and the devastation and death he witnessed that day wounded him for life.

Jim struggled to block out the traumatic events. He suffered a severe breakdown and was committed to an asylum which, sadly, was the common approach to mental health conditions in the 1930s.

'Something like that would affect anyone for life. There was no such thing as counselling in those days,' Gloria said. 'The experience left Jim in a terrible state, with little or no medical help. He was placed in an institution in Sydney.'

Only through Tom Fleming's kindness and genuine concern was Jim able to recover and lead a normal life.

Tom was a broken human being after losing his three children in the fire. The guilt was heartbreaking; his soul was empty and shattered, yet his kindness and love of family rose above the tragedy.

His inherent desire to help others still flickered and despite everything he'd been through, and everything he'd lost, Tom was there for his nephew.

'Tom later had Jim removed from the institution and placed under his care,' Gloria said. 'He took him under his wing. Later, Jim joined the army, married and had a family, and went on to live a pretty normal life.'

Tom and Nellie Fleming and their surviving children, Ronald, Pat and Flo, left the district. There were simply too many sad memories.

They relocated to Gunnamatta Bay near Cronulla, and tried to get on with their lives.

Tom was later employed as caretaker of Redfern Town Hall.

Three more children were born — twins Colleen and Bruce, and a son Darryl, known as Des.

Colleen and Darryl were named after siblings lost in the blaze.

Nellie died in 1967, aged sixty-one, and Tom later retired to Belmore, near Canterbury. He died in 1989 at the age of ninety-six.

Up until his death, he was the oldest serving justice of the peace in NSW.

Tom and Nellie are buried together in the Catholic section of Rookwood Cemetery.

CHAPTER 19

I SHOT HER BECAUSE
I DON'T LIKE HER

The pretty Italian girl spotted the four young Australian soldiers and was immediately smitten.

But it wasn't their rugged good looks that impressed her — it was the English brand of cigarettes they were smoking.

A deal was brokered and several packets of Turret, Craven A and Wild Woodbines were exchanged for an assortment of civilian clothing and apparel.

This covert exchange enabled the group of soldiers — all from the Garah district in north-western NSW — to embark on an epic escape across the Swiss Alps during World War II, on their way home to freedom.

In 1943 the war across Europe raged unchecked and was nigh unstoppable.

Brothers Paul and Carl Carrigan, their cousin Ron Fitzgerald — also from Garah, thirty-two miles north-west of Moree — and Lloyd Ledingham from Moppin, spent nearly two-and-a-half torturous years in Italian prisoner-of-war camps.

Italy surrendered to the Allies on 8 September 1943. During the subsequent chaos and confusion, thousands of prisoners escaped from camps across Italy.

Groups of allied soldiers defied the odds and crossed the Swiss Alps. Others headed south to allied lines and many more were rounded up by the Nazis and sent to PoW camps in Germany.

Fitzgerald, Ledingham and the Carrigan brothers crossed the border to freedom, wearing the civvies they traded for cigarettes with the pretty Italian girl.

The Moree boys, as they famously became known, were helped by sympathetic villagers and farmers as they made their way through rugged terrain across the Swiss Alps — a path to liberty Italian partisans called *sentieri della liberta*, or the Trails to Freedom.

It was the start of winter and conditions were appalling.

They left Biella in the foothills of the Swiss Alps north of Turin and one week later crossed the border at the Monte Moro Pass.

The Moree boys were members of the 11th Anti-Tank Battery. They were captured in Mekeli, Libya, on 8 April 1941.

Through the efforts of the Apostolic delegate to Australia and New Zealand, Archbishop John Panico, they were located safe and well at Campo 78 in Sulmona in the province of L'Aquila in Abruzzo — a holding camp where prisoners were grouped by rank and nationality.

They were later moved to Campo 57, a notorious prison at Grupignano, near Udine in the province of Fruili in north-east Italy, not far from the Yugoslav border.

Then, in early 1943, the Moree boys were four of nearly 800 Australian and New Zealand soldiers moved to Campo 106, a labour camp at Vercelli in the Piedmont region, in north-western Italy.

There were more than seventy PoW camps across Italy, holding thousands of allied soldiers and officers.

Archbishop Panico headed the newly created Apostolic Delegation Prisoners of War Information Bureau and the Moree boys were the first Australian soldiers traced by the Vatican.

In October 1941, about six months after being captured, Paul Carrigan penned a letter from Campo 78 to his parents, Alexander and Amy Carrigan.

He assured them all was well.

'The camp is proving to be quite a pleasant one,' Paul wrote. 'We are situated in a valley surrounded by high snow-capped mountains. The scenery is very pretty and the sun quite warm. The trip in the train was delightful. This is a very fertile land and everything seems to grow luxuriously. The country looks very nice, with its green crops and beautiful trees.'

The prisoners were confined to concrete huts. They were supplied with a bed, mattress, sheet, blanket and pillow, and soap and towels were on hand.

Red Cross food parcels containing butter, tinned milk, chocolate, biscuits, raisins, prunes and tinned jam and tinned meat were supplied regularly.

'The parcels are generally British, Scottish or Canadian. The Canadian parcels are the most popular,' Paul wrote.

Prisoners laid out a football field and also played cricket and basketball. There was a cinema and library, as well as a newspaper written, edited and printed by prisoners.

There was also an orchestra of sorts, as Paul wrote:

We have an excellent group of melody-makers, the instruments being a saxophone, cornet, violin and piano accordion.

There are three or four dances a week and the sight of men dancing together is no longer strange to me. I have seen the pastime practised at home by inebriated frolickers (but) I have not yet taken the floor.

We are all in the best of health and spirits and are

being treated very well, so there is no need to worry about us.

If Campo 78 was 'quite pleasant', Campo 57 was the complete opposite.

The prison was notoriously commanded by brutal fascist Colonel Vittorio Calcaterra, historically described as a 'sadist and a beast and an accessory to murder'.

Australian War Memorial records described conditions at Campo 57 as extremely harsh: 'Food was poor, and housing was crowded and insanitary. The prisoners had to improvise their own medical treatment.'

Pneumonia and kidney disease — known colloquially as the '57 twins' — were rife.

During the course of the war Campo 57 held more than 4500 allied servicemen.

The Australian War Memorial said Calcaterra's regime reduced the camp to a mass of neurosis 'as no-one knew when his turn would come to be victimised'.

Calcaterra died before he could be tried as a war criminal — he was slain by Italian partisans.

In April 1943, the Moree boys were moved to Campo 106 and put to work in the rice fields around Vercelli.

About five months later, with the Italian Government on the brink of collapse, rumours spread quickly that evacuation was probable. Most guards deserted the camps, leaving prisoners to either fend for themselves against the Nazis or find freedom.

As German troops descended on compounds around northern Italy, hundreds of prisoners — including the Moree boys — escaped to the nearby hills and made their way to freedom over the Swiss Alps.

After twelve months in neutral Switzerland, Fitzgerald, Ledingham and the Carrigan brothers were sent home to Australia. They were part of a large contingent of allied POWs repatriated from Italy, through Switzerland, as well as Germany, through Sweden.

The servicemen arrived in Sydney on 21 November 1944 and were reunited with loved ones waiting at Sydney Showground.

They spoke highly of the hospitality shown by neutral countries, where roast beef, baked potatoes, plenty of fresh fruit and Swedish beer were often served.

Paul and Carl Carrigan enlisted together, were captured together and escaped together.

They enlisted at Paddington and wore consecutive army numbers — NX51288 and NX51289.

On 27 November 1944, the Red Cross arranged a public homecoming for the returned men.

They came back to north-western NSW celebrated war heroes with incredible stories of survival, fortitude and bravery.

When the much-deserved pomp and ceremony subsided, these homebred heroes returned to peaceful life on the farm.

For Paul Carrigan, however, the ravages of conflict and the grim memories of prison camps never left him. Four years after returning home, in the middle of Moree's main shopping precinct, his demons surfaced in the most horrific way.

* * *

Alex and Joan Fingleton's trip to Moree on Tuesday 26 October 1948 from the family property Tyrone, near Gurley, was routine.

It gave the couple a chance to catch up with friends and

family, do the weekly shopping and tidy up business affairs and farming matters.

Moree's main street was abuzz with people and activity, as was the norm on any weekday afternoon in the late 1940s. Shops and cafés were doing a roaring trade. Banks had queues of customers finalising transactions before the close of business and hotels on the main intersection of Balo and Heber Streets were steadily filling with late-afternoon patrons keen to get in a few cold ones before 6 pm closing — the 'six o'clock swill'.

Traffic was bumper to bumper along both main thoroughfares and parking spaces were scarce.

Two PMG workers repaired lines on the Max Hotel corner and municipal council staff swept gutters and footpaths.

But on this pleasant spring afternoon in 1948, Moree's bustling CBD was silenced by the piercing crack of a single pistol shot that ended with the murder of a member of one of the district's most respected farming families.

* * *

Joan Estelle Fingleton died instantly when she was shot at point-blank range in busy Heber Street by her brother, thirty-one-year-old Paul Carrigan.

Mrs Fingleton, 38, was sitting in the family car, parked outside the Max Hotel. Her husband Alex, 52, was in the driver's seat and their fourteen-month-old daughter, Anne-Marie, was sleeping peacefully in a bassinet between her parents.

Mrs Fingleton's mother, Amy Carrigan, was in the back seat of the vehicle.

Paul Carrigan was a troubled man with deep-seated

psychological problems brought on by the shocking memories of war and times spent in Italian prison camps.

He was armed with a Savage automatic .32 calibre pistol. He took the firearm, belonging to his father, from the top of a chest of drawers at the family home at Welbon, Garah.

Carrigan saw the Fingleton's family car and approached the passenger-side window. He fired a single, fatal shot at his sister. The bullet pierced Mrs Fingleton's heart. She died instantly.

Alex Fingleton jumped from the vehicle and deftly disarmed his brother-in-law, who fled to a nearby vehicle and sped away.

* * *

In the late 1940s Australia was bubbling with enthusiasm and confidence. The war was over and a new dawn signalled a fresh beginning.

And while the end of World War II heralded prosperity and a much-needed economic boost across Australia, it also brought home shattered servicemen and women badly affected by the consequences of global conflict.

In the modern era, bruised and battered heroes — many of them emotional and psychological wrecks — are cared for, treated and given every chance to return to a semblance of their pre-war lives.

For many, post-traumatic stress disorder (PTSD) is the sad reward for defending one's country. The disorder is now recognised as a serious and very real illness, affecting thousands of returned service men and women.

But in 1948, when these war-ravaged heroes were lauded and back-slapped for their courageous deeds, their demons

— and dark despair — remained deeply embedded. Those affected didn't reach out and talk about their fears, emotions or depression. It simply wasn't the accepted approach, especially for war heroes returning home to family and loved ones.

The safer option was to keep a brave face, rather than admit frailty.

This was an era when the term 'shell-shocked' was whispered in hushed tones and quickly dismissed. The subject was taboo; the condition was everywhere, but no-one talked about it.

*   *   *

Paul Gerald Carrigan was a crushed man.

He returned to Australia a war hero and resumed his life — the broken, shattered shards of it — at Welbon.

He wore his uniform with pride and represented his country with integrity, but his pride and integrity couldn't deflect the horrors of war.

His family was worried. Carrigan wasn't the same man who left peaceful farm life a few years earlier.

And, on that spring Tuesday afternoon in Moree in 1948, his demons surfaced in the most wretched way.

Carrigan killed his sister in cold blood in front of a number of witnesses before jumping in a green utility and fleeing to the family farm, about ten miles from Garah.

He was followed by police and, after questioning, taken into custody.

The following day at Moree courthouse, Carrigan was charged with feloniously and maliciously murdering his sister and transferred to Maitland Gaol.

A coronial inquiry into the death of Joan Estelle Fingleton

was opened on 10 November 1948 before Coroner Henry Francis Brown.

Hotelier John Bourke Deery and barman James Rawcliffe were among numerous witnesses called to give evidence.

Carrigan called into the Royal Hotel about 2.30 pm and had one beer with Deery. He left the hotel but returned a few minutes later to the lounge bar with his mother, Amy.

'Paul ordered another middy of beer for himself and a glass of dry ginger-ale for his mother,' Deery said. 'They had their drinks and left their glasses at the table. Paul ordered a packet of cigarettes, which I got for him. He then left the hotel with his mother. He was quite sober but appeared a little more quiet than usual. He was in old clothes which I thought was a little unusual as he is usually well-dressed.'

When Carrigan left the hotel he walked up Heber Street to the Max Hotel.

Barman James Rawcliffe told the inquest Carrigan entered the hotel about 3.15 pm.

'I have known Paul for about ten years,' Rawcliffe told the coroner.

'I saw him have one middy of beer. He was on his own and said 'good day' when I spoke to him. He drank his beer and then walked out of the hotel. Paul was quite sober. A few minutes later I was in the lounge bar and heard a shot from the direction of the front of the hotel from the Heber Street side.'

Alex Fingleton said he parked the family car outside the Max Hotel in Heber Street and his wife Joan and their baby daughter remained in the car while he attended to some business.

While Alex was absent, Joan's mother, Amy, arrived at the vehicle and sat in the back seat, chatting with her daughter. She'd just been at the Royal Hotel with Paul.

'I returned to the car and got into the driver's seat. My daughter was seated next to me and Joan was on the outside of the front seat,' Alex said.

'As I sat in the car, I saw Paul approaching and Mrs Carrigan said to me, "talk to Paul and keep him occupied". I looked to my right and saw Paul walking along the side of Heber Street at the back of my car.

'He walked towards the back of the car and I said, "Hello, Paul". He kept walking and went out of my sight around the back of the car towards the side on which my wife and her mother were sitting. I did not turn around and just sat there. I then heard a shot fired and I looked around to my left and saw my wife fall back on the seat and gasp.'

Alex jumped from the vehicle and raced around to the passenger side.

'I saw Paul standing about a foot from the side of the car next to where Joan was sitting,' he said. 'His right hand was outstretched and there was a pistol in his hand which was pointed straight at my wife. I immediately placed my left arm around his body and with my right hand I grasped his right hand in which he was holding the pistol.'

During the struggle Carrigan dropped the pistol and managed to escape Fingleton's grasp, fleeing to his vehicle, parked nearby.

Fingleton told the coroner he and his wife were always on the best of terms with the accused.

'I have never seen him in any disagreement with any person,' Fingleton said.

'Mrs Fingleton had always been very fond of her brother and had been worried about him.'

Another brother, Frank, told the inquiry their sibling

had received psychiatric treatment since returning from active duty.

'Paul went with the armed forces in 1941 and saw service with the anti-tank brigade in Libya. He was captured and was a prisoner-of-war for about two years. He then escaped and went to Switzerland and returned home in 1944 in November,' Frank said.

'He came to Moree on three months' leave and on his return I noticed he became quieter. He was morose at times and seemed bitter towards life in general.'

Frank said his brother returned to Sydney and remained in the army for about another twelve months. He returned home as soon as he was discharged and went to live with his parents. At times, he went to his own property, Dumienda, at Mungindi.

'He was a moderate drinker, and drink seemed to affect him in that he became more morose,' Frank said. 'During the past twelve months I have seen Paul, at various times, and during the last three months I have seen him every day.'

He said Paul at times seemed very contented and at other times he appeared most unhappy and worried. He received treatment in Sydney for nervous troubles.

'The last time I saw Paul was on 10 October at my parents' home. He appeared very depressed and did not want to talk to me. I have never heard him express any threat against any person,' Frank said.

Police Inspector William Wright told the coroner, when he asked Carrigan whether he shot his sister, Carrigan replied: 'I shot her because I don't like her.'

Carrigan told Insp Wright he did not feel sorry about killing his sister. He refused to write or dictate a statement.

Police officers Henry Orman, William Parker, Albert Brown

and Reg Hueston, who found Carrigan at Welbon station, also gave evidence.

Sgt Brown, of the Sydney CIB ballistics section, said the pistol used was fitted with two safety mechanisms — one operated manually, the other, automatically.

'The manual safety was in good order, but the automatic safety was not in working order because the trigger lock was not assembled correctly,' Brown said.

PMG cable-joiner George Simpson and PMG linesman George James were working on the corner of Balo and Heber Streets when they heard the pistol shot.

'I looked up and saw a man with a pistol in his hand and he was near the front door of a sedan car,' Simpson said.

'I saw another man race up and knock the pistol from the other man's hand. The man that had the pistol moved smartly to a green utility vehicle.'

George James corroborated his workmate's testimony.

'On his way to the green utility he (the accused) paused and looked back at the sedan. I then went and rang the ambulance and doctor,' James said.

The coroner found Paul Carrigan 'feloniously and maliciously murdered his sister, Joan Estelle Fingleton'.

Carrigan was committed to stand trial at the Central Criminal Court, Sydney, on 22 November 1948 — exactly four years and one day since arriving on Australian shores a war hero.

On 2 December he was found not guilty of murder on the grounds of insanity.

Three doctors certified Carrigan was insane and suffering from a split personality.

Psychiatrist John McGeorge said he saw Carrigan in March

1946 — more than two years before the murder and about eighteen months after Carrigan returned to Australia.

'He was then vague in his statements and displayed little interest in what was going on,' Dr McGeorge told the court. 'He received treatment in an institution, his condition improved considerably, and he left the institution in May 1946.'

Six months later Carrigan's mental health deteriorated and he returned to Dr McGeorge for treatment.

Dr McGeorge examined Carrigan after the murder and told the court he believed the accused was currently, and at the time of the murder, certifiably insane.

'The patient told me he believed his actions were controlled in some way, and that some sort of influence was making him do things,' Dr McGeorge said.

Crown prosecutor Charles Vincent Rooney told the Central Criminal Court the facts were not disputed.

'Carrigan was a prisoner of war and his health had not been good for a number of years,' Rooney said. 'The Crown and the defence agree on Carrigan's mental condition.'

He was ordered by Justice Leslie Herron to be kept in strict custody at Long Bay Gaol until 'the Governor's pleasure is known'.

Paul Gerald Carrigan, born on 28 July 1917, died at North Ryde psychiatric centre on 4 November 1972. He was fifty-five.

He was buried at Macquarie Park Cemetery at North Ryde, Sydney — his demons finally silenced.

* * *

Joan Estelle Fingleton was born in 1910 at Goondiwindi, one of eight children to Alex and Amy Carrigan, members of a prominent pioneering family.

Mrs Fingleton was a well-known and popular figure in the Moree community and was a volunteer for numerous charitable organisations.

In 1929 she helped raise £5744 for the Moree District Hospital and Royal Alexandria Hospital when she stood as country queen for the Moree Hospital and Commercial Travellers' Carnival. This equates to more than $440,000 in new millennium dollars.

At least ten members of the Carrigan family, as well as three first cousins from the Fitzgerald family, enlisted during World War II, including leading-aircraftsman Ron Carrigan, with the RAAF in Canada; leading-aircraftsman Dominic Carrigan, in Lindfield; gunner Ernie Carrigan, with the anti-tank regiment in Grovely, Brisbane; gunner Andrew Carrigan, in Palestine; and brothers Carl and Paul Carrigan, gunners in the anti-tank regiment in Palestine. Lex, Max, Aubrey and Brian Carrigan joined the 24th Light Horse Militia before enlisting in the AIF Artillery.

Postscript:

In this day and age, Paul Carrigan's split personality would have unquestionably been diagnosed as post-traumatic stress disorder and treatable.

Andy Cullen, who left school in 1995 to join the Australian Army and reach the rank of major, fully understands Carrigan's mental anguish.

Cullen, a former explosive ordnance disposal technician, left the army after seventeen years' service.

About six months later he was hospitalised after suffering a complete mental breakdown.

Cullen and his wife Zoe now run the charity, PTSD Resurrected, which provides a holistic approach to healing and support to individuals and families suffering from trauma, PTSD and depression.

Cullen says Paul Carrigan would have nowhere to go or no-one to turn to in 1948 — support groups like PTSD Resurrected simply didn't exist.

'What an incredibly sad story,' Cullen said. 'However, the reality for Paul and many of his veteran colleagues who suffered from mental health issues following the war was that there was simply very little support available.

'Not a lot was known about PTSD or shellshock as it was then known and even less was done to help those suffering.

'Fortunately, today sufferers of PTSD as a result of service can find help in many areas of society and there are many varied treatments available to assist individuals and families to help them restore hope, find healing and redefine their purpose in society,' Cullen said.

'Unfortunately, we still lose too many veterans to suicide as a result of PTSD and more must be done as a community to help individuals and families who are often suffering in silence. The stigma of mental health is changing and as a society, we must band together to help people like Paul find peace and healing after war.

'We are not meant to live in isolation and fear; we are meant to participate in life together as a community of caring people ready to lend a hand to someone in need,' he said.

CHAPTER 20

OLD VEECH IS NEXT!

Escorting convicted criminal George Lorie from Walgett lock-up to Narrabri railway station was no easy task for Carinda police constable William Noble.

Lorie was found guilty of stealing more than fifty sheep from Quilbone station, a 10,000-acre spread near Quambone in western NSW.

Quilbone was owned by well-known squatter and western districts pioneer, Patrick Veech, a son of ticket-of-leave convict, Bryan Veech.

George and Emily Lorie, and their six children, lived next door. Lorie's selection — named Lulls Luck — comprised eight hundred acres on the edge of the Great Macquarie Marshes. The property was considered some of the best grazing country in the district.

At the Walgett Quarter Sessions on 21 March 1902, Judge Ernest Docker sentenced Lorie to four years' imprisonment for stealing Veech's sheep in October the previous year.

The court heard Lorie employed a Chinese labourer, George Gee Sing, to dig a deep trench near his house. He told Gee Sing he was establishing a fruit orchard and would use the carcases of his poorest sheep for fertiliser.

Not long after finishing the job, Gee Sing was awoken one night by strange noises near Lorie's sheep pens.

Gee Sing was curious. He crept across and covertly watched Lorie shear sheep under the glow of a crude lamp made from

George Lorie murdered pioneer Patrick Veech in 1905 before slicing his own throat as a police search party closed in (Image credit: Museums of History NSW — State Archives Collection)

Patrick Veech arrived in Australia as a child with his convict father, Bryan Veech, in 1838. Over the next sixty years, the Veech family prospered. They owned vast tracts of grazing and farming country around Wellington and Quambone, including the properties Quilbone and Mountain View. Patrick Veech was murdered by George Lorie on 11 September 1905 (Image credit: Museums of History NSW — State Archives Collection).

an old tin can and rag wick, known as a slush light.

Once the sheep were shorn, Lorie slaughtered the beasts, removed the heads and threw the carcases in the trench dug by Gee Sing just days earlier.

Gee Sing, still awaiting payment for the work, confronted Lorie the next day.

After a violent argument, Gee Sing went to the police. He alleged he was owed money for digging the trench and told police about Lorie's midnight shearing activities.

Patrick Veech was notified, and a quick muster and head count of sheep in a paddock adjoining Lorie's selection showed fifty woolly wethers were missing.

Further investigations revealed Lorie's seasonal clip was due to be put through the Quambone wool scour. Veech identified fifty fleeces, minus tar brands, as most likely belonging to Quilbone station.

Suspicions were confirmed when pieces of the missing brands were recovered in a separate bale.

When Lorie's land was dug up, five shorn and headless carcases were found and identified as Quilbone-bred. Aboriginal trackers also recovered the scorched jawbones of a hundred fully-grown sheep in the remains of a fire on Lorie's selection.

Judge Docker wasted little time slotting Lorie for four years.

As Lorie was escorted down the courthouse steps, he noticed Veech and threatened to kill the old pioneer. Apparently bad blood had been swirling between Lorie and Veech for years.

Constable Noble, tall and lean with a huge handle-bar moustache, told the prisoner to keep his mouth shut.

'Keep walking Lorie unless you want the judge to add a few more years to your sentence.'

The next morning, Noble and Lorie boarded a Cobb & Co coach bound for Narrabri, about 120 miles due east. The prisoner was chained and handcuffed. He wasn't going anywhere in a hurry.

Once in Narrabri, they would board a passenger train and head to Maitland.

Noble sighed; a few long days and nights across rough ground, dry gullies and endless miles of railway line lay ahead.

Lorie, also known by the name Sullivan, was short and wiry, with gaunt features and a tangled, unkempt beard. His face was weathered and lined, and he looked much older than his forty-two years. He was known around the shearing sheds as 'Chinese Sullivan', 'the white Chinaman' or just 'Chinnie'. He was feared across the NSW western districts and outback Queensland, and notorious for his heavy drinking, short temper and incredible strength and agility.

Legend had it Lorie was so good at his craft he 'could shear a sheep so clean the pink skin could be seen all over'.

Contemporary reports, however, suggest he was despised by fellow shearers as a morose, sullen figure who preferred his own company, rarely fraternised with workmates, and ate alone.

One newspaper suggested Lorie was given the sobriquet 'white Chinaman' because he only employed Chinese workers at his Quambone property.

Some shearers were a bit more creative. They said Chinese blood coursed through Lorie's veins, all because of an apparent lack of body hair. The claim made for a good yarn in the sheds at smoko time, but is more than likely just that — a good yarn.

In 1886, Lorie famously led a shearers' revolt at Beaconsfield station, near Longreach in central Queensland, despite being a non-unionist and not very well-liked in the sheds. District graziers had banded together and lowered the shearers' pay rate and Lorie was far from happy with the cockies' cartel.

About forty men were still prepared to work for the reduced rate, however — until five hundred furious shearers arrived at Beaconsfield station to convince them otherwise.

Beaconsfield, managed by Walter Anderson for pastoral behemoth George Fairbairn, was one of Australia's premier sheep stations and consistently ran about 100,000 head.

The same year that Lorie turned up with his blood boiling, an Australian record was established when twenty-seven horsemen moved 43,000 sheep forty miles from Barcaldine to Beaconsfield station.

Lorie, only aged twenty-seven at the time, stood before the angry mob and wielded a pair of rusty shearing blades high in the air. 'I've had enough of this business. The first man to put shears into wool in these sheds will get these through the guts!'

The men knew Lorie wasn't kidding and his violent threats won the day. The men packed away their blades until the graziers backed down and upped the pay rate.

The confrontation was a preface of sorts to the birth of unionism in the pastoral industry, and glorified Lorie as a working class hero.

But sixteen years later, this unlikely hero was on his way to Maitland Gaol to sit out a four-year stretch for knocking off sheep from his neighbour's place.

As the Cobb & Co coach trundled through the Pilliga scrub, Constable Noble dozed lightly.

Lorie saw his chance. He raised his cuffed, clenched fists and brought them down hard on the constable's head.

But Noble was too quick. He jammed his revolver into Lorie's mouth hard enough to draw blood. Lorie froze. The taste of cold steel against his tongue wasn't pleasant.

Overhead, driver Tom Lakewood sensed something amiss. He reined the horses and drew the coach to a halt.

Lakewood scrambled down and helped Noble shorten up Lorie's leg-irons and handcuffs.

'Looks like we've got us a live one here, guv'nor,' Lakewood muttered.

Noble nodded. He was dazed but otherwise okay. 'I'll be glad to see the back of this bastard when we get to Maitland.'

Lorie's desperate bid for freedom was a very real indication of what lay ahead — a pre-curser to the tragic chain of events that unfolded after he was later transferred to Goulburn Gaol and released from there in 1905.

* * *

Lorie's family life is unclear. Newspaper reports say he and Emily lived together 'as man and wife for many years'.

At one point they were in outback Queensland, where Lorie earned a living in the sheds.

Some family trees suggest Lorie married a young girl named Ellen Alma Mahaffie at Tenterfield in 1887. 'Mahaffie' was possibly her mother's surname.

When Lorie and Ellen moved to Quambone in the 1890s, Ellen became known as 'Emily'. By the time Lorie was sitting in Goulburn Gaol in the early 1900s, Emily adopted her father's surname and became 'Emily Kearnal'.

Her surname was spelt several ways, including 'Kanel', 'Keanell', and 'Kernal'. She was also known as Emily Smith, Amly Lorie and Emily Cora Capel.

Probate records refer to her as 'Emily Kearnal', and that

name has been used for the purpose of this story.

When George Lorie walked out the front gates of Goulburn Gaol a free man on 25 May 1905 he made his way back to Quambone — and into Emily's somewhat hesitant arms.

It wasn't long before Lorie returned to his old ways. And he quickly worked out there was something not quite right with Emily. She was different, somehow.

Lorie discovered Emily was seeing a shearer named David Harris. The affair apparently began when Lorie was doing time at Goulburn and continued after his release.

He learned Emily had sold off most of his livestock to Patrick Veech, his arch-nemesis. She disposed of some of their furniture and personal belongings as well and was planning to take off with Harris.

Lorie, his blood boiling, confronted Emily at their Quambone selection.

Children Frank, Mary, Beatrice and George were with their mother. Oldest son, Andrew, had not long left home to seek farm work and oldest daughter, Ettie, was working as a house servant for a family at Carinda.

'When I find that mongrel, I'll put a bullet through his heart, and that goes for old Veech and his mangy mob as well,' Lorie screamed.

Emily feared for her life. She and the children fled the cottage. Lorie gave chase a short distance on foot, levelled a pistol in their direction and fired several stray shots.

Emily took off to Carinda police station and reported the incident. She also gave police details about a bullock Lorie allegedly pilfered from Quilbone station and his murderous threats toward her lover and members of the Veech family.

'He said he would hunt down David Harris and the Veeches

and kill the lot of them,' she told police.

Lorie was quickly rounded up and charged with attempting to discharge a loaded firearm with intent to do grievous bodily harm, as well as stealing the bullock — a charge he vigorously denied.

Incredibly, despite his well-documented temper, a criminal history peppered with gaol time, and Emily's detailed statement to police officers at Carinda, Lorie was given bail and listed to appear at Coonamble Quarter Sessions on 21 September.

The minute he made bail on 5 September, Lorie sold his farm for £350 to Coonamble alderman William Young and set aside £50 to pay for legal representation at his trial.

On 10 September, he went gunning for David Harris.

Lorie found Harris with Emily at the Junction Hotel, a notorious roadside inn also known as The Shingle Hut, about thirty miles from Quambone. Harris and Emily were living nearby.

Lorie aimed a .22 calibre rifle at Harris and fired. Emily's lover raised his arms to protect himself and a bullet pierced his hand.

'Old Veech is next,' Lorie yelled.

Harris and Emily ran from the pub and hid in the scrub; Harris was wounded but okay. Lorie jumped on his horse and headed to Quilbone station.

Police were quickly notified and an urgent message was sent to the Veech family to be on the lookout for Lorie, who was armed, dangerous and baying for blood.

Early the following morning, 11 September, Lorie crouched in a pig pen on Quilbone station, not far from a set of workers' huts. He was camouflaged under some strips of stringybark.

About 8.30 am, Patrick Veech's sons, Cornelius and Barney,

were making their way to the station stockyards. As they walked past the pig pen, a gunshot shattered the stillness.

Cornelius, known widely as Con, felt a bullet rush past his ear.

'Look out, Con, I think Lorie is in with the pigs,' Barney yelled.

Both men scrambled back to the homestead and gathered firearms and ammunition. Inside the family home was their mother, Bridget and daughters Alice, Annie and Bridget. Housemaid Martha Young was with the family.

Another son, seventeen-year-old Malachi, was boarding in Sydney and studying at the technical education branch of the Department of Public Instruction.

As Con and Barney Veech guardedly made their way through the house paddock, they saw Lorie dart behind the workers' huts. Con mounted his horse and gave chase. Lorie aimed his weapon at Veech, who immediately jumped from his horse.

Lorie sprang to his feet and ran towards one of the workers' huts, where 74-year-old Patrick Veech and another son, Louis, had sought refuge. Also in the hut was Michael Frawley, an elderly gentleman, long retired, but still living on the property.

Lorie ran through the door and cornered Patrick. He fired but the rifle jammed. In a fit of rage, Lorie raised the firearm and struck Patrick in the head with the rifle butt. Patrick fell to the floor, blood pouring from the wound. Lorie raised the rifle high and struck the old man twice more.

The violent attack lasted less than a minute.

Neighbour Thomas Rutledge was arriving at Quilbone station as Lorie fired at Con Veech. The shot startled him. He saw a cloud of dust rise from the pig pen and Lorie running to the hut. Rutledge watched from a distance. A few minutes later, Lorie emerged from the building and took off along a creek bed and out of sight.

As Rutledge approached the hut, Louis Veech ran out and met the neighbour.

'Father is dead! Lorie has killed our father,' Louis sobbed.

Rutledge ran inside the cottage and found Patrick barely breathing. The old pioneer died minutes later.

*   *   *

An inquest into the death of Patrick Joseph Veech was held two days later on Quilbone station. District Coroner Henry Giles Shaw presided.

Dr Thomas Bertram told the inquiry Veech died from a fractured skull and other injuries to the head. He said the injuries were caused by a blunt instrument, most likely to have been the butt end of a rifle.

After hearing evidence from Veech's sons, Michael Frawley and neighbour Thomas Rutledge, Coroner Shaw returned a verdict of wilful murder against George Lorie.

*   *   *

The body of Patrick Veech was taken by special rail to Wellington, about 150 miles south-east of Quambone, and buried in the family vault at Wellington Catholic Cemetery.

The funeral was conducted by Archdeacon David D'Arcy and Wellington undertaker Christopher Shakespeare. The *Freeman's Journal* reported:

The late Patrick Joseph Veech was a very old resident of this state and part of his life was spent in the Wellington district. He was a native of County Meath, Ireland, and came to the colony at an early age. He was engaged extensively in pastoral pursuits, and amassed considerable property. He was a kindly man of somewhat retiring disposition, and was held in the highest esteem in the locality. His kindness to the poor, and even to the family of the man who caused his death, was proverbial.

Patrick arrived in Australia from Ireland in 1838 as a child with his convict father, Bryan Veech.

On 19 December 1837, his father was arrested in Palmerstown, County Kilkenny, and charged with being in possession of a wad of forged, thirty-shilling banknotes. The total haul was just over £11.

Veech, aged forty when arrested, claimed he received the money as payment for two heifers at Smithfield, north of Dublin.

Judge Johnston didn't believe the story and sentenced Veech to fourteen years' transportation. He arrived in Australia the following year on the convict ship *Westmoreland*, with six-year-old Patrick in tow.

On December 18, 1847, nearly ten years to the day he was collared on the streets of Palmerstown for possessing dodgy money, Bryan Veech was granted his ticket of leave and allowed 'to remain in the service of John Gardiner Esquire at the Macquarie River for twelve months'.

The same year, his wife Bridget, and their children Michael and Alice, arrived as free settlers on the *Waverly*. Bridget's widowed sister, Mary Anne, and her son, John, were with them. They joined Bryan and Patrick at Wellington, near Dubbo in central-western NSW, and the family prospered.

Within forty years they owned vast tracts of grazing and farming country around Wellington and Quambone, including the properties Quilbone and Mountain View.

Patrick was survived by Bridget and four sons and three daughters. The family lived and worked on Quilbone station.

Newspapers across the country weighed in on the Quilbone tragedy, with many asking why Lorie was granted bail. If Lorie had remained behind bars while awaiting trial, Patrick Veech would still be alive, they argued. The *Wellington Times* pondered "the great wonder how such a man could secure bail":

> He was well-known to be a desperate character, who had already served a lengthy term of imprisonment, having only been discharged from Goulburn Gaol in May, and other serious charges were against him. It is said he had threatened a course of murder, and people were warned of his evil intentions. The principle of releasing a man until the charge against him is proved may be all right as a broad principle, but under certain circumstances it is not always to be justified.

Shearer Harry O'Brien and Lorie were well acquainted.

'Lorie was acknowledged as one of the quickest and best to ever shear a sheep,' O'Brien said.

But there was a dark side to the gun shearer:

'He had little to say to anybody, and did not associate or fraternise with the other men of the shed. He preferred to have his meals alone and to sleep away from the others. Lorie was disliked by nearly everyone, especially the unionist shearers. For one thing he was a non-unionist, but it was his irritable, disagreeable temperament that made him so unpopular.'

Bill Edwards, one of the founding members of the Australian Workers' Union, remembered Lorie.

'I worked with some great old blade shearers in my time, such as James Sutherland, Tom McDermott, and Allan Cameron, but the fastest of the lot, in my opinion, was George Lorie, better known as "Chinnie Sullivan",' Edwards recalled in the *Australian Worker.*

Edwards worked alongside Lorie in 1894 at Waranna station, a vast grazing property near Coonamble owned by William Keogh.

'The sheep were big and full-fleeced. There were no rosellas among them (a slang term for sheep losing their fleece),' Edwards said.

'One morning Lorie never came to the shed until half an hour after we started shearing, and his tally was 198 for the day, and they were shorn well at that.'

Another shearer, who used the byline OC in the *Uralla News*, painted a much grimmer picture:

'I never heard of him being credited with one humane act nor ever heard any man speak kindly of him; he gloried in being a pariah and boasted in blasphemous language that he had no friendship with God or man.'

After murdering Veech, Lorie fled on horseback and hid out at an Aboriginal camp near Wallangambone station, owned by Joseph Green. He stayed at least one night.

A female Aboriginal elder, concerned about Lorie's presence at the camp, walked nearly seven miles to Wallangambone station shearing sheds and told Green.

Two shearers were sent to the camp to investigate, but Lorie saw them coming.

'Don't tell them I was here,' he told the Aborigines, and scrambled to his feet.

Lorie's rifle, used to bash Veech to death, was strapped together by two pieces of timber and fencing wire. He secured a Winchester rifle and ammunition from the Aborigines and told them he had 'a few more people to deal with'.

Lorie was now armed and desperate. He sought refuge at Pomeroy, a neighbouring property owned by Charles Wynne.

Lorie reached Pomeroy, about thirteen miles from Quambone, and asked Wynne for supplies. Wynne cautiously obliged and Lorie retreated into thick scrubland.

Inspector General of Police Thomas Garvin issued a statement: 'A warrant has been issued by the Quambone bench for the arrest of George Lorie, charged with the wilful murder of Patrick Veech, at Quilbone, near Quambone, in the Coonamble district, on 11 September 1905.'

Lorie was described as forty-six years of age, five-feet, four-inches tall, of medium build, with dark brown hair turning grey and grey eyes:

> He was discharged from Goulburn Gaol in May after serving a sentence of four years for sheep stealing. For this offence he was convicted at the Walgett quarter sessions. He has with him a single-fire .22 Remington rifle, and a supply of ammunition. On 12 September he procured a Winchester repeating rifle and ammunition, and is a dangerous man. It is thought that Lorie may make through the scrub via Carinda, Boorowa and Narran, and cross to Queensland between Tatalla and Goodooga from which place he came about nine years ago.

Dubbo Sub-Insp William Moss, Coonamble Sen-Sgt Richard Francis and Constable Robert Mitchell from Warren arrived at Quambone.

Moss had trucked a team of horses to Warren before riding sixty miles to Quambone with Francis and Mitchell. They arrived about 10 pm the day after Veech was murdered.

There was very little to go on. However, early on Wednesday morning grazier James McLeish, from nearby property Sandy Camp, rode to town and told the officers Lorie was seen at the Aboriginal camp at Wallangambone station.

'He told people there he was going to return to Quambone and murder his wife and David Harris. They think he might've gone into Wynne's place, Pomeroy, but he could be back at the camp,' McLeish told the officers.

Moss and his men saddled their horses and made their way to Pomeroy, where they were met by Charles Wynne's son, Eugene.

'We're on our way to the Aboriginal camp at Wallangambone; we have reason to believe George Lorie might be there. He's wanted for the murder of Patrick Veech,' Moss said.

'I don't think you'll have to go that far. Lorie was here this morning and there's every chance he's close by,' Eugene said.

Charles and Eugene Wynne took the officers to Pomeroy homestead to work out a strategy.

'Lorie had a cup of tea this morning and is in the scrub not far from here,' Eugene said.

Charles Wynne offered to go to look for Lorie. 'I'll persuade him to come up for dinner. Failing that, I'll try to get the rifle from him and convince him to surrender.'

Wynne set out in search of Lorie. He called him by name, stressing he was alone and unarmed.

After about an hour, Wynne found the wanted man hiding in thick undergrowth.

Lorie trusted Wynne — to a point. They spoke at length, at times quite amiably, but Lorie refused to surrender.

'I still want that wretched woman and the man she's tied up with, as well as that bastard, Con Veech,' Lorie said angrily.

Wynne eyed Lorie's rifle, but the fugitive held it tightly. 'Giving yourself up is the only way out of this, George. Surely, you can see that. The courts will be lenient when they hear your side of the story.'

Lorie was unswerving. 'If there's no way out, I'll shoot myself and my bondsman can do what he likes with my body.'

Wynne noticed a pocketbook and lead pencil among Lorie's pile of possessions. The pencil had seen better days. Wynne realised he was getting nowhere. Lorie had no intention of peacefully ending the hostile situation and surrendering to police.

Wynne returned to the homestead and told Moss what had happened. He gave the officers Lorie's exact location.

Lorie knew Wynne would tell the police everything and was convinced there were already officers on the place looking for him. He was dead right.

Lorie quickly packed up his gear. He retreated deeper into the bush and found shelter under a fallen tree.

He wrote furiously in his pocketbook. The pencil was worn to a stub. Lorie knew his time was up but wanted the world to know the circumstances that led to Veech's murder.

Police and Aboriginal trackers searched the area for the next two hours. The day was closing in on them. They heard what sounded like a muffled gunshot, or large tree branch snapping, and gingerly headed in that direction.

Sub-Insp Moss was mindful of Lorie's threat to commit suicide but told his men to take every precaution. 'Keep your rifles at the ready; Lorie is a desperate man capable of doing anything.'

But they had little to worry about. George Joseph Lorie was already dead.

Less than a hundred yards away, his body lay under a low, thick clump of wilgas. His throat was cut from ear to ear. A damaged rifle lay nearby. The cartridge was struck but had failed to explode.

When the officers found Lorie's body, blood was still flowing from the gaping neck wound. His clenched fist held a bloodied knife. His lips were grimly pursed and his eyes shone brightly against the setting sun.

Lorie's body was taken to Quambone and an inquest into his death was held before District Coroner Henry Giles Shaw who, two days earlier, headed the inquest into the death of Lorie's victim, Patrick Veech.

Sub-Insp Moss told the coroner Aboriginal trackers led them to Lorie's body.

'When we reached the spot, Lorie had just died. His throat had been cut from ear to ear with a sharp pocket knife,' Moss said.

'Blood was still trickling from the wound and the knife was clutched in his hand. He had a rifle by his side, but the barrel was bent. Part of the stock was broken and the lock was out of order. It was capable of being fired by using a little manipulation, but was very defective. There were three cartridges in the rifle magazine and one in Lorie's pocket.

'Evidently, Lorie planned to shoot himself. An examination of the rifle showed the hammer had struck one of the cartridges in the barrel but the cap snapped without exploding the charge,' Moss said.

A bag containing bread, mutton, tea and sugar was near Lorie's body as well as legal documents relating to the sale of his Quambone property. There were also two promissory notes, each for £150, made out to Carinda publican William Hardy. They were issued on 9 September and due for payment twelve months later.

A pocketbook with an account of Lorie's murderous ways and a full confession was found. Lorie made entries right up until his death.

Coroner Shaw returned a verdict of suicide.

*   *   *

Sub-Insp Moss praised the work of Aboriginal trackers and police officers engaged in locating Lorie. He especially praised the actions of civilian Charles Wynne.

'The community owes a debt of gratitude to Mr Wynne for the moral courage, duty and bravery he showed, which materially assisted the police in the execution of their duty,' Moss said.

He particularly lauded the efforts of Sen-Sgt Francis, who displayed tremendous courage during the manhunt.

Two months later, Francis was promoted to the rank of sub-inspector and transferred to Hay, in the western Riverina region of south-western NSW.

Lorie's lengthy, handwritten confession was detailed and precise. He laid the blame for his troubles squarely on the shoulders of Emily Kearnal.

In part, the confession read:

Oh, that wicked woman. I call my Lord to witness on my last day that I have not been guilty of 'illusing', or threatening to shoot her, though I may have said words I had no right to say, and so had she. Her wicked, false statement is the cause of my trouble, and her fancy man the cause of me committing murder, or intent to murder.'

Lorie wrote about the morning he murdered Patrick Veech:

I saw old Veech sitting down. I tried to fire on him but the rifle would not go off. I then hit him with the stock of it, but do not know whether I killed him or not.

Lorie firmly believed Emily colluded with Veech and Michael Harris to put him back behind bars:

If it had not been for that wicked woman, who so cruelly treated me, and drove me off my head with her wicked talk and false swearing, I would never have dreamt of doing what I have done.

But, after firing at her fancy man, I went to Veech's. It was not revenge for past wrongs and getting me four years. I forgave him that for my own good, as well as his. But this time, when he got me committed, he assisted her in every way to get me into more trouble.

When I came home I found everything gone, and I had not even a blanket to sleep under, nor a bite to eat. I started to look for the stock. I found the sheep, cattle, and pigs over at Veech's. He had bought them off her, sympathising with her in every way.

Lorie wrote he tried to keep his nose clean when released from prison:

> I never dreamt of doing anything wrong when I came
> home from my trouble, not even if she had left me and
> took all my property. I intended to go to work. But when
> she and Harris and Veech tried to get me in trouble the
> second time, it drove me to it. I would sooner die than
> go back to gaol.
>
> This is how I am served by the woman I loved. I gave
> her all the money that I earned and registered the stock
> brands in her name. This has been the cause of all my
> evil.

He also accused Emily of turning the children against him:

> I sincerely say I never intended or dreamt of hurting a
> hair on her head, or any part of her body, until she most
> wickedly swore my liberty away, and not even when
> she had Harris stopping with her at the Junction Hotel
> when I came home. They had sent my oldest boy away
> — where I don't know. And they had the other children
> tutored up so that they would not come to see me. When
> I begged my way to see them, they would stare me in the
> face and tell me wicked lies.

Lorie claimed his children were groomed to make false
statements to police:

> May the Lord be good to my children; I forgive them for
> the falsehood they used. May the Lord forever punish

them; I cannot forgive them. I don't think God can. May they live hard and die hard. It is hard for me to say, but I have been most wickedly treated. I hope I will die soon; may the Lord forgive me.

It was later suggested the ongoing feud between Lorie and Veech was the result of Veech desperately wanting to buy Lorie's land.

The selection apparently had a creek running through it, with a reliable water supply. The land was considered prime grazing country, some of the best in the district. Veech's biggest problem, however, was that Lorie steadfastly refused to sell.

The bad blood between the pair resurfaced when Lorie came home from gaol and discovered Emily was about to skip town with another man. He was pushed over the edge when he discovered Emily sold his livestock to Veech, the man he hated the most.

Probate showed the Veech estate owed £300 for the sale of the stock. The entry was made in the name 'Lorrie'.

Throughout the nightmare, Lorie strenuously denied stealing a bullock from Veech and claimed he was set up by Emily. Lorie's claim carried some credibility.

George Lorie was a desperate man, driven to the brink of madness by a series of events beyond his control — and he was a man who liked to be in control. The gun shearer, once known in sheds around western NSW and outback Queensland as 'the white Chinaman', was a wretched figure full of rage and resentment.

He was buried at Quambone Cemetery the same day his death was deemed a suicide by District Coroner Shaw.

*   *   *

Years later, William Noble, the young constable tasked with escorting Lorie to Narrabri railway station in 1902, recalled his brush-ins with 'the white Chinaman' in a 1953 *Sydney Morning Herald* article headlined 'Miscreant of the marshlands'.

I was a young trooper temporarily in charge of the little settlement of Carinda on the Marthaguy Creek in the police district of Walgett, Noble wrote.

Carinda in those days consisted of a police station, a post office and general store, the usual bush hostelry, billiard saloon, smithy, several private houses and a wool scour.

After taking stock of my new environment, I became interested in a mysterious character who roamed around every Saturday night, leading a good horse and closely followed by two well-trained sheep dogs. He was a sullen sort of individual who seldom spoke to anyone. Close on midnight he would mount and disappear.

From inquiries, I learned he was George Lorie, nicknamed 'Chinese Sullivan' and also known as the 'big gun shearer'. He occupied a reservation of 800 acres with his wife and young family in a secluded part of Merri-Merri Creek country, an overflow of the Great Macquarie Marshes. He ran 600 or 700 runty sheep of mixed breeds bearing no registered earmarks or brands.

Every station owner in the district suspected Lorie of being a clever sheep thief who operated alone and at night. One of the most absorbing topics in Carinda was how he had obtained his odd collection of sheep. Over the years this elusive marauder was never cornered in the act of stealing sheep. When pursued, he vanished into the bush along a maze of trails.

After his discharge from gaol, Lorie returned to find his selection had been forfeited and his wife was living with a shearer near a once-notorious grog shanty, The Shingle Hut.

Noble recalled escorting Lorie to Narrabri railway station by Cobb & Co coach.

'Lorie was a notorious character,' he said. 'He thought I was asleep and tried to bash my brains out with the handcuffs, but I thrust my revolver in his face. In forty years' service with the police, I did not encounter a more ruthless or vicious criminal than Lorie.'

Postscript:
Patrick Veech and his father Bryan also had difficulty distinguishing their own sheep from those belonging to others.

At Wellington in early 1863, when Patrick was thirty-two, they allegedly stole thirty ewes and thirty lambs from Mumble station, a neighbouring property owned by Sir William Verner.

They were charged with receiving and appeared before Justice Edward Wise at Bathurst circuit court on 5 September. Mumble station employee Edward Rhodes told Justice Wise he found Sir William Verner's sheep at Veech's Mountain View property.

'I went to Veech's station and found some of our sheep intermixed with theirs and immediately recognised our sheep. I was present when the constable produced a search warrant. Patrick and Bryan Veech were there when I took out some ewes and lambs from among a flock in their yard,' Rhodes said.

'I examined them and found our mark had been removed and a different brand put on their ears. This brand had evidently been fixed recently and I am familiar with Sir William's brand. I know the prisoners have lived on the boundaries of Sir William's station for some considerable time and I have seen them occasionally actually upon his station.'

Rhodes alleged Bryan Veech said: 'If you were inclined to act neighbourly, you would say I took Sir William's sheep by mistake.'

Justice Wise sentenced Patrick Veech to two years' hard labour at Darlinghurst Goal. His 66-year-old father was acquitted and discharged when Justice Wise found there was 'no evidence to send to the jury'.

On 11 September, six days after the trial, Bryan Veech died.

His son Patrick was murdered by George Lorie at Quilbone station on the same date, forty-two years later.

* * *

George Lorie's family circle is foggy at best — and the identity of his partner Emily much foggier.

According to several family trees, twenty-eight-year-old George Joseph Lorie married sixteen-year-old Ellen Alma Mahaffie at Tenterfield on 25 January 1887.

However, a thorough search for documented proof of this marriage ever taking place came to nothing.

George and Ellen lived in Queensland before relocating to Quambone in the early 1890s.

For reasons unknown, once they settled at Quambone, Ellen Lorie became 'Emily Lorie' and later 'Amly Lorie'. By 1905, when she took off with Michael Harris, she was known as 'Emily Kearnal'. There is evidence 'Kearnal' was her father's surname and 'Mahaffie' her mother's maiden name.

There is also a suggestion Ellen and Emily were not the same person.

To completely confuse matters, George Lorie's probate papers record 'Amly Lorie' as also being known as 'Emily Smith'.

She is referred to as 'Emily Smith alias Amly Lorie' several times in the 112-page document.

At the time of Lorie's death, probate listed Emily's children as fifteen-year-old Andrew Charles; thirteen-year-old Ettie Martha; twelve-year-old Creswick Francis; nine-year-old Mary Ann; seven-year-old Beatrice; and five-year-old George Grasden.

'All these children are illegitimate and with their mother, Emily Smith, alias Amly Lorie, in Coonamble,' probate records.

But a transcript of Mary Lorie's birth certificate, dated 21 July 1895, lists 'Ellen Alma Mahaffie' as her mother, suggesting Ellen and Emily were the same person.

Her probate testimony 'sworn by the deponent Emily Kearnal, generally known as Amly Lorie' before Commissioner for Affidavits Sidney Skuthorpe states: 'I was never legally married to the abovenamed deceased but I am generally known as Amly Lorie. I was living with (George Lorie) as his wife for a period of about thirteen years continuously immediately prior to 21 March 1902.'

Lorie was convicted of sheep-stealing on this date and sent to gaol. He returned to his selection, Lulls Luck, on 28 May 1905.

'I resumed living with (George Lorie) as his wife from that date, up until 17 July when he threatened to shoot me and presented a loaded revolver at me. I left him and ceased to live with him,' Amly Lorie testified.

'I have had six children by the abovenamed deceased during the period I resided with him.'

Amly Lorie, also known as 'Emily Smith', testified she was the mother of all six children but never once referred to herself as 'Ellen Alma Mahaffie' — despite that name being on at least one of the children's birth certificates.

Shortly after Patrick Veech's murder, newspapers widely reported: 'Lorie was released in May last, after serving a long sentence for sheep-stealing. Since his release he has been committed for trial for presenting a firearm at a woman named Emily Kearnal, also known as Emily Lorie, with intent to murder her. Emily Kearnal has been living with Lorie for sixteen years as his wife, and had reared a large family'.

Emily began planning her escape with David Harris when Lorie was locked up in Goulburn Gaol.

She most likely began using the surname 'Kearnal' about this time.

In July 1897, Emily was issued a stock brand in the name 'Mrs Amly Lorie' but by 1905 police knew her as Emily Kearnal. She was listed under that name in the NSW Police Gazette and Weekly Record of Crime when Lorie was charged with attempting to discharge a loaded firearm in her direction, with intent to do grievous bodily harm.

To further confuse matters, one family tree has 'Emily Cora Capel' as an alternative birth name for Ellen Alma Mahaffie.

This tree records Ellen marrying George Joseph 'Laurie' in 1887, which draws parallels with marriage dates in other trees — but still offers no documented proof that a marriage took place.

While there are some indicators Ellen Alma Mahaffie and Emily Kearnal were different people, great-granddaughter, Julie Yeomans, says they were more than likely the same person.

Julie's grandmother was Emily's fifth child, Beatrice.

Beatrice's death certificate records her mother's surname as 'Smith, also known as Emily Cara'.

'I also found a record of Ellen Alma 'Laurie' (born Mahaffie) with an additional birth name being Emily Cora Capel,' Julie said. 'She supposedly married a George Joseph 'Laurie' at Tenterfield on 25 January 1887. This adds credence to Emily and Ellen being the same person and gives a link to the name Emily Cara on my grandmother's death certificate.'

On 13 November 1906, about fourteen months after George Lorie murdered Patrick Veech and cut his own throat, Emily Kearnal married shearer Michael Harris at Trangie, a small town forty-five miles west of Dubbo.

The marriage was conducted by Presbyterian minister William Sharpe. The minister's wife, Isabella, and Alice Priddis were witnesses.

Emily recorded her parents as 'Thomas Kanel' and 'Sarah Mahaffy'.

Listing her mother as Sarah Mahaffy suggests Ellen Alma Mahaffie did exist at some point.

Emily registered her status at the time of marriage as spinster, rather than widow, indicating she was never married to George Joseph Lorie.

Countless newspapers covering the Quambone murder in 1905 referred to Emily's love interest as David Harris.

Was David Harris and Michael Harris the same person?

The answer is most likely 'yes'.

Harris conceivably switched names as part of the plan to run off with Emily — perhaps a ploy to put George Lorie off the scent.

However, when Lorie committed suicide, anonymity was

no longer necessary — Lorie was out of the way.

Three more children were born: Emily Amelia, Ellen Jane and Doris Phyllis.

Was middle child Ellen named after Ellen Alma Mahaffie or was that purely coincidental?

Eldest daughter Emily was born at Eenaweena station, near Warren, six weeks before her parents were married.

A transcript of Emily's birth certificate states her mother's name as 'Emily, formerly Keanell'. The next sentence, 'Emily Keanell (spinster), married to Michael Harris at Trangie on 13 November 1906', has been crossed out.

Emily's daughter, Mary Ann — her fourth child with George Lorie — married twenty-eight-year-old dentist Joseph Humphrey Williamson at Holy Trinity Church, Orange in 1914.

Mary Ann was nineteen years old and the wedding certificate acknowledges a letter of consent signed by the bride's mother, 'Emily Harris'.

The certificate also identifies the mother of the bride as 'Emily Capel' — one of the names used by Emily Kearnal before she married Harris.

The birth certificate of Doris Phyllis Harris, Emily's third child with Michael Harris, states her mother as being 'Emily Cara Harris' — yet another reference to 'Cara/Cora'.

Electoral rolls suggest Harris and Emily parted company at some point.

Emily lived at 62 Fitzroy Street, Dubbo, during the 1930s and 1940s and died at that address on 10 November 1948. The cause of death was myocarditis and coronary thrombosis. She was seventy-six.

Oddly, a transcript of her death certificate lists her parents as 'unknown'.

Emily Harris, also known as Emily Smith, Ellen Alma Mahaffie, Emily Cora Capel, Amly Lorie and Emily Lorie, is buried in the Church of England section at Wellington Cemetery.

CHAPTER 21

THE GHOST OF LITTLE EMMA QUINN

Locals feared a child-killer lurked in their midst when the body of twelve-year-old Emma Quinn was pulled from the Gwydir River near Biniguy on 16 April 1877.

Emma's body lay partly submerged in the river's murky, muddy water near Dan Eaton's Biniguy station for three days.

Two months earlier, another twelve-year-old girl, Mary Ann McGregor, was murdered at Ulamambri station, near Coonabarabran. Newspapers began making comparisons.

Mary Ann's alleged murderer, Thomas Newman, was behind bars at Dubbo Gaol, awaiting his day in court — and, most likely, the gallows.

Biniguy's tight-knit community was on tenterhooks. Locals feared a copycat killer was on the loose around the Gwydir district, 140 miles north-east of Coonabarabran. Villagers were shocked and saddened by the apparent murder of one of their own.

Biniguy, twenty-five miles west of Warialda in north-western NSW, was settled about twenty-five years earlier.

Pioneers now felt their idyllic patch of paradise — fertile farming and grazing country — was under threat.

Newspapers widely reported the latest death and the earlier murder. They warned 'the denizens of the remote bush' to never leave their families unprotected when 'so many ruffians are loafing about this country'.

Biniguy residents' fears worsened when district police

magistrate Patrick Brougham established Emma Quinn was brutally violated and strangled before being dumped in the river.

Brougham, based in Bingara, was not properly qualified to make such a judgement. However, the responsibility rested squarely on his shoulders because a doctor was not available to conduct a post-mortem examination on Emma's decomposed body.

The ruling, handed down at a hastily convened inquest the day after the girl's body was found, drew harsh criticism from the general public as well as widespread scrutiny from newspapers. The *Armidale Express and New England General Advertiser* commented:

> It seems to us the evidence as to the cause of the girl's death is by no means satisfactory, although we cannot speak positively on this point until we see the depositions. It seems incredible that at this season of the year, after less than three days' immersion in water, the girl's body should have been too far decomposed to conduct an accurate examination.

However, the newspaper did concede such a thing was 'perhaps possible'.

There was also speculation the young girl's death may well have been accidental. The newspaper suggested:

> It is consolatory to have some grounds for supposing the poor girl perished by accident. The girl was missed about eleven o'clock in the forenoon, an hour after she was sent to the river to wash some clothes. The place

where her body was found is near her parents' home and is surrounded by huts, and is not more than half-a-mile from Biniguy station, which is in sight. The girl's mother was not half-a-mile away dealing with a hawker at the time when her daughter's death must have occurred. All these circumstances seem to point to the girl's death being an accidental one. The police are, however, still endeavouring to unravel the mystery.

Magistrate Brougham's official verdict was 'strangulation caused by some person unknown', delivered at Bingara courthouse on 25 April.

The *NSW Police Gazette* recorded: 'The body was too decomposed to allow a post-mortem examination being made, but a medical witness (magistrate Brougham) deposed death was caused by strangulation.'

Brougham's credentials to record such a decision were questioned by newspapers.

'The bother has mainly arisen from the fact a non-professional man as regards to medicine (Brougham) presumed an opinion on a subject he did not understand, though he says he has been a barrister,' reported the *Evening News*.

An all-weather coat was found close to Emma's body. It was thought to belong to a stranger seen several times in the area during the days leading up to the child's death.

Witnesses said the slightly built stranger was no more than four feet, ten inches tall.

A police description in the *NSW Police Gazette* published on 18 April — two days after Emma's body was found — stated the stranger had dark hair, slight dark whiskers, a long, thin, wiry moustache, thin face and a long nose that 'appears to have been broken'. The stranger, name unknown, was believed to be heading west.

Shortly afterwards, another suspect was questioned.

Itinerant worker Hugh McCabe was hauled in and arrested by police officers but subsequently cleared of any involvement.

McCabe and two mates were camping near Pallamallawa and were allegedly seen near the Quinn farm about the time Emma vanished. However, McCabe and his mates proved beyond doubt they were a considerable distance away at Biniguy station enquiring about work when Emma disappeared.

*　　*　　*

On the morning of Friday 13 April Emma was entrusted to look after her younger siblings, ten-year-old Mary, eight-year-old Harriet, six-year-old George, four-year-old William and twelve-month-old Samuel.

Their mother, thirty-year-old Harriet, left Emma in charge of the large brood while she went the short distance to Biniguy station to purchase household staples and supplies from travelling hawker Alex McIntosh.

Harriet's husband, thirty-four-year-old George, was one of the district's earliest pioneers. He was diligently ploughing a paddock some distance away on the family's forty-two acre selection when his wife was organising the children.

George was born in Bathurst in 1842, one of thirteen children to John and Emma Quinn, and arrived in the district in the early 1860s when barely out of his teens. He married Harriet Jane Golby at Warialda in 1864 and the following year Emma — the first of twelve children — was born.

George grew wheat and corn and, over time, established an imposing orchard across three acres.

Oranges, lemons, apples, grapes, apricots, plums and persimmons grown on the small parcel of land were the talk of the district for decades.

First-born Emma was mature for her age, and considered 'next-in-charge' after her mother. She gave next eldest Mary strict instructions to watch over the younger children as she made her way to the banks of the Gwydir River to collect fresh water and wash clothes.

The country was in severe drought and the Gwydir, or Big River as it was widely known, was barely flowing. Emma, laden with buckets and dirty laundry, cautiously made her way down the bank. Finding a good spot to gather fresh water would be difficult, given the bone-dry conditions.

Meanwhile, more than five miles away, a settler was on his way to see Charles and Harriet Boughton, near Pallamallawa. The traveller's name has been lost in time, but his account of what he saw that day has been passed down through the generations and was recorded in newspapers years later.

It was a beautiful autumn morning, despite the unseasonably dry weather, and the traveller hummed contentedly as he rode. He was making good time and estimated he was within three miles of Boughton's Crossing.

As he trotted along the Gwydir River's northern bank, a sudden movement caught his eye on the opposite side. He noticed a young girl with her back towards him. He guessed she was no more than twelve or fourteen years of age.

He watched the young girl approach the water's edge.

A mob of cattle nearby was startled by her presence. They became extremely restless and began charging along the bank, but well away from the girl.

The traveller watched intently. He knew the girl might need help if the frenzied cattle turned the wrong way. Thankfully, they didn't. Instead, the mob ran away from the river and out of sight.

The traveller turned his gaze back to where he saw the young lass at the water's edge, but she was gone — she had simply vanished into thin air. He figured she found shelter from the stampeding cattle, which were long gone.

He continued his journey to the Boughton farm, armed with quite a story to tell Charles and Harriet.

The cattle stampede was confirmed by witnesses living nearby. However, the same witnesses did not see a young girl on the banks of the river.

The entire incident happened at least five miles downstream from where Emma Quinn was collecting water near the family home.

Later, when the traveller was told about Emma's disappearance, he came forward and told authorities about the incident downstream.

When he described what he saw to Harriet Quinn, Emma's distraught mother, she went white with shock — the mysterious young girl wore clothing identical to that worn by Emma the same morning.

The traveller was unaware a young girl in the district was missing until he arrived at Boughton's Crossing, where he was told a search party was under way to help locate the girl.

The peculiar sighting was enough to convince superstitious locals the traveller had witnessed the ghost of twelve-year-old Emma Quinn. The traveller's tale generated a ghost story that has been passed down through the decades.

There was no reason to suggest the traveller fabricated the sighting; he related the incident to the Boughtons immediately afterwards and, at the time, wasn't aware Emma Quinn was missing.

Emma's body was found three days after the mysterious sighting, about half a mile from where she was collecting water and washing clothes. Buckets and dirty laundry were found on the riverbank.

The spot where the traveller saw the ghostly young girl wearing clothes identical to Emma was five miles downstream.

An account of the traveller's sighting was published twenty years later:

> He learnt of the girl's disappearance and by the circumstances saw that by no possibility could the girl have had time to be where the alleged vision appeared — fully five miles away in an opposite direction. He told what he had seen to the mother and his description of the ghost's clothing was identical with what the girl was wearing when temporarily left at the river by her mother.

The traveller was never named, making the incident more folklore than fact — perfect fodder for a good, old-fashioned ghost story.

It is widely believed Emma's death was accidental and magistrate Brougham got the autopsy conclusion horribly wrong.

Observers claimed there was more guesswork than science applied.

'It is very unfortunate the services of a duly registered medical practitioner were not obtainable at the inquest. As far as we can ascertain after careful enquiry, the evidence in this respect is very unsatisfactory,' reported the *Armidale Express and New England General Advertiser.*

CHAPTER 22

THAT'S MY DADDY!

Curly-haired four-year-old Leo Kliendienst sat barefooted with his mother, Elizabeth, in the witness box at Moree courthouse and cast his inquisitive eye around the chamber.

He noticed his father sitting at a table. A stranger was with him. The stranger was dressed in a suit and looked very important. There were policemen in the room, too.

A big man sat at a much bigger table and watched everyone and everything. He seemed very interested in what all these people had to say. Out of everyone in the room, Leo figured, this man was the most important.

Leo's older brothers, seven-year-old Mervyn and eight-year-old Oswald, sat at the back of the courtroom.

Outside, sixteen-month-old brother Ernest was being nursed by a family friend. Sitting alongside them was twenty-two-year-old Hilda Evelyn Berger, a key witness in the proceedings inside.

Leo smiled broadly and promptly jumped from his mother's knee and ran to his father's side.

'My daddy,' he proudly declared.

Leo's father, thirty-one-year-old Alexander Joseph Kliendienst, sat before police magistrate George James Johnstone in the Moree court of petty sessions charged with bigamy. The man in the suit sitting next to him was the defence counsel, Moree solicitor William Cole.

Little Leo smiled broadly. Alexander smiled back and ran his fingers though his son's curly locks.

The child then ran across the floor to Constable Lockhart. Leo pointed to his father.

'That's my daddy,' he proudly told the policeman.

Everyone smiled bravely as little Leo ran excitably around the courtroom. It was a poignant moment during a committal hearing that shocked the district in the 1930s.

*   *   *

Kliendienst and Elizabeth Lindsay Corcoran were married by the Rev William Barker at the Methodist Church at Uralla, near Armidale in the New England district of NSW, on 27 January 1923. They were both nineteen.

The marriage produced six children but the family was beset by tragedy.

Their first child, Reuben, born in 1924, died at three months. He was rushed to hospital with an abscess, but died soon afterwards.

Leo's twin brother, Irwin, died at four months in 1929.

The four remaining children were present at Moree courthouse that hot Tuesday afternoon in early February 1934.

In September the previous year, Kliendienst had left his wife and children at Uralla and headed north-west to the Mungindi area on the Queensland border in search of work.

He was previously employed in the Postmaster General's Department at Armidale, but was laid off.

The Great Depression was all but over. Australia, and the rest of the western world for that matter, wasn't out of the woods just yet though. Dire economic aftershocks reverberated around the country.

Times were tough. Money — and employment — was scarce.

Within a few days of starting work at Mungindi, Kliendienst met twenty-two-year-old Hilda Evelyn Berger, who was employed at a local hotel as a domestic.

A romance quickly blossomed and, on 30 September 1933 — less than a month after meeting — they were married at All Saints' Church of England in Moree by the Rev Clifford Roslyn Rothero.

Hilda was lucky to get a ring on her finger after Kliendienst twice failed to make it to the church. The first time was a no-show. The second time, Kliendienst claimed his truck broke down en route to Moree from Mungindi.

Hilda, born in 1911 at Drake, a small village north-east of Glen Innes, to Bernard and Eliza Berger, was allegedly none the wiser. She had no idea her new husband was already married, with a wife and four young children waiting for him at Uralla.

As soon as they tied the knot, Kliendienst and Hilda packed up their belongings and headed to Queensland. They settled at Tiaro, a small timber town in the Frazer Coast region about 140 miles north of Brisbane, where Kliendienst found work timber-getting.

During the trip Kliendienst confessed everything. He told Hilda about his family at Uralla. She was gutted by the news but decided to stick. A whole new life lay ahead for both of them, she thought optimistically.

*   *   *

Back at Uralla, Elizabeth Kliendienst was getting worried. She saw neither hide nor hair of her husband since she said goodbye in late August and he drove away in a lorry belonging to her father, Phillip Corcoran.

Kliendienst promised to wire money once he found work, but not a penny arrived. It seemed he had simply vanished.

Uralla townsfolk said his disappearance was possibly the best thing that could've happened to Elizabeth. He was known in hushed tones around town as a 'street angel' by day and 'house devil' by night. He gave his wife hell.

To get by, Elizabeth and her four children relied on food relief and charity from Uralla church groups as well as help from family and friends and state government aid.

Police were called and the shocking truth quickly surfaced — Kliendienst had married again and left the Mungindi district.

The ever-reliable bush telegraph gave police quite a few leads and by late January 1934 the newlyweds were tracked down to the Frazer Coast region in Queensland.

They had been married — and on the lam, of sorts — for nearly four months.

On 26 January, Kliendienst was arrested for 'having gone through the form of marriage with Hilda Evelyn Berger, at Moree, NSW, on 30 September 1933 during the lifetime of his wife, Elizabeth Lindsay Kliendienst, whom he married at Uralla, NSW, on 27 January 1923'.

Prosecution was conducted by celebrated Sen-Sgt Florence Michael O'Driscoll.

Kliendienst was formally remanded by police magistrate Patrick Mortimer Hishon at Brisbane police court.

He was held in the Brisbane watchhouse until 2 February, pending the arrival of a police escort from NSW.

Boomi constable Tom Cochrane was sent to Brisbane to collect Kliendienst and escort him back to Moree.

'I have a warrant for your arrest on a charge of bigamy, committed at Moree,' Constable Cochrane told Kliendienst.

The clearly distressed father of four broke down and came clean. The charade had been going on too long and the weight of the lie became too much to shoulder. He willingly made a statement.

'I have been expecting this,' Kliendienst said. 'I know I should not have married Hilda. But I love her and knew she would not come away with me if we didn't get married.'

* * *

On 6 February 1934, Kliendienst appeared before police magistrate George Johnstone.

Elizabeth Kliendienst, a frail woman known by family and friends as Liz, held back tears as she produced a copy of a wedding certificate as proof she was married to the defendant.

'We were married at Uralla on 27 June 1923,' she told the court.

'The marriage was performed by the Reverend William Barker at the Methodist Church. Alex's father and mother, Jack and Kathleen Kliendienst, were present as witnesses,' she said.

Defence counsel William Cole objected, somewhat lamely. 'This marriage certificate should be a certified copy,' he declared.

Magistrate Johnstone quickly overruled Cole's wafer-thin objection and asked Liz Kliendienst to continue telling her story.

'We lived together at Uralla and Armidale, and then Alex left to go to Mungindi,' she said.

'He left me at Uralla about four months ago and has not been home since. We have four children together.'

The Rev Clifford Roslyn Rothero, who married Kliendienst and Hilda Berger at Moree, was called to identify the defendant.

'I recognise the defendant in court as the male party,' he said.

Again, defence counsel William Cole threw in a desperate objection — one last throw of the dice. 'There is no evidence the witness (Rothero) is authorised to celebrate marriages,' he argued.

When magistrate Johnstone put the question to Rothero, he all but rolled his eyes.

'I am properly registered as a person authorised to perform marriages,' the minister replied.

Moree resident Ruby Alma Troth, a witness to the union of Kliendienst and Berger, was called to identify both parties.

Magistrate Johnstone committed Kliendienst for trial.

* * *

Two days later the self-confessed bigamist faced Judge John Clancy at Moree Quarter Sessions.

Kliendienst pleaded guilty to the charge.

Moree police Sgt Pat McGrath told the court the defendant left his wife and family 'in destitute circumstances'.

'He went to look for work at Mungindi, travelling in a truck belonging to his father-in-law, Phillip Corcoran,' the sergeant said. 'Within about three weeks he met and married Hilda Berger, and they left for Queensland.'

'What is the girl's attitude in the matter? Did she believe he was a single man when she married him?' Judge Clancy asked.

'My understanding is that Hilda thought the defendant was single when they were married at Moree. He later disclosed the fact he was already married, just before they went to Queensland,' Sgt McGrath replied.

Defence counsel James Kinkead, as instructed by solicitor William Cole, argued his client knew he was doing wrong. He said the fact Kliendienst missed two wedding appointments indicated the defendant deliberately tried to avoid tying the knot with Hilda Berger.

'His failure to keep the appointments on two occasions clearly shows he realised he was doing wrong, and he was between two fires — he was between a rock and a hard place,' he told the judge.

Judge Clancy's jaw dropped.

'And he did all this in about three weeks?' he asked, somewhat confused.

Kinkead shuffled a few papers and conferred with his client.

'The timeframe was about five weeks, your honour,' he said.

Hilda Berger told the court she travelled to Queensland with Kliendienst despite knowing he was already married with four young boys. She was unaware of his marital status during their brief courtship. She was also unaware that Kliendienst left his wife and four children all but destitute and hungry.

'We lived at Tiaro, near Gympie, and I stayed with him until he was arrested,' she said.

She told the court there was no prospect of children in the second marriage.

Crown prosecutor Vernon Treatt said Kliendienst did not support his first wife, Liz, or wire money home after finding work at Mungindi.

'He has also intimated he did not intend to live with his wife, but was going to live with the second woman. He states the girl will "stick with him",' Treatt said.

As far as Judge Clancy was concerned, the case was cut and dried and he sentenced Kliendienst to twelve months' hard labour.

The judge did not hold back when summing up. He was a

good judge of character and knew in a heartbeat the type of person with whom he was dealing. Kliendienst was simply not a nice person, but a callous bastard, and Judge Clancy was fully aware of the fact.

'I am perplexed by your actions,' he told Kliendienst. 'You have left your wife and family. You may not have been happy in your situation but you left them in straitened circumstances to marry another girl, without bothering at all about the consequences.'

Judge Clancy directed Kliendienst to explain himself. 'I would like to hear what the defendant has to say,' he said.

Kliendienst bowed his head and cleared his throat. It was hard to look Judge Clancy in the eye.

He told the judge he and Liz were very young when they were married in 1923.

'We were not quite twenty years of age,' he said.

'But why did you do this?' queried Judge Clancy.

'Because I like the girl,' replied Kliendienst.

Judge Clancy shook his head. Kliendienst's shallow response left him all but speechless.

'The circumstances surrounding this case warrant me sending you to gaol,' he told Kliendienst.

Defence counsel James Kinkead requested Kliendienst be issued a good behaviour bond. 'At least that will give the defendant an opportunity to provide for his wife and family,' he argued.

Judge Clancy flatly refused to even consider the request. 'This case is far too serious for that. Your client has displayed a callous attitude. Quite frankly, it is an attitude I fail to understand under the circumstances. I sentence the defendant to twelve months' hard labour.'

Newspapers readily agreed with Judge Clancy's summation.

'One of the scandals attached to the administration of justice in this state is the free and easy manner in which convicted bigamists are treated by a lenient bench. One of the tribe, however, got his desserts at Moree a few days ago, when the court heard the details of one of the most distressing cases ever ventilated in that centre,' reported the *Richmond River Herald and Northern Districts Advertiser*.

*   *   *

On 25 October, while Kliendienst was doing time in prison, Hilda Berger gave birth to a healthy baby girl. She named her Margaret Ann.

Hilda and Kliendienst never reunited. Their brief marriage was annulled and Hilda and baby Margaret returned to Glen Innes. She later married Victorian Charles Gorrie.

When released from prison, Kliendienst quietly returned to Uralla, seeking forgiveness from Liz and the children.

He walked slowly up the front path of the family home and tapped lightly on the front door. The door swung back and his jilted wife slowly looked him up and down.

Kliendienst begged Liz to take him back, but she was more concerned about the clothes he was wearing.

'For goodness sake, Alex, who dressed you? Those trousers don't match those shoes!'

Despite everything that happened during the past few years, Kliendienst was welcomed back to the family fold.

But twelve months in gaol and a loving, forgiving wife weren't enough to change his ways. There was no fairytale ending to their marriage.

Kliendienst found employment with Gostwyck Shire

Council and was seen as a hard worker and good bloke. However, the man once described as a 'street angel' by day and 'house devil' by night was always there.

In 1937, Donald Lewis Kliendienst was born — a brother to Leo, Mervyn, Oswald and Ernest.

Alex Kliendienst gave his wife hell but through it all she bravely and lovingly raised five boys.

Kliendienst succumbed to throat cancer in 1977. He was seventy-four.

Liz died nine years later. She was eighty-three.

Her one dying request to family was not to be buried next to her husband.

Postscript:

Alex Kliendienst's bigamy case was not the first of its kind in north-western NSW.

In April 1930, Sid Collie pleaded guilty to a charge of bigamy at Moree police court and was committed for trial at Tamworth Quarter Sessions the following month.

When Collie, also known as Colley or Collett, was rounded up near Tulloona — midway between Moree and Goondiwindi — and handed a warrant by Moree police constable Tom Ellis, he did not deny the charge.

'I will plead guilty,' Collie told Constable Ellis.

'I have always found you an honest, hard-working chap. You have never given the police any trouble, and you are a well-behaved man,' Constable Ellis said.

Former wife Linda Corben told police magistrate Augustus Loftus at Moree police court she married Collie at Petersham, Sydney, on 25 March 1922. They were both eighteen at the time.

The newlyweds settled at Leichhardt and the marriage produced two children.

One afternoon in 1926, Collie allegedly said to his wife: 'I am going now to draw my wages. Be ready when I come home and we will go to the pictures.'

Linda told the court her husband never returned.

'I applied for a divorce. The case was heard on 24 March 1929, and I secured a *decree nisi*,' she said.

The decree was made absolute in September 1929. One month later she married Les Burton at Balmain.

Her first husband, Sid, however, couldn't wait for due process. He married Ethel King at Moree on 10 February 1927 — two years before the decree was granted.

'On that date I was still the wife of the defendant,' Linda told the court.

She said she was 'far better off'. 'It really worked out better since he (Collie) went away because we could never agree. It was to my advantage that he left.' she said.

The Reverend Albert Manefield recalled conducting the marriage ceremony between Collie and King at the Moree Methodist parsonage. Moree electrician Fred Buxton was a witness to the union.

'The usual declarations were made and signed. I witnessed the defendant sign his declaration,' Manefield said.

At Tamworth Quarter Sessions, defence counsel Richard O'Halloran told Judge Hugh Mocatta his client was a man of good character.

Judge Mocatta, however, said the offence was very serious. 'The accused married the woman Corben and, after three years, deserted her. She later took steps to obtain a divorce, but prior to that he married somebody else. The woman herself said it was for her own good that he left her. I can hardly sanction bigamy. It is a serious offence.'

After weighing up the evidence, Judge Mocatta deferred sentencing.

'The ends of justice will be met if I release the accused on his own recognisance of £50 and one surety of £50 to come up for sentence if called upon to do so within a period of two years,' said the judge.

He did, however, add one strict condition to the good behaviour bond. He ordered Collie to marry Ethel King within seven days of the rising of the court.

Defence counsel O'Halloran couldn't get out of his chair quick enough.

'Your Honour, Ms King is willing to marry my client as soon as possible. More than that, she is prepared to pay all fees,' he told the judge.

*   *   *

In 1915, Leslie Selina Hyland fronted police magistrate Major Frederick Crane at Moree courthouse, accused of marrying railway labourer John Gleeson while still legally married to coal miner, Jack Rees.

The court heard Hyland married Rees at the West Wallsend Presbyterian Church on 11 July 1912. Nearly three years later, on 4 May 1915, she wed Gleeson, under the name Leslie Reid.

In May 1915 a summons was served on Hyland at her Morton Street home by Constable James Gillis from Moree police.

'You have been married before. Why did you get married under the name Leslie Reid, when your name is Selina Rees,' asked Constable Gillis.

'I have my reasons. How did you find that out?' she questioned.

Hyland broke down and confessed to Gillis.

She said she used the surname Reid because her estranged husband was searching for her.

'I did not want my whereabouts traced,' she said.

'The first marriage took place about four years ago to Jack Rees, who is now working at Killingworth coalmines. The first nine months were fairly happy but then he started drinking and there were frequent quarrels,' she said.

She told Constable Gillis she was treated cruelly by Rees and complained at least three times to police about his conduct.

'Once, after a drinking bout, he took to me by the throat. I was lucky my dogs took to him,' she said.

At the time, police advised her to apply for a legal separation and Rees consented to the request. An agreement was drawn up by Newcastle firm, Bruce and Cohen Solicitors, and signed by both parties.

'After the agreement was signed I thought I would be free to act as I pleased and marry again,' Hyland said. 'He (Rees) told me I could live with whomever I liked and he would not bother me. He said he planned to go to the war,' she said.

At the time of the summons, Hyland said Rees was at the Liverpool camp, undergoing basic training with the Australian Imperial Force.

Rees went to war on 12 May 1915 and returned on 28 May 1919.

Hyland married Gleeson on 1 May 1915 and the couple settled in Moree.

The case was heard while Rees was serving at the Dardanelles.

Hyland pleaded guilty to one charge of bigamy and Magistrate Crane committed her for trial at Moree Quarter Sessions on 5 October. She was released on £100 bail.

At the trial hearing Judge Hugh Montgomerie Hamilton allowed Hyland to leave the courtroom until her sentence was read. When Hyland returned, Judge Hamilton stressed the seriousness of the offence.

Hyland burst into tears when the judge sentenced her to six months' imprisonment with light labour.

'I will never live that out,' she sobbed.

After conferring with defence counsel Tom Hogan, Judge Hamilton reduced the sentence to four months with light labour.

When released from prison, Hyland relocated to Tent Hill, near Tenterfield, with second husband John Gleeson.

Jack Rees returned home from the Great War and tracked down his estranged wife. He told her he would seek marriage dissolution on the grounds of misconduct.

'I expected as much,' she said.

At the Newcastle circuit court in 1919, Chief Justice William Cullen found the issues proved and granted the petitioner, Jack Rees, dissolution of the marriage.

CHAPTER 23

A MAN IS SHOOTING AT MR HOGAN!

Moree mayor Tom Hogan was known for attending church in a perfectly pressed white suit. A dapper man, Hogan was highly regarded and well liked across north western New South Wales.

But grand plans for a boxing stadium and a bitter battle between an aspiring fight promoter and council authorities, led to Hogan's murder as well as the attempted murder of former mayor Alfredo Zlotkowski.

Hogan, a solicitor and devout Catholic, was shot dead about 10 am on 11 December 1921 on the north-western corner of Auburn and Gwydir Streets.

He was on his way home after attending morning mass at St Francis Xavier's Catholic Church.

Hogan, 46, was confronted by a deranged gunman and shot eight times. He died instantly. His perfectly pressed white suit was saturated with blood.

Five years earlier the man who murdered Hogan in cold blood, John Jeremiah 'Jack' Curran, 45, was gaoled for two years for the attempted murder of Alfredo Zlotkowski, the mayor of Moree in 1897.

Curran, a shearer with an entrepreneurial streak and sense of showmanship, harboured grand visions of building a boxing stadium in Moree. He wanted to stage regular, world-class tournaments featuring headline boxers. The tall and lean Irishman with a pronounced nose and dimple, pledged his

*Shearer turned boxing promoter Jack Curran was
found guilty of murdering Moree mayor Tom Hogan in
1921 (Image credit: Museums of History NSW — State
Archives Collection)*

life savings to the project.

In early 1914, he began constructing the stadium on the southern side of Alice Street, between the intersections of Gosport and Warialda Streets. However, he was told by council authorities alterations were needed before tournaments could be held.

Curran built the stadium — with seating capacity for a thousand spectators — at a cost of £400 but ongoing battles with council saw only ten tournaments held at the venue in three years.

On grand opening night in March 1914, Duke Jennings overpowered Brownie Dixon in a twenty-rounder for £20 a side. The "house full" sign was hoisted proudly.

The following month Queenslander Frank Barrett defeated local hope Curly Kermond in the sixth round of the north-west championship and in July, Ossie Harrison took on Don Robinson in a twenty-round lightweight bout for £15 a side.

Harrison had Robinson's measure from the onset, but the fight was awarded to Robinson in the fifteenth round after the referee fouled Harrison for elbowing.

There was standing room only at all tournaments. Curran, it seemed, was on a winner and the crowds loved it. Local newspapers lauded the shearing contractor for his initiative and foresight.

The newly erected stadium is one of the best up-country institutions of its kind in the state. Mr Curran, to whom we are indebted for it, intends it not only for the exhibition of pugilistic encounters but for the encouragement of amateur boxing in general, the training of young boxers, and for the provision of legitimate sport for the winter months.

With more fights scheduled and the promise of some big-name boxers coming to Moree, Curran poured another £200 into the stadium to comply with council-required upgrades. But despite pulling big crowds to watch quality boxing, the stadium was empty for months at a time because of Curran's ongoing dispute with council.

By 1915, Curran was back working in the shearing sheds. When shearing at Bugilbone, he received correspondence from Mayor Hogan.

The letter said Moree Municipal Council had taken the liberty of giving the Australia Day committee permission to use the stadium to stage a fundraising event for the war effort.

Curran cordially replied to Hogan, saying he did not want the stadium to be used in the future. 'But as Mr Hogan had given permission (for the patriotic fundraiser) I hope the entertainment will be a success,' he penned.

Hogan duly replied, thanking Curran and informing him of the event's success and advising where the proceeds would be directed.

Curran returned to Moree to find the stadium had been broken into and the locks damaged. He complained to local police, who he claimed refused to take action.

Curran also alleged Hogan told him: 'Don't make a fuss. I think you'll get a licence for the place now.'

Curran stewed over the matter for more than twelve months. The following year he publicly questioned the whereabouts of money raised from the patriotic event held at his venue without his approval.

Curran alleged mishandling of funds by event organisers.

The public accusation brought about a writ for slander against him from one of the event's organisers, solicitor Alfredo Boleslas Fortunato Zlotkowski, who sat as Moree mayor in the late 1800s.

After the case was settled, Curran paid Zlotkowski out-of-pocket expenses as well as £25 to Red Cross funds.

About eighteen months later, about 11.30 am on 15 March 1917, Zlotkowski left his Frome Street office and made his way to Heber Street, a routine stroll to visit an acquaintance.

Curran, armed with an automatic revolver after being at shooting practice that morning, was standing near a tree in front of the Political Labor League rooms when Zlotkowski walked past.

Curran, described by the *Inverell Times* as "an atheist and anti-conscriptionist" claimed he was cajoled and jeered by a young boy, who allegedly yelled out: 'There goes your king; salute your king!'

Curran, riled by the remarks, fired the gun. The bullet passed between Zlotkowski's arm and body.

'You are a lucky man you did not get it through the head,' Curran roared.

He was quickly disarmed by shearers John Hartley and Les Fulham, who were chatting with him when the incident occurred.

Both men gave evidence at the subsequent trial at Armidale circuit court where bail was set at £500.

Curran told the court he never intended to shoot Zlotkowski. 'I merely wanted to create a disturbance so he could re-open the slander case,' he said.

Zlotkowski told the court: 'I saw Curran speaking to two

men named Fulham and Hartley, who were standing on the edge of the footpath in front of the PLL rooms'.

'I said "good morning" to Fulham and walked on. I had gone three or four paces when I heard a loud explosion quite close to me. I turned round instantly and Curran was standing there within a foot of me with a revolver in his hand. I grabbed hold of his two wrists with my two hands, and I said to him, "good God, man, what are you doing?"

'He said, "you are a lucky man you didn't get it through the head".'

Curran was found guilty of the attempted murder of Zlotkowski and given a two-year sentence.

He was admitted to Goulburn Gaol on 19 June 1917. After serving part of the sentence, he was transferred to Tuncurry Settlement, a prison farm where prison labour was used for planting pine forests.

When released in 1919, Curran still carried a deeply rooted grudge against Zlotkowski and Hogan.

He had no choice but to pull down the stadium and sell off the land, leaving him virtually penniless. At one point he used the building as a residence.

After years of fighting council, losing his life savings and spending two years behind bars, Curran had £45 to his name and was forced back to the shearing sheds to earn a living.

On a bright, sunny morning in 1921, two weeks before Christmas and after attending morning mass, Tom Hogan — resplendent in his white suit — was planning to spend the rest of the day with friends at the property owned by his mother-in-law, Catherine Moloney.

He made his way along Gwydir Street to Auburn Street, where he was accosted by Curran, who was convinced Hogan was involved in some way in the break and enter of his boxing stadium six years earlier. He was certain Hogan, as the mayor of Moree, had granted permission for the locks to be broken.

The enraged shearer pulled a handgun and pumped eight bullets into Hogan, killing him instantly.

As Hogan slumped to the ground in a pool of blood, Curran fled along Gwydir Street towards the Mehi River.

A young girl, Dorry Shanahan, witnessed the murder and ran back to St Francis Xavier's Catholic Church to alert parishioners.

'A man is shooting at Mr Hogan!'

Police, and a large group of volunteers, led by twenty-three-year-old Constable John Kearney and Mounted Constable Possie Wilson, searched for Curran.

About midday they found Curran on the Gwydir River at Solling's Paddock, adjacent to the Weebollabolla-Boolooroo stock route.

Curran, armed with a rifle, was crouched on the opposite bank, about a hundred yards from his pursuers.

He readied to fire at the group, however the rifle jammed so he attempted to flee.

Constable Wilson drew his service revolver and fired at Curran, who threw down his rifle and surrendered.

Curran made his way across the river and was taken into police custody at Moree lock-up.

When searched, Curran was in possession of a rifle, sheath knife, automatic revolver and 302 cartridges.

*   *   *

John Jeremiah 'Jack' Curran was born in Dunlavin, County

Wicklow, Ireland, in 1877. He arrived in Australia with his parents, John and Anne, on the *Sorato* in 1881.

The family lived in Victoria before moving to Queensland and later NSW, where Curran told authorities he 'knew poverty'.

Curran suffered serious bouts of sunstroke as a teenager and again as a young shearer. He said he was a child when his father died and watched his mother struggle to raise her family and educate her children.

It emerged in subsequent court hearings at Narrabri and Darlinghurst, Hogan promised to show Curran a letter from the Chief Secretary clearing him of any involvement regarding the damage caused at the boxing stadium.

The letter allegedly directed Hogan to 'break the locks' to the boxing stadium.

'You be damned. The Chief Secretary or Jesus Christ himself could not give authority to open my place,' Curran told Hogan days before the shooting.

Curran told the court the letter was never produced and the fatal meeting on the corner of Auburn and Gwydir Streets two days later was purely by chance.

'I can just recollect asking him if he would show me those documents,' Curran told the court.

He said Hogan replied, 'something about the police' and 'something that annoyed me'.

Witnesses called included motor mechanic Thomas Purtell, store manager Thomas Funnell, shearing workmate James Sullivan and council employee Alf Fairhall.

Purtell, who was with Curran at Moree Bore Baths as well as Peter's and Co Refreshments Rooms a few hours before the shooting, told the court he knew the accused had grievances with Hogan.

He said as they sat in Peter's and Co they observed Hogan walking by.

Curran allegedly remarked: 'there goes Holy Tom.' Purtell said the accused did not seem disturbed or upset.

Fairhall was at his residence near the scene of the murder. He said he heard shots fired.

He looked out on the street and witnessed Curran fire three more shots directly at Hogan as the mayor staggered and fell.

Curran fired one more shot in to the mayor's body as it lay lifeless and bleeding on the Auburn Street footpath.

Funnell said he saw Hogan passing by his store and moments later heard gunshots.

'I then saw Tom Hogan running and the accused running after him, firing several shots as he ran,' Funnell said.

Sullivan, a shearer who worked with Curran, said the accused often displayed anger and frustration when working the sheds and would repeatedly talk about losing his life savings.

'He would become excited when he discussed it,' Sullivan said.

Moree doctor Clyde Single told the court Curran fired eight shots.

'The fatal wound was in the heart. There were six others in the trunk as well as another in the head,' he said.

In April 1922, before Justice Alexander Gordon at Narrabri District Court, Curran was found guilty of murdering Thomas Rodgers Hogan, with the jury requesting leniency.

Curran was sentenced to hang by the neck until dead.

Three months later Justice Charles Wade, at the Full Court of Criminal Appeal in Sydney, set aside the conviction and ordered a new trial, with the principal ground of appeal being that, at the Narrabri trial, Justice Gordon misdirected the jury on the question of sanity.

Justice Wade said a man, though acting upon what were called 'insane delusions', might still be held criminally answerable for an act done contrary to law 'if the jury was satisfied on the facts that he was conscious of the physical quality of that act, and also of its wrongfulness.

'It was a matter of importance that all the evidence bearing upon that question of consciousness should be carefully considered by the jury. And this must most especially apply to that part of such evidence as bore upon the actual time of the commission of the crime charged.'

Justice Wade said the law recognised the same man might at one time be in such a condition as to know both the nature and wrongfulness of an act and at a different time not in such a condition.

'In the present case I have come to the conclusion that an error upon this point has unfortunately crept into the presentation to the jury of Curran's own evidence,' Justice Wade said.

At the subsequent trial three months later at Darlinghurst Central Criminal Court before Justice David Ferguson, a jury acquitted Curran on the grounds of insanity.

Chief government medical officer Dr Arthur Palmer said he and two fellow specialists examined Curran.

He concluded Curran suffered from 'delusion of persecution'.

'In such cases the sufferer in all other respects can be as intelligent as the average,' he told the court.

'Frequently, a paranoiac was more than ordinarily intelligent, but with regard to the particular subject of his aberration, he was quite impervious to reason.'

Dr Palmer said a person's conduct was the only means by which that person's sanity could be judged.

'Curran said to me that he had done no more to Hogan than Hogan did to him. He told me "he murdered me, as I murdered him" and that, in my opinion, was most distinctly the view of an insane mind.'

Dr Andrew Davidson, a 'mental specialist', substantially agreed with Dr Palmer's assessment of Curran's condition, the court was told.

Dr Lee Brown, resident doctor at Long Bay Gaol, told the court Curran suffered 'delusional insanity'.

Curran was ordered to be detained at the Governor's pleasure.

'He will be held under observation, and if certified insane, will be committed to the criminal ward of a lunatic asylum,' the court concluded.

Curran was transferred to Long Bay Gaol.

The day after the trial Curran's defence counsel, celebrated barrister Archibald McDonnell, told *The Sun* newspaper: 'I never doubted for a moment the jury would return any other verdict than that of 'not guilty on the grounds of insanity'.'

McDonnell was a highly regarded criminologist and authority on medical jurisprudence, famous for defending *pro bono* accused wife murderer Arthur Peden, who was acquitted of the crime after being twice sentenced to death in early 1922.

Curran's legal team also made public a letter received from a jury member who sat in the original trial at Narrabri.

In part, it read:

I was one of the unfortunate individuals compelled to act as a juryman in the Curran trial at Narrabri (and) I think it best to let you know of a little matter that could not have been known to you previously.

The fact that I wish to place before you is that one of the jury declared himself to be a personal friend of Hogan. I may be wrong, but I say that Curran's trial was not a fair trial. Do not misjudge my motives in writing to you. I am no friend of Curran. I had never seen him until the day of his trial. Neither was I an enemy of Hogan. If this letter should be of any use to you, then use it by all means as you think fit. Let me know when this letter has reached you so that I shall know that I have done what little one man may do in the interests of fair play.

In later years, John Jeremiah 'Jack' Curran was diagnosed with Parkinson's disease. He also suffered from sunstroke throughout his life and spent his final days at the Mount Royal special hospital for the aged at Parkville, an inner-city suburb of Melbourne.

Early in 1961, Curran was struck down with severe bronchopneumonia and treated by Dr Sophie Beecham.

He died on 7 January of that year aged eighty-four, and was buried at Fawkner Cemetery.

Postscript

Being a civic leader in Moree in the early 1900s was not an undertaking for the fainthearted.

In 1915 a case of mistaken identity led to seventy-six-year-old William Gillespie being charged with the attempted murder of Roger Delander, a Moree alderman and former mayor.

Delander was elected mayor for back-to-back terms in 1913 and 1914. He was also a well-known hotelier in the district.

At the time of the attack Delander was licensee of the

Sportsman's Arms Hotel on Alice Street in East Moree. Later, he would take over the Royal Hotel on the northern side of town.

Gillespie claimed he was attacked and robbed by a large group of people in the yard of the Sportsman's Arms at 3 am on 9 December 1915.

'Murder! Police! Thieves!' Gillespie screamed.

Delander, thinking all hell had broken loose, raced outside to investigate.

He saw Gillespie staggering about — the only person in the pub's yard — and deftly showed him the gate to Alice Street.

As Delander turned to head back to the hotel, Gillespie rushed him from behind and stabbed the Moree alderman.

Gillespie was arrested by Constable James Gillis and taken to Moree police station. He was charged with feloniously wounding Delander with intent to murder.

He was also charged with assault with intent to do grievous bodily injury.

Gillespie was defended by Moree solicitor William Moodie and appeared before Judge Hugh Hamilton at the Moree Courthouse Quarter Sessions.

He pleaded guilty to both charges.

Crown prosecutor Robert Jardine Browning told Judge Hamilton the defendant was 'bewailing the loss of some money'.

'He believed he'd been robbed, when Delander came up and put him out of the yard,' Browning said.

'Gillespie apparently mistook the landlord for one of the robbers and, in the struggle between them, Gillespie used his knife. Fortunately, the wound was not serious.'

Dr Matthew Harris said the knife penetrated the right side of Delander's body.

'If it was a little higher up, it would have penetrated the heart, and if a little lower, it might have penetrated the lung,' Dr Harris said.

Gillespie maintained he was sober at the time of the incident, although admitted he could have been suffering 'the after-effects of drink'.

He told the court four or five people robbed him and he was merely defending himself.

'You should think yourself a lucky man. The incident could have been a lot worse,' Judge Hamilton told the defendant.

The judge suggested Gillespie be committed to an aged-care facility.

'If the accused is prepared to go into an asylum, that would probably be the best place for him,' Judge Hamilton said.

'I will deal leniently with the defendant and not send him to gaol.'

Gillespie was acquitted of attempted murder but found guilty of assault with intent to do grievous bodily injury.

'Mr Gillespie, you will enter a surety of £40 to be of good behaviour so that you might be brought up at any time to answer the charge,' Judge Hamilton directed.

Three years after Delander escaped death in the yard of the Sportsman's Arms Hotel, he found himself on the wrong side of the law when accused of telling a female employee at the Royal Hotel he would 'sooner sleep with her than the queen'.

Daisy May Chapman, employed as a housemaid, also alleged Delander straddled her while she was down on her hands and knees scrubbing linoleum flooring.

Mrs Chapman and her husband William boarded at the hotel. However, William was home from Moree Hospital after spending four weeks recovering from serious illness and haemorrhaging.

On the morning of Saturday 20 July 1918, Delander presented William Chapman with an account for unpaid board, totalling more than £11.

Later, Mrs Chapman told her husband about Delander's alleged misconduct.

Outraged, Chapman confronted Delander. A scuffle, and 'highly offensive' language, followed.

At least two punches connected.

The Chapmans accused fifty-two-year-old Delander and his wife Emma, 47, of assault and insulting words and the Delanders counter-accused the Chapmans of the same offences.

When the matter got to Moree courthouse before police magistrate Major Frederick Crane on 30 July, Tom Hogan — mayor of Moree in 1915 and 1920 — appeared for the Delanders.

Alfredo Zlotkowski, mayor of Moree in 1897, defended the Chapmans.

The entire day's sitting was allocated to the hearing of five summonses between both parties.

Chapman admitted shoving Delander but denied using offensive language. He maintained his actions were due to Delander's alleged misconduct towards Mrs Chapman.

He said the confrontation brought on another haemorrhaging attack.

The assault cases against both parties were dismissed by Major Crane as 'trivial' however Delander and Chapman were both convicted of using insulting words and each fined £2, with both parties sharing court costs.

Mrs Delander was fined 10 shillings for using insulting words against Mrs Chapman.

The words used by Delander were described by Major

Bush Tragedies

Crane as 'most offensive'.

Major Crane advised Delander he should be mindful his actions gave the public the 'opportunity to learn such things as disclosed in the evidence', referring to the misconduct allegations made by Mrs Chapman — a juicy, small-town scandal ripe for gossip.

The court case didn't earn Roger Delander any friends in the local print media, either, despite his standing in society.

A _North West Champion_ editorial absolutely condemned the former mayor:

'We do not hold the view that, in the interests of morality, we should in such cases altogether adopt the "hush-it-up, smother-it-up" policy. A newspaper has a duty to perform, and there are times when the ends of morality are better served by lifting the veil, and revealing the character of some individuals we have in our midst,' the newspaper blasted.

'One of the most unfortunate incidents was that respectable women should have been compelled to figure in the case. The words for which Delander was fined were described by Major Crane as being 'most offensive'. It is surprising, in the circumstances, the penalty imposed on the defendant could have been so light. That the licensee of one of the leading hotels in Moree — and an ex-mayor — should be found guilty of having made use of such grossly insulting words, full of sordid suggestions, to a married woman employed by him as housemaid, and against whose character no imputation was made in the evidence, is almost inconceivable'.

514

www.ingramcontent.com/pod-product-compliance
Lightning Source LLC
Chambersburg PA
CBHW032046020426
42335CB00011B/216